DEMOCRACY

Paul Cartledge was the inaugural A. G. Leventis Professor of Greek Culture in the University of Cambridge, and President of Clare College, Cambridge. Between 2006 and 2010, he was Hellenic Parliament Global Distinguished Professor in the History and Theory of Democracy at New York University. Over the course of his distinguished career he has written numerous books on the ancient Greek world, including *The Greeks: A Portrait of Self and Others*, *Ancient Greece: A Very Short Introduction*, and *After Thermopylae*, all published by Oxford University Press. He has also served as historical consultant for the BBC television series *The Greeks*, and for four Channel 4 documentaries, including *The Spartans*.

Praise for *Democracy: A Life*

'*Democracy: A Life* is a magisterial and moving account of the fate of democracy....In an easy, graceful style, with flashes of revelatory personal expression, Paul Cartledge deploys his stunning mastery of several millennia of human history and deep knowledge of decades of scholarship to bring ancient democracy and its critics, modern as well as ancient, vividly to life.'

Danielle Allen, author of *Our Declaration: A Reading of the Declaration of Independence in Defense of Equality*

'The fruit of a lifetime's learning, this passionately argued book reveals what made ancient Greek democracy so remarkable and so different from the tamer version we have today. By showing how far we have come from the ancient Greeks, Paul Cartledge reminds us how much we still have to learn from them.'

David Runciman, author of *The Confidence Trap: A History of Democracy in Crisis from World War I to the Present*

'No library should be without this wonderful book, in which Cartledge has abundantly shared his love and knowledge of ancient Greece with us.'

Kirkus Reviews

'The clarity and zest with which he pursues his Snark-like quarry, the breadth and variety of his reading, and his cheerful persistence against odds (matching that of his subject) combine to make this an unexpectedly enjoyable page-turner.'

Peter Green, Books of the Year 2016, *Times Literary Supplement*

'A stimulating biography of democracy, both in theory and in all its practical manifestations....[A]lso a thoughtful response to those scholars who argue that democracy is not 'a quintessentially Western idea'. Cartledge's analysis suggests that it is just that.'

Classics for All

'A nuanced account of the meanings and meanderings of democracy.'

Catholic Herald

'Just what was ancient Greek democracy and why does it still matter? Scholarly giant Paul Cartledge answers those questions in this learned and readable book that glides gracefully from Aristotle and the stones of Athens to Rome, the Renaissance, the Age of Revolution, and today's era of globalization.'

Barry Strauss, author of *The Death of Caesar: The Story of History's Most Famous Assassination*

Democracy

A Life

Paul Cartledge

OXFORD
UNIVERSITY PRESS

OXFORD
UNIVERSITY PRESS

Great Clarendon Street, Oxford, OX2 6DP,
United Kingdom

Oxford University Press is a department of the University of Oxford.
It furthers the University's objective of excellence in research, scholarship,
and education by publishing worldwide. Oxford is a registered trade mark of
Oxford University Press in the UK and in certain other countries

First published 2016
First published in paperback 2018

Impression: 3

Published in the United States of America by Oxford University Press
198 Madison Avenue, New York, NY 10016, United States of America

British Library Cataloguing in Publication Data
Data available

Library of Congress Cataloging in Publication Data
Data available

ISBN 978–0–19–969767–0 (Hbk.)
ISBN 978–0–19–881513–6 (Pbk.)

Printed in Great Britain by
CPI Group (UK) Ltd, Croydon CR0 4YY

To Josh Ober in friendship and with admiration
And to the memory of 'Freeborn' John Lilburne (b. c. 1615, d. 1657)

CONTENTS

Contents

Contents

LIST OF ILLUSTRATIONS

LIST OF MAPS

PREFACE

THIS IS NOT MY first crack at democracy, mainly ancient Greek. In 2008 I published, in German translation, the book of a series of lectures I was invited to deliver at the University of Heidelberg (Cartledge 2008). This came about through the good offices chiefly of Professor Joseph Maran, aided and abetted by Professor Tonio Hölscher, to both of whom I owe a great deal, and not only for their immensely friendly hospitality. In 2009 I published a book on ancient Greek political thought (as opposed to theory) from Homer to Plutarch (roughly c. 700 BCE to CE 100), in which democracy served as the guiding red thread (Cartledge 2009b). And I have published a number of articles on aspects of democracy ancient and modern (e.g., Cartledge 1996a, 2000). But these were all early runs at the subject. The real work begins here.

The present book has been several years in the making. Most immediately, it is based squarely upon a set of advanced, final-year undergraduate lectures that I delivered in Cambridge over four successive academic years (from 2009 to 2013), both to undergraduate students taking the Classical Tripos and to those studying for the Historical Tripos. The lecture course was titled 'Ancient Greek Democracy—and its Legacies', although for reasons that will become apparent I would have preferred 'Ancient Greek Democracies'. Since all or most of the Historians who opted to take the course and the attached examination paper (about ten in each of the four years) knew little or no ancient Greek, the programme was firmly billed as a course in translation, a fact of which I tried to make a virtue. In this, as in many other respects, I had the shining example of the late Sir Moses Finley (Professor of Ancient History at Cambridge from 1970 to 1979) to guide me. It was to him (and also to the late Professor Pierre

Vidal-Naquet) that in profound homage I dedicated my *Ancient Greek Political Thought in Practice* (Cartledge 2009).

In advertising and executing the course of lectures I announced six principal aims:

1. To explore the meanings of 'democracy' both ancient (in Greek: *demokratia*) and modern (including current);
2. To enhance understanding of the special circumstances required to make possible both the emergence and the continuation of 'People Power' (*demokratia*) at Athens;
3. To compare and contrast the democracy (democracies) that were created in Athens with those to be found elsewhere in the Greek world, a world of—at most periods from about 600 BCE on—1,000 or so citizen-states (*poleis*);
4. To appreciate the development of ancient political thinking and theory about democracy, and not least comprehend their typically *anti*-democratic bent;
5. To track the devolution or degradation of the original Greek conceptions and practices of democracy through the Hellenistic Greek world, late Republican and early Imperial Rome, and down as far as early Byzantium (6th c. CE); and
6. To follow some of the trajectory of post-Ancient democracy, in the European Middle Ages and Renaissance, in Revolutionary England, America and France, and in its reconstituted or reinvented forms of the nineteenth century and beyond.

I further issued a prospectus, to the following effect:

All historiography may be contemporary history, but the historiography of democracy could hardly be more so. The current global preoccupation with democracy and (for some) its global extension makes constant re-examination of the original ancient Greek versions imperative. This course will thus be explicitly and determinedly comparativist from the outset, and one early pedagogical aim will be to problematize and defamiliarize Modern democracy and thus to sever any easy assimilation of it to (any) Ancient (prologue).

We shall not only be comparing and contrasting Ancient with Modern, I continued, but also—and at first equally or even more—comparing and contrasting Ancient with Ancient, and indeed Ancient Democracy with Ancient Greek Oligarchy (which could sometimes be represented as really quite 'democratic'). Aristotle (384–322 BCE), I advised, will be our guide in this as in so much else where ancient politics are concerned (here Chapters 1, 2, and 6). In his *Politics* he claimed to be able to distinguish four species of the genus *demokratia*. We shall follow along in the same line of thought, by comparing Athenian democracy, a version of Aristotle's 'last' or 'ultimate' species (itself a moving target, with quite distinct evolutionary stages and revolutionary moments) with other, of course far less well documented democracies, such as those of Mantineia and Elis in the fifth century BCE, or Thebes and Argos in the fourth (Chapters 4, 5, 9, and 11).

Ancient Greek, especially ancient Athenian, democracy (to 322/1 BCE) was to be the main topic of the course (Chapters 3–13). But the last third or so was advertised as addressing also its varied legacies. To begin with, therefore, we would continue the story beyond the Classical into the Hellenistic period, where at least the island-city of Rhodes kept some sort of democratic flag flying in the face of first Hellenistic Greek (Chapter 14) and then Roman assaults. Republican Rome, I would argue against strong contrary opinion, has no true place in a history of Ancient democracy properly so called, at least as that was anciently understood by the pre-Hellenistic Greeks (Chapter 15). This negative conclusion would be reinforced and confirmed by considering the devolution and devaluation of the term *demokratia* in the works of Cicero, Aelius Aristeides, and others in the central Roman era (c. 200 BCE–CE 200), and (well) beyond that into the sixth-century Byzantine world of Justinian (r. 527–565) (Chapter 16).

More briefly, I concluded, we would look finally at some foreshadowings or inklings of modern democracy as vaguely sketched in the European Middle Ages and Renaissance (Chapter 17), much more sharply focused in seventeenth-century England (the English 'Revolution' as witnessed to in the Putney-Leveller Debates, Chapter 18), and yet more explicitly announced in the claims to antique Greek democratic legitimacy put forward by some of the French Revolutionaries of the later eighteenth century (Chapter 18).

Modern democracy as such would not be our subject, but the resumption, really reinvention, of democracy (so called) in the nineteenth century, especially in the United States (Chapter 19) and the United Kingdom (Chapter 20), certainly would be; so that we would end on a paradox, one that I still find quite baffling, actually. Until the first half of the nineteenth century the dominant tradition of Western political thought both in and since Antiquity had been *anti*-democratic, opposed, specifically, to the more radical species of democracy theorized by Aristotle in the *Politics*. That long tradition has been and is still today being actively undermined, although it is as yet far from being overthrown, by various shapes and forms of direct democracy advocates, including those who point to the—technical—capacity of new information technology to realise the global democratic village. Against them, however, looms the spectre of a globalized political world order dominated by a country and state-form, the People's Republic of China, entirely lacking in any sort of Western-style democratic tradition whatsoever. Back to the future? It might well turn out to be just a pious wish (epilogue).

That prospectus was quite closely adhered to in the lectures, although they differed in detail and sometimes more than just in detail year on year, as they were always given *ex tempore* from—extensive—notes (supplied to students as handouts) rather than delivered as pre-conceived scripts. It has been likewise adopted as the guiding scheme for this book, as the chapter citations above are meant to indicate.

If I may end this preface on a rather personal note, I will relate how at a dinner with colleagues in Cambridge in about 1981, early in the Thatcher years, I was shocked to be told by a now deceased, extremely eminent professor of ancient and modern philosophy that for him democracy was, as it were, bunk. To be fair, I had no illusions myself about what I dismissed as 'bourgeois' democracy, but I did think there was still a good deal of life yet in the old dog of democracy that the Greeks had (as I still believe) invented: democracy as the rule of the masses, the political empowerment of the poor, on the basis of some workable definitions of freedom and equality. That at any rate in principle seemed much better than what it had replaced—rule either of the unelected and nonresponsible one (whether a hereditary monarch as at Cyrene in north Africa or a usurping tyrant as on the eastern Aegean island–state of Samos), or of the possibly elected but certainly not responsible (to the people) few (whether a more or less hereditary aristocracy or, as on the island of Aegina, a plutocracy; Sparta being, as often, a special case, both in practice and in ideological fiction).

The other personal factor that fuelled my quest for ancient democracy or democracies was the chance that I was raised in Putney on the south bank of the Thames in southwest London—not only the place of origin of King Henry VIII's *consigliere* Thomas Cromwell but also that Putney in which, when it was still just a village cut off from London, there occurred in October and November 1647, in the church of St Mary's, the eponymous Putney (or Levellers') Debates (Chapter 18). Here for the first time in English history and in a consciously non-traditional political forum, the prospect of a republic in the sense of a non-monarchical and in some sense 'popular' political regime was seriously debated—and of course it was shortly to be implemented, if hardly in a democratic form, under another Cromwell, Lord Protector Oliver Cromwell. St Mary's stands today; but so too—still unfinished—does the Levellers' great project of genuine republicanism.

ACKNOWLEDGEMENTS

I OWE HUGE THANKS, ONCE again, to the Oxford University Press and especially its New York editor, Stefan Vranka, and his able assistant Sarah Pirovitz; to former colleague Gareth Stedman Jones and current colleague David Runciman, for delivering lectures early on in the course on early modern, modern, and contemporary understandings of democracy, roughly from Robespierre to Noam Chomsky; to all those colleagues who have supervised (taught) the course in whole or in part to either Classics or History undergraduates or both, especially Robin Osborne, Paul Millett, Tom Hooper, and Carol Atack; to friends and colleagues who most generously read drafts and offered comments, including above all Carol Atack, Richard Cohen, Edith Hall, and Tom Hooper; to Lex Paulson for revivifying democratic enthusiasms; and last but not least to the one hundred or so students (several of them auditing) who attended them and provided me with invaluable feedback and a constant reality check.

I dedicate the book to two persons: one long dead but not forgotten—at least not by me—John Lilburne, guiding spirit of the English Levellers; the other my longstanding friend and colleague Josh Ober, now Constantine Mitsotakis Professor at Stanford University, formerly Magie Professor of Ancient History at Princeton, who—as we learn from an unusually revealing, indeed revelatory online interview—has been working on a general theory of democracy, from a political-scientific standpoint informed by a political-historical approach (see www.artoftheory.com/josiah-ober-the-art-of-theory-interview/).

TIMELINE

(All dates down to 508/7 are approximate or traditional.)
BCE = Before Common Era
CE = Common Era

Archaic Age

c. 700	Poems of Homer and Hesiod; introduction of hoplite fighting
c. 650–600	Law on office-holding inscribed at Dreros, Crete
621/0	Dracon's laws inscribed at Athens
594/3	Solon's laws at Athens
550	Achaemenid Persian empire founded by Cyrus (II 'the Great')
546	Cyrus defeats Croesus of Lydia
545 (to 510)	Tyranny at Athens of Peisistratus and son Hippias
508/7	Cleisthenes introduces Democratic reforms at Athens
505	Sparta's Peloponnesian League formed

Classical Age

499 (to 494)	Ionian Revolt: rebellion against Persia of Ionian Greeks and other Greek and non-Greek subjects
490	Battle of Marathon: Athens and Plataea defeat Persian invaders
480 (to 479)	Second Persian invasion, under Xerxes, defeated: Salamis 480, Plataea 479
480	Battle of Himera: Sicilian Greeks under Gelon defeat Carthaginians
478 (to 404)	Athens founds anti-Persian Delian League

466	End of tyranny, beginning of democracy at Syracuse
462	Further Democratic reforms at Athens: Ephialtes and Pericles
460 (to 446)	First Peloponnesian War: Sparta and allies versus Athens and allies
449	Peace of Callias (between Athens and Persia; existence and precise date disputed)
447	Thebes defeats Athens at Coroneia, establishes Oligarchic federal state; Parthenon begun (completed 432)
446	Thirty Years' Truce between Sparta and Athens (broken 431)
431	(to 404, with interruptions) Atheno-Peloponnesian War
421 (to 414)	Peace of Nicias
415 (to 413)	Athenian expedition to Sicily: Syracusan victory
405 (to 367)	Dionysius I becomes tyrant at Syracuse
404	Sparta, with Persian aid, wins Atheno-Peloponnesian War
404 (to 371)	Spartan hegemony
401 (to 400)	Expedition of the 10,000 Greek mercenaries to Asia: written up by Xenophon of Athens
395 (to 386)	Corinthian War: Sparta defeats Quadruple Alliance (Athens, Boeotia, Argos, Corinth)
386	King's Peace (first Common Peace): sponsored by Artaxerxes II of Persia and Agesilaus II of Sparta
385	Plato founds Academy at Athens
378 (to 338)	Athens founds anti-Spartan Second Sea-League, Thebes a founder-member
371	Battle of Leuctra: Thebans defeat Spartans; Theban ascendancy in mainland Greece (to 362)
366	End of Sparta's Peloponnesian League
362	Second Battle of Mantinea: Theban victory, death of Epaminondas; Common Peace renewed
359 (to 336)	Accession of Philip II of Macedon
356 (to 346)	Third Sacred War: Phocians versus Philip
346	Peace of Philocrates between Macedon and Athens: Philip rules Greece
338	Battle of Chaeronea: Philip and Alexander defeat Athens and Thebes; foundation of League of Corinth
336	Murder of Philip II, accession of Alexander III ('the Great')

336 (to 323)	Reign of Alexander
335	Alexander orders destruction of Thebes; Aristotle founds Lyceum at Athens
334	Alexander invades Persian empire
331	Foundation of Alexandria in Egypt; Alexander defeats Darius III at battle of Gaugamela
330	End of Achaemenid Persian empire
323 (to 322)	Lamian War: failed revolt of Greeks against Macedon
322/1	Deaths of Demosthenes and Aristotle; termination of Athenian democracy

Hellenistic Age

301	Battle of Ipsus; death of Antigonus I, founder of Antigonid dynasty of Macedon
300	Zeno of Citium (Cyprus) founds Stoic school at Athens
283	Death of Ptolemy I, founder of Ptolemaic dynasty of Egypt and of Museum and Library at new capital, Alexandria
281	Seleucus I, founder of Seleucid dynasty of Asia, assassinated; Achaean League refounded
263	Eumenes I succeeds Philetaerus as ruler of kingdom of Pergamum
244 (to 241)	Agis IV king at Sparta
238 (to 227)	War of Attalus I of Pergamum for mastery of Asia Minor
235 (to 222)	Cleomenes III king at Sparta
224 (to 222)	Antigonus III invades Peloponnese, founds Hellenic League
223 (to 187)	Antiochus III succeeds Seleucus III
222	Battle of Sellasia: Antigonus III defeats Sparta
221 (to 179)	Philip V succeeds Antigonus III
215	Alliance of Philip V and Hannibal of Carthage
211	Alliance between Aetolia and Rome: First Macedonian War (to 205); Rome sacks Syracuse
200 (to 197)	Second Macedonian War
196	Rome declares Greece 'free'
194	Rome evacuates Greece
192 (to 188)	Syrian War of Rome against Antiochus III

171 (to 168)	Third Macedonian War
168	Battle of Pydna, end of Antigonid dynasty
148	Macedonia becomes Roman province
147 (to 146)	Achaean (League) rising against Rome

Late Roman Republic

146	Sack of Corinth, Achaea becomes Roman protectorate
133	Attalus III of Pergamum bequeaths kingdom to Rome (becomes Roman province of Asia)
86	Roman general Sulla sacks Athens
31	Battle of Actium: Octavian defeats Cleopatra and Antony

Early Roman Empire

27	(to CE 14) Octavian/Augustus reigns as First Roman Emperor CE
CE 66–67	Roman Emperor Nero tours Greece, 'wins' at Olympics
117–138	Reign of philhellenic Emperor Hadrian

Later Roman Empire/Early Byzantine Age

324	Foundation (8 November) of Constantinople (refoundation of Byzantion) by Emperor Constantine
330	Dedication (11 May) of Constantinople
395	Emperor Theodosius I orders termination of all non-Christian religious worship, such as the Olympic Games
529	Emperor Justinian (527–565) orders closure of Greek philosophical Schools

Some post-antique landmarks

1215	Magna Carta (first version)
1453	Fall of Constantinople to Mehmet II, 'the conqueror', Sultan of the Ottoman Turks
1647	Putney (or Levellers') Debates
1776	American Declaration of Independence
1789	French Revolution begins
2004	M. H. Hansen and T. H. Nielsen (Copenhagen Polis Project) publish *An Inventory of Archaic and Classical Poleis*

DEMOCRACY

PROLOGUE

Lost in Translation? Modern and Contemporary Appropriations of Democracy I

For every person who knows how Athenians voted in the Assembly, there are hundreds who are aware that it was they who gave a name to what we pride ourselves on as a uniquely legitimate form of government. (Ryan 2012)

No constitution has ever given more weight to the decisions of the ordinary man than did the Athenian. (Forrest 1966: 16)

EVERY SCHOOLCHILD KNOWS THAT it was the ancient Greeks who invented democracy. But first it must always be remembered that there were some one thousand ancient Greek political entities, often very different, always radically self-differentiated, in the extended and diverse ancient Greek world of Hellas between say 500 and 300 BCE, when *demokratia* emerged, rose, peaked, and declined or was destroyed. So the question of which Greeks did so, and when and how precisely, is salient. And, second, suppose one were to argue that what the ancient Greeks—or at least the ancient Athenians—understood both practically and symbolically by *demokratia* was something much more like Lenin's revolutionary Bolshevik slogan 'the dictatorship of the proletariat'. Or, conversely, that what the average citizen of a modern democracy takes democracy essentially or substantively to be would have been dubbed, more or less dismissively or contemptuously, by a convinced ideological democrat of ancient Athens as—at best—disguised oligarchy. Those are positions I shall myself argue for. Or what if one were to claim, as is sometimes done by liberal interpreters of the term, that democracy was not a uniquely ancient Greek invention in any sense except, relatively trivially, the purely etymological? That is a position that I shall be firmly arguing against in this opening chapter.

Whatever view one takes of these positions, the dissonance or even contradiction in applied political terminology undoubtedly does raise the not unimportant question of why exactly it is—and how it has come about—that we (and not only Anglophones, of course) today gaily use as a loan-word a term that in its original Greek context or contexts bore quite such a radically opposed signification. That question becomes even more interesting, and problematic, if we track back a couple of centuries—to a time before democracy had become widely considered 'okay', let alone an obligatory positive good; to a period when it was used by its many diehard opponents in a sense not all that remote from the interpretation given it by its original ancient Greek, especially Athenian, opponents: namely, mob rule, the tyranny of the majority. That too is a question that I shall be addressing and attempting to answer, but only in the last part—Act V—of this book. Here, in Act I, I shall content myself with exploring some of the major, salient, and most pressing points of difference between democracy (really, democracies) ancient and modern, taking 'modern' to have begun by the time of—and to have been immeasurably boosted by—an influential lecture delivered in Paris in 1819 by the Swiss liberal Benjamin Constant. But first let me deal with the case recently mounted collectively by scholars grouped under the editorship of the Australian scholars Benjamin Isakhan and Stephen Stockwell—a case that has its congeners in recent writings of the Indian economist Amartya Sen and the British social anthropologist Jack Goody.

What these writers and thinkers mostly share in common is a desire to dethrone or at least devalue what they take to be the 'standard', that is Western or Eurocentric, line in the history of democracy: an approach, an attitude, that is for them at once too narrowly defined and insufficiently complex as well as being viciously ethno- or culture-centric. No doubt there are defensible political (as opposed to academic) reasons for wanting to hold and advocate such a revisionist position. But they go much further. They posit an alternative 'secret' history of democracy, which in their view shows both that it was developing in the Middle East, India, and China *before* classical Athens and that it clung on during the (European) Dark Ages in Islamic states, Iceland, and Venice; that it was often part of pre-colonial tribal life in Africa, North America, and Australia; and that it has since developed in unexpected ways through the grass-roots activities of Muslims, feminists, and technophiles. Those are several steps too far, I feel, although it is just the first part of that multiple claim that I wish to contest and refute here: that ancient Greece or specifically classical Athens did not pioneer democracy. As the philosophers say, that all depends— on what is meant by 'democracy'.

The ancient Greek root word is a portmanteau term, a combination of *demos* and *kratos*. There is referential ambiguity in the first of those two words: for *demos* here could mean either 'people' very broadly—as in Abraham Lincoln at Gettysburg's 'government of the People, by the People, for the People', that is, some notion of self-government by or in the name of a politically defined group as a whole. Or it could mean *demos* in the sectarian, class sense of the majority of poor citizens—however precisely that majority might be identified, and of course in ancient Greece there was never any serious doubt that the citizens in question were always free adult males. This ambiguity of the word *demos* was explored and exploited by major Greek writers and analysts, Aristotle not least. There was also ambiguity of reference in the second constituent member, *kratos*: unambiguously the word meant 'power' or 'control', being derived etymologically from the Greek verb meaning 'to grip' or 'to grasp'; but what was it that the *demos* was supposed to be grasping or gripping, having within or under its power—was it the organs of state governance, or was it the minority of citizens who were not poor, the 'few' (*oligoi*, likewise variously defined sociologically, or both)? I shall return to that in a later chapter. However, despite those acknowledged ambiguities, one thing was not in dispute or open to argument about ancient Greek *demokratia*: whether you loved it or hated it, it denoted and connoted power, or, more precisely, political power (the derivation of 'political' from Greek *polis* will require separate exegesis later on). Isakhan and Stockwell and at least the great majority of those scholars whose work they edit do not share that precise ancient Greek focalization and concentration on power. Instead they talk, rather airily as it seems to me, about public argument or deliberation or reasoning, involving some notion of equality of participation, perhaps, but not the collective decision-making by the majority voting of voters who are deemed in political principle and measured in practice as being exactly equal—one citizen (in ancient Greek terms), one vote, with everyone counting for one and no one for more than one; nor the exercise of executive power by popularly and collectively delegated and responsible officials or bodies.

Constant's point was a rather different one, and spoke to what I shall call the great divide between all ancient and all modern democracies: all ancient ones are direct, all modern ones representative. 'We, the people' do not rule directly but choose others to rule for—that is, instead of as well as on behalf of—us. (Lincoln's invocation of 'government by the People' is from this point of view formally misleading, if not actually false.) In antiquity, by contrast, 'the Athenians' (meaning, the duly and legally registered citizens acting as the *polis* of the Athenians) or whichever other *polis* one might choose to consider ruled themselves, in person, directly, as well as for themselves. More precisely, as Aristotle put it in the *Politics*, to which we shall return in Chapter 1, they 'ruled and were ruled in turn'. It is indicative of the participatoriness of ancient Greek politics that it was never 'Athens' that decided or did this or that but always 'the Athenians'; 'Athens' was solely a term of geographical reference. I shall argue, moreover, that for these political purposes Athens—and *a fortiori* all the other Greek *poleis*, most of which had much smaller citizen-bodies—were very strictly speaking 'face-to-face' societies.

But what exercised Constant most was what he took to be a key difference of socio-psychological orientation and evaluation as between all 'ancient' societies and all 'modern' ones when examined from the point of view of their respective conceptions and practices of 'liberty'. Whereas ancient societies were heavily or exclusively preoccupied with and predisposed towards public political forms of freedom, whether freedom from internal or external interference or the freedom to intervene and be effective politically in the public sphere, modern societies according to Constant's hypothesis privileged wholly or predominantly forms of freedom that could be enjoyed or exercised in the private—that is the non- or even anti-political—sphere. The distinction and opposition between these two ideal types were somewhat smudged by Constant's understandably less than totally correct understanding of the way classical, democratic Athens had in fact functioned—it was not after all until 1891, seventy-two years later, that the so-called *Constitution of the Athenians* attributed to Aristotle was published, commendably soon after its discovery on papyrus in Egypt. But the heuristic principle has proved a remarkably fertile one, rightly so, and this is one of the reasons why my study will not explore the details of the development of modern democracies in a historical way much beyond the middle of the nineteenth century.

I am, however, very interested, methodologically, in the quite extraordinary outpouring of research as well as agitational literature on the subject of democracy in the contemporary early twenty-first century, globalised world, in the spread—or attempted enforced spread—of what passes for democracy today. Especially gripping is the work of those scholars who believe that there is something in ancient democracy (by which is normally understood some version of ancient Athenian democracy) still worth retrieving, recuperating, perhaps even reapplying suitably modified and adapted to actually existing contemporary and likely future political conditions. On 24 September 2009 the *New York Review of Books* carried a double-page advertising spread paid for by the Johns Hopkins University Press, in which no fewer than six of the books advertised had either 'democracy' or 'democratization' in their title. The year before that, the then-professor of politics at my own university noted in his inaugural lecture that 'On any historical assessment, the achievement of some form of limited democracy in so many countries today is an extraordinary one' (Gamble 2009: 32). The more recent so-called Arab Spring gave further life to that notion on a regional scale, though without much in the way of comfortingly positive results to back it up thus far. There have also been numerous experiments with types of democratic decision-making within existing democracies (such as Finland) or at least major efforts at promoting the notion of greater popular political involvement at the grass roots, if only through such talking shops of 'deliberative democracy' as Power 2010, an initiative with which James Fishkin has been notably connected. Finally, for present purposes, and most immediately relevant to my own intellectual project, there has been a determined effort among some activist scholars to retrieve and promote what they take to be ancient Greek democratic virtues in order to counteract a widespread and growing perception that contemporary democracy, especially perhaps in those countries where something reasonably called democracy has been in existence the longest, is being diminished, managed, or hollowed out. In almost all these variously utopian or pragmatic scenarios the role of the Internet or more broadly electronic, digitised social media is hotly debated, both for and against. Is 'the net' merely or very dangerously but a 'delusion', if one is seeking somehow to liberate or empower the world?

I shall return to these issues and questions right at the end of this book. I want to conclude this opening chapter by engaging more closely with just one exposition of the sort of approach and point of view that I do find helpfully challenging, and one of the sort that I do not. As an instance of the former I take Martin Breaugh's *L'expérience plébéienne. Une histoire discontinue de la liberté politique*, a four-hundred-page tome that first appeared in 2007. Breaugh focuses his research on the theory and practice of emancipatory politics and radical democracy, and for the sake of demonstrating the validity of that approach historically he selects a series of key episodes in which the 'people' (or 'plebeians'; Breaugh consciously borrows Roman Republican political vocabulary) by means of concerted revolt have passed or rather projected themselves from a sub-political status to achieve political agency and express an alternative form of political power. Interestingly, Breaugh does not select an episode from ancient Greek history, though he might well have chosen the very primal scene of democracy in ancient Athens in 508/7—at least as that has been interpreted by one influential stream of thought. But what he does get right, it seems to me, is to focus squarely on the achievement and exercise of political power, albeit in antinomian forms. As one commentator on Breaugh's book has nicely put it, 'Those who follow the Occupy or the Aboriginal Idle No More movements will obtain fresh insight and exhilaration from Breaugh's ... account of these spontaneous struggles for dignity'. There is of course a huge danger in taking this stance of committing a vicious presentism, or anachronism, but it is an approach that ancient Greek radical democrats would surely have found highly congenial.

The challenge thrown down by Amartya Sen, the brilliant Indian Nobel laureate (for development economics), is of a very different kind: since at least the late 1990s he has contended that democracy is not 'a quintessentially Western idea, an immaculate Western conception'. His argument has some eight strands or props. He argues, first, that ancient Greece (by which clearly is meant ancient Athens above all) is not unique, even among ancient civilisations, in giving importance to public discussion and public reasoning; second, that to speak of democracy as an exclusively or peculiarly 'Western' phenomenon is both to indulge in 'an element of racist thinking' and to underplay the intellectual links binding ancient Greeks to ancient Egyptians, Iranians, and Indians; third, that other ancient peoples beside the Greeks, such as the Jains of ancient India, were egalitarians; fourth, that the ancient Greeks' democratic experience had little or no impact in the contemporary ancient equivalents of what became France, Germany, and Britain in Europe but had great impact on 'participatory governance' in post-Alexander Greater Iran, Bactria (Afghanistan), and India in Asia; fifth, that although democracy's impact in antiquity was always localized, thanks to the role of the Italian mediaeval city-republics and their ultimately global impact, the story of ancient democracy is still relevant to that of democracy on the global scale; sixth, that when in 1947–1948 India became the world's largest democracy (a status it still enjoys), it disproved practically the theoretical notion current until the eighteenth-century Enlightenment of Montesquieu and Rousseau that democracy could only ever be a local system; seventh, that Indian democratic thinking, as embodied in its modern multiparty constitution, embraced both Western and local Indian historic experiences of democracy, the latter being instantiated by the Buddhism of emperor Ashoka in the third century BCE and by the 'heterodoxy and pluralism' of Mughal emperor Akbar in the 1590s (according to the BCE/CE chronography), both of which tolerant regimes promoted open public discussion; and finally, eighth, that the 'large intellectual heritages' of China, Japan, East and South Asia, and—especially—India as regards 'the ideal of public reasoning' and the practice of 'associative reasoning' have been neglected. It is only fair to add that Sen, though obviously pro-democracy on some plane, nevertheless admits that the inherent qualities, and especially the 'informational role', of democratic institutions have not adequately addressed let alone prevented 'conspicuous deprivations', or guaranteed the rights of minorities.

I may well have failed to do equal justice to all eight of these strands or props of argument, or have placed them in the wrong order of Sen's own evaluative hierarchy. But although I must of course instantly agree with him that there is some inherent, essential connection between democracy and publicity and equality of discussion and reasoning about public political goals (the Greeks themselves, as we shall see, explicitly made just such a claim for their own democracy or democracies), what Sen's argument seems conspicuously to omit or come to terms with adequately is precisely the power of Greek *demokratia*, the democratic power of decision and control, whether over the central organs of governance or over the would-be oligarchic minority of citizens. It is in order to try to get a good grip on this extraordinary—and for its time unique—contribution to the history of politics and political thought that I have undertaken to write this life of democracy, from its ancient Greek origins onwards. And to do that, one must have some sense of the available sources of evidence, foremost among which must be ranked the work of the ancient world's most extraordinary—indeed giant—thinker, Aristotle, author of a treatise that is habitually (but misleadingly, as we shall see) translated as the *Politics*.

MAP 1.1

Greece and the Aegean. From Pomeroy, *Ancient Greece: A Political, Social, and Cultural History* (

BLACK SEA

Byzantium
Chalcedon
Perinthus
Nicomedia

PROPONTIS

Sangarius R.

othrace
CHERSONESE
Sestus   Lampsacus   Cyzicus
Hellespont
Elaeus   Abydus
Sigeum   Troy

M Y S I A

ANATOLIA

PHRYGIA

Gargara
Assus
Lesbos
Pergamum
Mytilene   *Caicus R.*

L Y D I A

Pitane   Cyme
Phocaea   *Hermus R.*   Sardis
resus

Chios   Smyrna
Chios   Clazomenae
Teos   *Cayster R.*
Erythrae   Colophon
Lebedus   *Maeander R.*
Samos   Ephesus   Tralles
Icaria   Priene   Magnesia   Aphrodisias
Samos   Miletus
Didyma   C A R I A

nos   Myndus
Naxos   Halicarnassus   Elmali

Amorgos   Cos
Cnidus   L Y C I A
ra   Xanthus

Ialysus   Rhodes
Camirus
Rhodes
Lindus

Mallia
Zakro

1.

SOURCES, ANCIENT AND MODERN

HISTORY—OR RATHER HISTORIOGRAPHY, THE writing of history—is nothing without sources. For, when lacking them, it is historical fiction, if not at best a historical novel. Not that the metaphor of 'sources'—pristine springs of relevant and otherwise valuable evidence gushing forth unbidden, unsullied—is an entirely innocent one. In order for evidence to count, it has to be, as Charles Darwin once put it, either for or against some theory, and theories, at least in the humanities, tend to be value-laden, if not overburdened with partisanship. Objectivity may be a noble dream, but it is a dream all the same. Nor is even the most professional, dry-as-dust contemporary historiography entirely devoid of fiction, since all history, as the Italian philosopher Benedetto Croce wrote, is contemporary history—in the profound sense that the historian is herself or himself a victim of contemporary pressures, and is writing or composing for a contemporary audience in terms that must make some sense to that imagined readership. Historians, in other words, make it up: they make history by reconstructing the past or rather *a* past, their version of the past, in and for the present (and, it is hoped, the future). But they do so, or should do so, strictly and ultimately on the basis of authentic testimony from, or bearing witness to, the times about which they write rather than those in and for which they write.

The very ancient Greek term *demokratia*, as already noted in the prologue, is fraught with essentially contested meanings. Those extant ancient Greek authors who wrote consciously and specifically about democracy as such, or about particular democracies, did not do so under any illusion or pretence of absolute objectivity. Indeed most of those, as we shall see especially in the final section of this chapter, wrote very consciously *against* democracy, either on

13

principle or on pragmatic grounds or both. But there is one ancient standout exception to this rule: a thinker, indeed a giant thinker, who both theorized ancient Greek politics and, with his pupils, conducted or supervised empirical research into the nuts and bolts of actual political systems. Although he was not an ideological democrat in an ancient Greek sense—that is, not a promoter of the rule and power of the *demos* of ordinary poor citizens over the wealthy minority of elite citizens and against the perceived best interests of the latter—he was not, either, a convinced ideological anti-democrat, as was (I would unhesitatingly argue) Plato, his teacher and mentor at the Academy of Athens that he had founded. I refer to Aristotle, son of Nicomachus.

Aristotle was not born an Athenian nor did he achieve Athenian citizen status, although he lived in Athens for fully three-quarters of his adult life. His birthplace Stageira (or Stagirus) in Chalcidice in northern mainland Greece was at the time of his birth in 384 BCE a small provincial town within the orbit of the neighbouring kingdom of Macedon; indeed, Aristotle's father Nicomachus served as court physician for Macedon's king Amyntas III (r. 393/2–369). At the age of seventeen—not yet an adult but no longer a child—Aristotle chose to migrate to Athens, the 'city-hall of Wisdom', as the man who was to be his master for the next twenty years had dubbed it, and join the community of the Academy, an informal intellectual circle grouped around their master and mentor, and so named for the grove within which they met to learn and discuss. When Plato died in 347, Aristotle left Athens and travelled in the eastern Aegean for the next dozen years or so, during which he conducted primary biological research on the island of Lesbos and got himself married to the ward of Hermeias, the intellectually inclined 'tyrant' (sole ruler) of Atarneus, a Greek city of northwest Asia Minor. By 335 he had returned to Athens, resuming the status not of citizen but of 'metic' or resident alien, now striking out on his own by establishing the higher research and education institute we moderns call familiarly 'the Lyceum'. This was again named for its location, also within a sacred grove, dedicated to the cerebral god Apollo in his 'wolfish' aspect (as a protector of flocks and herds from ravening wolves). Another name for the school of research that Aristotle founded was 'peripatetic', because of the master's habit of conducting his teaching on the hoof.

Somehow or other, he—with or without his many pupils' assistance—contrived over the next dozen years to compile a portfolio of some 500 titled works, most of which (the 'exoteric' works) were apparently designed to reach out to a public beyond the confines of the Lyceum. But of those 500 the only thirty or so to have survived more or less intact to our day are all works for internal, in-school consumption, being therefore so-called esoteric works. Of these, one has a special place in any history of ancient Greek democracy: the tract that is usually referred to as the 'Politics'. Here, however, lies another trap for the unwary. 'Politics' is the conventional English translation of Greek *politika*, which may or may not have been the title that Aristotle himself gave to a treatise essentially worked up by his students from lecture notes. Whether he did give it that title or not, what he would have meant by it is not what we understand by politics but 'matters concerning the *polis*'; and by '*polis*' he would have understood not any political entity or state-form in general but one very specific state-form in particular, the *polis* of the ancient Greeks. This to my mind is best rendered in English as 'citizen-state' (rather than the more usual 'city-state'). *Poleis* (plural) were not necessarily or indeed often highly urban-ised affairs, and Greeks spoke of these political entities as (say) 'the Athenians', not 'Athens', since they took the view that 'men are the *polis*', meaning by 'men' adult male full citizens. Moreover, Aristotle himself had a very particular and personal intellectual take on the Greek *polis*, which he understood as a 'natural', organic entity representing and embodying the end-fulfilment (*telos*, whence 'teleology') of all political entities or states as such. And since like all Greek political thinkers and theorists, Aristotle did not separate off and insulate ethi-cal judgment from cold 'scientific' analysis, for him the *polis* was an ethical entity, indeed the sole kind of political community within which the truly good life for social man could be fully achieved. That is what is meant by his decep-tively familiar definition of man (humankind) as a 'political animal'.

For us, however, it is possible to dissociate to some extent the overarch-ing philosophical armature from the more descriptive, empirical matter con-tained within the *Politics*, which is after all constantly referring back to and often firmly grounded upon a database of—for its time—unusually carefully and thoroughly researched political information regarding a significant pro-portion of the then-existing *poleis* in the wider Greek world: some 150 out of the 1,000 or so in all, which extended from today's southeast Spain to modern Georgia at the far eastern end of the Black Sea. That database of over 150 Greek 'constitutions' (*politeiai* in Greek, but the Greeks' conception of what counted as 'constitutional' was far broader than our own; see further Chapter 2) was gathered by students of the Lyceum and somehow collated there, and somehow circulated more widely. It is typical of the vagaries of our extant evidence that the sole surviving example of this dataset should be the *Politeia* of the Athenians, and that it should not have survived quite complete. That sole survivor, written on papyrus and preserved by the dryness of the Egyptian desert, turned up at the end of the nineteenth century; it was very promptly published, and at a stroke transformed our understanding of at least one ancient Greek democracy. Or rather it brought a renewed awareness of the fact that ancient Athens was not one single, uniform democracy but had over the course of almost two centuries experienced at least two moments or forms of democracy, thanks to its undergoing what the author of the *Constitution of the Athenians* labelled 'transformations'.

I use the neutral locution 'the author' advisedly. Debate and dispute persist, rightly in my view, over the extent to which the attribution of the work to Aristotle himself in person can be sustained. Probably the majority scholarly view today is that although the work is Aristotelian, it is not Aristotle's, or at least not entirely so. 'Pseudo-Aristotle' looks and sounds a bit harsh, but '?Aristotle' seems a perfectly fair way of referring to the work's author (or authors). Formally speaking, to oversimplify a bit, it is a game of two halves: first comes a chronologically ordered section tracing the transformations—thirteen identified in all—through which the city (political entity) of Athens progressed from at least semi-mythical kingship through aristocracy and timocracy (wealth-related oligarchy) and tyranny (unconstitutional one-man autocracy, not necessarily tyrannical in the modern sense) to various shades and forms of democracy, interrupted quite briefly by civil war and bouts of extreme oligarchy (collective dictatorship, junta-rule); the second half consists of a more or less systematic exposition of the democracy's chief institutions and their functioning as they currently operated at the time of the work's compilation, let us say in the later 330s and early 320s.

By using the combined evidence of *Politics* and *Ath. Pol.*, it is possible to obtain a really quite full and detailed picture of what ancient Greek democratic politics and at least one democratic polity were chiefly like, and what they were about, in the third quarter of the fourth century BCE. It is at any rate a happy coincidence, and perhaps much more than that, that the bulk of the surviving non-literary—that is, the epigraphic or documentary—evidence for the workings of democracy at Athens also belongs to that same quarter-century, as do the extant lawcourt and Assembly speeches of Demosthenes, Aeschines, Lycurgus, and Hyperides, and many of the pamphlets of Isocrates. About all of those much more will be said later elsewhere. But Aristotle in the *Politics* arguably offers a great deal more even than that. Being ancient Greece's foremost social analyst and taxonomist, he not only provides us with by far the fullest available discussion of what the Greek *polis*—any *polis*—was, what were its necessary constituents and conditions as opposed to its accidental, non-essential features; he also deconstructs or decomposes *demokratia* as such, that genus of 'constitution' as it were, into four sub-species, ranging along a spectrum from the most radical and 'left-wing' (what he calls the 'last' form of *demokratia*, a category applicable to Athens) to the most moderate, which most closely resembled and indeed overlapped with the most moderate or least 'right-wing' form of oligarchy. (The left-wing/right-wing terminology stems from the French Revolution; see Chapter 18.)

And he does more even than that: he also offers his own considered view of what it is that essentially—not accidentally—distinguishes all forms of democracy from all forms of oligarchy. Do not be fooled, he implicitly says, by the nomenclature: democracy, power of the many or masses, versus oligarchy, rule of the few. The real, essential criterion of distinction is not mere numbers but 'poverty and wealth': that is to say, democracy *is* the rule of the poor, oligarchy *is* the rule of the rich, and so much is that the case that even in a situation where the rich were *per impossibile* the majority of a city's or state's citizens, Aristotle would still classify and label it an 'oligarchy' and vice versa. (For his definition of 'citizen', see Chapter 7.) What then did he understand by 'rich' and 'poor'? The former admittedly was a group susceptible of a rather tauter if not necessarily mathematically determined definition: they were the leisured elite of the citizen body, those who did not have to work for a living, who did not live under compulsion from anyone else to work, and indeed typically would be able and willing to compel others—often unfree, slave others—to work for them. This perhaps helps explain an otherwise rather puzzling feature of the first, definitional book of the *Politics*: Aristotle's insistence, regardless of the intellectual contradictions this mired him in, on the necessity of there existing within the *polis* a class of 'natural' slaves, who indeed made the *polis* a realisable

FIGURE 1.1
Law of Eucrates, 336 BCE
At a moment of great crisis in 336 BCE the Athenian democracy passed a Law against Tyranny. The words of the law, directed emphatically against the ancient, originally pre-democratic Areopagus council, were reinforced visually by an image of the goddess Demokratia shown supporting the People of Athens, itself represented as an elderly citizen. © akg-images / John Hios © akg-images / John Hios

possibility. As for 'the poor', they were all the rest of the citizen body, the non-'rich', a far too broad grouping, of course, although he was forced by the facts to concede that some 'poor' citizens were much less poor than others and indeed that some might better be labelled 'middling', that is, in between the (clearly) rich and the (clearly) poor; and that at the bottom end it might be necessary to separate off the destitute and beggarly, those who possessed virtually nothing, from the merely poor.

If that sounds like a proto-Marxist class analysis of Greek politics, well, that is pretty much what Karl Marx himself thought it was and one of the main reasons why he labelled Aristotle a 'giant thinker'. For us, I think, one of its greatest services is that it does full justice to the *kratos* part of *demokratia*, the 'grip' or 'grasp' element. What was it that the *demos* had in its grasp or power? Obviously, at one level, the 'things' (literally) or affairs of state, the public organs of self-governance. But at another level—and especially when *demos* was given its full, class-related value of 'masses' or 'the poor'—it was the 'few' elite citizens, the *oligoi*, over whom the *demos* was exerting its power. That, for Aristotle as an ideologically driven moral-political theorist, was not a cause for celebration. Indeed, Aristotle was second to none in deploring the sectarian, self-promoting versions of democracy in which the empowered poor majority of citizens acted in their own selfishly exclusive interests, as they perceived them, at the expense of the unity, harmony, and general well-being of the polity as a whole.

If there was one thing that Aristotle was peculiarly sensitive to in the lived actuality—as opposed to the ideal conception—of many if not most of the Greek *poleis* of his own day and earlier, it was their unfortunate propensity to degenerate into civil strife, including all too often and easily outright civil war. Already in the later fifth century Herodotus (*Histories* 8.3.1) had stated his view that 'civil war within a kindred people is as much worse than a united war against a foreign enemy as war is worse than peace', but he was concerned with strife within the Greek people as a whole or between two or more Greek *poleis* rather than within a single *polis*. Aristotle, however, following in the footsteps of Thucydides and his brilliant analysis of the civil war that afflicted the island-state of Corcyra in 427, gave that judgment an intra-state application and a sociologically sophisticated underpinning; indeed, he devoted a whole book out of the eight-book *Politics* to identifying causes of civil strife and war and suggesting both preventative and curative solutions to the disease. And though he did not believe, as some non- or anti-democrats did, that democracies were by their very nature more prone to suffer from or generate civil strife than were oligarchies, it is necessary to repeat that Aristotle was not an ideological democrat himself. For democracy, according to the classificatory system adopted in Book 3 of the *Politics*, is a deformed or corrupted mode of governance. It may be the case that just as a feast to which many contribute is superior to one furnished by a single individual, so 'a multitude is a better judge of many things than any one man' (*Pol.* 1286a). This was an ancient version of the 'wisdom of crowds' nostrum. But rule of the poor was by definition sectarian rule and therefore, since most poor citizens were ill-educated, likely to be at best inefficient. Rather, for Aristotle—advocating as always the golden mean in all things—the city most likely to succeed pragmatically was the one in which the middling citizens held the political balance between the extremes of rich and poor with their diametrically opposed self-interests, although even such a city would still be operating at a level well below the optimal Aristotelian philosophical ideal.

In short, a careful reading of the *Politics* provides most of the necessary toolkit for analysing and understanding not just Athenian democracy (or rather democracies) but democracy in the late classical Greek world as a whole. And although we lack and always will lack the required substantiating evidence in detail, we must take the full measure of his observation that in his day most *poleis* enjoyed (or suffered) one or other version or variant of either democracy or oligarchy. There were, in other words, lots of other Greek democracies besides Athens, and most of them, it would probably be fair to suppose, were a good deal less extremely democratic too. It is only on this relatively secure basis of later fourth-century BCE evidence that it is at all justified for us to proceed backwards to try to guess what democracy might have been like in its earlier incarnations, whether in Athens or elsewhere. That does not of course mean that it is legitimate to assert that what was the case in say 330 must have been the case in 430. To try to determine the latter, we must move from literary to contemporary, documentary evidence.

It was once famously argued in a joint article by the comparative social anthropologist Jack Goody and the literary scholar Ian Watt (1962/1963) that the ancient Greeks' alphabetic script was inherently democratic. By that they meant in the first place that the simplicity of the world's first fully phonetic alphabetic script potentially enabled even a child of five or six to have access to information of the kind relevant to the running of such a system of popular self-governance. They also implied, however, that there might be some necessary connection between the development and possession of such an alphabetic script and the fact that it was the Greeks, that is the Athenians, who first invented democracy. Now, it is true that democratic systems of self-government were in part dependent upon the use of alphabetic literacy, which required the mastery of only between twenty-four and twenty-eight graphic symbols—as opposed to the 200 or so signs *plus* ideograms of the Greek 'Linear B' syllabary employed by the palace scribes of the Late Bronze Age 'Mycenaean' kingdoms, or to the 3,000 or so characters that are said to be required for the possession of basic literacy within any Chinese system of writing. Yet although the administrative organs of many Greek cities were fully literate, only about half of those cities at most could be properly described as democratic. Moreover, even within classical Athens—probably the most literate of all the Greek democracies, and the one that most demanded acts of mass literacy on a regular basis to further its ordinary routine practices of self-government—by no means were all citizens fully literate. Actually, something of a dispute rumbles on as to roughly what proportion of the citizen body could be so described: at one extreme, William Harris has contended that even for Athens, the proportion should be estimated at never higher than 10 per cent, whereas at the other end of the interpretative spectrum there are those, including myself, who would put it at 50 per cent or above. At all events, no one should quarrel with the proposition that literacy and above all the publication of corporately generated texts and documents for 'anyone who wishes' to read were of the essence of Athenian democratic ideology.

For purposes of illustration, therefore, I confine myself to classical (fifth- to fourth-century BCE) Athens, distinguishing initially between public documents of a 'national', all-Athenian character, whether of domestic or external import, and, on the other hand, those that might be called rather 'local', that is, affecting just one particular local sub-division of the Athenian democratic polity. I offer extracts from an example of each of those types, with brief commentary to indicate the sorts of issues that the documents raise, and the sorts of issues on which they may be expected to inform. Of course, there had also to be several documents that were hybrid in type, and I give an example of that genus too.

In 336 the Athenians enacted a law proposed by one Eucrates. By then the Athenians had for a long time (since 403/2) been distinguishing between laws (*nomoi*) and decrees (*psephismata*). Laws were general, not ad hominem, in their application and were formally evaluated, voted, and ratified not by the people as such but by a sub-group of the annually empanelled 6,000 jurors known as 'lawgivers'; both the panel and the jurors were selected by the democratic method of the lottery, and both were taken to *be* (not merely to represent) the Athenian people. Decrees, by contrast, were resolutions of less general scope and permanence and were passed by majority vote of those Athenians attending meetings of the Assembly (*ekklesia*), which by this time were held four times per civil month, or forty times per annum. Early 336 was a time of crisis: less than eighteen months before, the Athenians and their Theban allies had suffered a disastrous defeat at the hands of King Philip II, his son Alexander (later 'the Great'), and the Macedonians on the battlefield at Chaeroneia in Boeotia. There was a real possibility, and a genuine fear, that Macedon might do to Athens what it had done to other rebel or recalcitrant Greek states— that is, impose a pro-Macedonian tyrant. It was to that possibility and fear that Eucrates' law was a response.

Here is a selection from the published document, which was unearthed in the 1930s in the excavations of the American School of Classical Studies in the ancient Athenian Agora (civic centre):

> Eucrates son of Aristotimus of Peiraeus proposed: for the good fortune of the Athenian People be it resolved by the Lawgivers: if anyone rises against the People with a view to establishing a tyranny and joins in establishing a tyranny or dissolves the People of the Athenians or the democracy at Athens, whoever kills him who has done any of those things let him be without stain. If the People or the democracy at Athens is dissolved, let it be forbidden to every member of the Areopagus council to go up to the Areopagus hill or to hold a session or to deliberate about any matter whatsoever . . .
>
> [my own translation]

The text was not expected to deliver its message by itself; this is a member of the class of 'document reliefs', and above the text is a relief sculpture depicting a standing female figure in the act of crowning a seated, middle-aged to elderly male figure. There can be little doubt that these two represent personifications of democracy, understood as a goddess and a member of the official pantheon of deities to which the Athenians collectively paid religious cult, and the people (*demos*). The act of crowning originated in the sphere of athletic contests; a crown of sacred olive leaves, for example, was the prize for victory at the Olympic Games. But under the democracy at Athens, itself also a hugely competitive arena, the practice grew up of awarding golden crowns to citizens deemed to have performed some signal public service. The award was symbolic, in that the honorand did not actually receive the crown, which found its way into the state treasury of Athena on the Acropolis. So well known was the practice that in the same year 336 a proposed award to Athens' foremost orator and democratic champion Demosthenes was the occasion for major public bloodletting between the leading politicians of the day (see Chapter 10 for an account of the political trial of the accused proposer Ctesiphon). Viewers of this document relief, in other words, were to understand that the Demos itself rather than any particular member of it was being rewarded and honoured by its very own patron goddess simply for being that—a democratic People. The very continued existence of the democracy was thus being deemed a cause for public and eminently visible self-congratulation.

In a sense Eucrates was doing nothing very remarkable. The democracy's myth of origin, its founding charter, was the myth of the Tyrannicides (see Chapter 3). Tendentious or false as history, this was extremely powerful as

(a)

(b)

FIGURE 1.2A AND FIGURE 1.2B

Athenian silver tetradrachm

The silver four-drachma coin was the Athenians' equivalent of the Byzantine solidus, the French Louis, and the English sovereign: at the same time a standard unit of monetary exchange and store of value but also an imperial token. © Courtesy of the American Numismatic Society

ideology. Democracy at Athens, in other words, was from one point of view identified precisely and fundamentally as anti-tyranny. But, apart from articulating the threat of the democracy's being overthrown and replaced by a possible tyrant ruler, Eucrates' text also goes on to make clear from where, more specifically, it was feared that such anti-democratic counter-revolution might emerge—that is, from which political organ of state: namely, the Council that took its title from the place below the Acropolis where it sat, the Hill of Ares (God of War). Of all Athens' democratic organs, the Areopagus was the least democratic: it had been founded well before the democracy had even been dreamed of, and originated as an organ of political domination by the wealthy, aristocratic elite. Only members of certain families were eligible for election to the qualifying office of Archon, from retiring holders of which the Areopagus was automatically recruited, and the 300 or so Areopagites then served for life—in contravention of the normal republican and democratic principle of rotation. From 508/7 and the reforms of Cleisthenes on, that principle had been embodied in the new—popular, non-aristocratic—Council of 500 recruited on non-gentilicial lines and soon also by the democratic method of the lottery. If the Areopagus was allowed to continue in existence, that was in deference to or in veneration of ancient tradition, and did not preclude institutional innovation: in the 480s recruitment to the Archonship was thrown open to the democratic procedure of the lottery, and in 462/1 the reforms of Ephialtes removed from the Areopagus its last remaining vestiges of independent political power or initiative, reducing it to a lawcourt charged with judging only certain non-political types of case. Every so often there were moves initiated by conservatives to try to restore to it some of its imagined or real past power, and the post-Chaeronea crisis seems to have been one of those occasions. In 336 it was nevertheless a pretty soft target, however much nostalgic conservatives willing to co-operate with autocratic Macedon in dismantling the democracy might have wished it otherwise. Eucrates, in other words, may very well have been playing to the gallery rather than articulating a genuine concern.

The foreign affairs of the Athenian democracy as they stood in (probably) the mid-fifth century BCE may be illuminated by a document found in Athens but since lost; all that now survives of it is a copy of a copy. A standard modern sourcebook (Fornara 1983) prints two alternative English translations, in order to convey graphically the 'comparatively wide range of interpretation' possible. And that is just interpretation of what may have been written in the original text, not of what that text might mean. All the same, there is sufficient agreement over the particular passage that interests me to make discussion of the so-called Regulations for Erythrae of (probably) 453/2 BCE worthwhile:

> Among the Erythraeans lots shall be drawn for a Boule of 120 men. The man allotted to the office shall undergo scrutiny in the Erythraean Boule. No one shall be allowed to serve as a member of the Boule who is under thirty years of age. Prosecution shall lie against those found guilty, and they shall not be members of the Boule for the space of four years. The allotment shall be carried out and the establishment of the Boule effected for the present by the Episkopoi and the Phrourarch, in future by the Boule and the Phrourarch. Each future member of the Boule at Erythrae shall, before he enters the Boule, take an oath to Zeus and Apollo and Demeter, calling down destruction upon himself if he swears falsely and destruction upon his children. The oath shall be sworn over burning sacrifices . . .

By what right, or through what power, was the Assembly of the Athenians justified in seeking to impose, or enabled to impose, such a set of regulations upon another Greek *polis*, even though one of that institution's cardinal ideological features was that it should enjoy freedom and autonomy from just such external intervention and imposition? The answer, in short, is that Erythrae on the coast of Ionia (in western Turkey today) was an ally of Athens, a member of the so-called Delian League, that is, the offensive and defensive alliance that Athens had taken the initiative in forming in the winter of 478/7 in the wake of the Greek allies' defeat of the grand Persian invasion of mainland Greece in 480–479. The League had three main objectives: revenge and reparation for the material and spiritual damage inflicted by the invading Persians; the immediate liberation of those Greek cities which still remained subjects of the Persian Empire; and the permanent liberation of all Greek cities threatened with loss of their liberty as long as that empire existed. The longer answer is that from very early on after the foundation of the alliance in 478/7 the place of Athens within a supposedly equal alliance had noticeably gravitated from that of acknowledged 'leader' to that of overlord, and by the mid-fifth century the alliance might be referred to rather as an 'Athenian rule' (*arkhe*, often translated as 'empire').

One clear symptom and symbol of this change of status are the offices of Episkopoi ('Superintendents') and Phrourarch ('Garrison Commander') mentioned in the Erythrae decree. These were Athenian officials selected from and answerable to the Athenian citizen body, empowered by a decree of the Athenian Assembly. The formal, legal justification for this apparently drastic intervention by Athens in Erythrae's internal affairs transpires later on in the decree, as part of the terms of the oath of allegiance and office that every new member of the Erythraean Boule was required to swear:

> I shall not rebel from the People of the Athenians or from the allies of the
> Athenians . . . Nor shall I receive back any of the exiles . . . Of those who
> fled to the Medes . . . I shall not banish those who remain in Erythrae
> without the assent of the Athenians and the People . . . If someone is
> caught betraying the city of the Erythraeans to the tyrants, he shall with
> impunity be put to death . . .

Athens' intervention, in other words, had been motivated—or at any rate officially justified—by the alleged 'medism' (taking the Persians' side) of a presumably very small number of Erythraeans who wished Erythrae to be back within the Persian Empire rather than a member of the Athenian alliance. The fact that they are smeared with the wholly negative label of 'tyrants' suggests further that they were not merely pro-Persian but also anti-democratic. And that in its turn is entirely congruent with the nature of the Boule that the Athenian Superintendents and Garrison Commander are tasked to introduce and protect. For it is to be a candidly democratic Council, just under one quarter the size of the Athenians' own Council of 500 but selected likewise by the democratic mode of the lot, and placed under religious oath to serve patriotically and democratically under pain of extreme religious sanction in case of infringement. It appears that the historical moment at which Athens chose so to intervene at Erythrae—and no doubt elsewhere—was one of great crisis for the alliance and its objectives, in the immediate wake of a disastrous anti-Persian intervention in Persian-governed Egypt that had come to grief in

454. But it does raise the question (to which we shall return in Chapter 9) of the extent to which the Athenians deliberately and purposefully used or abused their power and prerogatives under the terms of their anti-Persian alliance in order to promote the extension of democratic government within the citizen-states of the eastern Mediterranean Greek world. Can democracy indeed be imposed?—a question for our times, no doubt, as well as theirs.

From the 'national' I move on to the local level, that of the administrative unit known as the deme (from *demos*, the same word as *demos* = 'people', but here meaning village, parish, ward); and to illustrate the way Athenian demes operated, I have selected a magnificent marble stele, its inscribed text largely intact, from the important deme of Thoricus in southeast Attica. Thoricus owed its importance not least to its proximity to the silver-bearing lead mines in the region, which were worked by the labour of many thousands of slaves privately owned by some of Athens' richest citizens. It was from the silver ore of the Laurium district that the Athenian state minted the often strikingly beautiful coins that I shall be discussing in the next section.

The Thoricus stele itself stands about a metre and a third high and is inscribed on both its front and its two lateral faces. It has had a chequered modern history. Though its existence seems to have been known to an American classical scholar in or around 1960, it was first brought to public scholarly attention only in 1975 by the doyen of Attic (Athenian) epigraphical studies, Eugene Vanderpool. Four years later, however, it was whisked from its Greek homeland to the Golden West, bought by the fabulously well-endowed Getty Museum in Malibu, California. Just over thirty years later, happily enough, the Getty decided to return it to Greece, to the care of the Epigraphical Museum in Athens, an adjunct of the National Archaeological Museum, where its return was properly celebrated and trumpeted in 2011. For this locally produced and oriented stele is a gem of the classical Athenian democracy—a brilliant system of self-governance that imaginatively combined the local with the national, and indeed based the latter on the former. To become and to function as Athenian citizens, relevant adult males had to be inscribed on the citizen register of their local deme. Only then might they participate in national affairs. But membership of a deme was not merely a formal qualification for full active citizenship: the deme was also where one practised being a citizen, in the twofold sense of 'practised'. Not only did demes have 'national' functions to perform, but citizens might also try their hands in local government at the sort of decision-making and administration that they would be required to perform at national level too. Besides being exceptionally lively forms of local government, demes might also offer a rich social life too. Thoricus, for example, possessed a rather fine theatre.

Demes functioned democratically not least in the sphere that we describe as 'religion'. The text of the Thoricus stele is in fact a month-by-month calendar of religious sacrifices. It lists what sacrifices of which animals and in what amounts must be offered up on which days of which month to which god or hero—forty-two of them in all, including the local eponymous hero Thoricus, as well as Helen, Heracles, and many more. The date of the stele is reckoned somewhere between 440 and 420, a period of huge upheaval in the fortunes of the Athenian democratic state, running from the revolt of one of its most important allies, the island-state of Samos, to the end of the first phase of the great Atheno-Peloponnesian War fought between alliances headed by Athens and Sparta respectively. We shall return of course to those huge struggles in another place, but here it is the religious dimension to which I wish to give pride of place.

The Regulations for Erythrae stele discussed above contained the following clause: 'The oath shall be sworn over burning sacrifices'. Such animal blood-sacrifices, burnt upon an altar within a sacred enclosure often adjacent to a temple, were of the essence of all ancient Greeks' religious experience. This was the chief way in which they communicated with and acknowledged the superior power of the divine or superhuman beings they worshipped. The organisation and management of a whole year's such sacrifices were therefore among the very most important duties of each deme's *demarchos* (roughly 'mayor', as that Greek word is used today). National festivals too—the Panathenaea or the Great (also known as City) Dionysia, for conspicuous examples (see Chapter 8)—comported animal blood-sacrifice as a key moment of the communal identity they implemented and reinforced. But the more humdrum sacrifices conducted at the local level, such as those prescribed by the Thoricus calendar for the Rural Dionysia, for instance, will have served equally to regulate the ordinary Athenian citizen's sense of himself as an Athenian, and to order his place within the universe overseen by the pantheon of deities to which the Athenians communally subscribed.

As an example of a document inscribed locally but with national implications I choose the rather fine document relief made of Pentelic marble that was set up within a shrine at Acharnae north of Athens, probably in the 330s. The shape of the stele mimics the front elevation of a temple, alluding to the actual Temple of Ares that the shrine uniquely boasted. Temples of Ares are a rarity in all Greece, and the bellicose orientation of the demesmen of Acharnae was sufficiently distinctive for Aristophanes to make them the eponymous chorus of his 425 BCE *Acharnians*; the plot of this comic drama was driven by the hero Dicaiopolis' overwhelming but hopeless desire for his city to make peace with the Spartans. Formally the stele was an offering made jointly to Ares and to the city's patron goddess Athena in her martial aspect by Ares' priest, Dion son of Dion; but this was a monument and document with much wider—indeed city-wide—aspirations and implications. The interest of the document, historically speaking, lies in the fact that it then records the texts of not one but two oaths. The first is contemporary, since it is the oath sworn by all Athenian Ephebes (eighteen- and nineteen-year-olds) undertaking a form of national service before reaching full adult maturity and entering the city's armed forces. The regularisation of such service was an innovation of the 330s and part of a movement of civic re-armament spearheaded by the statesman Lycurgus in response to Athens' crushing defeat by Philip and Alexander at Chaeronea in 338 (see further Chapter 12).

The second oath text on the stele is much more curious and potentially even more revealing. It purports to record the very words of the oath sworn in 479 by Athenians (and presumably other loyalist Greeks united in alliance against the Persian invaders) immediately before the decisive land battle of Plataea—that is, some six generations ago. The Athenians had a special connection to Plataea, since they had been allied with the Plataeans since 519, and the Plataeans alone had stood shoulder to shoulder with them at Marathon in 490. Time and again, the Athenians supported little Plataea: now against its Boeotian would-be overlord Thebes, now against Thebes' ally Sparta. But although the Athenians had sent 8,000 heavy-infantry troops under Aristeides to Plataea, it was not they who had played the key role in the stunning Greek victory that ensued. That heroic role fell to the Spartans, who were also the overall leaders of the anti-Persian Greek alliance. After Plataea, a major victory monument was dedicated by all the allies collectively at Delphi, spiritual heartland of all Greeks, and the name of the Spartans headed the list of allies inscribed on the bronze coils of the so-called Serpent Column (remains of which are now to be seen in the ancient hippodrome of Byzantine Constantinople, modern Istanbul; there is now a copy of the Serpent Column *in situ* in Delphi). But it seems that the Athenians were never entirely happy to concede priority to the Spartans for the Greek victory over Persia, not even in the case of the Plataea battle. The Acharnae stele of the 330s, therefore, was just the latest thrust in an ongoing campaign of Athenian self-promotion, which at that date would have had the particular extra point of appealing to the sensitivities and interests of the Athenians' Macedonian overlords.

For, after winning Chaeronea, Philip of Macedon had in 338/7 been appointed by the Greek alliance he formed and dominated as supreme commander of a 'panhellenic' campaign to invade Persia and liberate the Greeks of Asia from Persian control. The Spartans had in 338/7 refused to join the alliance that had voted for the Persian campaign, despite having their home territory invaded by Philip. They had thereby excluded themselves also from sharing in a panhellenic enterprise that was being promoted ideologically by Philip as an act of revenge for the damage both material and spiritual that the Persians had inflicted on Greece in 480 and 479. (In 334 Philip's son and successor Alexander sought to reinforce the point when he made a victory dedication at Athens, upon the very Parthenon, in the name of himself and all the Greeks 'except the Spartans'.) It was this alienation and isolation of the Spartans that the Athenians, I believe, were seeking to capitalize upon by the inclusion of the Plataea Oath text in the Acharnae stele. The Athenians, it implied, were the true saviours of Greece from the Persians in 479 and genuinely loyal allies of the Macedonians in the 330s. By linking the Plataea Oath to the Ephebic Oath, moreover, the drafters of the document were also conveying the message that the Athenian youth of the 330s, in order to prove themselves true patriots, should seek to emulate the towering achievements of their heroic ancestors of 479. That the Plataea Oath was—arguably—spurious in whole or in part was beside the point.

Without leaving epigraphy behind entirely we may turn next to numismatics, the study of coinage, which is a peculiarly rich source for the history of the Athenian democracy and its foreign relations in the fifth century BCE. Coins by themselves are often datable fairly precisely, by means of hoard associations, stylistic development, findspots, and so forth. A standard mid-fifth-century Athenian silver owl represents what was then the most extensively produced and widely distributed issues of the entire Greek world. The imagery of Athena's symbolic owl associated with an image of the goddess's crowned head and spray of her familiar plant, the olive, had been combined on Athens' official silver coinage since the last quarter of the sixth century, when Athens was ruled by the tyrant Hippias. Such owl coins then performed a number of functions— payments to mercenaries, payments for court fees, fines, or taxes; and they might also be used in high-value commerce. But from the second quarter of the fifth century onwards these intrinsically valuable coins came also to assume the new symbolic function of an imperialist token, since allies of Athens typically paid their cash tribute in such specie, and examples were symbolically paraded in the theatre by allied representatives as part of the opening ceremonies of the annual Great Dionysia play-festival. The Athenian Assembly, conscious of the coinage's fundamental economic and political importance, periodically issued legally enforceable regulations regarding its production and usage.

Either in the 440s or more likely the late 420s to early 410s, the so-called Standards Decree prescribed throughout Athens' alliance the common usage of certain specified weights and measures of capacity—and forbade the usage of any other silver coinage than the official Athenian issues. (The coining by other cities of metals other than silver, such as electrum, was not formally outlawed, and these remained legal tender within the alliance.) Whatever economic advantages this measure brought—and there is no doubt but that it would have eased the task of the Athenian imperial officials responsible for collecting, storing, and accounting for the money tribute the Athenians demanded of the great majority of their 150 to 200 allies—a major function of this prohibition was to emphasise the Athenian-ness of the anti-Persian alliance. That it may also have generated resistance is one possible inference from the fact that the Assembly found it necessary to pass, on the proposal of one Cleinias, a decree regarding tribute-collection. Like the Standards Decree, the Cleinias Decree is of disputed date. But whenever they were passed, what is strikingly noticeable in both decrees is their hardline tone: these are not measures passed for an alliance of equals, but an imposition by an imperially minded suzerain on its subordinates.

Iconography is also the keynote of my penultimate class of evidence for the history of ancient Greek democracy and specifically democracy at Athens. Greeks and especially the democratic Athenians went in for public sculpture both freestanding and architectural in a huge way. It helped of course that they had readily accessible major sources of particularly fine workable marble on nearby Mount Pentelicum and elsewhere in Attica, and a slave labour force to quarry, transport, and in part work it. The Parthenon, the huge and elaborate marble temple of Athena Parthenos built on the Acropolis between 447 and 432, is—when read from a political point of view—a massive ideological statement with the most powerful implications. Not for nothing did Pericles make sure to have himself appointed one of the project's overseers. But for the purposes of this immediate discussion I fix rather on a pair of freestanding statues, representing the so-called Tyrannicides, which were made not of marble but of the copper alloy usually referred to as bronze. By the end of the sixth century and throughout the fifth bronze was the medium of choice for the most strikingly innovative and individualistic freestanding sculptures.

I refer to the Tyrannicides as 'so-called' because, as the sceptical historian Thucydides would protest a century later, in around 514 the Athenian aristocrats and lovers Harmodius and Aristogeiton had not killed the ruling tyrant Hippias but only his younger brother Hipparchus, and they had done so not in the name of any grand political ideal, but in pursuit of a sordid inter-aristocratic familial quarrel. For the vast majority of Athenians, however, most of the time Harmodius and Aristogeiton were nevertheless celebrated as democratic heroes, champions of democracy. Indeed, as mentioned, their action was taken to be the foundation or charter myth of the democracy itself, democracy itself as a system of self-rule being essentially perceived and projected as anti-tyranny. Aristocratic drinking songs (*skolia*) soon after the event had celebrated the pair as having been responsible for introducing *isonomia* to the Athenians, meaning perhaps something like restoring to them the rule of law as opposed to arbitrary dictatorship. Following the Cleisthenic reforms of 508/7, however, *isonomia* was appropriated as a peculiarly democratic slogan standing for equality of status and respect under the laws, and the aristocratic pair were also appropriated and re-imagined in order to serve new, popular and democratic ends. Thus when the Persian emperor Xerxes chose in 480 to loot the original sculptural pair fashioned by the Athenian Antenor in around 505 and remove them to his capital of Susa, this was taken as a heinous affront to Athens' civic and democratic pride, and a replacement pair was commissioned from sculptors Critius and Nesiotes and erected in c. 477 in the central civic Agora of the city, the most powerfully symbolic public space after the Acropolis. For a very long time indeed (until the 390s) they were the only mortals to receive such hallowed treatment here.

Finally, taking it as a source in a different sense, and bearing in mind earlier remarks about the element of creative fiction present in all historiography, I conclude with a brief look at one of the very best books of the past quarter century not just on ancient Greek democracy but on democracy as such: *Athens on Trial: The Antidemocratic Tradition in Western Thought* by Jennifer Tolbert Roberts (Roberts 1994). The key lies in the subtitle. 'We are all democrats now', it might plausibly be claimed—whether we are social democrats, Christian democrats, subjects of a 'people's democracy', and so on and so forth. But although in the Greek world as a whole between say 450 and 300 BCE a good number out of the 1,000 or so Greek *poleis* had experienced some form of *demokratia*, so labelled, the tradition of thought about politics that started with the age of Herodotus was resolutely and overwhelmingly anti-democratic. Of the articulate and extant witnesses to that political world the number who can with any confidence be called ideologically pro-democratic can be counted on the fingers of only one hand: Herodotus himself, perhaps, Pericles as represented by the famous funeral speech attributed to him in Thucydides' *History*, Protagoras the drafter of democratic laws for the new city of Thouria, Democritus the atomist, Demosthenes the ideologically driven practical politician ... and from around 300 BCE until approximately CE 1850 hardly anyone was so again. Why not? The answer must differ according to period and place, but Roberts' book offers helpful answers, not least by herself attempting to reconstruct ancient democratic theory as a consciously anti-elite, class-driven mode of political thought (see further Chapter 6). She shows too in detail how, and to what extent, *anti*-democratic thinking and practice prevailed from Socrates and the Socratics (Plato, Xenophon, Aristotle), through the time of Republican Rome in the last centuries BCE (represented in historiography by the Greek Polybius), right down until the eighteenth or nineteenth century of our era.

However, besides documenting anti-democratic thinking, she also faults Athenian democrats for excluding women from the political process. The Greeks did inevitably recognise that women were half the human race, but almost no Greek male conceded that they possessed the natural potential for full and equal political empowerment. The conceptual underpinnings of such chauvinism, in terms of biology or psychology, differed according to place, time, and individual, but Aristophanes' grotesque caricature in his *Women in Assembly* (*Ekklesiazousai*) of 393 or 392 is a distorted reflection of standard ancient Greek chauvinism, which—to bring us back to the point we started from—achieved its philosophical apogee (or nadir, to some of us) in Aristotle's *Politics*. However, before we point the finger or worse at the chauvinistic Greeks, we must recall that the total political exclusion of women was also the practice almost everywhere in the world right down to the latter half of the nineteenth century. *Alia tempora, alii mores.* All the same, Roberts' perhaps too presentist critique of ancient Athenian democracy is I would say less harmful than those watered-down understandings of democracy that I criticised in my prologue. To those, the understandings of politics, the political, and democracy that were developed by the ancient Greeks offer the sharpest possible contrast.

2.

THE EMERGENCE OF THE *POLIS*,
POLITICS, AND THE POLITICAL

Modern and Contemporary Appropriations of Democracy II

IN THE PROLOGUE I LOOKED briefly at the series of arguments marshalled by Indian Nobel Laureate Amartya Sen both in defence of the proposition that democracy was not a peculiarly European story or achievement, and in attack upon those versions of democracy's history which attributed a special, or even a unique, role to the cultures of ancient Greece and their post-classical reception. Sen has been widely and impressively supported on both counts. The Australians B. Isakhan and S. Stockwell have co-edited a volume provocatively titled *The Secret History of Democracy* (2011), contributors to which line up to provide multi-cultural, global documentation of the thesis that democracy is as much a Chinese, Japanese, East and Southeast Asian, or Indian phenomenon— or achievement—as it is a European or Western one. From within the classicist fold Marcel Detienne in *Comparer l'incomparable* (2009: 85) has attacked what he claims to be the widely held view that democracy dropped from the sky, once for all, in fifth-century BCE Athens; and ancient historian Kostas Vlassopoulos in *Unthinking the Greek Polis* (2007b) has inveighed against historicist eurocentrism with reference especially to the political sphere and very specifically to the ancient Greek institution with which this chapter will be largely concerned, the *polis*—which, he argues, should be repositioned within a much wider, multi-level, interlinked system of Mediterranean and Near Eastern exchange.

Finally, but very much not least, the venerable Cambridge social anthropologist Jack Goody launched (also in 2007: esp. 49–60) a ferocious tirade against the legacy of Moses Finley (1912–86), who apart from writing *Politics in the Ancient World* (1983) also edited a volume on *The Greek Legacy*, which he subtitled *A New Appraisal*, and in which he himself wrote on ancient Greek politics (1981). The title of Goody's work says it all: *The Theft of History*—Finley and others, in other words, have in Goody's jaundiced view conspired to deprive other, non-western cultures of the credit for pathbreaking cultural achievements—such as democracy—which they erroneously attribute uniquely or preferentially to the ancient Greeks. Coming from one who was the co-author of a study on literacy that was not unhappy to link the ancient Greeks' development of alphabetic literacy causally to their pioneering achievement of democracy, this is quite an about-face. But is it justified?

Against this revisionism there stands a tradition of scholarship on ancient Greek political history going back to George Grote in the second quarter of the nineteenth century, which holds that ancient Greeks did pioneer politics and democracy and, moreover, that what they created may still offer useful examples for contemporary would-be democratic reformers. The names of—besides Finley, above—Mogens Herman Hansen (in Europe) and Josiah Ober (in the United States) spring at once to mind as contemporary exponents and upholders of this tradition, which requires constant critical analysis—itself a legacy of ancient Greek ways of thinking—but can be defended. It is from ancient Greece that a very great deal of contemporary political vocabulary is derived—monarchy, aristocracy, oligarchy, and tyranny, among others, and of course politics itself: linguistically European in origin, of course, but not by reason of that necessarily also Eurocentric in contemporary usage, which far exceeds the bounds of Europe on any definition. Nor is the establishment of this historical fact in itself a cause, let alone an excuse, for Western triumphalism.

So, it is crucial first to define what one understands by 'politics'. And here—as in the case of democracy—I propose to operate with a strong definition: the taking of collective decisions in public on matters both operational-pragmatic and ideological-conceptual of crucial, central importance to the decision-taking collectivity as such, following an agreed process of open debate among the decision-takers who for the sake of this argument will be called empowered citizens, that is, have the executive power to enforce those decisions.

'Citizens' as it happens comes to us from Latin not Greek, via the exceptionally powerful tradition of Roman 'civil' law: that is, the law governing *cives*, citizens, originally of the Roman 'Republic' (*res publica*, the 'thing of the People', 509–27 BCE), then of the Roman Empire (established by the first emperor, Augustus, who ruled from 27 BCE to CE 14; see further Chapters 15–16). The Greek word that we translate as 'citizens' is *politai*, literally '*polis*-people', in the masculine gender. Full, active, participatory citizens in ancient Greece were all by definition adult males. The feminine form of *politai* did exist, *politides*, since in certain Greek communities such as democratic Athens women were considered the non-active half of the citizen body or *politeuma*, and thus indispensable at least for passing on passively the potentiality for acquiring citizenship by hereditary descent to their sons. But nowhere in ancient Hellas were women granted active political privileges, let alone equal political privileges with their menfolk. What is this *polis* from which so much ultimately is derived?

Exhaustive research for over a decade by Hansen and his colleagues and associates within the Copenhagen Polis Project funded by the Royal Danish Academy yielded a string of admirable collective works on various aspects of various Greek *poleis*, together with an encyclopaedic volume devoted to all the then known *poleis* identifiable anywhere in the Greek world between 600 and 300 BCE, some 1,000 of them in all. The chief lineaments of the Greek *polis* as such are therefore rather well understood by now, and what is known—often far too little—about the many individual Greek *poleis* is at any rate far more easily accessible than ever before. Two main senses of the word *polis* may therefore be distinguished: first, *polis* as a physical entity, the central settlement and location of the most important political activity conducted by a *polis* in the second sense, that is, of a political community constituted by its *politai*-citizens. The former sense is found as early as the Homeric poems (perhaps put together c. 700–650 BCE in their monumental form), but the latter sense does not appear until towards the second half of the seventh century, for example in an inscribed text from the small *polis* of Dreros in eastern Crete (see further below).

Some debate still surrounds the question of how best to translate *polis* into English. The standard older translation 'city-state' runs up against the two difficulties that many, if not most, *poleis* could hardly be described as ever being genuinely urban and that many, if not most, lacked certain essential defining characteristics of what political scientists or political sociologists would be comfortable describing as 'states'. The former difficulty is the more easily addressed: by substituting 'citizen-' for 'city-state', one both captures the ancient Greek notion that its citizens *were* the *polis*, a notion reflected in the ancient political terminology, which did not speak of 'Athens' or 'Sparta' doing this or that but always of 'the Athenians' or 'the Spartans', and sheds the unwanted anachronistic associations of 'city'. The problem of 'state' remains, however, but so long as one thinks of an entity that has political functions rather than of an entity with full-blown 'State' (capital S) institutions (bureaucracy, civil service, government, standing army, etc.), it will serve its purpose adequately.

However, the process whereby the citizen-state emerged—the 'rise of the *polis*'—is hard to grasp, given the available sources. A combination of archaeology (the physical remains of central places and their associated religious sanctuaries and cemeteries, together with visual images on artefacts such as painted pots), contemporary written sources including poetry (e.g., the iambics of Archilochus of Paros and Thasos, the elegiacs of Tyrtaeus of Sparta, or the lyrics of Alcaeus of Mytilene), and epigraphy (e.g., the Dreros inscription just mentioned) strongly suggests that the process of *polis*-formation in the Aegean and coastal Asia Minor heartlands extended over a longish period of perhaps a century, going on faster or more slowly depending on the region. It indicates further that that process both led to and was assisted by the establishment of new overseas settlements of Greeks striking out from those heartlands at first for the central Mediterranean (south Italy and Sicily) and then eventually, by 550 BCE, settling around both the Mediterranean and the Black Seas. Plato's humorous simile 'like ants or frogs around a pond' nicely conveys the littoral nature of this pattern of dispersal. 'Colonization', on the other hand, once the standard term, radically distorts its political nature. For most of these new colonial settlements were *poleis* in the strong political sense of citizen-state from the word go. That is to say, no less than their 'mother-cities' (metro-*poleis*) they asserted their freedom and autonomy, their independence, as an essential condition of *polis*-hood.

There is another, possibly even more controversial reason for not translating the ancient Greek *polis* as 'city-state'. The conceptual category 'city-state' is actually quite widely distributed and applicable in human history. Mogens Hansen and collaborators have identified getting on forty of what they call 'city-state cultures', including, for example, Singapore today. But in my view the utility of the concept is not so much to draw attention to what these different cultures have in common as to bring out and emphasise what characteristics they do not share. One way of bringing out the peculiar qualities of the ancient Greek *polis* is to trace briefly the trajectory of the word *polis* and the thing or things it can signify, from the poems of Homer onwards.

Is there a *polis* in Homer? The answer is both 'yes' and 'no'. Yes, the 'polis' word is used there (alternatively spelled *ptolis*), but no, the *polis* in the full political sense of citizen-state is not present. The latter institution may be hinted at or implied, but it doesn't operate as such in the poems, for very good institutional reasons: there are no citizens properly so called in either the *Iliad* or the *Odyssey*, and, although there are assemblies described—both on the battlefield at Troy and back home on Ithaca—there are no properly empowered decision-making assemblies or indeed any body that could function as such. The nearest that the poems come perhaps to depicting the sort of actual political community that might have existed in the time of 'Homer', that is at the time the poems were achieving their monumental form in the decades around 700 BCE, is to be found in *Iliad* Book 18: that is, in the lengthy description of the artwork decorating the outer face of the magical shield fashioned for heroic Achilles by lame craftsman-god Hephaestus at the request of Achilles' divine mother Thetis. Somehow or other—but this is epic fantasia not sober realism—Hephaestus had crafted thereon depictions of not just one but two cities: one a city at peace, the other a city at war. But even the city at peace is not a city without bloodshed: the scene portrayed is one of elite judges who have been summoned to arbitrate over the claims to compensation lodged by the family of a murdered man. Nevertheless, the dispensing of public justice in place of the rough private justice of the *lex talionis* (an eye for an eye) was indeed a cardinal feature of the lawfully embodied early *polis*. However, in Homer it is revealing that the most patriotic hero on display is not a Greek but Hector, crown prince of Troy. Famously it is he who utters the stirring sentiment 'one omen is best: to fight in defence of the fatherland' (12.243). Even if this may be interpreted as expressing a sort of incipient patriotism, it is the *patris* (fatherland) not the *polis* of Troy that is the object of his patriotic devotion.

The real Greek diaspora of the eighth and seventh centuries BCE also has its counterpart in Homer, but in the *Odyssey* rather than the *Iliad*, which in other ways too is the more 'modern' of the two poems. The island of Scherie inhabited by the Phaeacians, which lay within striking distance of Odysseus' own island-kingdom of Ithaca, was later taken to be the island of Kerkyra (Corfu). This had in fact been founded from Corinth as an *apoikia*, a 'home away from home' or overseas *polis* foundation, traditionally in the third quarter of the eighth century. In the *Odyssey*, however, it was no less a kingdom—if a rather benevolent autocracy—than any other of the heroes' domains, and if King Alcinous ably assisted by his queen Arete dispensed a form of regal justice, he did so purely informally, on his own terms, unfettered by civic constraints. But as the poet is careful to remind his listeners, on Scherie we are in never-never land: the ships of the seafaring Phaeacians travel to their destinations under their own steam as it were, without the need for merely human intervention. There is little or nothing of the real political world of the early *polis* to be detected here.

The prominent theme of mortal justice is taken up again, and greatly developed, by another poet contemporary with the period that saw the crystallization of the monumental Homeric poems. But with this crucial difference: whereas not even the ancient Greeks were quite clear who, or even how many, 'Homer' was, they were left in no doubt by the poet himself that Hesiod was a unique individual set within a veristic and very specific political context. The putative scenario of his long, hexameter (epic metre) poem titled *Works and Days* is briefly as follows: Hesiod's Ascra, a village later established as a subordinate settlement within the *polis* of Thespiae in Boeotia, is ruled by non-responsible, greedy, antisocial 'kings' (*basileis*)—not monarchs, as Homer's Agamemnon or Odysseus are supposed to be, but petty local aristocrats; a court of these kings has ruled against Hesiod and in favour of his allegedly feckless brother Perses in the matter of their immigrant father's disputed land-inheritance. Hesiod gets his own back, symbolically, in the poem by showing up Perses as a mere tool of the immoral 'bribe-swallowing' rulers (*WD* 38–9). For Hesiod, at any rate, the current generation of mankind—the fifth and so far the worst in an ever-degenerating sequence—is the Iron Generation, which is portrayed as a bad time to be living through, though still not quite as bad as a possible future one in which there will be no true justice or true respect left. But why then does he represent himself as having no other concrete political remedy to appeal to or to apply, and powerless therefore before the *basileis* of Ascra? And how were his listeners meant to interpret his fable of the hawk that has caught a helpless nightingale and contemptuously taunts her that it would be folly to resist (*WD* 202–12): does the hawk stand for the kings, and the nightingale for poor helpless Hesiod? Or does the hawk rather stand for supreme Olympian god Zeus, and the nightingale for the kings, who are being assured metaphorically by Hesiod that Zeus' inexorable justice will catch up with them fatally in the end?

At any rate, Hesiod was apparently not materially destitute. His competence in composing verses—not only the *Works and Days* but also the influential *Theogony*, a sort of Greek Genesis—argues otherwise. So too does his ideal prescription, ostensibly addressed to Perses, of a life of constant hard, agricultural toil, but one that is to be alleviated nevertheless by the enforced assistance of a slave underling (*dmôs*). He may not be the semi-aristocrat he has been taken to be, but he is probably a more than merely middling peasant farmer. The source of his political powerlessness may therefore arguably have lain in the failure of Ascra thus far to have developed militarily in the direction that, according at least to one peculiarly acute later commentator, might have given power to his elbow. More precisely, Thespiae in about 700 BCE probably did not yet possess a significant force of the type of heavy-armed infantrymen known from their shield (*hoplon*) as hoplites. It is a modern hypothesis that the emergence of warfare between massed phalanxes of hoplites, however exactly that occurred, played a key role in transforming the nature of politics in a number of the most important early Greek states. This hypothesis is, however, already sketched retrospectively by Aristotle in his *Politics* (1297b15–28), where he outlines a politico-military schema of historical evolution from an aristocratic mode of government employing cavalry as its principal arm to a mode of governance dominated by the next-wealthiest segment of society who fight now as hoplites or heavy infantrymen. What is particularly tantalising is Aristotle's further statement that these early hoplitocracies were called democracies.

As we shall see, there was indeed one early Greek *polis*, namely Sparta, in which the linkage between political recognition of the *kratos* of the *demos* and the development of full hoplite phalanx warfare was seamlessly tight, and it may be that Aristotle had no other city in mind or no other empirical basis for his general claim beyond that one. However, the process may perhaps also be illustrated by the early history of another central Greek *polis*, Megara, not far from Thespiae and next door to Athens, as reflected through the elegiac poems of Theognis (c. 550). Later sources talk of some sort of social upheaval, possibly even political revolution, taking place in the early sixth century at Megara. There is also talk, presumably not unconnected, of a Megarian 'tyrant' called Theagenes, who would have flourished in the 630s and 620s, and who was the father-in-law of Athenian aristocrat Cylon (to whom we shall return). Theagenes, according to Aristotle (*Pol.* 1305a24–5), 'slaughtered the flocks of the rich'. Not, be it noted, the flocks of the 'nobles' (as would have been appropriate at Ascra), but of the economic elite, who were not necessarily all well-born (*eugeneis*). There is at least a hint here of a 'class' approach, of the autocratic, monarchic tyrant's emerging as a champion of the ordinary, non-wealthy people (*demos*) against the wealthy few (*oligoi*). If so, the factor that could have made the difference, at least in some of the thirty or so cities where tyrants are attested in the seventh and sixth centuries BCE, is the development of hoplite armies. Tyrants, it must be added, did not necessarily rule tyrannically; what distinguished their rule was that they seized or held sole power outside any existing legal framework. One *polis* that never experienced a tyrant in this sense was Sparta, and it may well be that its early constitutional development was framed precisely to avoid that unwelcome contingency.

It is ultimately to Aristotle in a lost work on the *Polity of the Spartans* (*Lakedaimonion politeia*), one of the 158 that he and his Lyceum students compiled (see previous chapter), that we owe our knowledge of a prose document known as the Great Rhetra, the Magna Carta of ancient Sparta. This famous text, so labelled to distinguish it from a number of lesser *rhetrai* or 'enactments', is preserved in a *Life* of the Spartan lawgiver Lycurgus written many centuries later (c. 100 CE) by Plutarch, who derived it directly from the Aristotelian work. Actually, as Plutarch virtually concedes from the outset of the so-called biography, his Lycurgus was an at least semi-legendary figure, one to whom the Spartans themselves paid religious cult as either a hero or a god. Over time, he came to be regarded as *the* Spartan lawgiver, to whom all sorts of disparate ordinances of different dates became attached. (A somewhat similar mythologizing process affected the tradition on the Athenian Solon, although he was quite certainly historical: see Chapter 3.) Yet even apart from Lycurgus' alleged authorship, the Great Rhetra remains a huge puzzle and of uncertain provenance and authenticity. Formally, it is presented by Plutarch as an oracular utterance of Apollo of Delphi, a god to whom the Spartans were indeed especially attached; and being exceptionally pious, they were quite likely to have wished to place their political arrangements under the sign and protection of the Olympian god to whom all their major annual religious festivals were devoted. The terms of the Rhetra—poetic in expression, and not transparent in meaning—also favour the notion that this was a religious document with practical political application.

However, the language used radically complicates interpretation. There is mention of tribes (presumably the three pseudo-kinship tribes common to Dorian cities) and obes (residential districts). There is mention of the kings in the plural and a Gerousia (Senate) of thirty including the (two) kings. Then comes a clause, imperfectly preserved in Plutarch's Greek text, which seems to mention *kratos* and *damos* (the Doric form of *demos*) together. What is not at all clear is what relationship is intended or presupposed between the tribes and obes, on the one hand, and the kings, Gerousia and *damos*, on the other. The *damos* is said to mark the feast of Apollo, or alternatively to hold assembly, 'season in season out', but it is no more clear what relationship is to subsist between the Gerousia and the *damos*, especially when a final clause adds that in case the *damos* speaks crookedly the Gerousia shall be 'setters aside' (of their wishes or decision). Moreover, besides its lack of transparent clarity of expression, the text as presented omits what at any rate was later to become the chief executive office of the city, the Ephorate, an office to which all members of the *damos* were eligible for election. For the moment, however, I focus solely on that conjunction of *damos* and *kratos*, easily the earliest such conjunction on record anywhere in early Greece. Whatever precise meaning is to be attributed to either term, let alone to their use in conjunction, it is unthinkable that any *polis* would have hit upon such a formulation before the evolution of hoplite warfare. It is not therefore merely coincidental that Sparta was, if not actually the first, at any rate one of the very first hoplite polities. War and politics, as often in Greece, went hand in glove, and more so in Sparta than anywhere else.

It would be very wrong, though, to treat the Great Rhetra (even if genuine and accurately preserved) as enshrining the very first example of ancient Greek democracy. In fact, Sparta never became a democracy, for reasons to which we shall return elsewhere. What Sparta may plausibly be claimed to have pioneered, rather, is a strong notion of citizenship—and I think it's not an accident that the earliest attested usage of *politai* in all Greek literature is in a poem of the mid-seventh century BCE Spartan warrior-poet Tyrtaeus (*P.Oxy.* 3316). Later, these citizens were referred to collectively as *homoioi*: not 'equals', as that is often mistranslated, but people who were 'same (*homos*)-ish', alike in one or more but not all respects. Socially and economically, blatant inequalities existed among them and indeed were exacerbated over time, but politically all Spartiates (the formal title for full citizens, another word that occurs first in Tyrtaeus) were equal members of the legally empowered *damos*. Sparta too, at least as the patriotic Tyrtaeus represented it, was one of the earliest Greek *poleis* to achieve a major goal of them all, namely *eunomia*. By this term was understood not so much the enactment and enforcement of 'good' laws (*nomoi*) but rather the happy condition of lawfulness or law-abidingness, whereby citizens knew their place and obeyed the laws and law-enforcers.

But for what is possibly the earliest documented use of the term *polis* in its strong political sense we must look not to any major Greek town or city but to little Dreros in eastern Crete. In an inscribed text from the Agora of Dreros that is datable to the second half of the seventh century there appears for the first time the formula 'it pleased the *polis*'. Who exactly constituted the *polis* in this sense is not specified, but what it pleased them to do clearly is: namely, to place fixed-term conditions on the tenure of the top political office of *kosmos* (literally 'orderer'). Given the very early date, we are surely dealing here with a narrowly restricted, probably elective oligarchy of the wealthiest and most honoured citizens, a group not unlike the *basileis* of Ascra perhaps. But what distinguishes their situation most obviously from that of Hesiod are the very formality and publicity of the document; indeed it seems to have been a peculiarly Cretan political characteristic to wish to display written legislative enactments in public spaces from an early period, and that may be a function of the fact that there were so many *poleis* competing with each other in such a relatively restricted space.

To conclude, I return to the mainland and to Theognis of Megara. Not all the verses attributed to him are certainly his, but those addressed to one Cyrnus appear authentic. Their author is confident that the *polis* should consist of its active political element of the free, landowning, arms-bearing citizens who enact the laws in their assemblies. But, clearly aristocratic in his social outlook at least, he resents most bitterly intermarriage or rather miscegenation between members of the old aristocracy and those whom he calls the socially 'worthless', nouveaux riches:

> With horses, rams, and asses, Cyrnus, we seek out
>   Good blood, and everyone wants pedigree
> To breed from; yet a man of class, if offered wealth,
>   Doesn't mind marrying from worthless stock
>
> (lines 183–6, trans. M. West)

To put that in non-moralistic terms, borrowed from the Roman Republic, what he objects to is the rise of a patricio-plebeian elite of wealthy men who monopolise the offices of oligarchic government in Megara. His objections are delivered from above, as it were, but we would surely not be far wrong in supposing that poor Megarian peasant farmers and other 'poor' Megarian citizens were likewise voicing their objections to the political status quo from below. For that latter process, however, the best documentation comes not from Theognis' Megara but from Solon's Athens.

II

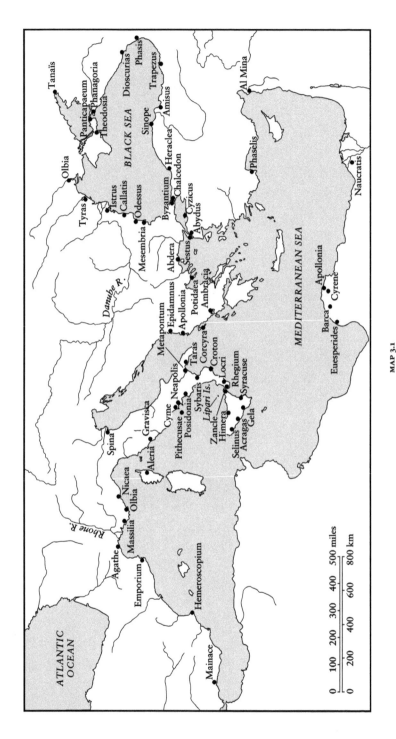

MAP 3.1

Greek Colonization. From Pomeroy, *Ancient Greece: A Political, Social, and Cultural History* (1998).

3.

THE EMERGENCE OF GREEK

DEMOCRACY I

Archaic Greece

'Archaic' in contemporary parlance is either a derogatory term at best or even a downright abusive one, but for students of early historic (post-Bronze Age) Greece it is both descriptively neutral and evaluatively positive, often simultaneously. It is the label conventionally applied to a period of past Greek time, but the decision as to how to circumscribe that (or any) chunk of the past as a 'period' always bears in itself an evaluative load. The term is by no means applied only by historians of ancient Greece to 'their' Archaic period. For it is applied by historians of other cultures too in the way it is here, that is, to mark out a period that is deemed to be inchoate, or formative, one looking forward to or bearing the seeds of a more mature or fully formed 'Classical' era or epoch. In numerical terms, Greece's Archaic Age is normally deemed to run, at the outside, from c. 800 BCE to 480/79 (the date of the Graeco-Persian Wars occasioned by Persian emperor Xerxes's invasion of mainland Greece), or at a minimum from around 700 to 500.

The thinking behind the broadest definition is that already by c. 800 there are sufficient signs and indications that at least the most 'progressive' areas of the Greek world had definitively emerged from the so-called Dark Age (variously defined, most usually from c. 1100–800) that fell after the end of the Mycenaean or Late Bronze age. Indeed, the utility of the very notion of a Dark Age—marked by catastrophic population decrease, political decentralisation, and loss of basic craft skills—has been called into question: was it not precisely during these supposedly dark centuries that a metals technology based on the working of the more plentifully distributed and more practically effective material of iron superseded the usage of bronze for key cutting-edge tools and weapons that had given the Bronze Age its name? True, but it has to be said that at any rate in one of the most important regions of the former Mycenaean age, Laconia in the southeast Peloponnese (where historical Sparta was to rise to greatness from c. 750 on), there is little or no reason as yet to doubt the aptness of the label Dark Age.

The thinking behind the narrowest definition of the Archaic Age is that before 700 all is still pretty much mist and myth and prehistory (or at most protohistory), since there are either no or insufficient written texts on which to base a properly historical account; and that at the lower end at least certain parts of the Greek world had already by 500 taken steps marking a definitive break out of Archaism and into Classicism. Of those steps the one that features most prominently in most accounts is the emergence of democracy—an early and inchoate form of democracy, to be more exact—at Athens. That, however, is controversial in several ways, chiefly because, even though the earliest and best ancient Greek historian does retrospectively so label it (Herodotus 6.131), by no means all historians accept that the *politeia* that had emerged at Athens by around 500 really was a democracy. On the other hand, there are some— many fewer—historians who wish to apply democracy to an even earlier phase of Athenian constitutional development, as far back as c. 600 BCE.

We shall return more than once to the issue of the proper classification of the Athenian polity in the latter half of the (ex hypothesi) Archaic period. The key point here is methodological. In retrospect, one may specify the necessary and sufficient conditions for the emergence of something labelled 'democracy', but what one may not legitimately claim is that democracy of some sort had to happen sooner or later, let alone happen how and where and why it actually did. Anachronistic, teleological thinking must at all costs be avoided, even though it has some ancient 'authority' in the thinking behind the work attributed to Aristotle that is known for short as the *Ath. Pol.* (*Athenaion Politeia*). For my present purposes it is not necessary to draw a hard and fast line between an Archaic and a Classical Greece, but it is necessary to expunge any modern anachronistic notions that may attach unconsciously to the former term.

This was, rather, an 'age of experiment', and more precisely it was an age that saw radical, even revolutionary thought-experiments which had a direct relationship to—and I would argue impact upon—the world of practical politics. Already in Homer, indeed, in the conspicuously ill-favoured shape of the agitator Thersites, there are signs of plebeian, anti-aristocratic thinking, even perhaps political thought. What might be called, a touch anachronistically, the demagogic rabble-rousing of Thersites provokes—from the irate mouth of King Odysseus—the remarkable abstract noun *polukoiraniê*, literally 'many-kingness' (*Iliad* 2.204). That state, declares Odysseus, is not at all a good thing, either morally or pragmatically—this is supposed to be the tenth year of a monumental siege, after all; and to it he opposes, not aristocracy or aristocratic oligarchy nor any other theoretically articulated mode of rule, but the traditional monarchic sovereignty embodied in the person of generalissimo Agamemnon. However, not content with abstract phrase-making, Odysseus also concretely thwacks Thersites with Agamemnon's divinely bestowed sceptre of kingly authority. Thersites is deeply pained both physically and emotionally, whereupon the mass of assembled Achaeans (Greeks) laugh out loud at—and thereby aggravate—his very public humiliation. The message for Homer's original readers and auditors was surely unambiguous: do not even think about questioning the political status quo, which is literally god-given, ordained ultimately of the greatest, best, and most powerful divine overlord, supreme father Zeus himself. But the very fact that it was spelled out in this way likely hints at a subtextual anxiety, at an at least vague sense of popular discomfort with or even resistance to the rule of those who are both in Homer and later also in Hesiod called 'kings' (*basileis*). Later, when monarchical sentiment was at a lower ebb, these elites liked to call themselves the 'fine (or beautiful) and good' (*kaloikagathoi*). For the ancient Greeks, good looks were the outward and visible sign of an inward, spiritual, or rather socio-political superiority.

More indications of a deep current of non- or even anti-aristocratic political thinking in Archaic Greece have been plausibly detected in the works of a number of post-Homeric elegiac or lyric poets of the seventh and sixth centuries. To these 'middling' poet-citizens—in other words, men situated both sociologically and ideologically between the *basileis* and aristocrats and the ordinary members of the *demos*—has been attributed the espousal of a 'strong principle of equality', an egalitarianism which in its turn can be seen as eventually undergirding the democratic turn of the late sixth and early fifth centuries. But long before that, probably the best illustration of this 'middling' sort of political thinking are the poems and the reforms they subserved of the Athenian lawgiver Solon. Poems—and reforms: for although he both advocated and tried to justify his reforms through his verses, nevertheless the two have to be kept conceptually and interpretatively separate. On the one hand, his extant verses, many preserved through the *Ath. Pol.*, are the sole authentic and contemporary evidence for the reforms. On the other hand, at various times since their passage, and not least during the upheavals of the end of the fifth century and the renewed internal contestations of the latter part of the fourth century BCE, 'Solon' was invoked as a talisman by different, sometimes violently opposed tendencies—some on the 'left', as it were, claiming him as a democratic pioneer, others further to the 'right' as a more moderate reformer. As a result, not only why he proposed the reforms he did, but even what exactly his reforms were, became matters for dispute.

Some aspects of his work are, however, tolerably clear. In around 600 BCE Athens was racked by deep and acute crisis, both economic and social, and therefore in our terms also political or moral-political. In 594/3 (probably) Solon was appointed by the then political establishment of the Athenian *polis* as an extraordinary Archon or Arch-Mediator (*diallaktes*). On the economic side, Solon foreshadowed or echoed another politically minded elegist, Theognis of Megara (see Chapter 2), in seeing money and wealth as the root of all, including political evil. On the political side, he praises orderliness (one of his poems has the very Spartan—see below—title 'Eunomia'), and warns against the possibility of Athens falling under a tyranny, even claiming that he had been urged to make himself tyrant but had refused to do so on principle.

Solon represented himself instead as a moderate, the advocate of a middle way between two extremes. Yet the nature of such of his reforms as are tolerably documented and established makes it clear that the political struggle he was arbitrating was not twofold but tripartite: between, on the one hand, the old 'Eupatrid' (scions of 'good' fathers) aristocracy and the less- or non-nobly born nouveaux riches (hoplites and above), and, on the other, between those two groups, broadly 'the rich', and the more or less impoverished masses (*demos*). Solon claims optimistically to have given to each of the contending groups what they deserved (not necessarily what they demanded or expected): to the old aristocracy retention of at least some of the privileges and offices that the right of birth allegedly justified, including all the major public priesthoods and (for women of certain families) priestesshoods; to the new rich access via election to the top offices, including the annual Archonship, and so to membership of the original aristocratic Areopagus council that was composed automatically of ex-Archons, and possibly also—but the evidence for this is controversial—to a new Council of Four Hundred; to the mass of the poor citizens (newly defined, see below) access to an Assembly (Heliaea) which functioned as a court of appeal against the judgements of—still, inevitably, mainly—aristocratic officials.

The latter measure—and in a sense the whole political package—was premised upon a fairly radical and fundamental economic reform known for short as the Seisachtheia ('Shaking-off of Burdens'). This comprised the abolition of existing debts and, for the future, outlawry of debt-bondage; it was thenceforth illegal for a citizen to contract a debt on the security of his own person, so that should he fail to repay the principal or the interest demanded he could not legally be made a bondsman by his creditor. Thus was instantiated nothing less than a new definition of civic-political freedom, encapsulating a new, more inclusive and sharper definition of citizenship. The overall significance of the reforms was indeed partly symbolic. Solon's new laws were inscribed publicly in the Agora, on durable wooden tablets, making the point that governance was no longer a secret process to be kept locked within the breasts of innately privileged aristocratic individuals beyond the reach of the laws. But their significance was also practical, especially as far as the new Heliaea was concerned—and it may well have been in the Heliaea that the counting of individual votes was introduced for first time.

The significance of this innovation cannot be overestimated. It implied the equation one citizen = one vote, whether the citizen was rich or poor, noble or commoner. That probably helps to explain why retrospectively, and anachronistically, the author of the *Ath. Pol.* (see Chapter 9) included the privilege of appeal to the Heliaea as one of the three 'most demotic' of Solon's measures. The other two were, first, the ban, already mentioned, on the securing of loans on the person (which indeed drew a sharp legal line between the citizen and the slave) and, second, the legal empowerment of 'anyone who wished' to act as a volunteer prosecutor in public, non-personal, or familial cases known as 'writs', whereas in private cases only the directly injured party or parties was entitled to prosecute. In the later fourth century 'demotic', which literally means 'belonging to' or 'favouring' the *demos*, could be used as an alternative shortened form of 'democratic', but it is not certain that that is how the author intended his adjective to be taken, and, even if he did, was he right?

To sum up on Solon: some years ago Vassilis Lambropoulos wrote presciently that 'It is time to restore Solon to his rightful place in philosophy, politics, law and poetry, recognizing him as a major early figure' (1997: 26). That restoration and recognition have since been achieved, in spades. Indeed, it has been argued that Solon's introduction of the Heliaea was tantamount to introducing a form of democracy; to which I would respond that, although that may have been a partial precondition of the later emergence of democracy at Athens, it was not in itself a sufficient condition, let alone a decisively definitional move. The same, I shall argue below, goes for the reign of the Peisistratid tyrants, in the sense that they unwittingly and unwillingly set in place further preconditions for the emergence of proto-democracy. But before looking at them we should turn our gaze away from Athens for a moment, and first of all to the eastern Aegean offshore island of Chios, where a potentially momentous popular innovation in governance occurred not long after Solon's activity at Athens, but clearly did not have anything like the same immediate or eventual institutional consequences.

The evidence is epigraphical: a stele first published in 1909 but re-examined and fundamentally reappraised by the doyenne of Archaic Greek epigraphists, L. H. Jeffery, who dated it with some inevitable imprecision in the first half of the sixth century BCE. Only the back of the stele is preserved at all well, but it is the text on this face that concerns us most nearly. The front face mentions two officials, a demarch ('mayor?', or possibly the Chiot equivalent of Athens's eponymous Archon) and a *basileus*; the latter means literally 'king', but perhaps that should remind us rather of Hesiod's 'kings' or more particularly the 'King' Archon at Athens, who was the annual official with principal oversight of civic religious affairs. On one of the two sides of the stele allusion is made to the appeal of a judgment, again recalling Solon's Athenian Heliaea, and on the other side there is reference to the obligation to swear an oath in a particular month. But it is the back side that carries a dynamite charge:

Let him appeal to the Boule [Council] of the People. On the third day
after the Hebdomadaea [the seventh day of a month, dedicated to the
Ionians' chief god Apollo] that Boule shall assemble which is the People's,
[which] can inflict fines, and which consists of fifty men from a tribe . . .

For this is the earliest certain extant reference to a Council that is explicitly called 'of the People', and that may therefore be properly labelled popular,
although precisely who counted as the 'People' we cannot unfortunately say.
It would be to go too far to argue that the very existence of this Chiot popular Council alongside—presumably—a non-popular (i.e., a traditional aristocratic) Council corroborates the authenticity of the alleged Solonian Council
of Four Hundred. But at the least it shows the forward march of another city's
demos—besides those of (in their very different ways) Sparta and Athens—in
the sixth-century BCE Archaic Age.

Other possible cases of the advance of a *demos* to political incorporation
and significant empowerment during the sixth century include Heraclea
on the Black Sea (a Megarian foundation), Megara itself, Eretria and Chalcis on
Euboea, Mytilene on Lesbos, Cyrene in north Africa, Lipara (off Sicily), Naxos,
and Ambracia in northwest Greece. These have all been carefully investigated
if perhaps over-optimistically assessed by Birgalias (2009a), who advocates the
application to them of the analytical category of *isonomia*. For him this is a
type of regime to be located somewhere between a superseded aristocracy or
tyranny and a full-blown or at least unambiguous democracy, and represents a
compromise between the elite 'notables' and the citizen masses (in a numerical
sense) leading to the transformation of a social into a political majority.
Isonomia thus would have represented a definite advance on Sparta's and Solon's
eunomia, which meant good order or lawfulness. Certainly, it became a buzzword in Athens in the latter part of the sixth century, and will be scrutinised as
such later in this book. But unfortunately it is not attested concretely in the very
poor and usually much later sources for any of these other Archaic *poleis*—to
which Birgalias adds the early fifth-century (and so post-Cleisthenic) cases of
Argos and Elis. Much less moderate and even less persuasive is the view of Eric
Robinson (2011) that by c. 550 there existed 'a number of *demokratiai*'. This
seems to me to be quite literally a terminological inexactitude. It is time to
return to post-Solonian Athens.

Solon had allegedly warned the Athenians against tyranny, and that was easily construed with hindsight as a warning very specifically and personally against the tyrannical ambition of one Peisistratus, a Eupatrid (see above) aristocrat boasting a line of descent going all the way back to a Homeric hero. But actually, if we may believe the conflicting and conflicted accounts that made their way down to Herodotus and some even later writers, Peisistratus' road to supreme power was rocky and winding, and it was not before 545 that he achieved anything like a stable rule, and then only after a major military showdown involving heavy use of foreign mercenaries paid in the newfangled medium of silver coin.

One technique of rule-consolidation that Peisistratus seems to have employed to great effect—and perhaps needed to employ—was the promotion or invention of great unifying 'national' or 'ethnic' religious festivals. The Panathenaea or all-Athens festival devoted to the city's patron goddess Athena was organized (or rather reorganized) according to the traditional dating in 566, thus well before Peisistratus's first seizure of power (c. 560?) on anybody's chronology. The motivation behind it was, moreover, not peculiarly Athenian but rather pan-Hellenic, 'all-Greek': that is, it represented Athens' not entirely successful attempt to respond to the very recent linkage of the long-established Olympic Games festival with three other Games—the Pythian in honour of Apollo at Delphi, the Isthmian in honour of Poseidon at Corinth, and the Nemean in honour of Zeus at Nemea—into a four-yearly cycle or circuit of 'crown' athletic festivals (the sole material reward for victory being a symbolic crown or wreath). The Panathenaea, even when celebrated every fourth year with especial magnificence—with games and contests of various kinds open to all comers, not just Athenian citizens—never quite managed to elevate itself into the top, genuinely pan-Hellenic league, and offered material value-prizes from the start.

However, it was apparently during the period of Peisistratus's tyranny that the next most prestigious—and also importantly international in its appeal—religious festival was inaugurated: the annual Great or City Dionysia, in honour of the shape-shifting god who was thought to delight especially in the performance of plays. Initially, these involved only one actor-producer and a chorus of singer-dancers, but here were planted the seeds of that flowering of tragic and subsequently comic drama that vitally informed Athens's democratic culture in the fifth and fourth centuries (see Chapter 8).

As important in its own way was the Athenians' enhanced involvement under Peisistratus with the cult of the two Goddesses, Demeter and her daughter, whose sanctuary at Eleusis was set within comfortable walking distance along a Sacred Way running to west of the city of Athens. This happened at both the official and the individual levels. Most Athenian citizens and many other Greeks besides chose to become initiates in the Eleusinian Mysteries (so called from the secrecy of the rituals). Archaeology corroborates the extent of Peisistratus' investment in public building here, and more especially on the Acropolis and in the Agora: financing works that will have had both economic (employment) and symbolic (both 'national' and dynastic enhancement) pay-offs for the regime. It was also Peisistratus, finally, who promoted Athens's image and reach abroad by way of enhanced participation in the Delia festival: the chief religious celebration of the Ionians' patron god Apollo held annually on Delos, the island of his birth. In that, unwittingly, lay the seeds of a related fifth-century Athenian achievement, the establishment of a notionally pan-Hellenic military alliance centred symbolically at first on Apollo's Delos rather than at Athena's Athens, and so known as the 'Delian League' (see further Chapters 7 and 8).

In the realm of institutional politics, both Herodotus and Thucydides remark that Peisistratus or the Peisistratid family dynasty preserved (that is, actually, made to work) Solon's reforms—except, Thucydides significantly adds, that they fiddled things so that supporters of theirs were always in the 'offices', especially, one assumes, the chief executive office of the Archonship. That comment may apply more particularly to the reign of his oldest son and successor Hippias than to that of Peisistratus himself, who died in about 527, of natural causes. For over a dozen years Hippias continued the dynastic regime's clever policy of accommodating itself to the fundamentals of the Solonian system. Indeed, Hippias may have surpassed even his father in his willingness and ability to achieve détente with the tyranny's fiercest critics and opponents in order to enable that 'Solonian' constitution to continue to work. For as a find from the Athenian Agora made in the 1930s has proved beyond a shadow of doubt, in 525/4 Cleisthenes, son of Megacles of the Alcmaeonid family, held the office of eponymous Archon—in blatant contradiction of the family tradition passed on to and believed by Herodotus, which held not only that the Alcmaeonids were prime movers in working for the tyranny's overthrow (as we shall soon see) but also that they had been in exile throughout the tyranny—that is, from at least c. 545 until 510. Not so! That same surviving fragment of the Archon list also shows a Miltiades holding the eponymous Archonship in 524/3 and Hippias's son Peisistratus doing so in 522/1: in other words, after a decent interval the tyranny reasserted its prior claim over the leading members of the main rival families.

It was under Hippias too that Athens's first properly civic silver coinage was struck, known for short as the owl coinage after the iconic device of its patron goddess's familiar totem (the little owl). The silver used, extracted from lead by cupellation, was drawn from Athens's own slave-worked mines at Laureum. Apart from serving as a 'national' status symbol, the coinage, which was struck in large denominations, was useful mainly for making exceptionally big payments or for the storage of exceptionally large amounts of wealth. It is not impossible, however, that it had a role to play in one of Hippias' grandest national projects that did not actually achieve fruition in his reign—or indeed for over six centuries thereafter: an ultra-grand temple dedicated to Olympian Zeus. This failure should not perhaps be accounted a major setback. But within little more than a decade the Peisistratid political structure had begun to crack irreparably.

With the coolness of hindsight it is possible to credit the Peisistratid family tyranny with making a decisive or at least facilitating contribution to the next, 'Cleisthenic' step on Athens'—and Greece's—democratic road. However, the Athenians themselves, collectively, chose to see things rather differently, attributing a massive and fundamental ideological meaning to an act that may not actually have had either the significance or the consequences that they imputed to it retrospectively. Such is history—or the myth of history, or history as myth. Anyhow, in about 514 Hippias' younger brother and coadjutant Hipparchus was murdered—and it was this public assassination by the erotically connected couple Harmodius and Aristogeiton that the newly democratic Athenian state chose to look back upon as its founding, authorising moment. Actually, as the sobersided and not wildly democratic historian Thucydides observed, in a deflating digression (6.54–59), Hipparchus was not the tyrant, so that this was no act of tyrannicide, and the motivation of the assassins, so far from being ideologically liberationist let alone democratic, was instead sordidly personal.

To rub Attic salt in the wound, Thucydides also pointed out that the Athenians did not in the end liberate themselves from the Peisistratid tyranny, but had to have the job done for them by the Spartans.

On this point he was for once in agreement with Herodotus, who preserves a very full and unambiguously clear account of the facts of the case, even if he does leave the exact nature of the Spartans' motivation for intervention considerably unclear. Herodotus was sure that the exiled Alcmaeonids had bribed the oracular priestess at Delphi known as the Pythia to respond to any and every official enquiry of the Spartans that they must free the Athenians from the tyranny of Hippias—but was himself puzzled as to why the Spartans should have been willing to obey the injunction and so overthrow a family dynasty to which they were supposedly tied by the near-sacred bond of ritualised guest-friendship. At all events, in 510 King Cleomenes I, who had earlier advised the Boeotian city of the Plataeans to ally themselves with Athens allegedly in order to set them permanently at loggerheads with the much more important Boeotian city of Thebes, intervened personally in Athens and ended the tyranny. Hippias fled Athens—and sought refuge with another Greek tyrant, at Lampsacus: only Lampsacus on the Asiatic side of the Hellespont (Dardanelles) and its tyrant were vassals of the Persian empire—more seeds were thus sown here, in this case of future Graeco-Persian conflict on the grandest scale, from Marathon to Plataea and beyond.

The occupying Spartans'—or perhaps more particularly Cleomenes'—subsequent gross diplomatic error was to try to dictate what sort of post-tyranny regime Athens should have, and in particular to try to impose the rule of another Athenian as tyrant, and a subservient, pro-Spartan tyrant into the bargain. That move, however, was considered to constitute a flagrant breach of Athens' freedom (*eleutheria*) and independence (*autonomia*) as a polis. The unintended and undesired result—after a sharp bout of *stasis* or civil discord in 508/7—was the enactment of the reform bill attributed to the leading Alcmaeonid Cleisthenes. That really was—or so I shall argue in the next chapter—the founding moment of democracy at Athens, indeed in all Hellas. And the world. But if it was founded under any one label or slogan, that would have been *isonomia*, not *demokratia*.

MAP 4.1
Attica. From Pomeroy, *Ancient Greece: A Political, Social, and Cultural History* (1998).

4.

THE EMERGENCE OF GREEK

DEMOCRACY II

Athens 508/7

B Y THE END OF the sixth century BCE (in round figures by 500), the mid-dling political thinking discussed in the previous chapter and exempli-fied most notably and practically by Solon at Athens had been trumped and superseded by something far more radical—nothing less than an intellectual revolution. So at any rate, argued the brilliant social historian of early Greek myth and thought, Jean-Pierre Vernant. It will be argued here that not only was this alleged revolution a fact, but that it also played a direct role in the political revolution instantiated at Athens in the package of reforms enacted in 508/7 and ascribed en bloc to the quite exceptional aristocrat Cleisthenes.

To summarise Vernant's case very briefly: he detected in the Archaic Greek world the emergence or rather a breakthrough by 500 of a new mode of think-ing, which had two aspects. It was, first, a rational mode of thinking in the sense that when attempting for the first time to explain the non-human natural world of nature (the Greek *phusis* means literally a process of growth) and the ordered and orderly universe (*kosmos*), it explicitly denied or held in suspen-sion the power of the gods and goddesses to explain or even affect both of those. Thales of Miletus (*floruit* c. 600–585) was apparently the ultimate pro-genitor of this line of approach, to which he may perhaps have applied the term *historia*—'enquiry' or 'research'. Probably the most famous result of this type of thinking was his speculation—or rather stipulation (there was no way that he could have tested this empirically as a working hypothesis)—that the ultimate element and constituent of all perceptible matter was water. A counter-intuitive intuition, no doubt, but not a bad guess, and especially impressive coming from one who was credited with the aphorism that everything was 'full of gods'.

It would be misleading to describe his mode of thought as 'scientific', but it would be perfectly legitimate and helpful, on the other hand, to characterise it, with Vernant, as 'abstract': that is, it deliberately deprived objects of the limitless capacity to change, to metamorphosize, attributed to them by the hitherto universal and dominant thought-mode of 'myth'. The Greek word *muthos* from which English 'myth' is derived meant originally anything spoken, but for sixth-century intellectuals such as Thales it came to acquire a secondary and not entirely complimentary implied meaning of mere stories about gods and heroes (and other divine, or otherwise supernatural and superhuman powers): tales that were empirically untestable and so whose content was epistemologically speaking unknowable. It was the combination of those two aspects—the rational and the abstract—within this new, revolutionary current of thinking that eventuated in, for example, the 'natural theology' of Xenophanes of Colophon—another Ionian Greek. It was probably not accidental that Ionia on the western coast of Anatolia took the leading role here, since not far inland from Ephesus lay Sardis, which in turn via the enabling highways of the mighty neo-Assyrian, Median, and lastly Persian empires gave access ultimately to the advanced mathematical and scientific thought of Babylonia; and since, by a different, nautical route that led to the Greek entrepot of Naucratis in the Nile delta, Ionian Greeks had links into another older, more advanced civilisation, that of Pharaonic Egypt. Xenophanes is the first on record to put forward a naturalistic explanation of the Greeks' profound urge since at least the time of Homer and Hesiod to anthropomorphise their gods and goddesses. But, wrote Xenophanes in a splendid flourish of humanistic *historia*, if lions or horses had hands and could draw, they would draw their gods and goddesses in the shape of lions or horses. Consider too the (non-Greek) Thracians: their gods and goddesses have blue eyes and red hair—naturally (or rather, conventionally) enough, since that's what they themselves by nature have.

To begin with, these Ionian intellectuals and their followers outside Ionia had shown themselves interested primarily in the non-human *kosmos*, and hence they came to be known as 'natural philosophers'; Xenophanes, for example, travelled as far west as Sicily, where he speculated upon the meaning of the marine fossils he saw embedded deep down in the stone quarries of Syracuse. Or else they had concentrated on the thoughtworld of myth as that was applied to, or freely invented, supernatural powers. But around 500 BCE a change of direction towards human affairs is signalled by the pioneering work of Hecataeus, who like Thales—no mere coincidence, surely—hailed from Miletus. Hecataeus composed and somehow published either one or two works: *Genealogies* and *Journey Around the World* (*Periodos Gês*). In a programmatic preface he set out his stall: 'The tales (*muthoi*) told by the Greeks are many—and ridiculous'. Reference to 'the Greeks' seems to imply some standard of comparison with non-Greeks. At all events, if he had any hope of corroborating his claim to be performing a 'world' circuit, he will have had to encounter non-Greek 'barbarians' in the eastern Mediterranean, who in some cases lived cheek-by-jowl, if not actually among or even together with, Greeks. One such case was the Dorian Greek settlement of Halicarnassus in Caria, home to the first Greek intellectual who we know for certain boasted of practising *historia*: Herodotus. It can be no coincidence, either, that Herodotus did not just report Hecataeus' priority but also measured his own achievement against— and of course above: Greeks were famously agonistic—that of the Milesian. One good way of appreciating Herodotus' achievement would be to observe that his *Histories* married the scientific speculation of Thales to the humanistic rationalist rejection of myth by Hecataeus in order not merely to expound and to celebrate, but also to understand and to explain the single most momentous human process of his age, the Graeco-Persian Wars (see further Chapter 5).

Vernant's contribution to our understanding of late Archaic Greek political thinking and practical politics is far from exhausted by his 'intellectual revolution' concept. He—together with his Paris colleague Pierre Vidal-Naquet—also applied himself to explicating the role of myth in another sixth-century cultural breakthrough, the invention of tragic drama. We have already seen that in order to foster and shore up his rule, tyrant Peisistratus had actively patronised a number of 'national' religious festivals—among them the annual Great or City Dionysia. Conceivably, the new genre of drama pioneered there allegedly by Thespis (hence 'thespian') in the 530s would have evolved for purely artistic reasons to do with the coincidental development of the combined arts of music-making, choreography, and poesy, and would have done so with no

specifically intellectual, let alone political, content or application. Vernant, however, is to me entirely persuasive when he places the creation of the public art-
form to which the Athenians gave the rather puzzling name *tragoidia* (literally
'goat-song') under the sign of what he called a 'tragic moment': that is, a fruitful
clash between the old, myth-based explanation of both the natural world and
of human society and the new, revolutionary, human-centred view of the world
that was beginning to express itself politically in what with hindsight may be
called proto-democracy, a form of rational political self-empowerment. This
in my view is where Cleisthenes and his reform-package come in. For it was
no accident that it was in about 500 BCE, half a dozen years after the package
was implemented, that the scene of Athenian drama was removed from the
Agora to a dedicated space on the southwest slope of the Acropolis, a space that
would henceforth be known—after the *theatai* or spectators who filled it—as a
theatron: the theatre of Dionysus. Indeed, it would not be stretching a point too
far to suggest that the old festival of the Great or City Dionysia was now made
over, reinvented, as a democratic festival or festival of democracy. But let us
first explore and calibrate the Cleisthenic reforms.

Cleisthenes himself was born in c. 570, the son of an Athenian aristocrat called Megacles and of Agariste, daughter of Cleisthenes of Sicyon, the
Peloponnesian tyrant ruler after whom he was named. The story of his parents'
matchmaking is humorously told in Herodotus, but the first sober documentation of its issue, Cleisthenes, is provided by the Athenian official Archon-list of
c. 425 BCE, which (as noted in the previous chapter) records him as holding the
office of Eponymous—chief—Archon in 525/4. That would have been news to
Herodotus, who for good and for ill is our main narrative source on Cleisthenes
and his doings, abetted rather feebly by the *Ath. Pol.* and by Aristotle in his own
right in the *Politics*. From the machinations of Cleisthenes senior, the Sicyonian
tyrant, and of Cleisthenes' father Megacles, who played a double or even tri-
ple game in the career of Athenian tyrant Peisistratus, Herodotus could have
inferred that young Cleisthenes' career was unlikely to be smoothly conventional. In fact, as we have seen, he believed that Cleisthenes spent most of his
life from his mid-twenties until his mid-fifties in exile from Athens and his
ancestral lands, and that he was not above bribing the Delphic priesthood to
help bring about his restoration. But what that account leaves out is consideration of what sort of an Athens he imagined or hoped he would return to,

other than one without the Peisistratid tyranny. Was he—had he become—a principled believer in 'freedom' from non- or extra-constitutional government, or even something more positively radical and popular, even populist? Or was he also an ambitious politico intent on regaining the sort of power an aristocrat such as he might have felt was his due?

The latter, certainly, is the impression Herodotus wants to give; and presumably that was the story that his aristocratic (including Alcmaeonid) sources spun to him. Herodotus after all was self-confessedly obliged to 'tell what was said', what his sources told him, no more and no less (7.152.3); and conventional aristocrats might not have wished to be reminded or to reveal to an outsider that it was a black sheep of their own flock who had gone over to the dark, democratic side. Anyhow, after the overthrow of the Peisistratids in 510 (by the Spartans, to repeat), Herodotus' Cleisthenes engaged in what is represented as being at first nothing more elevated than a head-to-head struggle for honour and power with rival aristocrat Isagoras—thereby embroiling Athens in the sort of *stasis* (civil strife, even civil war) that Herodotus himself deplored (8.3). Their forces were evenly matched, indeed so much so that each felt obliged to turn for extra support to highly unconventional sources. But whereas Isagoras looked outside to Sparta and King Cleomenes to bolster him (and possibly also secure for him a tyrant's throne), thereby incurring the conjoined enmity of patriots and anti-tyrants, Cleisthenes turned inwards—to the Athenian *demos*, a *demos* that in Herodotus' ambiguous words (5.66) had been 'formerly despised' (either by all leading political actors, or possibly just by Cleisthenes).

This demotic turn is cloaked by Herodotus (or by his aristocratic sources) in what at first seems thoroughly conventional language. For he says that Cleisthenes 'added the *demos* to his *hetairia*', in effect treating all ordinary, non-elite Athenian citizens as if they were his *hetairoi*—an elite term for aristocratic bosom buddies. Yet in the circumstances that language is paradoxical and metaphorical, for that was a truly maverick, opportunist move or manoeuvre; and, however egalitarian, it was by no means wholly honourable. But it worked; it did the trick. It put Cleisthenes in a position eventually to carry through the reforms that Herodotus succinctly summarised as 'introducing the tribes *and the democracy* for the Athenians' (6.131). But did he? What did Herodotus mean by 'introducing the tribes', and was it in truth democracy that Cleisthenes (also or thereby) introduced?

The evidence being what it is, extreme caution is in order, even when stating what Cleisthenes did, let alone why and with what effect. Let's take our lead from Herodotus and start with those 'tribes', since clearly they were somehow at the heart of the matter. 'Tribes' translates Greek *phulai*, but that should not conjure up visions of what ethnographers and social anthropologists understand by 'tribal' societies: that is, non-western, pre-political societies lacking any elaborate mechanisms of communal decision-making and organised socially in real or artificially constructed ('classificatory') kinship groupings. Early historical Greece was, I have argued, pre-political, in the sense of pre-*polis*, and, if Homer may be relied upon, possessed *phulai*. But already these early historical 'tribes' were no longer natural, wholly kin-based groupings; and, as for the three Dorian 'tribes' of, say, the *polis* of Sparta at the time of Tyrtaeus (c. 650 BCE: see Chapter 3), the very name of one of them, Pamphuloi or 'all-tribespeople', betrays its artificially made-up character. All Ionian Greeks, such as those of Miletus or Athens, liked to imagine that they were ultimately descended from a common male ancestor, Ion, and most of them celebrated their common identity by annually celebrating the Apatouria festival (as most Dorians celebrated their Dorian-ness through the religious festival of the Carneia in honour of Apollo.) But this was not celebration of a genuine kinship, but rather of a pseudo-kinship, and there were social groupings politically more important than the four Ionian 'tribes' at Athens. These were known as *gene* (akin to our 'genetic'), and, however precisely these religio-political corporations were constituted (they too proclaimed their pseudo-kinship basis), it seems highly likely that it was through membership in these that Athenians gained admission to citizenship. Almost certainly, too, they were controlled either by members of the old aristocracy or of the new, birth or wealth aristocracy. If therefore a political reformer wished to alter the very basis of Athenian citizenship, he would have had to dismantle or bypass the existing 'tribal' structure, and that, we may safely infer, is what Herodotus meant when he stated bluntly that Cleisthenes 'introduced (or established) the tribes for the Athenians'.

In practice, Cleisthenes—or more likely Cleisthenes and his team of expert advisers—for all-important purposes of self-government, replaced the existing Ionian pseudo-kinship tribes with new, locally based 'tribes'. The new basis of citizenship was made enrolment in a deme: confusingly, the same word *demos* as in 'People' here meant 'village' or 'ward'. Eventually there were 139 or 140 demes, which were grouped into thirty *trittyes* (thirdings), which in turn were distributed, ten apiece, among the three broad sub-regions into which the territory of Attica was now divided for political including military purposes: the city, the inland region, and the coast. Out of the thirty *trittyes* were formed the ten new political tribes, by the expedient of combining one *trittys* from each region, thus: 1 'city' + 1 'inland' + 1 'coast' *trittyes* = 1 tribe. Some demes grew sufficiently urbanized to resemble mini-Athens-es, but most—like those of the plain of Marathon—remained 'composed of farmlands dispersed over the plain, which might here and there have been grouped into a small settlement consisting of a few houses, perhaps of related families' (Steinhauer 2009: 85).

There was no doubt plenty of scope for argument and disagreement—over exactly where the boundary of a deme lay, or which *trittys* should go with which others to form a tribe, or (not least) to which deme a citizen should attach himself at the initial (and thereafter hereditary, set-in-stone) allocation.

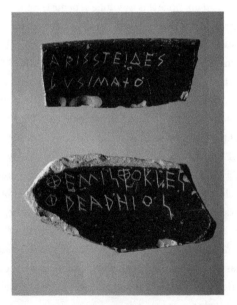

FIGURE 4.1
Ostraca
Inscribed potsherds (*ostraka* in Greek), such as these examples directed at Aristides and Themistocles in the 480s, served as ballots in the controversial democratic procedure of ostracism. © Gianni Dagli Orti / The Art Archive at Art Resource, NY

The deme engendered immense loyalty: when under duress from Spartan invasions in and after 431 Athenian rural dwellers were forced albeit briefly to abandon their homes and take up temporary residence in the city of Athens, they were put out at having to abandon what was to them their own little *polis* (Thuc. 2.15–16). Engendering loyalty in the new and far more artificial regional tribes was rather more difficult. In order to endow them with something approaching a quasi-family identity, each was named after a legendary tribal 'hero', to whom religious worship was paid at regular tribal gatherings. Other expedients included organising the hoplite army by tribal regiments, recruiting decision-making or advisory political bodies and composing boards of officials on the basis of equality of tribal representation, and seating citizens or competing with choruses in the theatre by tribes. But there was no questioning the radical novelty of the whole scheme as such, which—so far as our hopelessly limited evidence allows such an inference—was up and running within a tolerably short space of time.

We should like to know a great deal more about how exactly the initial lists of citizens were drawn up, since this was done at deme level, and for this among many other reasons, both practical and symbolic, it was the deme that was the ultimate basis of the entire superstructure. What bolsters the inference of swift efficiency in implementation is the fact that, as we shall see in the next chapter, one of the things that most forcibly struck outside observers about post-Cleisthenic Athens was how much more militarily successful it quite suddenly became. Each new tribe was to elect one new-style General; and the new annual boards of ten elective Generals thus formed were firmly in place at least from 501 BCE. Yet they somehow coexisted alongside the old-style, annual office of War Archon: a touch of conservatism, if not political reaction, in deference perhaps to the old guard. Indeed, right up the Battle of Marathon in 490 at least, the latter was technically in overall command of any Athenian land army. Each new tribe, as noted, had to contribute one regiment of hoplites to the army; there was no significant Athenian navy until the 480s, and the Athenian cavalry force was still, and would generally continue to be, feeble and largely symbolic. Depending on fellow tribesmen for one's life was well calculated to foster genuine mutuality.

Each new tribe was also required to provide one-tenth of the members of a brand-new Council. The very existence of an earlier, Solonian Council (of Four

Hundred) is in dispute, let alone what its powers and responsibilities might have been. The Cleisthenic Council of 500 was unambiguously slated from the word go to be the steering committee of the newly re-empowered Assembly, the *Ecclesia*, in order to help it perform its primary function, which was to take final decisions on policy. The *Ecclesia* was so called because its constituents on any one occasion of its meeting were 'called out', summoned by a trumpeter or herald or some other means to a designated meeting place. Under the Solonian dispensation that place of meeting had been the Agora, but from 508/7 onwards it became the nearby hill lying in the shadow of the Acropolis and known as the Pnyx (from a Greek word meaning 'squeeze tight together'). Athenians attending an Assembly meeting here squeezed together by sitting or squatting down, each citizen occupying on average roughly half a square metre. It is estimated that in 508/7 and indeed until well into the fourth century no more than 6,000 Athenians could be accommodated reasonably comfortably in the space available. But that number was judged to be a sufficiently representative—both quantitatively and quantitatively speaking—proportion of the entire citizen body; that, if we may believe Herodotus' (5.97) probably overgenerous round figure estimate, was of the order of 30,000 in 500 BCE, when Aristagoras tyrant of Miletus came to make his plea for military aid.

We shall return shortly (Chapter 5) to the nature of his business. To wrap up our account of the Cleisthenic package, we must discuss a number of legal matters that vitally affected the status and behaviour of citizens under the new democratic dispensation. For, in accordance with Aristotle's democracy-leaning definition (*Politics* 1275), the citizen was he who was entitled to an actively participatory share in both office-holding and in the passing of legal judgments; and all the new Athenian citizens—some of whom were of foreign birth, others freed ex-slaves—were formally entitled to a participatory share in both. On socio-economic grounds, however, we may safely imagine that only relatively few would have been in a position, let alone keen, to put themselves forward for election to the Archonship, the Generalship, or any of the major financial offices such as Treasurers of Athena. Indeed, specific legal restrictions on eligibility remained in place until well into the fifth century. On the jurisdictional side, too, Cleisthenes had left untouched the existence and privileges of the old aristocratic council of the Areopagus, not least that of the impeachment of officials for high crimes and misdemeanours, thereby leaving unresolved an issue that was to move to centre stage four decades later (Chapter 5). But he had also left alone the Solonian Heliaea appeal court, so that it was presumably through this key popular institution that ordinary Athenians could activate their privilege of legal judgment by means of the casting and counting of their equal votes.

Such judicial votes were delivered secretly. Originally, perhaps, this was done using a pebble, *psephos*, whence by transference *psephos* came to mean a 'vote' (and hence too our 'psephology'). But in the fifth century the medium in use was no longer of stone but bronze—to which we shall return in connection with the next major revamp of the exercise of power (*kratos*) by the Athenian *demos*. Votes in the *Ecclesia*, however, were open, and delivered by show of—right—hands, hence the name *kheirotonia*, 'extension of hands'; normally too they were 'told' or guesstimated rather than individually counted, both for reasons of time-saving and because normally opinions would not be all that closely divided. Nevertheless, each public vote did potentially risk division in the sense of divisiveness, and even, at worst, *stasis*—civil dissension or outright civil conflict. That was also an essential consideration in the matter of one final, highly controversial legal measure attributed to Cleisthenes: ostracism (*ostrakismos*).

The very procedure was remarkable enough in itself, although its precise details are not entirely agreed among our sources, all of whom were writing very much later than the period in which ostracism was actually put into operation (intermittently between 488 and 416). At a stated moment in each civil year the Assembly was asked whether it wished to conduct an ostracism. If the vote were positive, plans were made for the voting to take place on a given day later in that same civil year, thereby allowing for a possible cooling-off (or perhaps hotting up) of the feelings that had led to the initial positive vote. Votes were cast in the shape of *ostraka*, potsherds, inscribed (either scratched or painted) with the name of the one citizen whom the voter wished to see formally exiled from Athens and Attica for a period of ten years; though he would not be deprived of his citizen status or his ownership of property, but rather of the physical possibility of exercising his citizenship or managing his property in person for the duration of his exile. (If, proverbially, 'a week is a long time in politics', ten years must count as an eternity.) On the appointed day, voters would rock up in the Agora and present to an official teller their inscribed ballot, whether it was they who had actually inscribed it or not.

For some voters were of course illiterate; this gave rise, inevitably, to the fable of a peasant countryman unfamiliar with city politics who innocently and ignorantly asked the famous Aristides to write 'Aristides' on a potsherd. But why him? asked the famously just Aristides—because I'm sick of hearing him called 'the just', replied the mindless ignoramus. Others took the opportunity to spoil their ballot by voting to ostracize, for example, 'starvation', and yet others—not only literate but witty—enhanced theirs by adding a little message such as 'Aristides, Datis' brother' (an accusation of 'medism', being soft on the Persians, which was literally correct for once, since Datis was in fact a Mede not a Persian) or 'May Kimon go away—and take Elpinike with him!' (a none-too-subtle implication of incest between this brother and sister). For the ostracism procedure to be valid, there had either to be a minimum of 6,000 votes cast against any one candidate, or—much more likely—there had to be a minimum of 6,000 proper *ostraka* cast in all, and the 'winner'—that is the loser—was he against whom the plurality of those 6,000-plus valid votes was directed.

Whatever might be said about the equity of this procedure—Aristotle for one ranted against its monstrous injustice, though he was not an Athenian citizen, and in his day it was a dead letter—it was certainly, formally speaking, thoroughly democratic in the later accepted strong sense of that term: that is, it involved the *demos* passing judgment collectively and on an exactly equal basis on its would-be leaders and advisers (whether they were holding any office at the time or not). Socially, it carries the further, highly interesting implication that at least a good percentage of those 6,000 minimum voters would be literate, or literate enough; that is, even though they might not be able to write a name themselves, they might reasonably be expected to be able to recognise the letters written or painted (the Greek for 'to write' could also mean 'to paint') for them on a potsherd. Alphabetic literacy of the ancient Greek type was not in itself necessarily democratic (cf. Chapter 2), but it was entirely compatible with being given a specifically democratic expression, as here. However, the procedure was also open to non- or even anti-democratic abuse, in one of two main ways. A cache of 190 *ostraka* has been excavated in the Athenian Agora, each one bearing the name 'Themistokles' and written in only a small number—not 190—of different hands. This looks very much like a set of *ostraka* pre-prepared by his opponents for distribution to willing or gullible voters on the day, as part of an orchestrated campaign to 'fix' the vote. Whether they were actually used or not, Themistocles was indeed ostracised—but not until the end of the 470s, whereas this cache had been designed for use in the 480s, when Themistocles had survived a whole series of ostracisms prompted or at least overshadowed by the burning issue of how Athens should respond to the post-Marathon Persian threat.

The ostracism procedure as such also survived that 480s series, even though it had led to very serious inconvenience: some of Athens' likeliest military commanders were actually in ostracised exile when the Persians under Xerxes did arrive, in massive military force, in 480. Sensibly, the Assembly of the Athenians voted to override these earlier judgements and recalled them all, not least Aristides—who on the strength of his achievements in 480 and 479 was to go on to play a leading role in post-Persian War Athenian policymaking. However, in 416 political chicanery over the conduct of one ostracism did not just have catastrophic consequences in the immediate term but effectively put an end for good to the institution's practical application. The leading candidates of the day were the more conservative Nicias and the more adventurous (and self-regarding) Alcibiades; the issue was not only or primarily personal but rather the future conduct of a war against Sparta and the Peloponnesians that technically, legally, was in suspension. (A peace agreement had been sworn in 421, which indeed bore the very name of Nicias, its principal Athenian negotiator and advocate; but Alcibiades was bidding to renew the fighting by reopening the western, Sicilian theatre.) Yet the plurality of *ostraka* was cast against a third, far less significant but still prominent figure, Hyperbolus. The following year the decision was taken by the Assembly to mount a simply massive expedition to Sicily, which ended in total failure at a stupendous cost in lives, equipment, and communal morale. A chastened *demos* never again actually voted to hold an *ostrakophoria*, although not even the cautious revision of the statute books undertaken between 410 and 399 (Chapter 9) formally revoked and expunged the procedure.

That was no doubt due to an exaggeratedly conservative reverence for what was called optimistically the 'ancestral constitution' or 'constitution of the fathers'. One of the potential 'fathers' was Cleisthenes, and, according to the *Ath. Pol.* (22) and other more reliable sources, it was Cleisthenes who had introduced ostracism. That would fit well with the general pro-democratic tenor of his reforms, since at this time it would have been the one quasi-legal means whereby ordinary Athenians might pass judgment on their political leaders, whether they had been elected or did not hold any office, and whether they had been charged with any offence or not. However, one difficulty with accepting the attribution of ostracism to Cleisthenes is that none actually took place until twenty years later, in 488/7. Another difficulty is that the alleged motive for the practice's introduction was a desire to prevent a recurrence of tyranny, yet the procedure would have been both a clumsy and an ineffective means of achieving that goal, and anyway that alleged motive looks like a false inference from the fact that the first Athenian to be ostracised was a member of the Peisistratid tyrant family. Its original aim, more plausibly, was to pre-empt, or to abort, *stasis* in the sense of outright civil war, arising from conflicts of persons and policies between would-be leaders or champions of the people. It also had the salutary, quasi-religious function of symbolically ridding the community of a potential source of pollution. Those two aims and functions seem to me entirely compatible with the ascription to Cleisthenes, who had emerged to his position of authority from out of a bout of *stasis*, and it would have sat very well with the establishment of a new, clean heroic cult of the 'tyrannicides'. One final point: ostracism, though it originated at Athens, was not unique to Athens. Under different names forms of it were practised elsewhere, but always in other democratic cities: Argos, Syracuse, perhaps Miletus, and perhaps also Megara. But it was only at Athens that it aroused quite the same degree of political passion, both contemporaneous and retrospective.

How, then, should one interpret the Cleisthenic reforms? What, if any, single-word label captures the quintessence of the 'transformation' (the phrase of the Aristotelian *Ath. Pol.*) that the total package embodied and represented? Modern interpretations of the 508/7 episode have been many and various— and often mutually incompatible. According to David Lewis, following a lead offered by Herodotus or his sources, Cleisthenes was nothing more than an Alcmaeonid schemer, manoeuvring to promote his own aristocratic family; but that interpretation runs fatally up against the overall thrust of the reforms, which were so clearly designed to obviate precisely the possibility of any one individual (or his more or less extended family members) gaining an undue amount of influence simply by using the system newly put in place. Antony Andrewes rightly emphasised the care and cleverness that had gone into constructing the package as a whole and into presenting it persuasively to the *demos* in the Assembly. Josiah Ober inferred from Herodotus' account the occurrence of some sort of popular uprising, which he saw as directed chiefly against outside Spartan intervention and its aim of re-imposing a foreign-backed tyranny; of this already populist, anti-tyrannical uprising, he argued, Cleisthenes and his immediate supporters seized brilliant advantage to push through their well-considered reforms. This to me assumes a rather too high level of development of popular political consciousness, although it undoubtedly did not harm Cleisthenes' cause that he could appeal to patriotic sentiment in his support. The French scholars Pierre Lévêque and Pierre Vidal-Naquet contrived to write a whole book around the reform of Cleisthenes, in which they laid particular stress on what they took to be its 'theoretical' underpinnings in terms of spatial organization, and especially its application of a version of decimalization. For Gregory Anderson, however, Cleisthenes was an opportunist, though less personally/familially motivated than Lewis', and his chief achievement was somehow to persuade (or fool?) ordinary Athenians into believing that his reforms were less innovatory than restorationist, taking Athens back to a good old pre-tyrannical golden age, while at the same time through them he was constructing an imagined political community of solidarity and equality for an actually heterogeneous and newly empowered *demos*.

The scholarly tendency according to which Cleisthenes' reforms did not usher in democracy properly so called, but rather something on the cusp of it, is brilliantly represented by Kurt Raaflaub. For him, it is not merely accidental or coincidental that the term *demokratia* is not attested until (probably) the 420s, although it may have been in existence a couple of decades earlier. This is because in his view it was not until after the further reforms proposed in the late 460s by Ephialtes, with Pericles as his junior adjutant, that Athens actually achieved a system of governance that could rightly be so labelled. Against that tendency, however, it can be argued both that there are positive indications that the term *demokratia* had already been coined before Ephialtes made his proposals (the personal name 'Demokrates' from the 470s, a poetic periphrasis of Aeschylus in his *Suppliant Women* tragedy, datable plausibly to 463), and that what those Ephialtic reforms did was institute a fuller, more developed, more demotic democracy than the democracy which—as even Herodotus (6.131) had had to concede—'Cleisthenes introduced for the Athenians'.

That position was argued most forcefully by G.E.M. de Ste. Croix in a posthumously published collection of essays (in private circulation since the 1950s). For Ste. Croix, moreover, taking the exact opposite line of that of Lewis, Cleisthenes was a confirmed, principled reformer, even if he did not yet know that he was also a democrat. Two main arguments are brought forward in corroboration: that the political system he gave his name to was immensely carefully thought out, and so constructed as to ensure in combination a maximum equality of participatory intensity locally (via the deme) with a maximum of 'mixing up' of citizens from all over Attica (via the tribes and their expressions in the Council and army); and, second, that the system began very quickly to work and work very well, one of the conditions of which is likely to have been that the citizens in their overwhelming majority wanted it to and willed it to so work. I myself have also argued for the view that post-Cleisthenic Athens was an early form of democracy—though not yet that in name. More specifically, it was a hoplite democracy, empowering differentially that better-off portion of the sub-elite *demos* who could afford to serve as hoplites in the new-model tribal army.

If I were to give the new system a single-word alternative title, it would be either *isonomia* or *isokratia*. Both those terms, however, are formally speaking ambiguous—or even ambivalent: they may be laid claim to by oligarchs no less than by democrats, depending on which citizens are being counted as relevantly equal (*isoi*) and to what (power or powers) the equality on offer is being applied. Proto-democrats—the majority of Athenian citizens—would have argued for the widest possible application of political equality, while recognising pragmatically that some were more able than others to avail themselves of the equality on offer in terms of the active exercise of participation and decision-making through election to the new Council and new offices including the Generalship, and attendance at the Assembly. It was no accident therefore that when the pro-democracy speaker in Greece's—and the world's—first attested example of political theory (an invented debate) was advocating the system with the 'fairest of names', he chose to call it *isonomia* (see further Chapter 6).

5.

THE EMERGENCE OF GREEK

DEMOCRACY III

Athens 507–451/0

A NUMBER OF KEY EVENTS between 508/7 and the next major bout of reforms of 462/1 can be pointed to as reinforcing or enhancing, though not always straightforwardly, the democratic thrust of the Cleisthenic package deal. To begin with, it seems that the Assembly got very wrong Athens' diplomatic relations with the Persian empire. Its former tyrant Hippias had fled to Lampsacus, a place of safety within the Persian imperial ambit, and Persia liked to operate control of its far Western Asiatic, Greek-speaking possessions through a small handful of pro-Persian local Greek tyrants, such as the tyrant of Lampsacus. Yet in 507 so anxious were the Athenians about a renewed Spartan intervention, and so desperate for outside support, that envoys of theirs actually gave over the token 'earth and water' that symbolised submission to Persia in return, presumably, for a promise of Persian financial aid. That mistake, if that is what it was, was at once overridden by the Assembly, one of the first decisions that the new democratic Assembly steered by the new Council of 500 had to make. Viewed unsympathetically by a non- or anti-democratic observer, however, this episode of trial and error could easily be seen as illustrating the stereotypical fickleness of the ignorant, stupid, and feckless 'masses'. That at any rate was exactly how another major foreign policy decision of the Assembly taken towards Persia half a dozen years later was viewed by Herodotus, as we shall see.

But if the early Assembly did not cover itself with glory, the early post-Cleisthenic army did, twice over. In 506, at the particularly insistent urging of that same King Cleomenes I who had got himself into such a tangle at Athens in 508, a large Spartan/Peloponnesian expedition was mounted against Athens. With what objective? Surely it can have been none other than politically motivated, to overthrow the Cleisthenic regime; a century or so later Thucydides (1.19) could generalise from a wealth of past evidence that the Spartans in their foreign policy always supported oligarchies—meaning not only existing oligarchies but also ones that they helped to impose by force. (The one gigantic exception to that rule occurred at Athens in 403, after the end of the war that Thucydides had set himself to narrate and explain.)

In practice, the expedition got no further than the western borders of Attica before it broke up in high dudgeon and amid fatal dissensions both between Sparta and one of its major allies, and between the two Spartan kings. Emboldened by that failure, the Athenians struck two further blows against hostile neighbours—Chalcis on the adjoining island of Euboea, and the Boeotian federal state led by Thebes. The Athenians themselves naturally enough made a great song and dance of these unaccustomed hoplite victories; less predictable was the paean of praise they provoked in the by no means always eulogistic Herodotus. For to him they demonstrated the ineffable superiority, at least for military purposes, of what he called 'exact equality of free public speech' (*isegoria*, echoing *isonomia, isokratia*). Herodotus took that to connote also metaphorically a twofold freedom: freedom *from* tyranny and freedom to fight *for* themselves, *for* their own freely chosen ideals, rather than under external compulsion. He clearly, if anachronistically, had in mind also the comparable energising spirit that the democratic Athenians would show a decade and a half later—on the battlefield of Marathon in 490, if not also on the sea at Salamis in 480.

Offshore to the east of Attica ran the very large island of Euboea, and to the south of Attica lay the tiny islet of Salamis. The Athenians now sent out settlers to both, but whereas those who became Euboean effectively surrendered their Athenian citizen privileges, those who went to live on Salamis were incorporated within the deme system, as Salaminioi. Relatively small in scale, these early population exports anticipated the far larger wave of Aegean-world Athenian emigration that was to mark the middle decades of the fifth century. As yet, it is highly unlikely that many, if indeed any, Athenians could seriously have entertained imperial ambitions, though the more farsighted of them might already have been concerned to secure extra supplies of grain, in the form of bread wheat, from the northern shore of the Black Sea (Ukraine and south Russia today). Nonetheless, that did not stop a majority from deciding in 500 to respond positively to a request from Aristagoras, the then tyrant of Miletus, for military aid, including manpower, in support of those Greeks of Asia who wished to revolt from the Persian Empire.

Herodotus—with the benefit of hindsight, laced perhaps by some anti-Ionian prejudice—poured withering scorn on this benighted decision: the beginning of many evils as he saw it not just for the Asiatic Greeks but for all Hellas—the Greek world—more generally. One can see what he meant. Aristagoras was an unstable and unreliable figure, and what is usually if misleadingly referred to as the Ionian Revolt of 499–494 BCE did turn out in the end to be an abject failure. But the Athenians, notwithstanding their grief at the Persians' destruction of Miletus in 494, did not suffer any direct material loss from that catastrophe and in 493 felt bold enough to lend support to a different kind of uprising much nearer to home, a proto-democratic putsch on the neighbouring island of Aegina. That too, however, was a failure, more significant for its intent and ambition than for its outcome. As for the Persians, after imposing a new imperial settlement in the West of their empire that affected the non-Greeks of Cyprus as well as the Greeks of Cyprus and Asia Minor, they set their minds to gaining control of much of the Aegean and to devastating Eretria on Euboea (which had also sent aid to fellow Greeks of Asia in 499) before punishing Athens.

Eretria was destroyed, and its surviving population enslaved and transported far to the east, but against the Athenians and their sole allies from Boeotian Plataea the expedition came famously to grief on the plain of Marathon in eastern Attica—a further triumphant corroboration of hoplite democracy. Herodotus reports that of the 9,000 Athenians a mere 192 (precisely) lost their lives, as against the rounded figure of 6,400 on the Persian side; he gives no figures for the Plataeans, whose very participation indeed tended to be suppressed at least by Athenian sources. Those 192 were permitted to be buried on the battlefield, an unusual honour, and were thereafter officially celebrated as heroes—that is, were paid the religious worship accorded to mortal men whose feats entitled them to more than merely human post-mortem veneration.

FIGURE 5.1
Persepolis tribute relief
Persepolis (in Persian Parsa), in southern Iran today, was the chief ceremonial capital of the
Achaemenid Persian Empire. The monumental entrance stairway to the Apadana (audience chamber)
represented visually the Persians' imperial reach through ethnically differentiated images of tribute-
bearing subjects. © pbk, Berlin/ Art Resource, NY

It was also in a spirit of celebration and thanksgiving that between 490 and 488 the Athenians embarked on the construction of the so-called Older Parthenon: the predecessor temple built on more or less exactly the same site on the Acropolis as the completed Parthenon was erected between 447 and 432. This was dedicated to the city's patron goddess Athena in her guise as a Virgin (indomitable, impenetrable, untamed by no male: somewhat akin to 'virgin' Queen Elizabeth I in this respect). But the Persians would surely be back, sooner or later. And the political events and the politicking at Athens of the following decade were shadowed constantly by this Persian threat, beginning as early as the prosecution in 489 of Marathon hero Miltiades (father of Cimon) by Xanthippus (father of Pericles) for failure to capture, compounded by alleged religious misdemeanours committed on, the Cycladic island of Paros. At issue here, apart from the purely personal rivalry and enmity, was what policy Athens should pursue in regard to this sensitive and recently

Persian-dominated region. Miltiades was found guilty, and fined hugely, a debt
his son Cimon discharged manfully following his father's painful death.

There followed the first completed ostracism in 487—of a relative of the
tyrant family whose senior member, Hippias, was in Persian exile. In 488 or
487 too the Archonship, the top annual executive office after the Generalship,
was significantly made sortitive (filled partly by lot), and thus opened up to less
notable Athenians than before. Further ostracisms followed, as Athens found
itself at war with neighbouring Aegina while simultaneously having to decide
on its policy towards Persia—a choice between sullen defeatism and outright
opposition. In 483/2 the die was cast: the Athenian Assembly was persuaded
by Themistocles, ostracism survivor and rampant democratic champion, to
vote to spend a huge windfall from the state-owned silver mines not on a mass
handout but on building an entire new fleet of triremes—ostensibly for immediate use against Aegina, but the exceptionally far-sighted Themistocles had a
greater object in his longer-term sights. These three-banked oared warships
were a kind of maritime guided missile (see Chapter 8, Figure 8.2). But they
also bore important political and class implications: each was powered by 170
economically unprivileged citizen-sailors, who had to be somehow trained,
fed, and materially rewarded or compensated. By 480, when the time came,
the brand-new Athenian fleet was sufficiently large and efficient to contemplate taking on the mighty Persian navy (of mainly Phoenician and Greek
warships).

In that year Darius' son and successor Xerxes finally, after some four years
of preparation, personally launched his amphibious attack from western Asia
Minor by way of the Hellespont. The land army suffered a serious hold-up and
losses at Thermopylae, thanks chiefly to the Spartans (who were the overall
leaders of such allied Greek resistance as could be mounted), but ploughed
on relentlessly to Athens, which it unceremoniously sacked, not excluding the
sanctuaries of the gods and heroes in the Agora and on the Acropolis. Things
went very differently at sea. A first inconclusive engagement was fought off the
island of Euboea, at Artemisium, in which the Persians again suffered serious
losses. But off Salamis, in a narrow strait into which Xerxes had rashly been
lured, the Greek allies led by Athens won a famous victory, equal in military
significance to that at Marathon. But the political implications of the two for
Athens were significantly different. Salamis marked the tipping point in the

composition of the city's armed forces from being an essentially amateur force of moderately rich farmer-hoplites to being predominantly a semi-professional fleet of sailors drawn from the swelling ranks of the Athenian poor. The title of the Athenian chief executive office remained General, but in practice Generals on active service were more often admirals of the fleet, none more so than Cimon. From the winter of 478/7 on, the Athenians through the offensive-defensive alliance they formed on the sacred island of Delos (hence the entirely modern term Delian League) pursued three objectives: those of liberating any remaining Greeks still under Persian subjection, taking revenge and reparations for Persian sacrilege and material damage, and trying to ensure the permanent freedom of all Greeks from the tentacles of the admittedly still very dangerous and threatening Persian Empire. The success the pursuit of them brought corroborated the growing equation of *demos* with the navy and—probably by 470—the coinage of the very term *demokratia* in the sense of the rule of the poor masses.

Culture, moreover, reinforced politics, as it had done under tyrant Peisistratus, but now in a democratic, explicitly anti-tyrannical way. I have mentioned already the official cult of the so-called Tyrannicides: Harmodius and Aristogeiton were unquestionably the first purely human beings (as distinct from the ten Eponymous tribal Heroes) to be accorded the accolade of having statues representing them erected at public expense in the Agora—and indeed they were the last to be so honoured for over a century. So keenly did the Athenians resent the theft of the original pair by Persian king Xerxes in 480 that one of their first official acts after the Persian threat had been beaten back was to commission in 477 a handsome, bronze replacement. It is the latter that gave rise to copies of varying size and in various media of this literally iconic duo (Figure 5.2). No less germane to the growth of democracy than these static visual representations of its adopted founding heroes were the dramatic representations staged from about 500 in the newly built Theatre of Dionysus; from 486 on these included comedies in addition to the tragedies and satyr dramas.

Aeschylus' extant tragedy *Persians* of 472, one of a group financed by Pericles (performing an official 'liturgy' as *chorêgos*), is the standout production. Exceptionally, its scenario was drawn from the near present, the Battle of Salamis and its aftermath at the Persian capital of Susa; normally, tragedians

FIGURE 5.2
Athenian Tyrannicides: Roman copies in marble of bronze originals
Harmodius and Aristogeiton (d. c. 513 BCE) were not in fact 'tyrannicides', since they killed the tyrant
Hippias' younger brother not the tyrant himself, nor were they democrats, but they were transformed
into icons of liberty and democracy and were the first humans to have named statues (of bronze)
erected in their honour in the Athenian Agora. © Album / Art Resource, N

drew their material from myth and legend, and not necessarily Athenian myth
and legend, of yore. Conventions were honoured by not actually mentioning
Themistocles, the prime architect of the Salamis victory, by name. But no one
in the audience would have been in any doubt that one of the play's surely
intended political effects was to associate Themistocles with the freedom
and democracy that that victory had assured. Xerxes, in polar contrast, was
depicted as the oriental autocrat from central casting, and his Persian courtiers
as the very type of effeminate, servile, barbarian subjects, not manly, free, self-
governing citizens. Special emphasis was placed on the fact that Xerxes was
'not subject to audit'—that is, not accountable to his people in the way that all
Athenian officials, even the highest and mightiest, were accountable, through
the Council, to the Athenian People. Whatever the Athenian audience made of
this hymn to democracy and civic-republican freedom, however, it did not save

FIGURE 5.3
Pericles
Pericles (c. 493–429 BCE) was born into the highest Athenian aristocracy, but threw in his lot with the common Athenian citizen and championed democracy during a long and mostly successful career both on and off the battlefield. © Album / Art Resource, N

Themistocles from being ostracised, probably in 471 or 470. For him by then, and for some time previously, it was not Persia that was Athens' bogeyman, but rather Sparta. When he embarked on his obligatory ten-year exile, he chose, with heavy symbolism, to spend it initially in Argos, perennial Peloponnesian rival and enemy of Sparta.

I spoke just now of the *Persians* as a 'hymn to democracy', but that word was not, and probably could not comfortably have been, actually used in the play. Even if already coined by then, it would have stuck out like a sore thumb, being far too glaringly modernist in tone. But Aeschylus was in his way glaringly modernist, and less than a decade later, probably in 463, he produced another of his extant plays, the *Suppliant Women*, in which the issue of how a monarch should properly rule was placed centre stage. The monarch in question this time was Greek, not Persian, and a ruler from way back in mythical time, but the city he ruled was Argos, which was a bit of a hint, and the manner in which he ruled was strikingly, anachronistically, democratic. Before deciding whether or not Argos should give sanctuary to these (non-Greek, Egyptian) suppliants, he declares that he must first consult the people of Argos, in a public assembly meeting, and through a popular vote. At line 604 of the play, in order to convey the fact that a large majority of the assembled Argives had voted in favour of the king's proposal, Aeschylus speaks of the 'authoritative or powerful hand of the People'; this is a poetic periphrasis for majority voting by the raising of right hands, one citizen one vote, as was in fact done regularly in the real-life, contemporary Athenian *Ecclesia*.

Small wonder that quite apart from his exceptional dramatic talent, Aeschylus' plays should so often have been commissioned by the chief Archon of the year, and financed by wealthy citizens such as Pericles. In 458, with his extant *Oresteia* trilogy, Aeschylus went one step further in his playing of politics by other, dramatic means. By then Athens was more or less at open war with Sparta (the so-called First Peloponnesian War), and by setting the opening play (the *Agamemnon*) in Argos—not Mycenae, as in Homer—he gave a strong clue to its ideological orientation; so too did an openly supportive reference to the need for Athens to make alliance with Argos (as in historical fact it already had done). But the main ideological thrust of the trilogy was internally directed, not externally, since the culminating play, the *Eumenides*, dramatised the very inauguration, by Athena no less, of the Areopagus as a jury court, convened ostensibly to try the refugee Orestes for the murder of his mother Clytemnestra. Now, the Areopagus was every bit as much a current Athenian political institution as the *Ecclesia*, but there was one huge, situational difference. Just a few years before, in 462/1, the old Areopagus council had been one of the central focuses of a major package of democratic reforms promoted by Ephialtes together with, in a supporting role, the still very junior Pericles.

Hardly anything is recorded about Ephialtes the man or politician, but the very fact of his assassination shortly afterwards shows that he, and not the barely thirty-something Pericles, was the chief reformer. Likewise clear is that the main institutional target of Ephialtes' reformist zeal was the Areopagus. This was indeed the most ancient council still operating, and not only its functions but also its membership and the method of its recruitment—from ex-Archons automatically—had, it seems, been left untouched by Cleisthenes.

But in 487, soon after Marathon, as noted, the Archonship had been thrown open to the lot (no longer filled solely by election), and from 457 eligibility for the office was opened to the hoplite status group of citizens and thus ceased to be the exclusive preserve of the old Eupatrid families or even of the Athenian plutocracy. What, then, was Ephialtes' beef? It seems that, negatively speaking, he had three main quarrels with the status quo: first, that major political trials (impeachment, for instance) were in its power, at least as a court of first instance, although there is also evidence that impeachment trials were held in the Assembly; second, and more vaguely, that it was the Areopagus that still was the ultimate source of legality in the Athenian *polis* by virtue (or as he saw it, vice) of its 'guardianship of the laws', possibly including under that title the supervision and audit of officials, although the evidence here is not only as usual much later but also likely tainted by anachronism; and, third, he seems to have accused either individual members or the body as such of being corrupt.

To put that more bluntly and pragmatically: the Areopagus, while acting ostensibly on principle as a supreme court, might reasonably have been thought to be operating in practice in a disproportionately anti-democratic sense, convicting democratic leaders and Generals or acquitting non- or less democratic leaders and Generals. In any case, what Ephialtes formally claimed to be doing was stripping the Areopagus only of its 'acquired' or 'additional' powers—the implication being that these powers were somehow not authorised by either the Solonian or the Cleisthenic dispensation; and reducing it to a court with still important but far more restricted and primarily religious responsibilities (unintentional homicide, for instance, or tampering with sacred olive trees belonging to the community).

The positive side of the Ephialtic reforms is by far the more important. Such legal powers as were lost by the Areopagus were transferred to the Heliaea founded by Solon, now re-empowered and also known as the Dikasteria or (People's) jury courts. These were courts of first instance, not only of appeal, presided over in a purely supervisory sense by one or other of the Board of nine Archons, and staffed by jurors who were also judges. Court sessions were held on between 150 and 200 days each year, and the jurors assigned—by lot—to any one court were drawn from the annual panel of 6,000 citizens who had put their names forward and also been selected by lot. Thanks to a proposal of Pericles in the 450s—and this is his one indisputable contribution to the new Ephialtic dispensation—all such judge-jurors were paid a small per diem for performing judge-and-jury service. Jurors tended on average to be on the poorer and older side and could be satirised by Aristophanes in 422 (the *Wasps*) as being venomously keen to bring in a guilty verdict, especially in cases where the penalty involved a fine.

Public pay was possibly also introduced around this same time as compensation for the exercise of certain military functions and for the holding of certain offices—for instance, membership of the Council of 500. Such political pay became for democrats a badge of honour as well as a practical necesssity for many poorer citizens. It was seen as due recognition of the *kratos* of the *demos*, almost what their *kratos* was for, and democratic citizens were proud to be buried with their bronze juror's token. Contrariwise, for their oligarchic opponents the dispensing of public political pay was a badge of shame, a black mark of the greed and laziness of the feckless masses that also enabled them to exercise *kratos* over them, the 'natural' rulers, and so a stigma to be removed at the earliest feasible opportunity (which did not arise until 411).

We have met Pericles three times already—as son of an Alcmaeonid mother related to Cleisthenes and of the Xanthippus who had tangled publicly with Miltiades after Marathon (then been ostracised but recalled to co-lead the united Greek naval effort against the Persians in 479); as impresario for Aeschylus in 472; and as supporter of Ephialtes in 462/1 and, after the latter's death, guardian and consolidator of the thrust of his reforms in the 450s. Since he later became so famous, or notorious, thanks not least to the comic poets and to the historian Thucydides, it is salutary to reflect that in the 450s, when he was still only in his late thirties and early forties, Pericles was a politician on the make, a honey-voiced and silver-tongued demagogue as well as—or rather than—a statesmanlike *demagogos*. That, I suggest, is the true context and spirit in which to try to understand the most radical measure of his entire thirty-year career: the Citizenship Law of 451.

According to the Cleisthenic citizenship reform of 508/7, henceforth only those could be enrolled and inscribed as citizens who, being adult (eighteen-plus), freeborn and legitimate, had a citizen for a father. The latter, normally, would then be responsible for seeing that his acknowledged son or sons were duly inscribed on the register of their ancestral deme. According to the Periclean citizenship law of 451/0, however, it was no longer enough to have a citizen father in order to qualify for becoming an Athenian citizen: one must also have a citizen mother, and (probably) those two citizen natural parents had also to be legally married to each other at the time of the birth. What were the motives and aims of this new double-descent rule? The ancient sources—none

FIGURE 5.4
Erechtheis tribe casualty list, 459 BCE
Athenians, who engaged in war on average some two years in every three during the fifth and fourth centuries, made a fetish of commemorating their war dead, both in spoken words and in permanent memorials on stone; here, starting with two elected Generals, are listed the dead from a single one of Athens' ten tribes, Erechtheis, in a single campaigning year (459) on Cyprus and in Egypt and Phoenicia as well as at three sites in Greece itself. © RMN-Grand Palais/ Art Resource, NY

of them authoritative—offer variant readings, and modern scholars have been no less fertile in their suggestions.

One way forward perhaps is to consider some of the more blatant and unavoidable consequences of the successful enforcement of the new law. Aristocrats such as Cimon, who had chosen to marry a foreign, non-Athenian girl, would no longer legitimately and legally be able to procreate Athenian citizen sons to carry on their father's name and inherit his property. The law was not retroactive, but Pericles was surely neither unaware of nor averse to this particular practical consequence—though it has to be added that under the new rule Cleisthenes too would have failed to pass the citizenship test. Less noble or non-noble Athenian citizens who chose to marry the daughters of the ever-increasing number of 'metics' or resident aliens (a status that included freed slaves), perhaps for economic or other business reasons, were likewise to be deprived of the right to pass on their citizen status to their male or female offspring. That would have enhanced the marriageability of all Athenian daughters, however humble, however poor, however unprepossessing, and especially those who were heiresses, daughters of fathers without legitimate male citizen issue, since on their father's death these had by law to be married to their nearest male relative (even if he were already married). The size of the citizen body—or at any rate the rate of its increase, which seems to have been particularly great in the middle decades of the fifth century—might thereby be significantly reduced. The *Ath. Pol.* indeed states that Pericles had introduced his measure 'because of the number of citizens', perhaps with a view to limiting the numbers of those entitled to the new state benefit of public pay. A first formal test of the effect on the total size of the citizen body was perhaps conducted in 445/4, when it had to be decided which citizens were to benefit from a public dole of wheat drawn from a politically motivated gift by an Egyptian rebel pharaoh (in rebellion from Persia). Correlatively, the Athenianness of the new-style citizen body would have been appreciably reinforced—and it is surely no coincidence that the Athenian 'autochthony' myth (according to which all true Athenians were ultimately descended from the very soil of Attica) first appeared in force round about this time.

Finally, the significance of the *demos* in that word's other sense of deme—which is where the citizenship was granted and tested—would likewise have been enhanced, with all the social implications this would carry for the multiple social, political, religious, economic, and military functions of this microcosm of the overall political universe. That is to say, more precisely, for each deme's specifically democratic functions: for whatever else may be said of the Ephialtic-Periclean reforms, one thing about them is tolerably clear. They midwifed a new, improved *demokratia* at Athens, in name now as well as in fact, at once a *kratos* of the *demos* and of the demes.

6.

GREEK DEMOCRATIC THEORY?

I HAVE INSISTED FROM THE start on two fundamental propositions, or equations. Ancient (Greek, Roman, whatever, but anyhow Western and pre-modern) Democracy = Direct Democracy: the *kratos* of the *demos* was exercised directly by the *demos*, though no doubt on occasions with elements of representation; whereas modern Democracy = Representative Democracy: 'We the People', insofar indeed as We are granted even formal or token *kratos*, are in principle acted *for*, by 'our' governments—'Them', not 'Us', albeit that modern representative systems may contain elements of directness. However they may be qualified—for all governmental systems are more or less hybrid, and there is a great potential variety of both direct and representative systems—these two propositions are fundamental. Indeed, I would go further: it is precisely because of this most fundamental of distinctions, which is a matter ultimately of openness and transparency, that the ancients did not develop a theory or theories of democracy in the way that has become de rigueur for all modern, representative systems, not excluding Soviet Communism. They did not do so because they did not require them.

There is something of a parallel here with the contrast of and opposition between ancient and modern notions of imperialism. It is not the case that the ancients had no ideology of imperialism, since they too liked to represent it not as a sheer will to power and gross desire to indulge greed at the expense of subordinated others but as a positive good for the peoples imperialised, or as part of a divine plan, and so on. It is the case, however, that the force underlying all forms of imperialism was less disguised by the ancients both because they felt less need to disguise it (this was a world of outright chattel slavery, after all, the ultimate dehumanisation and depersonalisation of human beings), and because the modes of imperialist exploitation available or used were typically far more transparent and open than those indulged in by modern imperialist powers.

This is not, however, to state or imply that the ancient Greeks failed to come up with anything that we should wish to dignify with the label of a 'theory' of democracy. 'Theory' is of course a word of ancient Greek etymology, meaning at root contemplation. For Aristotle indeed—perforce an armchair intellectual, though not an ivory-tower thinker—such contemplative activity at a distance was the very highest form of virtuous activity he knew or could theorise. But in this sphere, unlike in some others, his thought was not original, even if among his peers he was one of the best informed empirically and most profound conceptually (Chapter 1). And for once the fact that the Lyceum, his institute of advanced research and learning founded in c. 335, was located at the heart of Athens when Athens was still a democracy was of little help to his reflections. On the one hand, although there were in any case relatively few Athenian political philosophers, those that there were (the 'Old Oligarch', Antiphon, Plato) were to a man not just non-democratic but anti-democratic in their ideology. On the other hand, those practical Athenian politicians who did indulge in some general reflections on the nature of democracy (like Demosthenes in the surviving prefaces to some of his non-extant speeches) or who did make casual appeal to such reflections did not do so for theoretical reasons, nor did they attain the plane of theory at any very elevated level. Where then should one look for sources of democratic theory, and how should one best read them?

In a fundamental article of 1953 (reprinted in Jones 1957/1978), A.H.M. Jones took what he saw as the absence of evidence for developed ancient Greek democratic theory to be evidence for its actual absence in antiquity. Instead, he interestingly and still fruitfully attempted to work backwards from the main extant theoretical criticisms of democracy (especially those to be found in Plato) to try to determine what a pro-democratic ideologue or philosopher could or might have theorised in its favour. But actually there is ancient democratic theory out there, positively expressed and not just negatively inferable, although admittedly it either is to be found in unlikely looking contexts or has survived only in disjointed and hard to interpret 'fragments' of ancient writings.

The word *demokratia* is first attested either in the *Histories* of Herodotus (born c. 485, published c. 425) or in the Athenian Constitution wrongly ascribed to Xenophon (*Ath. Pol.*, c. 425?; see further below). But regardless of whether Herodotus' *Histories* appeared the earlier or not, his work is certainly the first to preserve an example of Greek political theory—as opposed to political think-ing or mere ideological prejudice. This comes in the remarkable form of the so-called Persian Debate in the third book (3.80–82), based as that debate is on the theoretical intuition that all governmental systems may be assigned to one or other of only three, jointly exhaustive categories or genera: rule by one, rule by some, or rule by all. It thus brilliantly exemplifies one leading charac-teristic of all Greek theoretical thought, no matter what its sphere of applica-tion: its genius for significant analytical generalization from multiple empirical instances. Somewhat paradoxically, at first sight, the word *demokratia* is not actually used here, even by the one speaker of the three noble Persians who—as Herodotus himself later makes plain—was actually advocating a version of it. But a very good explanation of that absence or avoidance can be offered.

To put the debate in broad context: all ancient Greek historians from Herodotus onwards included speeches in their works, for a variety of reasons and with a variety of effects or purposes in view. Thucydides, however, was exceptional for reflecting most explicitly and analytically upon the manner and matter of his speeches from the point of view of accuracy and authenticity. But even he could not have aimed to re-present anything resembling very closely the actual words of the original speakers. *A fortiori*, Herodotus, who took a relatively simple or even simplistic approach to the matter, mostly composed speeches like those of his ultimate model, Homer. They were lively and dra-matic, a good way to catch or maintain the attention of a primarily listening audience and to highlight key moments of decision, but only secondarily were they used to characterise the speakers or to explain the historical situation in any depth.

The one glaring exception to that rule, however, is precisely the Persian Debate. Its putative authenticity (including to some extent its content) mat-tered so greatly to Herodotus that he took the trouble later (6.43) to defend it specifically as regards the speech that concerns us most here, the one that he put in the mouth of Persian noble Otanes. The debate's more or less imag-ined and imaginary scenario is briefly as follows. We are in c. 522 BCE, and the Achaemenid Persian throne has been usurped and occupied by a pre-tender, whom seven noble Persians are conspiring to overthrow. But with what governmental system should the restored legitimate regime be endowed? That is the question, at least as posed by Herodotus; and that is the issue which three of the magnificent seven proceed formally to debate through set speeches of varying length, detail, and persuasiveness. Otanes speaks first and longest, advocating a version of rule by all, he is followed and answered by Megabyzus, who prefers a version of rule by some. Finally, triumphantly, future king and emperor Darius I advocates his idea of rule by one.

The speeches are notionally by Persians, but the political theory is wholly Greek. In hard reality, there can never have been a smidgin of doubt that the post-usurpation Persian regime of imperial governance would be a restoration of the political status quo ante: dynastic, autocratic monarchy exercised by a member of the Achaemenid royal house or tribe. Herodotus, however, seems to have been under the illusion that the question of regime was indeed genuinely debatable and debated. Moreover, he compounds that error by seeming to believe that the governmental system advocated by Otanes in c. 522 for the entire Persian Empire was the same sort of thing as the *demokratia* he credits the Persian grandee Mardonius with having instituted in the subject Greek cities of Ionia some thirty years later, in 493 (6.43). Yet actually Otanes had not advocated *demokratia* by name, but had given his preferred ideal regime the significantly different appellation of *isonomia*, meaning exact equality before or under the laws. Why so?

One good reason why Herodotus' Otanes did not use *demokratia* would be that in c. 522 the word had not yet been coined; another, that Cleisthenes had not yet instituted an early form of *demokratia* at Athens (so called by Herodotus in his own voice, 6.131.1). So even the terminologically casual Herodotus might have balked at attributing this radically innovatory Greek term to a Persian speaker in political debate several years earlier. Yet that is not actually the reason Otanes himself gives for choosing to call his preferred regime *isonomia*: namely, that to him *isonomia* is or has 'the fairest of names'. Since what he is in fact advocating is democracy, and a pretty radical form of it at that (below), his choice of *isonomia* was thus in context a rhetorical ploy to deflect or mitigate the hostility he knew he would have aroused if he'd called a spade a spade, advocating straight out, in-your-face *demokratia*, which would have been taken by his two opponents as meaning nothing less than mob rule. Besides, *isonomia* was a current slogan in late sixth-century Greek political discourse. Etymologically, however, even *isonomia* had its disadvantages, since it might be appealed to by both sides in the argument or quarrel over its application. Equality is good, so long as it is equals who are being treated, or advantaged, equally. Likewise, lawfulness or lawabidingness (the meaning of *eunomia*) is an admirable and desirable thing, so long as the laws treat equally, that is fairly, all those deemed relevantly equal. But everything depended on who was being counted as equal, and in what respects, and that was an issue that radically divided democrats and non- or anti-democrats. So let us turn to the specifics of Otanes' supporting arguments.

That he was no mealy-mouthed proto-democrat transpires from the three qualities which, he argues, collectively distinguish his *isonomia* from and above anything his opponents in the debate can pitch. For he does not confine his advocacy to majority rule, giving an early version of the somewhat vague and anodyne slogan Government of the People by the People for the People (Chapter 19). Instead, he comes right out and says that all offices—no matter what their function, or what qualifications might be required to perform them well—should be sortitive, that is, filled solely by the use of the lottery. For (to spell out the thinking) this random method of appointment is an equalising procedure that puts on a level the ordinary citizen with the extraordinary (in wealth, talent, family, or whatever). Moreover, Otanes implicitly rejects not only the exact opposite, oligarchic view—that all offices should be elective—but even the compromise view that actually was instantiated in the Athenian democracy of Herodotus' own day, whereby some (the top, the most demanding, financial and military) offices were elective, the majority sortitive. Finally, he adds, all offices should be responsible—that is, subject to audit, to be conducted by, it is implied, the People. That principle of responsibility was wholly operative at Athens—and indeed used by tragic playwright Aeschylus in his *Persians* of 472 as a way of sharply differentiating Greek (Athenian) from barbarian (Persian) political practice.

But Otanes doesn't confine himself to recommending his own preferred system; he also calumniates and derogates those of his two opponents. Or rather, just as he proposes what he takes to be the best form of his rule by all, so he attacks what he takes to be the worst versions of the rule by some and rule by one advocated or to be advocated respectively by Megabyzus and Darius. Megabyzus' version of rule by some, aristocracy, is thus transmogrified into faction-ridden oligarchy. Darius' all-wise, all-beneficent, enlightened, and traditional monarchy is traduced as or at least transformed into vicious, self-gratifying, despotic autocracy. Who dares, wins? Just so, although of course Darius *had* to win in order for the debate to conform to the historical actuality of Darius' restoration of the Achaemenid dynastic monarchy. And perhaps significantly, Darius did not win only through the persuasiveness of his speech, but also through a display of cunning intelligence of which Homer's Odysseus would not have been ashamed.

Arguably, indeed, Herodotus was a very political writer, and quite certainly he was very interested in philosophy in a non-technical sense; but was he capable—even if he had had the interest—of writing up a full-dress political-philosophical discussion in dramatic, quasi-dialogue form? It is much easier surely to imagine him borrowing from and adapting an existing treatise by a writer who specialised in writing such works—and, it hardly needs adding, a writer who was thoroughly imbued with a Greek cast of political thought and discourse. At least for the prototype author of the pro-democracy speech, which is noticeably longer and more finely developed than the other two, and comes first in order, as if to be knocked down, there are two very good candidates, both from the same northern Greek city of Abdera: Protagoras and his slightly younger contemporary the 'atomist' Democritus. The political thought of neither is at all well preserved, and for Democritus we have merely a few aphoristic remarks to go on. But Protagoras certainly visited Athens, the then-cultural capital of the Greek world, in the third quarter of the fifth century, and is indeed credited with being appointed to write the first laws for the new *polis* of Thouria/Thourii in southern Italy in the mid-440s; this was a multi-ethnic foundation, which was the brainchild of democratic Athens and in governmental form a democracy.

The evidential problem here is that we do not have extant Protagoras' own words and work but only a dialogue of Plato composed many years later and named after him, and, especially, an argument placed there in his mouth—but written by Plato—that is compatible with a version of democracy. Yet for Plato, Protagoras was doubly a target to be demolished rather than sympathetically explicated: not only was he pro-democracy but he was also a member of the accursed breed of 'Sophists', pseudo-wise men in Plato's eyes who claimed to know what they could not possibly know and moreover claimed to be able to teach their counterfeit form of 'knowledge' to gullible young men willing to pay them handsomely for the privilege of being so taken in. This is not at first sight a promising beginning. But it has nevertheless been plausibly argued that all ancient Greek political theory, and not least Plato's, should be seen as a response to democracy, and at the very least, in my view, some strong connection between the speech of Otanes in Herodotus and the democratic political theory of an intellectual circle including the likes of Protagoras and Democritus may quite plausibly be posited.

Further evidence is hard to come by. Defences or justifications of *demokratia* do, as mentioned, turn up in the fourth-century Athenian orator-politicians, for opportunistic rather than theoretical reasons. A Syracusan speaker in Thucydides, with the suggestive name of Athenagoras (something like 'he who honours Athena in the *agora*'), is likewise attributed with a pro-democratic utterance at a time when Syracuse was indeed democratically governed. A stronger case can be made for there being one peculiarly Athenian genre of public oration in which democratic theory is not just appealed to but somewhat developed, and that is the funeral oration. Only a couple of actually delivered examples, however, survive. That attributed to Pericles by Thucydides is no doubt significantly Thucydidean, at least in style, but Thucydides himself was no radical democrat, and the oration is less of a hymn to democracy in a constitutional sense (2.37 is an exception) than to the Athenian democratic way of life more generally: what Aristotle would call 'upbringing and customs/ habits' (*Politics* 1292b15–18). As for that attributed to Lysias, even if it was composed by him it could not have been delivered by him, since he was not a citizen of Athens but a resident alien of Syracusan origin. The *Epitaphios* of Hyperides is thus the fullest authentic example surviving, delivered in 323 more or less as the very death knell of the democracy was being sounded.

Such pro-democratic discourse, however, no matter how faintly theoretical, is hugely overweighed by a torrent of anti-democratic theory and prejudice, beginning at Athens with the short, punchy essay on the 'Athenian *politeia*' misattributed to Xenophon but most likely issuing from frustrated oligarchic circles in the 420s, well before there was a realistic chance of democracy's actually being overthrown at Athens. The author of this tract—or jeu d'esprit?—in effect says that although he abhors democracy for all sorts of ideological and principled reasons, he nevertheless has to concede that the hated and despised

Athenian *demos* does know how to further its own best interests, as it sees them—that is, in largely materialistic terms; and he does not blame them for doing that, since that is just exactly what one would expect of such morally and socially low-class types. The people whom the author does blame are those—and he may have had Pericles specifically in mind—who step out of and turn against their own social class to back the political interests of another, opposed class.

For a truly philosophical attack on the very foundations of the democratic edifice we have to turn elsewhere, to Plato. Besides his *Protagoras*, he was also the author of the *Gorgias* of c. 380, another dialogue named for one of the most distinguished and influential of the 'ancient' Sophists. Gorgias hailed from Leontinoi in eastern Sicily, visited Athens as his city's official ambassador in 427 (just about exactly the time of Plato's birth), and allegedly mesmerised the Assembly with his mazy rhetoric. That alone would have been enough to raise Plato's philosophical hackles, since he was committed on principle to countering such merely specious rhetoric with true philosophical knowledge and understanding. And it is in the *Gorgias* that Plato constructs a dialogue of the deaf between Socrates the all-wise master of the true art of politics and one Callicles (probably a composite imagined portrait rather than a real Athenian politician), who is targeted as a representative of the dreaded breed of Athenian 'demagogues' (Chapter 7): politicians as bogeymen, a species conjured up long since by Aristophanes and Thucydides. Rather than improving the masses, Socrates avers, even the most respected of former Athenian political leaders (such as Themistocles) did no more than titillate and pander to the base sensual appetites of their mass audiences—in that, they were no better than pastry chefs, really.

Plato, however, for all his dislike of meretricious Sophists, disliked the *demos* and democrats even more. It is in his very long work of the 370s titled in Greek either *Politeia* or *On Justice*, but which we call after its Latin title the *Republic*, that he gives fullest rein to this profound antipathy. It is not irrrelevant that the dialogue is set in the most democratic of all Athenian districts, the port city of Peiraeus, in the house, not of an Athenian citizen, but of a rich metic, the father of the pro-democratic speechwriter Lysias. At the most elevated, philosophical level all existing political systems—not just democracies—were for Plato radically and incurably defective, since the ruling element in all of them did not have access to the only kind of truth on which good government could properly be based. Hence his paradoxical claim—placed once again in the mouth of his 'Socrates'—that only if Platonic-style philosophers came to power in the Greek cities of the day or existing rulers became Platonic-style philosophers would they cease from their present ills and enjoy good governance (*Rep.* 473d). But quite apart from this paradigmatic but practically unattainable governing ideal, when Plato was dealing apparently with the real political world he envisaged a hierarchy of existing regimes, all in a state of more or less degradation or degeneracy by comparison with the perfection of the ideal state; and democracy festered at the very bottom of the Platonic heap (*Rep.* 555b–562a). Indeed, in states that were ruled democratically, Socrates ventures, even the donkeys would assume airs—donkeys not being considered then any more than now the very apogee of sensitivity and intelligence. The ideal state of the *Republic*, given the non-specific speaking name of 'Fair, Fine or Beautiful City' (Callipolis), may have been intended as just a thought experiment, a castle in the air. But the much more tangible and fungible ideal city contemplated in Plato's final and long meditated work, the *Laws*, was given both a name and a reasonably precise location in space: Magnesia on the island of Crete. It was also equipped with a very carefully drawn code of laws and regulations—so codified as to rule out definitively in advance anything even remotely resembling people-power for the precisely 5,040 citizens of the brand-new foundation. Here, Plato's final political-theoretical thoughts seem to have tended in a strongly theological, not to say theocratic direction; the very opposite of the place accorded the gods in the real democratic Athens within which Plato had been raised and spent his entire very long life (see further Chapter 10).

It may be thought that Plato's was a classically academic rant against a form of self-government that systematically favoured the less intelligent (lumped together in a standard assimilation with the poor) over elite intellectuals such as he. But there were other theoretical or more properly intellectual arguments (as opposed to mere snobbery or prejudice) that could be and were mounted against democracy. One of them held, in a sort of anticipation of George Orwell's 'some animals are more equal than others' (*Animal Farm*, 1945), that some citizens are as it were more equal than others. The alleged theoretical justification for this formally paradoxical claim was the assertion that equality was not all one single thing, but there were two kinds of equality: 'arithmetic' and 'geometric'. Under the former, comparatively crude equation all citizens were deemed not just to count as but to be exactly, mathematically equal. That was the democrats' kind of equality. The more subtle version saw equality rather as a matter of proportion: some—few—citizens simply were superior (in birth, intellect, education, physical attributes, and so on) to the rest, and it was therefore only fair, right, and just that they be given a larger share of respect and ultimately power than the majority. That was the oligarchs' equality. Compromise, or even dialogue, between adherents of the two kinds was not really possible— or indeed envisaged by the proponents of the 'two kinds' view, the very purpose of which was precisely to sabotage the strictly egalitarian notion of citizen equality that had underlain the *polis* from its inception but which had now in their jaundiced eyes been enlarged unacceptably to empower the humble poor masses at their own expense.

The other main anti-democratic argumentative tack was to claim that democracy of the Athenian type, though called *demokratia*, was not really democracy at all, but rather a disguised form of tyranny: the collective and constitutional tyranny of the masses over the elite few, not the older form of extra-constitutional, one-man autocracy as exercised by say Peisistratus. A very neat example of this variant of anti-democratic propaganda happens to survive in a collection of musings put together by Plato's contemporary Xenophon, which purports to be the memorable thoughts and sayings of the author's (and of course Plato's) mentor Socrates, and is known usually under its Latin title of *Memorabilia*. In the passage in question a cardboard cut-out Pericles in his pomp is imagined as being in dialogue with and twitted by the much younger Alcibiades (in reality, Pericles' ward) on the meaning and function of law (*nomos*) in a democracy. Unwisely, Pericles concedes to Alcibiades that anything that a ruling power enacts may legitimately be called a *nomos*. What, ejaculates Alcibiades, even when it is a tyrant who enacts measures contrary to the wishes of the subjects? Yes, says Pericles. So—Alcibiades presses home his advantage—when a democracy (meaning the dictatorship of the proletariat), acting like a tyrant, enacts measures contrary to the wishes of the elite few, that too is '*nomos*'? Yes, says Pericles—but stop bothering me with these footling debating tricks that I used to be very smart at myself, when I was your age. Ah, concludes Alcibiades, I wish I'd known you then, Pericles, when you were in your prime …

As with Herodotus' Persian Debate, this dialogue may well not be Xenophon's own original composition. Pericles had died in 429, Alcibiades in 404, and their peculiar salience as characters in a debate about democracy was probably exhausted well before Xenophon published the *Memorabilia* some time in the second quarter of the fourth century. But the issue had even then lost none of its theoretical salience for thinkers like Xenophon and his older Athenian contemporaries Plato and Isocrates; the more they were impotent to do anything practically to revise, let alone abolish—what democrats called 'destroy'—the all too solidly established Athenian democracy of their day, the more they resorted to imaginary anti-democratic utopias of evasion and criticism.

More profitable by far was the line taken by Plato's star student Aristotle and, under his guidance, his school's pupils. In Chapter 1 I argue that by combining the evidence of Aristotle's *Politics* with that contained in the Aristotelian (but not Aristotle's) *Ath. Pol.*, one might obtain quite a full picture of democratic politics at Athens at least in the third quarter of the fourth century (350–322). But that by no means exhausts Aristotle's exceptional utility. Whatever his own political views may have been, and whatever one may think of whatever they were, he is in a class of his own when it comes to doing political analysis and political sociology from a theoretical point of view—and not just of the Athens of his day, but in principle of all Hellas. He and his pupils at the Lyceum were engaged in a multi-volume collective project of classification, codification, and analysis of a whole series of Greek (and one or two non-Greek) political entities. The fruits may be partially glimpsed in the *Politics*, highly unsatisfactory though this is as a composition. Like Plato, Aristotle too was a utopian thinker, concerned to formulate some sort of ideal polity in words; but Aristotle's eutopias were far closer to the ground than Plato's outopias, and they were conservative and preventative in intention rather than positive and revolutionary. For Aristotle wished to help prevent the besetting sin of the *polis*, namely *stasis*, from breaking out, and he thought that the best—in the sense of most practical—way to do that was to suggest ways in which imperfect ('deformed') actual polities might be improved so as to make them as *stasis*-proof as possible.

Aristotle was not uninterested in monarchy, including tyranny as well as, at the other end of the spectrum, an ideal 'all-kingship'. But he was aware that the vast majority of Greek cities in his day enjoyed or suffered some form of republican regime, either democracy or oligarchy. 'Some form': for Aristotle the political 'scientist' it was not enough to speak just of *demokratia* or *oligarchia*, since each should be broken down (analysed) and subdivided into four species. The resulting spectrum ran as it were from the far left, the most extreme species of democracy, through the less extreme to the most moderate species of democracy, which in turn most closely resembled the most moderate of the four species of oligarchy; oligarchy then resolved itself into ever less moderate species until, on the far right of the spectrum, lay the most extreme. What differentiates the species of each are chiefly four variables: first, the matter of eligibility—who can vote, who can stand for office, or for which offices; second, the type of Council—whether it's administrative (democratic) or ruling/governing (oligarchic); third, whether the officials are or are not responsible to the *demos*; and, fourth, whether or not there is a popular justice system. Aristotle, as we shall see, automatically rejected extremes, and, although he could see some virtue in a 'wisdom of crowds' sense of democratic decision-making by consensus, he had little taste for the 'last', most extreme form of democracy, in which the *demos* rules by decree and considers itself above the laws.

But besides his analytical, classificatory interest in subdividing democracy and oligarchy, Aristotle was no less theoretically interested in what it was that really divided all oligarchs, however extreme or moderate, from all democrats. With unerring accuracy he as usual put his finger on the nub of the matter: despite oligarchy's literally meaning 'rule of the/a few', and 'demos' being capable of being construed as either 'majority' or 'masses', the essential difference between any *demokratia* and any *oligarchia* was not a matter of sheer or mere numbers, of the differential empowerment of the 'many' and the 'few'. Nor was it a matter of residence (town versus country) or of trade or type of occupation (farmer versus merchant). No: for him, democracy is the rule of the poor (over the rich), and oligarchy, vice versa. What, then, does Aristotle understand by 'poor' and 'rich'? Greek language distinguished between those who were more or less without means and resources and those who were absolutely down-and-out beggars. So 'poor' (*penetes*), when used as a binary term in opposition to 'rich' (*plousioi, euporoi*), meant not having enough resources to enable one not to have to work for a living, whereas being rich meant not having to work at all: that is, being able to command the labour power of others, and having the requisite leisure to live the good life of—ideally—active contemplation, the kind of life lived by Aristotle himself.

For Aristotle, being Aristotle, the political-theoretical mean was golden, and the middling polity was the one that was both the best conceivable and the best possible in pragmatic terms. Indeed, and rather confusingly, he actually gave to this middling sort of polity the generic name 'polity'. Its key features were that it combined the best elements of democracy and oligarchy but avoided sliding over into either of those two potentially extreme forms, because there were sufficient numbers of middling citizens—middling rich and middling poor—to hold the balance between them. If pushed, he would probably have said that most of the middling citizens he had in mind would be wealthy enough to serve as hoplites, thus falling into the top third or so in economic terms. However, as usual with him, reality and realism immediately broke in, and he conceded with regret that in the real Greek world there never or hardly ever were enough of them to make polity a practicable goal. On the other hand, there is no doubt at all that what lay behind his advocacy of such a middling compromise was his fervent desire to avoid or avert the endemic civil strife or civil war that at least since the 420s had afflicted the Greek world. If one wants to get a sense of the flavour of political struggle that gave rise to political murders, betrayals of cities and, at the limit, outright civil war, one need only read the bloodcurdling, violently anti-democratic oath that the most extreme oligarchs in some cities are reported by Aristotle to have sworn amongst themselves: 'And I will be evil-minded to the *demos* and will plot whatever evil I can against them'.

Not that Aristotle was alone in seeking some sort of moderate, middling constitutional state. The earliest expression of approval of a political-constitutional mixture of democracy with oligarchy is actually to be found in Thucydides, who—speaking for once explicitly in his own person—specially commended the moderately oligarchic regime that Athens experienced between 411 and 410 after the end of the extreme counter-revolutionary oligarchy of the Four Hundred. This he accounted as the best (either pragmatically or in principle) that he personally had known (though he was in exile from Athens at the time), since it represented a 'moderate blending, in the interests both of the few and of the many'. The 'many' here are the *demos* in the sense of the poor majority of citizens, the 'few' are the rich elite, those who are earlier (8.64) said to believe they deserved the greater share of power because they contributed more to the state in terms both of resources and of personal service. But the nature of the blend, too, was clearly of key importance for Thucydides—not just the mere fact of a blend, as it was also for Aristotle, who wrote that a 'well-blended oligarchy' was the type of oligarchy nearest to his (ideally desired) polity.

We shall return to the concept of the mixed constitution in a later chapter, on the Roman Republic (Chapter 15), where we shall see that whereas Thucydides and Aristotle seem to have envisaged the mixture in terms of a 'pudding', Polybius envisaged rather a 'seesaw' system of checks and balances, thereby anticipating and indeed influencing the conception of the United States' constitution.

7.

ATHENIAN DEMOCRACY IN PRACTICE

C. 450–335

I T IS A FACT not perhaps much emphasised outside the scholarly community that the overwhelming bulk of the evidence for 'the' Athenian democracy is concentrated in the thirty years—roughly an Athenian father–son generation—between about 350 and 322. It is to this period the last twenty-one, systematic chapters (42–62) of the contemporary Aristotelian *Ath. Pol.* are directed, and this is the period from which most of the extant documentary inscriptions—such as the Law on Tyranny of 336—have emerged. This means that any attempt to represent or understand how the democracy worked earlier, for instance in the so-called age of Pericles, must necessarily be a composite collage bringing in data from well after the date of Pericles' death in 429. But there is a further, even more fundamental conceptual difficulty. In 404 the democracy that was probably still in most essentials the one Pericles had known, and indeed had materially helped to usher in and in some sense presided over (see below), was abruptly terminated by the Spartans. For about one year thereafter Athens was ruled by what the Greeks called a *dunasteia* (whence our 'dynasty'), a very narrow, collective tyranny.

So bloodstained and brutal, however, was the happily brief junta of the Thirty Tyrants that even the normally pro-oligarchic Spartans were persuaded by their unusually enlightened king Pausanias to allow the Athenians to return to democratic self-governance. But was the 'restored' Athenian democracy of 403 and after the same as the democracy of 404 and earlier (since 462/1)? Certainly not: all scholars are agreed on that. What they are not agreed on, however, is whether the post-403 democracy was sufficiently similar to the pre-404 version as to make no real difference analytically speaking, or sufficiently different to make it necessary to infer a difference of kind.

Three issues lie at the heart of this dispute: the legal distinction now drawn between decrees of the Assembly (*psephismata*) and 'laws' enacted not by the Assembly but by specially designated 'law-makers' (*nomothetai*); the increasing use of the legal procedure of 'writ against unconstitutional proposals', both as a supposed defence of the existing laws and as a technique of inter-politician backstabbing; and, third, the increasingly sharp distinction to be observed between the functions and careers of (elected) Generals and (informally, non-constitutionally self-selected) professional politicians. To all of those I shall return—but let me declare at the outset that in this dispute I myself take the side of those who believe there was no essential, qualitative change after 403, except perhaps in tone and atmosphere; moreover, quantitatively speaking (in terms of the percentage of citizens actively engaged at any one time), it is arguable that post-403 Athens was more not less democratic than it had been in 404 and earlier. Curiously, that puts me in the same camp as the *Ath. Pol.*, which alleged that after 403 the democracy just went on getting more and more democratic (down into the early 320s when the work was presumably completed): 'The *demos* controls everything by means of decrees and jury courts in which the *demos* is plenipotentiary' (41.2).

Quantity is one thing, quality another—was the spirit or ethos of the restored democracy significantly similar to or different from what had gone before? The introduction of public political pay for attending the Assembly in the 390s might be an argument for difference, but it could also be interpreted as a purely pragmatic response to the extreme immiseration of large sections of the Athenian poor as a direct consequence of Athens' defeat by Sparta in the Peloponnesian War and subsequent loss of imperial lands and revenues. I shall return to that also below. But there is one further possible disjunction or disruption to mark, again one caused by or a consequence of defeat in a major war by a foreign enemy. In 338 Athens, by then allied to a Thebes that had itself been a democracy since the early 370s, suffered a catastrophic defeat at Chaeronea in Boeotia at the hands of Philip II King of Macedon. What followed is sometimes known—on the analogy of the 'age of Pericles' and the 'age of Demosthenes'— as the 'age of Lycurgus' (336 to 322; Chapter 12), from which comes the already mentioned Law on Tyranny. Again, to anticipate, one of the key questions that this age raises is the extent to which Athens' democracy changed—was the final (as it turned out) phase of democracy at Athens also a new kind of democracy? In short, to speak of 'Athenian democracy' may well prove to be seriously misleading, since there could have been as many as four Athenian democracies in all: 508/7–462/1 (or 451/0); 462/1–404; 403–336; and 336–322. Which happens— or perhaps does not just happen—to be the same number as that of the subspecies of democracy identified by Aristotle (Chapter 6).

In the third book of the *Politics* Aristotle defined the citizen generically as the (free, legitimate) male *polis*-member who has a share in decision-making, including passing legal judgement (*krisis*) and in ruling, that is office-holding (*arche*), adding that practically speaking that definition applied more closely to citizens of democracies than of oligarchies. But before an Athenian citizen could exercise either of those powers he had first to assert and have validated his credentials as a bona fide citizen. And that meant being entered on the official register of citizens kept by each deme, membership of which was hereditary after 508/7, regardless of where one normally resided. Confirmation of status required the attendance of sworn witnesses—family members and fellow members of the pseudo-kinship associations called phratries, people who had witnessed the parents' wedding and could vouch for the legitimacy of the offspring—and inspection of the candidate's genitals. The age of majority was formally eighteen, and at least in the fourth century, when such 18- and 19-year-olds were labelled *epheboi* (on the threshold of full adult maturity at 20), they were obliged to swear a formal oath; after c. 335 they could be enrolled in the city-run military-cum-religious *ephebeia*, a sort of national service. This oath is preserved on a well-cut stele of expensive Pentelic marble that was dedicated to Ares and Athena Areia by one Dion son of Dion, Ares' priest in the deme of Acharnae. Though locally produced and erected, the stele also had national pretensions, since together with the Oath of the Ephebes there was associated on the stele the text of a supposed Oath of Plataea, purportedly sworn by all Athenians immediately before the decisive battle of Plataea in 479 (see further Chapter 1, Chapter 12).

Periodically, as in 445 and 347/6, the city carried out a global revision of all deme registers. It was in the latter sweep that a client of Demosthenes found himself unceremoniously disfranchised by the deme assembly of little Halimous (the historian Thucydides' deme), even though he had previously held the post of mayor (*demarchos*). Riskily, he challenged that local decision in a central jury court, the huge jeopardy being that if he failed to win his appeal he would be summarily sold into slavery as an alien who had falsely claimed to be and acted as a citizen. But he did at least have a youngish Demosthenes on his side as supporting advocate, and a version of the speech Demosthenes wrote for him survives, which may suggest he was successful in his plea. At any rate, the defence that the client adopted allows us to see on what two main grounds his enemies had at first got him kicked off the Halimous register: his mother had served as a wet nurse to the children of others, which was represented as evidence of her servile status, and she had sold ribbons in the marketplace, which was allegedly evidence of her metic, possibly ex-slave, status. It was always easier to attack a man in court through his—often inert, always silent or silenced, never present—female relatives. But the defendant rejoined robustly and to us quite plausibly that those admitted facts were evidence not of his mother's sub-citizen status, but of the family's temporary impoverishment due to the Peloponnesian War.

Such a window into deme-level skulduggery is unfortunately a rarity. Far more typical are the deme decrees preserved on stone that honour local benefactors, or the stones such as that from Thoricus, which record in lavish detail the local calendar of obligatory sacrifices to be performed month by month in honour of a huge number of both local and national gods, goddesses, and heroes (Chapter 1). The strong impression conveyed by these documents, which is confirmed in some cases by quite elaborate sacred and secular public architecture, is of the deme as being—or wishing to present itself as—a microcosm of the *polis*; indeed, in 431, according to Thucydides (2.15), rural demesmen felt that they were being obliged to abandon nothing less than their *polis* when compelled by Spartan invasion to reside only temporarily in the city of Athens. The deme documents also help buttress the claim that it was the deme that was 'the basis of the Athenian democracy'. Deme officials—elected or chosen by lot, above all the mayor—had to manage the regular deme assemblies, the deme lawcourts, the choice of members to represent the deme (and so tribe) on the central Council of 500, the collection of any irregularly imposed property tax, and the handling of any military call-up. Small wonder that Euxitheus, the speaker of Demosthenes 57, had to contend with the likes of his accuser Euboulides, since there was such potential scope for underhand graft or at least the exercise of 'influence'. One might have thought that an aspiring politician with ambitions to make a name for himself on the big stage in Athens would hone his skills at deme level in arenas less demanding than the Assembly (up to 6,000 citizens present) or a popular jury court, often with 500 jurors, almost five times the size of the total citizen list of Halimous in the 340s; see further below. But the evidence doesn't seem to back that supposition up. For ordinary citizens, however, regular participation in routine deme politics was a school of democratic prudence.

Total numbers of citizens fluctuated over time. No general census is recorded before the last or penultimate decade of the fourth century, after the democracy had been terminated and when Athens was under Macedonian overlordship and ruled by a proxy dictator, Demetrius of Phalerum. There were allegedly already 30,000 Athenian citizens in 500 BCE, according to a tale in Herodotus (5.97), but that round figure probably errs on the side of excess; yet even if the true figure were, say, 20,000, still Athens would have been already between ten and forty times larger than the modal (most frequently occurring) size of the 1,000 or so Greek *poleis* attested in the fifth and fourth centuries. By 480 Athens may have put in commission as many as 200 triremes, and that would have required a total complement of some 40,000; but not all need have been Athenians. Those who were will have been drawn from the poorest of the four post-Solonian census classes known as *thetes* (literally, labourers).

These sub-hoplites will always have been the largest single group of the Athenian citizen population, usually constituting well over 50 per cent. Normally social mobility in any Greek city was likely minimal, but in Athens between c. 480 and 430 thanks to the Athenian 'empire' there developed the greatest scope for improving one's social lot and moving upwards into the hoplite group (*zeugitae*, literally 'yoke-men'). One fortunate individual actually climbed further up, into the second highest census group of *hippeis* ('cavalry'). But to be in the census of the *pentakosiomedimnoi* ('500-bushel men'), and so a member of the top 5 per cent or so economically, one normally had to start out seriously rich by inheritance.

Modern guesstimates of citizen growth at Athens go up as high as 60,000 by 431, though most would settle for a rather lower figure; and it has to be remembered that at that time quite a number of Athenian citizens were permanently settled outside Attica, as colonists owning and working or drawing revenue from land that had formerly belonged to the citizens of other *poleis*. By 404, it is generally agreed, citizen numbers had dropped back again to 20,000 to 25,000, owing to severe war casualties both on land and at sea and to the devastating 'great plague' that struck in 430 and carried off thousands, including the sexagenarian Pericles. Between 404 and 390 Athens was very seriously impoverished overall, which both occasioned demands for a restoration of some sort of overseas empire and triggered the introduction of pay for attendance at the Assembly. Assuming a slight rise followed by a fairly steady-state situation, one reaches a figure for 404–322 of around 25,000 to 30,000. In 322, another kind of disaster struck: the termination of the democracy by Macedon, with the grateful assistance of local diehard anti-democrats, resulting in the striking off of either 12,000 or 22,000 citizens (our inadequate sources differ) from the total list.

Cleisthenes' Council (*Boule*) of 500 (50 from each of his 10 new tribes) was his masterstroke (Chapter 4). If the primary Assembly (below) was to be the city's genuinely decisive body, it had to have an adequate smaller body in more or less permanent session to act as its steering committee—both to prepare the business of its regular stated meetings and to see to the proper carrying out of its decisions by the relevant officials. It was through the Council that after the Ephialtic reforms one of the three chief democratic functions lauded by Herodotus' Otanes (3.80; Chapter 6)—the accountability of officials to the people—was effected. Councillors were chosen by lot from all eligible demesmen, and each of the 139 or 140 demes had its allotted quota to fill, implying a notion of representation. Had the demes all been of the same size, or had it been felt necessary in the interests of some notion of equality that each deme should contribute roughly the same number of Councillors each year, then the average figure for each deme would have been about 3.8 or between three and four. As it actually was, at least by the time we have actual figures for the quotas (not before the later fourth century, as usual), there were huge differentials: between 22 per annum for the most densely populated deme, Acharnae (which was allegedly—Thucydides 2.22—capable by itself of providing no fewer than 3,000 hoplites to the Athenian hoplite force of normally some 10,000–15,000) and as few as three for little Halimous, or even fewer. Citizens moreover were legally debarred from sitting on the Council more than twice, and those maximum two terms of office could not be served consecutively (owing to the requirement for Councillors to be audited on leaving office by the relevant sub-committee of the incoming Council); as a result, most Athenians would have had to serve at least one term.

This, then, was a participatory democracy with a vengeance, given the intensity and frequency with which the Council sat. For it was in session on about 300 days out of each year (omitting only certain religious festival days); for 35 or 36 days at a time (one civil month) the 50 men representing one of the 10 tribes were said to be in or holding the 'presidency', that is, were responsible for organising the Assembly's agenda and presiding over any Assembly meetings that fell during that month; and of these one-third had to be on permanent watch duty, sleeping overnight in the Council Chamber.

The provision of political pay—or rather subsistence rations—was for many Councillors not a luxury but a necessity, especially for those whose usual residence was far from the city centre or who had no relatives or friends in the city, and will have been introduced in 462/1 or probably soon after. It remained available until abolished by the counter-revolution of 411: the oligarchic revolutionaries despised all forms of public pay, since it enabled poor Athenians to participate actively in the governing process, whereas they piqued themselves on their differential economic ability to contribute to the public good.

Apart from auditing the previous years' Councillors, the Council also conducted audits of any officials who had in their charge the spending of public funds. It was the Council too that awarded such public contracts as those for public construction projects, the two biggest of which were the Periclean programme of the 440s and 430s on the Acropolis and in the Agora, and the rebuilding of the city walls (destroyed in 404) in the later 390s, followed by the Lycurgan programme of the 330s and 320s. Since the 480s Athens' primary military arm had been its navy, and it was a committee of the Council that decided how much public money should be allocated to the building of the enormously expensive (about a talent each) trireme warships, and the housing of them in shipsheds in the Peiraeus and elsewhere. In short, being on this body really did give an Athenian a sense that he was involved directly in the running of the state. It is very noticeable that big politicians such as Demosthenes somehow managed to time their periods of service on the Council to coincide with really crucial moments.

The doings of the Assembly (*Ecclesia*) are best attested in 'the age of Demosthenes' (b. 384, d. 322). It bears repeating that the details of practice given in the *Ath. Pol.* as applying to the 330s and early 320s do not necessarily hold for the situation even twenty years earlier, let alone for the whole period from 508/7 on. For example, it is a quite remarkable fact that in the 330s and early 320s four Assembly meetings were supposed to be held every civil month; that is, 40 per annum or one roughly every nine days. Extraordinarily demanding. But for how long had that been the case? Only, it seems, from c. 350 on, before which only three meetings per month were stipulated. So, how many stated Assembly meetings had there had to be in, say, the age of Pericles? That is anyone's guess, quite literally; many of us are of the view that just one per month would not have been unthinkable. On top of which, of course, there would have been added the extraordinary meetings called, for instance, to face the crisis in relations with Sparta and is allies that was developing since 445 and especially after the extremely unpleasant repression of a revolt by the oligarchically run, strategically crucial island-state of Samos in 440/39.

And what about the numbers of attendees, whether regular or occasional, and their regional distribution in terms of their demes of origin or residence? For the fifth century—apart from the absurdity of Herodotus 5.97 (who on the face of it has all the supposedly 30,000 citizens agreeing to support the Ionian revolt)—there is just the one total figure preserved, and that comes from a deeply tainted, oligarchic source reported by Thucydides (8.72). According to the oligarchic counter-revolutionaries of 411, not even as many as 5,000 citizens had ever yet attended any one meeting of the Assembly. Of course, these men had an interest in minimising the figure, both since it was their contention that Assembly decisions had been taken only by a small and in some sense unrepresentative proportion of the total potential citizen body, and because they themselves were trumpeting their proposed anti-democratic reduction of the fully empowered citizen body to a notional 5,000 citizens. But it is the case, archaeologically speaking, that in the fifth century the area on the Pnyx hill available for meetings attended by seated Athenians each occupying roughly half a square metre of space would have accommodated a maximum of six thousand. (Ostracisms, which required a quorum of 6,000 voters, were held in the Agora.)

In the fourth century, and especially in the 330s, it seems that the meeting space on the Pnyx was somehow enlarged. At all events, some issues put to the Assembly for a vote, at least in the fourth century—for example, voting on setting in motion the law-making procedure (below) or voting honorary citizenship to a Pasion (an ex-slave metic, for public services rendered) or a Paerisades (a Thracian ruler, for hoped-for future economic benefits)—required a quorum of 6,000, or roughly 20 per cent of the 'normal' total of 30,000, the latter at two consecutive Assembly meetings. Given the purely physical constraints of the Pnyx (its name appropriately derived from a verb meaning 'to squeeze'), attendees at an Assembly meeting must have been regarded as representing—and indeed as representative of—the citizen body (as was the case for the People's Courts, below). Any gathering of 5,000 to 6,000-plus, in other words, might be expected to contain roughly the same mix of town- and country-dwellers, and of people pursuing a roughly similar gamut of rural or urban occupations. No pay for attendance was considered necessary or desirable in the fifth century: evidence either of a greater spread of wealth or of a greater public-spiritedness, or both, than were on offer when pay for Assembly attendance was introduced in the 390s. At first, though, the sum on offer was a mere obol (one-sixth of a drachma, the latter then a decent craftsman's daily wage), but very soon, thanks to a competitive bidding war between rival politicians, it had reached the same level as that paid for a day's jury service, half a drachma. It is noteworthy that Aristophanes' comic satire on the powers of the Assembly and the alleged ease with which a meeting could be 'packed', the *Ecclesiazusae* ('Women Attending the Assembly'), was produced in c. 393 when Assembly attendance was clearly a top-priority issue. (I shall be returning to consider the status and stature of Athenian citizen women in the next chapter.) Later still, when a distinction was drawn between the principal (not necessarily the first) meeting of any month and the other three ordinary meetings, a bonus was paid for attendance at the principal meeting, at which state security, the military, and religious affairs had to be debated as matters of obligatory routine. By the time of the *Ath. Pol.*, pay for this particular participation had reached the dizzy heights of a drachma and a half. It is worth noting that Athens was not the only democracy to offer political pay—but it was far and away the most generous.

The mode of delivering and counting votes seems never to have changed: extending of the right hand (*kheirotonia*) was the order of each and every

Assembly day, the numbers of votes cast being 'told' (assessed) not counted one by one. This was a matter not of ideology—for that, the individual counting of votes, as in the Heliaia from Solon's time on (Chapter 3), was critical—but of pragmatics: meetings had to be held in the hours of daylight and business concluded within a single day. (Rain could stop play, of course.) When the debate and initial decision over Athens' punishment of revolted Mytilene on Lesbos in 427 were reopened in the Assembly the following day, that was a matter for surprised note and report by Thucydides. After the initial ritual purifications and prayers had been concluded and the president for the day had announced the first item on the agenda, a crier bellowed out, 'Who wishes to speak?' (the word for 'to speak', *agoreuein*, being derived from the basic word for a political assembly, *agora*). This was a matter of fundamental democratic principle: that of *isegoria*, the exactly equal entitlement of each and every citizen present and in good standing (or rather sitting) to make public political speech; an important corollary of *isonomia*. (On freedom of speech, a different but also democratic concept, see Chapters 8 and 10.) But in practice, it seems, very few citizens would get up on their hind legs, ever. Which is one reason why professional politicians could be referred to as orators and full-time politicians.

By no means all citizens were equally well equipped—physically or mentally—to make persuasive speeches in the Assembly or even in the quieter, smaller environs of a Council meeting. A comic poet (Eupolis, a rival of Aristophanes) wrote of Pericles that 'persuasion sat on his lips', and Peitho ('Persuasion') was worshipped as a goddess at Athens; but he was quite exceptionally talented. Indeed, not all professional politicians were also public orators; some were what we would call technocrats—specialising behind the scenes in complex matters of public finance or the logistics of war or, as in the case of the arch-oligarch Antiphon, preparing briefs for oligarchs both Athenian and non-Athenian to help them cope with the rigours of a Council sub-committee or, more terrifyingly, a popular jury court. The separation between politicians and orators mirrored that between politicians and Generals; both were to some extent products of the same tendency towards specialisation of expertise that was a feature of the years from the 430s on. By the mid-fourth century it would have been extraordinary if either say the financial expert Eubulus or the all-round

political adviser Demosthenes had also been a proficient general, or if generalissimo Phocion had been a leading orator. Not that this break was entirely a
post-403 innovation: already in the 430s and 420s Phormion and Demosthenes
(not to be confused with his later namesake) had been generals (and admirals)
pure and simple, whereas it was only by accident that Cleon, having achieved
eminence as a politician partly thanks to his fiery rhetoric but also to his financial nous, also became a general (and a fatally bad one, at Amphipolis in 422).

Cleon was the historian Thucydides' *bête noire* and nemesis; he gets a
rough ride also from Aristophanes, who—belonging to the same urban deme,
Cydathenaion—also had personal bones to pick with him. It is largely thanks
to those two powerful writers, and to the equally potent Plato, that the notion
has gained traction that after the death of the statesmanlike Pericles Athenian
politics descended into an unseemly series of spats between mere 'demagogues'.
These were supposedly low-class—or at least lower-class—politicos who brought
democracy into (deserved) disrepute, since they merely pandered to the base
desires of the unwashed masses; whereas Pericles had led the People and even
forthrightly told them what they ought to decide and to do. That, however, is all
pure ideology, modern as well as ancient. The word *demagogos* by itself means
'leader of the demos' (in the sense of all the People); it is only when such leaders
or would-be leaders are viewed from an oligarchic-conservative standpoint that
it comes more often to mean 'rabble-rouser', or misleader of the masses.

The nineteenth-century pioneer of ancient Greek history George Grote,
in a famous chapter of his *History of Greece* (ch. 67), had rehabilitated the
so-called Sophists from Platonic vituperation and denigration. A century
later, Moses Finley, revisionist American historian of ancient Greece at
Cambridge, performed a similar rescue act for the Athenian demagogues.
As he succinctly put it, they were a structural feature of the Athenian democratic way of doing politics, which—in the absence of either a modern party
system or mass informational media—could not have functioned without
them. Pericles was thus every bit as much a demagogue as Cleon, and, conversely, every bit as vulnerable to the moodswings of the *demos*. This was
made brutally clear when they first sacked him in 430 from his office of
General (to which he'd apparently been re-elected without a break for at least
the past fifteen years) and fined him, but then at once re-elected him. To the

conservative, non-democratic Thucydides, who liked to imagine Pericles as a sort of uncrowned king raised above the hurly-burly of mundane politicking, this was just a classic instance of the horrors of rule by a fickle, ignorant, stupid crowd; in an obituary notice for Pericles (2.65), who died of the plague in 429, he made the triumph of demagoguery into a key part of his explanation for Athens' defeat in the Peloponnesian War a quarter of a century later. To an ideological democrat, on the other hand, the treatment of Pericles was just exactly what the *kratos* of the *demos* meant. If and when the policies that Pericles had so persuasively advocated in honeyed words were widely perceived to be failing in practice, not even he was considered immune from popular retribution.

It is important to remember that in democratic Athens, unlike say Republican Rome (Chapter 15), it was perfectly possible to be a major political player without holding any office. In fact, in a democracy such as the Athenian, unlike in a Greek oligarchy, offices as such (*archai*) and the powers of office-holding were relatively unimportant by comparison to the power wielded by the *demos* in Assembly and jury court. The three exceptions to that rule were the administrative Council of 500; the top military offices (Board of 10 Generals); and the top financial offices (the Board of 10 Treasurers of Athena, and also in the fifth century the imperial treasurers, called Hellenotamiae, or Stewards of the Greeks). All of the latter two kinds of offices were elective, not sortitive; the Athenians here in theory put pragmatic efficiency above democratic egalitarianism, but they also exercised accountability even more stringently over these privileged officials, sometimes to a fault. Altogether it seems that, including the 500 Councillors, there were year on year some 1,200 domestic offices to be filled; and if we believe the *Ath. Pol* (24.3), another 700 in order to manage the fifth-century Empire. Most were not only chosen by the lot but also collegiate, typically grouped in Boards of 10 to cater for universal tribal representation. In the fourth century, however, two new elective top offices were created that were perhaps harbingers of further changes to come: one was something like the equivalent of a chief secretary to the treasury or chancellor of the exchequer, that is, a financial supremo separate from and superior to the long existing financial boards; the other was a water commissioner, possibly a sign of population pressure or a measured response to excessive use of precious water for non-essential purposes.

And so, last but very much not least, we come to the jurisdictional dimension of the *demos' kratos*. I long ago lost count of the number of undergraduate
essays I read on the topic 'How much *kratos* did the *demos* really exercise in
the Athenian democracy?' that failed even to notice or mention the existence
of the People's Court or popular jury courts. So let it be stated loud and clear:
the *demos* exercised its *kratos* in the courts, not only in the Assembly—a peculiarly democratic phenomenon, if we embrace Aristotle's definition of the citizen canvassed at the beginning of this chapter, and recall *Ath. Pol.* 41.2 (quoted
above). Hence the significance of the oath taken individually by each of those
6,000 citizens annually empanelled, by lot, at the beginning of the civil year as
potential jurors for the year to come:

> I shall cast my vote in accordance with the laws and with the decrees
> passed by the Assembly and by the Council but, if there is no law, in
> accordance with my sense of what is most just without favour or enmity.
> I shall vote only on the charge and I shall listen impartially to prosecutors
> and defendants alike.

Hence too the dominant presence of courtrooms in the architectural layout
of the Athenian Agora.

After 462/1 popular jury courts were courts of first instance, not merely of
appeal. Moreover, decisions by the allotted juror-judges were formally inap-
pellable. The only way in which a disappointed plaintiff or defendant could
reopen a case or challenge a verdict was by prosecuting one or more of the
opponent's witnesses on grounds of perjury. Jurors for any particular case were
chosen by lot from those of the 6,000 who chose to put their name forward for
selection on the court days in question. The allotment was done in different
ways at different times in the fifth and fourth centuries; the system we know
most about is the latest, according to which jurors handed over their bronze
juror's token, and these were placed in a stone allotment machine; white and
black balls decided respectively whether a row of juror's tokens was or was not
selected. All trials were presided over—but not judged—by one or more of the
nine Archons, each with a different sphere of competence; the Basileus (King)
had charge of religious cases, for instance, the trial of Socrates in 399 for impiety. From the 450s on, thanks to Pericles, jurors were paid 2 obols per case, and

some time later, thanks to Cleon, that sum had been raised by 50 per cent to 3 obols, or half a silver drachma. That may not seem a lot, but it has been calculated that it would have been adequate compensation for the time a juror had to take away from his farm or trade or other daily occupation.

Courts sat, it has been estimated, between about 150 and 200 days a year, making attendance as a juror potentially almost a full-time occupation; on average probably most jurors were both elderly and rather poor. This partly explains the vitriol directed at all jurors as a breed in Aristophanes' comedy *Wasps* of 422: the Chorus are designated wasps because they allegedly liked only to convict and then to sting the convicted for the heaviest possible penalty available. But it was not only an economic but also a political disaster when for a considerable period in the 360s court sessions had to be interrupted and suspended for lack of available money in the public coffers to pay the jurymen. So attached indeed were volunteer jurymen to their bronze juror's token that relatives found it quite natural to include it among a dead kinsman's burial goods. By extension, Athens acquired a reputation in the outside Greek world for its exceptional litigiousnness; this was partly because in its days of greatest imperial power between about 475 and 430 it had been able even to compel non-Athenians to attend courts in Athens and be tried before Athenian jurors if they were suspected of conspiring in their home cities against what most Athenians took to be the alliance's best interests. But the reputation also justly reflected the democratic centrality of litigation and jurisdiction.

Crimes (e.g., 'impiety') were not carefully defined. Procedures were considered more important, and for some crimes more than one procedure was available to a potential litigant. There were no barristers; the rules of evidence both oral and written and rules of procedure were lax. There was no notion of precedent; and equity was the nearest they got to anything like strict 'justice'. Rather than the strict guilt or innocence of the defendant as charged, the jury often considered whether conviction or acquittal was better for the Athenian *polis* as a whole: the trial of Socrates was in this respect utterly typical. Punishments were fitted to the criminal rather than to the crime. Some types of case, like Socrates' alleged impiety, carried no fixed penalty, opening the way after the initial verdict of guilty for rival bids and yet a further chance for jurors to sit in judgment on their peers—and very often on their social superiors, since most jurymen seem to have been poor and humble, whereas some defendants were exceptionally high-profile. Within Aristophanes' *Wasps* there is staged a domestic mock trial in which the defendant is a dog accused of theft—but this was a subterfuge and satire on a real near-contemporary trial of a major politician for public peculation, a charge which carried the death sentence.

Among the odder cases on record must be counted the trial in either the 420s or the 410s of a leading Athenian called (patriotically, ideologically) Demos, whose father had been an associate of Pericles, on a charge involving his possession or use of a private collection of peafowl (see further Chapter 10). The legal consultant for the prosecution was Antiphon, the first Athenian semi-professional speechwriter and legal consultant on record to circulate publicly versions of his lawcourt speeches. In 411, however, he found himself having to deliver in person a forensic speech he had composed on his own behalf, on trial as he was for high treason and subversion of the democracy as leader of the counter-revolutionary oligarchic regime of the Four Hundred who had ruled Athens for some four months. He was, predictably, found guilty and executed, but Thucydides, possibly a former pupil of his, considered it the best such speech he knew, although he must have had to read it cold rather than hear it live, since in 411 he himself was in exile from Athens for having failed the democracy as an elected general.

Thucydides' nemesis, as mentioned, was the then-leading demagogue Cleon, who was also the chief butt of Aristophanes' prizewinning *Knights* in 424, the year of Thucydides' relegation. We do not know exactly which procedure of prosecution Cleon employed against Thucydides, but it would have been some form of public as opposed to private suit. The distinction of procedure between a public writ and a private suit goes back to Solon: in the absence of a public prosecutor, any citizen who wished could bring a 'writ', and did so formally on behalf of the community of the Athenians as such, whereas only those directly affected (e.g., the alleged victim of assault and battery) could bring a private suit. But the institution first of democracy, and then of the People's Court system, massively increased the attractiveness of writs. The emergence of a class of professional prosecution litigants was an inevitable side effect; they were abhorred by their usually rich victims and vulnerable to the legal charge of being 'sycophants' (literally 'fig-sayers'), but yet they also served the undoubtedly positive democratic function of helping the masses represented by the jury to keep the whip hand over the elite.

Of all the many and various kinds of writs, one in particular stands out for its democratic political function, and this is the 'writ against unconstitutional proposals'. It is first attested in c. 415, and that may be no mere coincidence. The year before had seen a failed ostracism, and that quasi-legal procedure—somewhere between a vote in the Assembly and a vote in the jury courts, with an added ritualistic, scapegoat dimension (discussed in Chapter 4)—was never used again. Pericles had been exceptional in not being ostracised, having 'won' a decisive contest with Thucydides the son of Melesias in perhaps 443. His former ward, the maverick Alcibiades, also 'won' an ostracism, that of 416, but the result of that vote was the reverse of decisive, since the wrong candidate, the lesser politician Hyperbolus, was ostracised rather than either himself or Nicias. Other ways had therefore to be found for the future of deciding between such rival high-profile politicians, and of aborting *stasis*, and the writ against unconstitutional proposals neatly fitted the bill. One fourth-century politician, Aristophon, boasted that he had survived no fewer than seventy-five such accusations, but we may legitimately feel that he did protest considerably too much—and too many.

Oligarchs or crypto-oligarchs always hated the power over them that the democratic court system provided to the *demos*. Both in 411, when a rigged Assembly held outside the city walls in wartime voted the democracy out of existence, and in 404, when Athens was handed over by Sparta to the untender mercies of the Thirty ('tyrants'), that system of jurisdiction was at once dismantled. And it has to be said that in 406—following the flawed naval victory at Arginusae, with its accompanying heavy loss of poor citizen lives—the Assembly did not cover itself in glory when it arrogated to itself the prerogative of the courts to try generals for high treason, and moreover breached the city's own rules of procedure in so doing. All eight generals who had been in command at Arginusae were prosecuted for high treason; six of them unwisely showed up at the ensuing Assembly meeting, which turned into a kangaroo court and condemned them collectively to instant death, although legally they should have each have received an individual trial before a properly convened lawcourt. The Arginusae trial went down in infamy, especially among those of an oligarchic tendency or temperament such as the exiled Xenophon, who was happy to record the alleged mob-rule shout that it was 'monstrous if the People were not to be allowed to do just whatever it pleased'. That was one reason why after 403 the Assembly was no longer permitted—that is no longer permitted itself—to legislate. From then on a strictly legal distinction was drawn between a decree of the Assembly and a law, that is, a legal decision of general application and in principle permanent validity that had to be passed by a separate body of law-makers or legislators.

However, that was actually not quite such a derogation from direct popular power as it may at first sight seem, since the law-makers who technically passed judgment on a proposed law by putting it as it were on trial were themselves drawn by lot from the annual panel of 6,000 juror-judges, and such general laws were anyway few and far between: only a few dozen are known. One is worth mentioning specifically, though it is unusual. The Law on Tyranny of 337/6 was both a law and an Assembly decree. That is, first the Assembly passed the text as a decree, which was then sent for 'trial' to the law-makers, who duly passed it. Moreover, the courts remained a crucial political decision-making arena right to the end of the democracy on any definition, as attested for conspicuous instance by the Crown Affair of 330: the trial of Ctesiphon under prosecution by Aeschines for having illegally proposed a crown of honour for Aeschines' deadly political rival Demosthenes. The published versions of the respective prosecution speech by Aeschines and the speech Demosthenes gave as supporting litigant of Ctesiphon make illuminating if not always edifying reading (see in detail Chapter 10). The result was a thumping victory for Demosthenes, and the end of Aeschines' career and indeed residence in Athens; although in the wider context of an Athens under the thumb of a dominant Macedon perhaps that didn't count as much more than an empty, last-gasp gesture of old-style democratic defiance.

The one area of legal practice where the *demos* did not necessarily rule as such was in the post-Ephialtic, politically shriven Areopagus. Symbolically, this august body remained of huge importance, as its central role in Aeschylus' *Eumenides* of 458 attests, and there are even hints that in the third quarter of the fourth century, as Athens reeled under the impact of superior Macedonian power, this body of ex-Archons for life may have made some attempt to reassert itself politically: its explicit mention in the Law on Tyranny is witness to that apparent recrudescence. But by and large its role after 462/1 was purely jurisdictional, although far from unimportant at that. Religious charges such as unintentional homicide and interfering with the sacred olive trees grown to provide the oil for prizes at the Great Panathenaea were included within its province. And that leads us on very nicely to a discussion in the next chapter of precisely the cultural dimensions of the democracy.

8.

ATHENIAN DEMOCRACY

Culture and Society c. 450–335

---

*P*OLITEIA, ONE OF THE root words of the ancient Greek political vocabulary, seems originally to have meant 'citizenship', in the sense of the qualities
or attributes of being a *polites*. The latter term turns up first in a Spartan text—
a mid-seventh-century BCE elegy by Tyrtaeus partially preserved on a third-
century CE papyrus rescued from Oxyrhynchus in Egypt. This some may think
entirely appropriate, as Sparta has also yielded one of the earliest documents
to spell out a version of the constitutional arrangements of any Greek *polis*: the
so-called Great Rhetra of arguably about the same date as the Tyrtaeus fragment. That was the second, derived sense of *politeia*, denoting what Aristotle
called the *taxis* (ordering, disposition) of office-holding and other such political institutions. The usual English translation 'constitution' approximates this
sense. However, by his day (and possibly long before) *politeia* had acquired yet
a third meaning, signifying what Aristotle called the 'way of life' and Isocrates
called the 'soul' or 'animating spirit'—our 'life and soul'—of a *polis*: denoting,
that is, something above and beyond its purely formal political–institutional
arrangements.

Thucydides seems to preserve an early version of this last sense when he
speaks of—or rather deplores—what he calls 'the secrecy of their *politeia*', referring to the fact that secrecy and secretiveness were engrained in the very fabric
of the Spartans' society and politics. What prompted that derogatory comment
was their neither unpredictable nor inexcusable unwillingness to divulge to
him, an Athenian enemy, exactly how many Spartans, and Spartans of which

social classes, had perished on the battlefield of Mantineia in 418; indeed, one might think the Spartans were well within their rights not to betray such a sensitive war secret, especially given that shortage of citizen manpower was already playing a crucial role in the development of Spartan society and politics and would do so even more fatefully over the next half-century.

Thucydides elsewhere draws attention to another peculiarity of the Spartans' society and culture, which is no doubt intimately related causally to their *politeia*'s alleged systematic secrecy: the existence of a servile body, much larger than the citizen body, called Helots ('captives'), who unlike most slaves and other unfree people in ancient Greece were themselves Greeks by birth and culture and yet were treated by their Spartan masters as a defeated and alien enemy within, and were moreover enslaved collectively as a subject community or people rather than individually owned, as most slaves in Greece were. More than once, Helots rose up in politically motivated revolt, aimed at securing not only individual freedom but also—for the majority among them—political independence and statehood as 'the Messenians'. It was to pre-empt this happening again that, probably some time in the mid-420s, the Spartans carried out an exemplary cull of those 2,000 or so Helots thought to be the most potentially subversive and rebellious—'and no one could tell how each of them was killed', adds Thucydides rather sinisterly, drawing attention once more to Spartan secrecy, if of a more morally vicious kind. I cite this striking episode, however, not in order to indict the Spartans of moral cruelty, but to draw attention to the fact that every Greek *polis* was by Aristotelian definition a 'community' or 'commonwealth', and that the Spartan polity was an unusually strong, close-knit, and tightly controlled example, reinforcing its sense of unique selfhood by the most extreme 'othering' of the Helots whom by an annual proclamation of their chief executive officials they declared formally to be enemies and thus liable to summary execution or murder.

As it happens, religion was another of those features that were common to every Greek *polis* but that the Spartans took to unusual, if not unique extremes. For all Greeks, religion was the lifeblood of their society and polity; so ubiquitous indeed and so deeply embedded were what they called alternatively 'the things of the gods' or 'the divine' that they had no separate, special word meaning 'religion'. Herodotus twice specially remarked upon the Spartans' valuing of the things of the gods above those of mere mortal men. But then all Greeks did that. What he was drawing attention to, therefore, was the Spartans' exceptional willingness to carry religiosity—the absolute necessity to observe religious ritual obligations—to the point even of placing their and other Greeks' communities and ways of life in extreme jeopardy. For the democratic Athenians, no less than for the non- or anti-democratic Spartans, festivals were their religion's beating heart. Three stood head and shoulders above the rest in the long run of annual and monthly festivals by which the Athenians' national and local (deme) calendars were punctuated: the Great or City Panathenaea, the Great or City Dionysia, and the Mysteries of Eleusis. All three were in some sense Peisistratean; that is, the Peisistratid tyrant family (Chapter 3) had lavished special attention upon them for propaganda purposes. But all were also given thorough democratic makeovers, partly to disembarrass them of their tyrannical associations.

The Great Panathenaea, as noted in Chapter 4, was revamped in 566. The coincidence of date makes it clear that this was the Athenians' local and emulous response to the establishment in the 570s of a Circuit of major Panhellenic (all-Greek) athletic games: the Olympic, Pythian, Isthmian, and Nemean. Like the Olympics and the Pythian Games, it too was held on a grand scale every four years and required the appointment of special commissioners who looked after the very complicated financial and other arrangements. But the Athena in honour of whose 'birthday' the Panathenaea were staged was Athena 'of the City' (Polias), patron goddess of the city of Athens. Other Greeks refused to concede to a female divinity so closely tied to one city equality of status with the male and more universal Zeus (the Olympics and Nemean Games), his brother Poseidon (Isthmian at Corinth), and his son Apollo (Pythian at Delphi). The Athenians themselves grudgingly conceded as much by including events that were open only to Athenian citizens: for instance, a kind of masculine beauty contest (the Euandria) and a trireme boat race held off Sunium, both of which were organized on a tribal basis. Moreover, in the sharpest contrast to the 'crown' games of the Circuit, for which only symbolic token prizes were awarded (all the more valued and valuable for that), the prizes at the Panathenaea were expensive, material-value prizes: specially pressed sacred olive oil (Athena's special plant) contained within distinctively shaped and beautifully painted transport-and-storage pots, the number awarded being carefully calibrated in accordance with the perceived importance of the event.

Hence the winner of the flashiest, most glory-bringing, blue-riband event—the four-horse chariot race—carried off the largest number. In about 500 BCE, not long after the democracy had been instituted and maintained in the teeth of Spartan intervention (Chapter 4), that event was won by a Spartan—and no ordinary Spartan, either, but King Demaratus, who had fallen out with his fellow king Cleomenes precisely over Sparta's policy towards Athens. How the politics of that victory played out—whether at Athens or back in Sparta—sadly no source survives to say.

I may have given the impression that, from a religious point of view, the athletic and other events of the Games were the most important element of the Festival; if so, that false impression must be corrected at once, since the key and central religious element was the procession from the Pompeion (Procession-building) at the city's Dipylon Gate through the Agora and up on to the very top of the Acropolis ending at the shrine of Athena Polias ('of the City'). The point of the procession was to convey the new robe woven every four years to bedeck an ancient, aniconic (non-representational) olive-wood statue of Athena, and to display the city of Athens to itself as well as to the goddess by giving a role and function to representatives of all the main social divisions—apart from slaves—of the population of the *polis*: that is, to both male and female free people, and to resident aliens as well as citizens. For this integrative function one might perhaps want to compare (and contrast) the Hindu Kumbh Mela festival: the soul of the Indian nation, as it has been called, but held only every twelve years and involving some 30 million rather than 30,000 persons. It is widely believed that the famous continuous frieze that adorned the temple we know as the Parthenon, constructed between 447 and 432, either depicts directly or at least alludes to this Panathenaic procession, and that may well be so; although I am myself most attracted to the hypothesis that the procession represents a mythical occasion, as opposed to any real-time human celebration, possibly the very founding act of the cult of Athena Polias itself imagined as having occurred in some distant, timeless past.

At all events, the very existence of the Parthenon temple, devoted to Athena Parthenos ('Virgin'), is something of a problem in religious terms, since the temple seems to have had no dedicated altar of its own, as every other cult-sanctuary anywhere else in the Greek world by definition did. Instead, Virgin Athena seems to have had to share with Athena of the City, and that means that the heifers (unmated, virgin cows) sacrificed to Athena at the end of the procession were slaughtered and cooked on an altar that more 'naturally' was attached to the sacred building we know as the Erechtheum. In its most famous form, from the 420s on, that temple included the literally iconic caryatid porch, boldly female and highly feminine images. But within the shrine were sacred spaces devoted not only to the eponymous Erechtheus, a legendary early king of Athens, but also to Athena Polias and to Poseidon assimilated to Erechtheus. A patriotic myth imagined that Athena and Poseidon had once upon a time been in competition for the role of patron divinity of the city, a contest won by Athena. Housing those two jealous divinities together with Erechtheus in the one shrine in a conspicuous spot on the Acropolis was a massive attempt at religious and political compromise, greatly to the Athenians' credit. But that leaves the Parthenon as having to perform some other, not purely religious function or functions, which fortunately are quite easy to divine. The new, 'Periclean' Parthenon (Pericles served as a public official on the building's administrative works committee) stood for imperial Athens in relation to the outside world; it was a sort of equivalent of St Paul's Cathedral as opposed to Westminster Abbey, the latter being London's equivalent of the Erechtheum.

Unlike the quadrennial Great Panathenaea, the Great or City Dionysia was an annual festival, celebrated in early spring; it was held in honour of a politically rather interesting Dionysus, Dionysus Eleuthereus. Although that looks like Eleutherios ('liberator'), which at Athens served as a cult title of Zeus (who was granted a fine Stoa in the Agora), it actually means Dionysus from the border town of Eleutherae. This was not incorporated as an Attic deme, and indeed was not even Attic in origin but Boeotian, so the Athenians had somehow grabbed Eleutherae from the Boeotians but not been able or willing to incorporate it fully within the new democratic *polis* system. Yet this literally marginal (in its geographical origin) cult of Dionysus was installed at the very epicentre of the city of Athens on the slopes of the Acropolis, where it was endowed with a peculiarly dramatic function and a dedicated theatre (mainly wooden at first) from about 500 BCE.

This dramatic Dionysus was the god not only or more particularly of wine but rather of metamorphosis, shape- and role-shifting in general, a function that was symbolized externally by the masks worn by all actors and chorus members and enacted through an extreme degree of impersonation and role-playing. All

FIGURE 8.1
Marriage Athenian-style, Lebes gamikos
Athenian weddings were legally speaking private affairs but had massive public consequences, in the shape of legitimate offspring and future male citizens. They called for heavy investment in pomp and ritual, including specially shaped painted terracotta vessels like this one, in which the specially consecrated water for the initial bridal bath was stored. Image copyright © The Metropolitan Museum of Art. Image source: Art Resource, NY

players had to be male, though they often played female roles, and all of course were human beings, though they often played gods and goddesses; all too were Athenians, though often they played non-Athenian characters, and all were free in their personal and civic status, though sometimes they played slaves. Tragedies and satyr dramas had their origins well back in the sixth century, but the Dionysia play-festival seems to have been formally reorganized around 500 BCE, no doubt as a reflection of the Cleisthenic reforms. In 486 they were joined by comedies, and all plays were staged as competitions (*agones*, whence our 'agony'), with prizes going to the winning playwrights, impresarios and lead actors ('prot-agonists'). These prizes were decided by small, democratically selected juries acting in the name of all Athenians attending the plays; up to 17,000 persons in all may have attended any one performance, though not all would have been Athenians and, if women were allowed to attend, not all would have been Athenian citizens of full political status.

An ancient paradoxical aphorism held that the tragic plays, though staged in honour of Dionysus, had nothing directly to do with him. Though true, up to a point (Euripides' *Bacchae* is a potent counter-example), that is beside the real point: for tragedy's democratic function, or one of its main ones, according to a modern reading that I find wholly persuasive, was to question the city's fundamental tenets and ideals. The slippery, ambiguous, and ambivalent nature of Dionysus (deadly violence alternating with ecstatic release) made his worship an excellent medium and arena for such profound questioning without running the ultimate risk (always lurking in the Assembly) of causing outright revolutionary upheavals. It is of course a separate issue whether any playwright or play or group of plays (each tragic playwright offered a set of three tragedies followed by a satyr drama) had a particular and discernible political agenda.

Comedy played to a peculiar strength of the Athenian democracy in another way. The Athenians had two words both of which we might translate as 'freedom of speech': *isegoria* and *parrhesia*. Their semantic space overlapped, but their core meanings were significantly different. Whereas *isegoria*, exact equality of public political speech, had a particular application to speech made in a political assembly, and could indeed serve as a synecdoche for democratic equality and indeed democracy as such (as in Herodotus 5.78: Chapter 4), *parrhesia* had a broader scope and reference. This was just the kind of free speech that the theatrical genre of comedy (*komoidia*: from *komos*, meaning a revel, and *ode*, a song) could have been invented to exploit. But, as is well known, freedom of speech has its costs as well as its benefits, and it seems that even the carnival context and atmosphere of comedy at the Great or City Dionysia could not be left entirely without some formal, legal restriction. Certain types of comic abuse were at least at certain periods expressly outlawed, and—at least if conservative critics of democracy may be believed—comic playwrights were careful as a rule not to abuse the very system of democracy as such, as opposed to its supposed and heavily caricatured abuses (as in, e.g., Aristophanes' *Wasps*). In its way, too, the trial of Socrates is another powerful reminder that the Athenians placed no absolute value on freedom of speech as a democratic virtue. Indeed, as we shall see (Chapter 10), a comic fantasy play could even be made to seem relevant to the real-world charge of impiety brought against him. Finally, as with the genre of tragedy, so with that of comedy there is always a question mark over the precise political aim or impact of any play or playwright; I, for example, am one of those who believe that Aristophanes was a very political playwright, in the strong sense of having and wishing to persuade his fellow citizens of a particular political agenda, but by no means do all critics agree with me on that.

But again, as with the Great Panathenaea, it is important to remember that the central religious function of the Dionysia was fulfilled not only or so much by the plays but by the procession of celebrants culminating in the ritual slaughter of bulls (as many as 240 in 333 BCE) on the altar within the god's sacred precinct that included a temple as well as the theatre. There followed a massive beef supper, affording a chance both to reintegrate and renew the local community after the winter, and, since this was a festival open to non-Athenians, both to present the city to the outside world and to incorporate foreigners temporarily within it. For instance, during the time of the Athenian empire of the fifth century it was at the Great Dionysia in late March or early April that representatives of the tributary allied cities were invited (or required?) to demonstrate their panhellenic loyalty and solidarity by parading in the theatre, each one bearing a symbolic talent of silver, before the actual play performances began. (I shall return to the cultural function of the plays within the democracy in my discussion of women in the democracy, below.)

Third, there were the Eleusinian Mysteries, held in honour of earth-mother goddess Demeter and her daughter Persephone not within the city walls of Athens but in an Athenian deme, Eleusis (the deme of Aeschylus), not far to the west; formally, they were under the management of two hereditary priestly families, but, as we shall see, the central city authorities were careful to exercise a very close and regular supervision of them. The Mysteries, as their name implies, were secret rites of initiation, individual not corporate, and, unlike the two previous festivals, were a genuinely panhellenic affair, open indeed not just to ethnic Greeks but to anyone—male or female, free or unfree—who commanded enough Greek language to be able to follow and engage in the rituals. The latter promised initiates a happy afterlife, and it seems that almost all Athenians at least would have had themselves initiated. That is one reason why for his comedy *Frogs* Aristophanes chose to form the main chorus from initiates in the Eleusinian Mysteries. The play takes its name, however, from its exceptionally comic and memorable—*brekekekek koaxkoax*—secondary chorus of frogs. So relaxed were the Athenians about making fun of the gods, in this exceptional time of festival at least, that the very god of the festival,

Dionysus himself, could be humiliatingly caricatured and parodied in this play as a cowardly ignoramus, ignorant not least of the finer points of tragic drama. Yet not only did the play win in 405, but it was actually re-staged, as a mark of special public honour, probably the following year.

However, to the Athenians the Eleusinian rites themselves, and control of them, were anything but comic. Again and again, the Assembly legislated for or regulated them—one of the best-preserved sets of regulations was that passed in probably 422/1, in which the Athenian *demos* made clear the ideological as well as imperialist functions of central civic control. In 414 a number of Athenians and metics, most prominently Alcibiades, were tried and found guilty of impiety for profaning the Mysteries; the penalty automatically imposed was death, although Alcibiades himself escaped that fate by flight to Sparta (and so by committing treason—for which he was later forgiven). But the democracy was also very careful not to interfere too overtly with the rights and privileges of the two aristocratic priestly families in whose charge they had been since time immemorial. In 403, at a deeply solemn moment of the deadly *stasis* that had engulfed the *polis* thanks to the regime of the Thirty Tyrants, it was a member of the Eleusinian Kerykes (Heralds) priestly family who stood forth and pronounced a healing oration, aptly heralding the comparatively peaceful period of restored democracy to come.

Those are just the festival highlights. Before moving on, let us recap—anticipating our discussion of the trial of Socrates (Chapter 10)—the extent to which democratic Athens publicly and politically was a city of gods as well as of men. After 462/1 the Areopagus, though politically diminished, nevertheless retained charge of very important religious matters including the management of the sacred olive trees of Athena. All empanelled jurors in the Heliaea swore a religious oath, violation of which would bring down the wrath of the gods on violators' heads. Every meeting of the Assembly was started with a religious ritual of cleansing—and could be stopped by rainfall, interpreted as a negative divine sign from Zeus. Moreover, every principal Assembly meeting at least after c. 350 had to include discussion of sacred matters, that is, relations with the gods.

One illustration of this preoccupation is the Assembly's set of regulations for the Mysteries cult at Eleusis that we have just mentioned. Even more spectacularly illuminating is the case of the Sacred Orgas, also involving Demeter and Persephone, two goddesses, which flared up yet again in 352/1. In ancient Greece neighbouring states often had niggling or worse boundary disputes, and 'Attic neighbour' was a proverbial phrase for being a very bad neighbour. Athens, however, managed to have two more or less permanent such boundary disputes, both religious. The lesser of the two concerned Oropus on the northeastern border with Boeotia, within which lay the important oracular and healing shrine devoted to Amphiaraus. The other affected relations with the *polis* of Megara to the west and centred on a tract of land devoted to Demeter and Persephone and labelled the Sacred Orgas; as the Athenians saw it, this belonged to them, so that in their eyes it was not only illicit but also sacrilegious for the Megarians to cultivate it. Bad relations with Megara, then a subordinate ally of Sparta within the Peloponnesian League, had been one of the contributory and precipitating causes of the outbreak of the Peloponnesian War in 431, and during that war's first phase Athens had dealt very severely with Megara by means of biannual invasions by land, led at first by Pericles. By the late 350s, however, Athens was considerably weakened once again by its recent defeat in the so-called Social War (War of the Allies within the Second Athenian League) of 357–355, and it seems that Megara had taken advantage of this weakness to remove Athenian boundary markers from the Sacred Orgas. Athens had to respond, but this time lacked the necessary military force; instead, divine support was called in aid.

Part of a very long (over eighty lines) but not well preserved decree of the Athenian Assembly survives, inscribed on a stele of Pentelic marble and found at Eleusis; it testifies to the two main concerns Athens then had in this area. The first was the precise determination of the boundaries of the Sacred Orgas; it is noteworthy that, alongside the hereditary Eleusinian priestly officials and the city's chief annual religious official (the 'King' Archon), the Areopagus also was specifically detailed to sit in judgment on the matter. The second concern was over whether or not land currently in agricultural use should in the future be rented out or left untilled. To determine that, however, the Athenians felt they needed the further divine intervention and authorization of Apollo of Delphi, and they therefore sent an embassy to consult his oracle. This procedure had three main advantages: it could help solve issues not obviously amenable to merely human practical reasoning; it could shift responsibility for deciding such ticklish matters from an Athenian political body to the god; and it conferred upon the decision a supernatural authority that would place it beyond easy challenge. But the Athenians went one step further, by constraining Apollo's response to an either/or question. For what they asked him, through the Pythia (his oracular priestess), was whether they should act either according to the instruction written on a piece of rolled-up tin wrapped in wool and placed in a gold *hydria* (water jug), or on that inscribed on another identically treated piece of tin placed in a silver *hydria*. The answer from Delphi was negative—'it was preferable and better that they did not cultivate' the edge lands. But what a rigmarole! At least, as it may well seem to us.

So far, by and large the discussion in this and the preceding chapter has been confined to the male half of the Athenian citizen population. What about the female half? A good question, and a difficult one to answer. For Athenian females both *were* and *were not* of the democracy. They both were fully recognized as equal and indispensable partners of the citizen men and yet also

FIGURE 8.2
Trireme reconstruction
The three-banked trireme warship (*trieres* in Greek) was the Classical Greek ship of the line, to the skilful manoeuvring of which the Greeks owed their victory at Salamis, and the Athenians their fifth-century empire. The 170 oarsmen were drawn from the poorest ranks of the citizenry, and their key naval role was the perfect complement and corroboration of their political power. © The Trireme Trust

could be treated legally as little better than slaves, almost as un-persons. This huge, seeming paradox will appear a little less strange after a reading of one of the opening portions of the first Book of Aristotle's *Politics*, in which he is seeking to define what are and what are not the essential constitutive elements of the *polis* (any *polis*). In this definitional exordium he concedes that women are necessary to the creation and perpetuation by sexual reproduction of the household (*oikos*), which is the basic building block of the *polis*. But within each household the relationship between the male and the female components—specifically the husband and the wife—must not be 'political', that is, reciprocal and equal. The man must always be on top, because of women's essential and therefore unchangeable nature. And to explain what he understands by that, Aristotle uses an analogy: whereas the natural slave— the person who is by nature slavish (itself an eminently challengeable construct)—lacks altogether the ratiocinative or deliberative power of the mind, soul, or spirit (*psukhe*), women (at any rate, the naturally free ones) do possess that power, but in them, unlike in free men, it is not 'authoritative', that is, it lacks executive capacity. By which he seems to mean that it regularly or even normally tends to be overwhelmed and overridden by the emotional or appetitive elements of the soul, so that women's resulting behaviour is not rationally determined.

Further confirmation of Aristotle's negative view of women's role in politics is forthcoming in Book 2 of the *Politics*. What he objected to so violently about Sparta's social and political arrangements were the power and independence of the adult citizen women: above all, they could own property in their own right, such that almost two-fifths of all privately held land was in their possession, and this seemed to Aristotle to be tantamount to rule by the women over the men. To him this was a reversal of the natural order—and led, inevitably, to disastrous practical results. Not only was half the Spartan state as it were unregulated, since the women were allowed to abandon themselves to all sorts of indiscipline; but also, and at a crucial moment in the city's history, when it was under direct attack for the first time ever by an outside invasion force (a massive Theban-led expedition in midwinter 370/69), the Spartan women were so terrified at seeing their city's and their own lands being destroyed under their very noses that they actually caused more harm to Sparta's cause than the enemy! By definition, they lacked the requisite quality of manly bravery.

We may beg to doubt the literal truth of that last claim, just as his opinion of women's essential nature may well strike us as excessively retrograde and even grossly sexist. But we get the message: Aristotle, by formalizing and giving a supposedly philosophical account of these women's issues, was reflecting and representing very fairly the views of the average free Greek male citizen. That helps to put into perspective what appears at first sight to be the quite blatantly disempowered condition of the citizen-women of Athens, especially as com-pared to the relative political and legal empowerment of their menfolk, even the humblest and poorest among them. But was Athens a phallocracy as well as a democracy? Up to a point.

Women as citizens existed at Athens, and they were labelled *politides*, the feminine form of *politai*; but they were not citizens in any active political sense, precisely because they were formally debarred from almost all activity, let alone decisive action, within the public sphere of Athenian democratic politics. Hence their normal appellations were purely geographical: 'the female inhab-itants of Attica', or 'the female inhabitants of the city of Athens', but not the feminine equivalent of male Athenian citizens. The very title of Aristophanes' comedy *Ecclesiazusae* ('Women Attending the Assembly') of c. 392 BCE was a joke, intended strictly for the comic stage: for, ideally speaking, real Athenian women were not even to be seen in public, let alone, as the play's opening sce-nario fantastically postulated, to be seen and heard making a decisive interven-tion in male disguise at an Assembly meeting.

Ideally speaking—in actual physical fact, however, it was impossible to keep even most adult Athenian citizen women out of sight all of the time, as Aristotle rather ruefully had to admit. For the women of poor households, wives whose husbands were poor, had no choice but to leave home regularly to earn extra income or, since they could not afford to own household slaves, to fetch water from the public fountains and other water sources. Besides, there was also one generally recognized exception to the ideal rule of home-concealment for females—participation in religious ritual events such as funerals and festivals (including some few that were women-only) outside the house, and in some few cases the exercising of public religious functions as priestesses. It was one of the little ironies in the life of the Athenian democratic *polis* that one of its chief religious officials was a woman, the high priestess of Athena Polias—and not just any woman, but a woman drawn always from one particular, aristocratic family; by contrast, after c. 450 priestesses of the cult of Athena Nike were selected democratically by lot from all eligible Athenian women. Sometimes the woman holding the office of Athena's high priestess was widely known by name, although this contravened another ideal norm, as expressed by Thucydides' Pericles in the Funeral Speech of 431/0 (2.45.2), which maintained that respectable Athenian citizen wives and other female relatives should never be named in public, outside the household—either for praise or for blame. Pericles' own live-in partner, Aspasia, vividly exemplified that rule, in reverse: not being Athenian and so not being able to be married to Pericles, she was considered fair game for the vilest, tabloid-style public abuse, especially after Pericles' death in 429.

One neat index of Athenian women's invisibility is that in sharp contrast to the notoriety of Aspasia of Miletus, we do not know even the name of Pericles' first and only lawfully wedded wife. Another mark—or stigma—of Athenian women's inferior social status is that even such a woman as the (divorced) wife of Pericles, who came presumably from one of the wealthiest and most aristocratic families, would have had to endure exceptionally limited property rights. In the index entry *s.v.* 'women' of a standard work on the Classical Athenian law of family and property there appears just the one word: 'disabilities'. It would not be stretching the imagination far to suppose that in sexual matters too Athenian women found themselves very much not equal partners. Hence the humour—or so it presumably seemed to the largely male audience—of Aristophanes' sex-war comedy *Lysistrata* of 411: women taking the sexual initiative and withholding sexual gratification from men? The very idea of it!

That, however, is just a fantasy. The sober reality was that women's place, ideologically, was in the home. The more that ideal could be met in practice, the higher the status of the men inside whose households the women were kept. When a new bride was brought to her new husband's home, she was welcomed with a ceremony not unlike the one that greeted the arrival of a new slave. Residence in Athens was virilocal: wives, who might often be as young as twelve to fourteen and who had been married off at the behest of their male guardian (literally 'lord and master') without their own say-so, had to accommodate themselves to their husband's domestic space. The ritual marital-engagement formula—'for the ploughing of legitimate offspring'—made explicitly clear what the primary function of every legal marriage was;

but if the wife performed it satisfactorily, and if the offspring were male, then she achieved what only she—as an Athenian citizen wife—could achieve after the passage of the restrictive, double-descent citizenship law of 451/0: the creation of a potential new citizen. The paramount need for an Athenian citizen husband to establish the legitimacy of especially his male children explains the publicity carefully accorded to the wedding ritual, the introduction of a new wife to the husband's phratry (a social, pseudo-kinship association), and, finally, the huge song and dance made about the birth of a son. The more witnesses the merrier.

Indeed, if the husband were poor, the production of a male child by and through his (anonymous) wife was the most important thing he could do, physically, for the state community as a whole; with the exception of serving with his body on a trireme warship, which has been well dubbed a 'school of democracy' (see further on the Peiraeus below). He will not therefore have been so concerned about the successful implementation of the Eponymous Archon's opening pledge on entering office to preserve intact the property-relations of the citizens throughout his term. On the other hand, he will have had to tolerate the indignity and shame of seeing his wife having to go out of the home to raise extra funds either by, for instance, serving as a wet nurse to another citizen's child or by selling ribbons in the marketplace (the scenario suffered by the impoverished family of the speaker in Demosthenes speech 57; see Chapter 7). It is often wrongly believed that ancient Greek wives were kept in some sort of deliberate purdah or at least seclusion, since that—ideologically—was the public ideal. But that ideal was realizable only by the families of the well-to-do. Ordinary poor Athenian women had no choice but to leave the marital home.

Aristotle was by no means the only member of the Greek social elite to regret this unavoidable social phenomenon on moral–social grounds. But he was probably almost in a class by himself in the rigorist, sexist way in which he defined the 'nature' of women on analogy to that of 'natural' slaves. On the other hand, the very fact that Aristotle was so desperately keen to justify, philosophically, the holding and exploitation of slaves within the *polis* is a massive clue to their actual and perceived indispensability. An awkward question that has to be raised and answered is, 'Was Greek (and so Athenian democratic) civilization based on slave labour?' Various answers have been given, ranging from the wholly negative to the wholly affirmative; my own is close to the

extreme end of the affirmative pole. Slaves—and at Athens that means deper-
sonalized, dehumanized, socially dead, and usually non-Greek chattels—were
in many key areas of society and economy found indispensable, and therefore constituted a basis of the Athenian democracy. 'Location, location, location'—the realtor's mantra—applied intensely to the function and significance
of ancient slavery: it made all the difference in the world, for example, that
the silver ore extracted at Laureum was furnished by slave labourers working in literally lethal conditions, or that rich Athenians requiring a permanent
extra-familial labor force for their estates invested in the purchase of typically
'barbarian', non-Greek slaves. Slaves were, moreover, good to think with, from
an Athenian citizen's point of view: being an Athenian citizen meant, by definition, not being a slave.

The guesstimation of slave numbers—both absolutely or proportionally—is
a very hard game to play at any time. The figures of 400,000 slaves at Athens
(attributed to Aristotle) or 150,000 (stated by the politician Hyperides) are
either physically impossible or grossly inflated. More soberly, Thucydides
(7.27–8) reports, on what he clearly thought to be adequate evidence, that
between 413 and 404 more than 20,000 of the Athenians' slaves ran away and
were permanently lost to the Athenian economy; a slightly later source implies
that many were corralled by the occupying Spartans at Decelea and sold on as
war booty to new Theban owners. The very richest Athenian plutocrats such
as Nicias (d. 413) might plausibly be thought to own as many as 1,000, but
fifty was considered to be a very large private holding indeed. If we postulate
that the wealthiest 400 Athenian citizens (those required regularly to perform
tax liturgies) owned on average fifty each—as did, for example, the father of
Demosthenes the politician—that would make a starting figure of 20,000. On
top of those, let us assume that those (10,000–15,000) Athenians who could
afford to equip themselves and serve as heavy-armed infantrymen owned at
least one slave apiece—that would give a further 10,000 to 15,000 slaves, and so
an absolute minimum figure of 30,000, or about one-tenth of a total population
of some 250,000 to 300,000 souls. But to these we must add the slaves owned
by metics (10,000–15,000 in all), the wealthier of whom owned several, and,
taking account of the ubiquity of slaves and slavery in Athenian discourse, a
far likelier total figure is of the order of 80,000 to 100,000, representing about
one-third of the total population.

When considering the role of slaves and slavery in Athenian democracy, it's important not to forget that for its proper functioning on a daily basis it required a certain number of routine functionaries (archivists, clerks, policemen, etc.), the roles of which were filled by 'public' slaves of the community. One of these, Nicomachus, after being publicly manumitted, was entrusted with supervising a commission tasked with revising the Athenian constitution post-410. Athenian politics being as it was, and particularly so in this revolutionary era, Nicomachus was almost inevitably prosecuted, but the new, revised code he had presided over was enacted into law. Public slaves like him (or the public coin-tester) sat at the very top of the servile heap. The hierarchy below them among the privately owned slave population extended down from skilled craftsmen, some of whom were permitted the luxury of living apart from their owners; farm bailiffs; and domestic servants (male and female) to the virtual chain-gangs forced to labour pitifully in the Laureum mines.

We noted above that the citizen–slave status distinction was good to think with. The principle of distinction was marked at Athens in several ways: for example, a freed slave did not become—as he might have done at Rome—a citizen, but an Athenian resident alien (metic), still therefore requiring a citizen to act as his guarantor and patron. In lawsuits, for the witness testimony of a slave to be admissible and valid it had to have been extracted from him or her under physical torture, whereas citizen witnesses swore oaths and were in principle protected from all forms of corporal punishment. Of course, one mustn't be too legalistic—the boundaries between citizens and slaves were no doubt quite often blurred in practice (slaves after all did the same jobs as citizen and metic women). But they were not anything like as blurred as some would like to maintain. It was only in extremely few cases—a Pasion, a Phormion, both known to us through lawsuits—that a slave did succeed in emerging not just from slavery to freedom but from freedom to citizenship. When the anti-democratic pamphleteer nicknamed the Old Oligarch objected that you couldn't distinguish a slave from a citizen on Athenian streets, he had in mind only the relatively privileged among them.

The Athenians were collectively and as a polity considered to be notoriously litigious, both by outsiders and by themselves. 'It can't be Athens', says a character in Aristophanes' *Clouds* of 423 BC, when the city's pointed out to him on a map of the whole world, 'I don't see any jurymen in session' (lines 207–8);

the following year, Aristophanes staged the comedy *Wasps* around the highly controversial practice of litigation in democratic Athens. It was controversial then not so much because it wasn't generally agreed that personal disputes or major political disagreements should be settled in a court rather than through violence, as because critics of democracy did not like or even hated the fact that a key part of the *demos*' political power was exercised in and through the People's jurycourts, indeed by their sitting in judgment on them and, as they saw it, at their expense. It did not help to soften the critics' views that in some court cases justice was literally seen being done, since courts in the Agora were open to inspection by bystanders who did not hesitate to add their quotient of uproar and might even hope to influence the jurors' decision thereby—typical democratic demagoguery! The Athenians' judicial practice is controversial today, among scholars, for a rather different reason. They cannot agree whether Athenian-style litigation promoted the rule of law, and was indeed expressly designed for that purpose, or whether it was the continuation of feud by other, legal means in a system of social relations operated as a zero-sum game. A test case is the function and status of litigators known tendentiously and derogatorily as 'fig-sayers' (*sukophantai*, whence 'sycophants'), against whom legislation was passed in an effort to prevent vitilitigation, exploitation of the system for purely financial gain by legalised extortion; on the other hand, one person's sycophant could alternatively be seen—in the deliberate absence of a public prosecution service—as someone else's public-spirited citizen selflessly prosecuting anti-democratic malefactors on behalf of the *demos* and for the good of the *demos*.

One principal arena for such litigation was the Athenian Agora or civic centre, where there occurred an inextricable intermingling of private and public, political and commercial, religious and secular interests. The City Hall (Prytaneion) was located here, as was the Tholos, where Councillors were housed. Likewise the public mint was to be found here, as well as purely private market stalls, and trade was transacted in both human (slave) and impersonal goods. Aristophanes, ever alert to the day-to-day mundane realities, gave the 'speaking name' of Agorakritos ('he who is picked out in the Agora') to the leading character, a grossly demagogic sausage-seller, at the end of his *Knights* of 424. Getting on for a century later, a particularly colourful private lawsuit preserved in the Demosthenic Corpus (no. 54) presents the prosecution side in a case of alleged assault and battery inflicted in the Agora. Dionysius

I, tyrant of Syracuse (reign 405–367), was supposedly urged to read the plays of Aristophanes if he wanted to gain a good idea of what the Athens of which he'd just been made an honorary citizen was like.

Penultimately, let us take a brief look at the Peiraeus. This had begun the fifth century as only the second port of Athens (after the Phalerum roadstead), but over its course it became almost a second city of Athens. From the standpoint of the *polis* administration, it was an Athenian deme. But its population, besides being far more diverse ethnically and culturally than that of an average deme, far outstripped the purely citizen component numerically, and in its multiple functions it far exceeded those of any normal coastal or maritime deme. Not only did it possess three harbours, including commercial as well as naval, but it acquired its own walled fortifications on top of the Long Walls that from the 450s linked it to the city of Athens eight kilometres away. Here lived what its critics liked to dismiss as the 'naval mob'—hired metics as well as citizens— who rowed the trireme warships, or built and maintained them. It has been argued that rowing triremes was in itself a kind of 'school of democracy'; that certainly might help explain the extreme antipathy towards the trireme style of warfare expressed by Plato in the *Laws*. Here too were located the docks, where were effected the absolutely key commercial transactions that brought bread-wheat (mainly from Ukraine and the Crimea) and other vital commodities into Athens, and through which were exported Athenian olive oil, fine pottery, and silver. Such was its sprawling development—an early case of urban blight—that orthogonal master planner Hippodamus was called in from his native Miletus (an Athenian ally) to bring some sort of order and rationality by means of egali-tarian zoning. At the end of the fifth century, however, the very physical and economic development of the Peiraeus had a politically explosive effect: the 'men of the City' was how the oligarchs were named in their civil war stand-off of 403 with 'the men in the Peiraeus', a stand-off that the Peiraeus democrats handsomely won. Truly he Peiraeus was a 'world apart'.

The Athenian navy would never again after 404 be the force that it had once been, though the architect-designed arsenal built in the 330s between the Hippodamian Agora and the shipsheds was something of a wonder, and the Athenians regularly had up to 400 triremes on the stocks. They continued to be paid for through public–private partnership: a combination of public funds for their construction (overseen by the Council) and private funds raised through the liturgy system of taxation for their maintenance and for the payment of citizen and foreign crews. But commercially the fourth-century Peiraeus went from strength to strength, becoming the major port for the entire eastern Mediterranean. The conservative Athenian rhetorician Isocrates hailed it in a pamphlet of c. 380 as a deliberate invention by the Athenians for the good of mankind. Demosthenes' so-called counter-indictment speeches (nos. 32–38), named for the procedure used in these commercial lawsuits, brilliantly illustrate both the cosmopolitanism and the complexity of traders and trading in and through the Peiraeus in the third quarter of the fourth century. The Athenians, sometimes lambasted for their lack of commercial savvy, rose magnificently to the challenge by framing new laws and devising new kinds of legal procedures and courts to facilitate and indeed promote this kind of activity, most of the protagonists of which were not citizens but metics, transient foreigners, or indeed slaves.

Finally, and aptly enough, we address death—or rather the Athenians' democratic attitudes to death and disposal of the dead. A very striking rise in the number of Athenians accorded formal rites of burial in the later eighth century is thought to mark the beginning of that egalitarian attitude to the disposal of the dead, which may be said to be a characteristic of the Athenians' democratic spirit and democratic institutions of the fifth and fourth century. Being a citizen in life entitled one to decent treatment at and after one's death. The public funeral ceremony and funeral oration, introduced probably in the 460s for the city's war dead, represented the apogee of public commemoration of dead citizens as heroes. The tribal casualty lists of war victims that began to be inscribed about the same time were a further instance of the state's taking over from the deceased's family the function of public celebration and commemoration. Already under Solon, formal legal measures had been taken to curb excess of expense and publicity indulged in by wealthy families seeking to make a political point through their notionally private and familial obsequies. That same egalitarian movement was reinforced under the democracy by the cessation of the aristocratic-plutocratic practice of commissioning hugely expensive grave markers in the form of lifesized painted-marble statues (naked for males, clothed for females), and indeed between about 500 and 430 any very lavish grave markers of any sort. But from about 430, perhaps because of the availability of expert masons working on the Acropolis programme, the erection of superior markers in marble resumed, and even the democracy could not fore-close the erection of a monument such as the lavishly carved marble relief stele set up in the city's principal central cemetery, the Cerameicus, for the twenty-year-old cavalryman Dexileos, who was killed fighting against the Spartans at Corinth in 394/3; but the family did feel obliged most unusually to specify the honorand's age in order to remove any possible imputation or suspicion that he might have been in any way mixed up on the oligarchic side in the all too recent civil war of 404/3.

A last word for the slaves: probably most of them—and certainly most of those who died in the silver mines—were disposed of casually, and so have left no trace of their existence in either town or country. But there were exceptions; there are always exceptions. Favoured household slaves, both male and female, might earn a place—and even an honourable mention—in the grave plots of Athenian citizens. One Atotas, originally from Paphlagonia in Asia Minor, earned for himself a laudatory funerary epigram (dated between about 350 and 330) that celebrated not only his royal descent and heroic great-heartedness, but also his skill at mining.

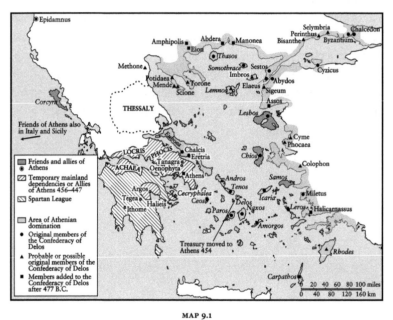

MAP 9.1
Athenian Empire. From Pomeroy, *Ancient Greece: A Political, Social, and Cultural History* (1998).

9.

GREEK DEMOCRACY IN CREDIT

AND CRISIS I

The Fifth Century

IT IS A BESETTING sin of popular commentators, critics, and pundits to imagine either that ancient Greece, the birthplace of democracy, was a single political entity or that in ancient Greece (whenever that was) there was only ever the one democracy, that of Athens. Some compound the basic error in all sorts of ways by speaking of 'Periclean democracy'. Arguably, even Athens alone had four or more, more or less sequentially, down to the democracy's forcible abolition by the Macedonian superpower: 508/7 to 462/1; 462/1 to 404; then either 403 to 322 or 403 to 336 (see Chapter 12); and 336 to 322. Indeed, some scholars, as we shall see (Chapter 14), are prepared to talk of Athenian democracy even after 322, indeed well into the third century, although by then the meaning of 'democracy' had taken on a different hue, if not form.

The aim of this chapter, however, is not to labour the point that 'Athenian democracy' or 'the Athenian democracy' are contestable and contested labels, but rather to emphasise—building upon a key analytical and classificatory insight of Aristotle's in the *Politics*—that Greek *demokratia* may and indeed should be analysed further into different degrees or even sub-types or species; Aristotle himself identified four. The high-water mark of Greek democracy was achieved within the second quarter of the fourth century BCE (Chapter 11). But of the several hundred Greek *demokratiai* that ever existed in ancient Greece, by far the majority did not belong to the category that Aristotle labelled 'the last', by which he meant the most extreme or the most developed, and to which he assigned the Athens of his own day. The vast majority of Greek democracies, in other words, were more or less moderate, or at any rate more moderate—less democratic, more oligarchic—than the best documented democracy of them all, Athens. Yet the democracy of Athens was not only the best documented; it was also an outlier, far removed from any Greek norm, and not to be confused with such.

It is probably safe to say that at least in the first half of the fourth century, there were several hundred Greek democracies or democratic *poleis*, but all we have by way of evidence to corroborate that crude approximation is the general statement of Aristotle that in his day most of the then-existent Greek *poleis* were some version of either democracies or oligarchies. The number of the 1,000 or so *poleis* of which we may state for certain or at least with great assurance that they were at some time within the fifth or fourth century some form of *demokratia* is unfortunately very much smaller. Quite recently, Eric Robinson has looked beyond Athens to identify those political entities—both individual *poleis* and federated *poleis*—that experienced what he calls somewhat vaguely 'popular government' and has come up with a total figure of something over fifty, the chief of those being Athens, Argos, Corinth, and Syracuse. I have already criticised (Chapter 4) what I consider to be his unacceptably loose application of *demokratia* to pre-550 *poleis*; in my view, there was no *kratos* exercised by any *demos* anywhere until at Athens in 508/7. On the other hand, I entirely welcome and share his critique of Athenocentrism directed against the too widespread view that 'Athens was the one and only "true" democracy' (2011: 219–22), and his two books are marvellous reference points for exploring the (admittedly jejune) evidence for early extra-Athenian democracy. I shall return to the maximum extension of Classical democracy in the Greek world in the fourth century, and to its acute crises in that century (Chapter 11); here I shall confine discussion to those phenomena within the fifth century—an arbitrary cut-off date, but one that happens to coincide rather neatly with one of Greek democracy's major crises, the tragic Athenian events of 404/3 and their aftermath.

Athens was a democracy from 508/7, an intensified democracy from 462/1; between those dates, Athens in the wake of the loyalist Greeks' victory over the Persians established in 478/7 a brand-new, multi-state naval alliance that moderns call the Delian League (since it was on the sacred Cycladic isle of Delos that the founding oaths of alliance were sworn, and there too that the alliance's original headquarters was established). Technically it was a hegemonic symmachy: an offensive and defensive alliance in which all allies were allied to the leader, Athens, but not necessarily with each other. Athens took the lead in establishing the alliance and laying down terms of membership—for this reason it might quite usefully be considered as ATO, the Aegean Treaty Organization. The alliance's three explicit aims and objectives were the exaction of revenge and reparation on the Persians for the damage caused in 490 and 480/79; the liberation of any Greeks still subject to Persian domination; and the permanent freedom of all Greeks from Persian control, for so long as the Persian Empire should exist and constitute a threat to Greek liberty. Athens was in 478/7 a democracy; the vast majority of the (eventually) 150 to 200 member allies were not, not then or ever. However, some—including some of the most important—either were already democracies in 478/7 or became such after 478/7, and in at least one case the Athenians so impinged upon a member state's freedom in the sense of right to political self-determination as either to impose or at least to support a democratic constitution.

There is no doubt therefore that the Delian League alliance, which very soon was converted into an instrument of Athenian external power-politics—an empire, if a minor example—was a factor in the extension of democracy in the Greek world in the fifth century. How significant a factor was it? And how conscious or deliberate was the role of Athens in this regard? Aristotle interestingly does not say that Athens went around establishing democracies but rather that they 'used to put down oligarchies', whereas Sparta contrariwise habitually overthrew democracies everywhere. On the documentary side—and there very clearly is a direct connection between Athenian democracy and the Athenian 'epigraphic habit'—the decree regulating relations between Athens and its subordinate ally Erythrae in Ionia, probably in the later 450s (Chapter 1), is unambiguous: had it not been for Athenian power and interventionism, which at least officially was in line with one of the alliance's major, anti-Persian objectives, Erythrae would not have become a democracy then and in that way. But can one generalise? Relations with Samos in 440/39 might usefully serve as a test case.

Such was the strategic importance of Samos to the functioning of the Athenian alliance and to Athens' naval control of the Aegean that its internal politics were never merely a local, domestic affair. The island-city was ruled by an oligarchy when it entered the Delian League alliance in 478/7, and it was one of the minority of the allied states that provided ships and crews from the start and continued to do so rather than switching to money tribute. It remained both an oligarchy and a ship-contributor for some four decades, until in the summer of 440 it went into open revolt from Athens and the alliance, aided and abetted by the nearest Persian satrap, based at Sardis in Lydia. Athens deputed Pericles to the overall command of the siege, which was to occupy nine months; it would cost a small fortune in material, financial terms and exact such a toll on Athenian morale that Pericles was debited, credibly, with resorting to morally dubious extremes of cruel torture on the prisoners of war. But though it is well documented that Athens punished Samos by depriving it of its fleet and walls and imposing severe reparation payments, what is not at all clear is whether—even after this most major of revolts—Athens imposed on Samos as a condition of its continued alliance a democratic mode of governance. Here, if anywhere, one might have thought, this would have been a second-nature, tactical as well as ideological, reaction—and yet, the clinching evidence is not there. At all events, one must keep quite separate from what may or may not have been done in 439 what happened on Samos in 412/1, when, against the run of play in that Ionian sector of the Great War, Samos became a democracy, fiercely active and demonstratively anti-oligarchic and pro-Athenian. Of course, it made a difference that for a brief moment in the summer of 411 the centre of Athenian democracy was no longer in Athens, where an anti-democratic coup had taken place (see below), but on Samos, where the devotedly democratic fleet was based, but by itself that does not entirely account for either the massacre of Samian oligarchs in 411 or the fact that Samos remained a loyal pro-Athenian democracy right down to the bitter end of the war in the spring of 404.

Indeed, such were the loyalty and such the unswerving democratic outlook of the Samian democracy after 411 that in 405 Athens took the unprecedented—and not repeated—step of engaging in a pact of isopolity with the Samians: under its terms any Samian citizens who wished to reside permanently in Athens might do so—and enjoy all the rights, duties, and benefits of

Athenian citizenship; and reciprocally vice versa for any Athenian citizens who wished to relocate permanently to Samos. From the fourth century onwards, and into the Hellenistic era, isopolity between formally independent *poleis* became a far more frequent phenomenon, but in 405 it was practically confined to cities of the same ethnicity that were members of federal *poleis* such as that of the Boeotians.

Of course, the pact between Athens and Samos was concluded in extremis and may well have had more of a symbolic than a pragmatic motivation and effect, but it does by its singularity point up the fact that the extension of Athenian citizenship was *not* normally a technique of empire, in the sharpest possible contrast to the Roman empire, for which the extension of Roman citizenship to allies and subjects regularly was. Well did the Roman Emperor Claudius contrast Athenian with Roman practice in this key regard, and explain the relative brevity of Athens' empire precisely in these terms.

Another useful test case of Athens' imperially motivated extension of democracy is the revolt of Mytilene and its suppression in 427, but here we must remember that by then Athens and its alliance had been been at war with Sparta and its alliance for four very tough years. Moreover, if Thucydides is to be believed, it was precisely from 427 that ideologically driven interventions on both warring sides became noticeably more frequent, indeed endemic: oligarchs, whether ruling or not, appealed to Sparta (which always on principle made a point of supporting oligarchies elsewhere; Thuc. 1.19), democrats vice versa to Athens. In 427 Mytilene, one of the five *poleis* on Lesbos (like Samos, an offshore east Aegean island), was ruled by an oligarchy, as indeed were three of the other four—the one democratic exception being Methymna. Already in 428, during the celebration of the Olympic Games, the Mytilenaean oligarchs had actively solicited Spartan intervention. In 427, with a Spartan fleet nearby, they had gone into open revolt, supported by the other three Lesbian oligarchies, whereas democratic Methymna stayed loyal to Athens and the alliance. Athens, together with those allies who could still provide ships and marines, blockaded Mytilene, in which crisis exacerbated by food shortage the oligarchs took the decision to supply hoplite weapons to the normally un-armed *demos*. No sooner had they received them, however, than they turned them on the Mytilenaean oligarchs. But was this because of the poor citizen masses' underlying pro-Athenian democratic ideology, an instance of what a speaker in the

Athenian assembly later that year was to claim to be the prevailing attitude of sympathy among the lower classes of the empire and alliance? Or was it due more simply to hunger, to the desire to end the siege as soon as possible? To conclude, as far as the behaviour and attitude of imperial Athens go, the safest answer to the question of its promotion and extension of democracy abroad within its alliance seems to be that of Roger Brock (2009: 161): 'It did not do so consistently, nor with a consistent ideological commitment.'

After Athens, the best attested cases of Classical democracy are Argos, Corinth, and Syracuse. Discussion of Argos and Corinth I shall defer to Chapter 11, not least because in 392 they entered into an isopolity agreement on democratic lines like that between Athens and Samos in 405, except that, rather than having a long space of sea between them, the territories of the two *poleis* were physically contiguous. But it should be recorded here that it was not the least important feature of Argos' history in the fifth century that some time after 494 it became a democracy and as such allied more than once with democratic Athens against its hereditary enemy, pro-oligarchic Sparta. It is unfortunate that the only diplomatic treaty involving Argos in the fifth century of which the terms are preserved is between oligarchic Argos and Sparta in 417.

For Syracuse, however, the evidence relating to its fifth-century political vicissitudes is distinguished precisely by Syracuse's revolutionary political transformation from governance by a powerful tyrant dynasty to its experience of a democratic interlude between 466 and 405. It was thus as a democracy that Syracuse resisted the democratic Athenians' ultimately disastrous attempt to subjugate it and perhaps all Greek Sicily between 415 and 413, prompting Thucydides to attribute Syracuse's successful resistance in significant part to its democratic constitution. Ancient democracies did fight each other. As at Athens, democracy at Syracuse succeeded the overthrow of a tyrant dynasty, but unlike the Peisistratids the Syracusan Deinomenids (Gelon, Hieron, and Thrasybulus) did not only rule the single *polis* of Syracuse—the largest *polis* in Sicily, founded from Corinth in about 730—but also possessed a sort of mini-empire in southeast Sicily and beyond. So it was not just 'the Syracusans' who overthrew the tyrant Thrasybulus 466, but the Syracusans helped by allies from cities all over Greek Sicily including Acragas, Himera, Gela, and Selinous. Syracuse, moreover, was one of those Greek 'colonial' cities—another was Heracleia on the Black Sea—that had managed to secure an unfree, serf-like native (Sicel) labour force with a distinctive collective name (Cillyrii or Callicyrii), and significant numbers of these too aided the tyrant's overthrow, perhaps in the (no doubt disappointed) hope of better treatment under a democracy.

Moses Finley, in his general history of pre-mediaeval Sicily, rightly made the point that the *polis* as such seems not to have become as rooted an institution in Greek Sicily as it was in Old Greece. He pointed to the regular recurrence of property confiscations and mass exilings of political opponents, taken even to the point of transfers of population that recall the practices of other, much more recent tyrannies. Sicilian tyrants, moreover, not only had employed very large foreign mercenary forces, but were in the habit of granting them citizenship; the local historian Diodorus (admittedly writing some four centuries later) reported that even after the tyranny's overthrow there remained some 7,000 of them still in Syracuse, who were summarily deprived of citizenship and expelled. The little evidence we have for the form and workings of democracy in Syracuse prompted Finley to suggest that 'the government almost looked like the Athenian'; the Syracusans even practised a form of ostracism. However, the council and officials were elected, not chosen by lot, there was no pay for public political service, and from a passage in Aristotle's *Politics* it would appear that it was only after the defeat of Athens in 413 that Syracuse experienced the transition to a form of democracy even remotely resembling that of their defeated enemies: what Aristotle says is that in 412 'the *demos* having been the cause of the victory in the war against the Athenians made a revolutionary transformation from *politeia* to *demokratia*'. 'Politeia', in Aristotle's special terminology, was a mixed regime inclining to democracy, not a form of democracy itself.

That would at any rate explain the influential, leading-statesman role of the aristocrat Hermocrates in and after 424 BCE; and, in order further to explain why Syracuse had not progressed as far as Athens down the democratic road, one might perhaps invoke fear of the Sicels—not only of the free, unsubjugated natives of the interior but more particularly of the unfree Cillyrii or Callicyrii (above); this will probably have been greater than the Athenians' fear of their own large but heterogeneous and polyglot body of mostly privately owned chattel slaves. Successful resistance to Athens' assault between 415 and 413 damped down internal *stasis* in Syracuse, although the Athenian general Nicias had claimed to be in touch with a potential fifth-column of presumably democratic traitors. But, when the *demos* 'transformed the government from a *politeia* to a *demokratia*', including the use of the lot for some offices, that provoked an equal and opposite reaction from the old oligarchic elite of Gamoroi ('owners of shares of the land', the richest landowners descended from the original settlers) and their followers, until Dionysius, a former follower of Hermocrates, rode the tiger of class and factional politics and succeeded in making himself tyrant. Not the least of his qualifications was to pose, successfully, as the saviour not only of Syracuse but of all Greek Sicily from subjugation by Carthage. Indeed, not only did Dionysius rule—under the emolliently 'republican' titles of Archon and Strategos (General)—for almost forty years (405–367), but he turned himself into the very type of 'the Tyrant', used for the edification of future students of political theory (not least by Plato and his pupils) and a model for would-be emulators. He even features in Dante's *Inferno*.

After Syracuse the pickings to be gleaned from the extant sources for other fifth-century democracies are sadly slim indeed. Here follows a selection drawn from Robinson's listings, ordered geographically—rather than chronologically—from east to west. In some cases it is not only the chronology that is uncertain, alas. About the time that democratic Athens was attempting to intervene, unsuccessfully, in support of a popular revolution at Aegina in 493, the Persian supremo in the West, Mardonius, allegedly 'placed the cities under democratic rule'. Or so Herodotus (6.43) would have his readers believe, but that is a very dubious claim (cf. Chapter 6). Far more likely is that Mardonius, by tolerating moderately oligarchic regimes, thereby granted to these Asiatic Greek *poleis* at least the semblance of what they most keenly desired—*autonomia*, independence from external rule: at any rate, a form of political liberty greater than they had enjoyed or rather suffered previously under their pro-Persian tyrants.

That extremely limited degree of 'freedom' was not considered by the Persians to be incompatible with the continued requirement enforced upon the Ionians, as upon all Persian subjects, to pay tribute in cash or kind, and their subjugation to the overlord of Asia, the Great King of Persia, via his local satrap or viceroy. Fifteen years later, however, all Ionian Greek cities had been liberated from Persian control and were required to contribute rather to an Athenian-led alliance; the experience of Erythrae within this new diplomatic framework has already been alluded to earlier in this chapter and discussed in Chapter 1.

The situation of Naxos, the largest of the Cycladic islands, is every bit as interesting. Again, our source is Herodotus, and the initial scenario he depicts relates to the immediate preliminaries to the outbreak of the so-called Ionian Revolt. 'The Naxians who currently hold the city' were 'the mass of the people'. As typically would happen in class warfare of this sort, the masses had not only taken over the reins of power, but ejected a number of those who had previously held them. Herodotus refers to the latter as 'fat cats' (in Tom Holland's new translation—the Greek literally calls them 'the thick'); these are the largest property owners, the rich few. As was to happen all too frequently later in the fifth century, these fat cats looked to Persia to restore them to their homeland and to power, and so they appealed to the most influential among their ritualised guest-friends, Aristagoras, the deputy tyrant of Ionian Miletus, because he happened to be on good terms with Artaphernes, the local Persian satrap of Lydia based at Sardis. The Persian expedition engineered by Aristagoras, however, proved a fiasco, and it was not apparently until 490 that a Persian fleet under Datis and the same Artaphernes—en route to punishing Eretria and Athens for having supported the Ionian Revolt—exacted a delayed revenge. The Naxian masses (or significant numbers of them) fled to the mountainous interior of the island, but the Persians 'enslaved those of them whom they caught and torched both religious shrines and the town'. What Herodotus does not add is that they also no doubt replaced the democracy with a compliant oligarchy of the richest and most pro-Persian Naxians, and that presumably remained the case until 478/7 when the island-city was enrolled as a founding member of the Athenians' new anti-Persian alliance, the Delian League, contributing ships and crews to allied anti-Persian expeditions.

Even if no regime change was then involved, the Naxian ruling elite must at least have been required overtly to soften their pro-Persian stance. Within a decade, however, Naxos was the first ally to stage an open revolt from the League—which the Athenians felt they had to suppress with exemplary severity. Not only were the Naxians required to surrender their ships and pull down their walls but they were also, in Thucydides' formulation, 'enslaved contrary to established usage'. 'Enslaved' is clearly being used metaphorically here, meaning deprived of full political autonomy and independence; but to which 'established usage' is Thucydides referring—normal Greek interstate relations, or specifically the conditions of alliance laid down for membership of the Delian League in 478/7? Either way, my own feeling is that Thucydides intended to highlight negatively Athens' interference in the internal political affairs of Naxos, and specifically its support for the installation or re-installation of a democratic government.

Democratic moves were also afoot in the Peloponnese early in the fifth century, not only at Argos, Sparta's enemy, but even within Sparta's own alliance. The Peloponnesian League (a modern term) was technically a hegemonic symmachy; the alliance was both offensive and defensive, and all allies recognised Sparta as their collective leader. But in ancient Greek it was referred to either as 'the Peloponnesians' or more formally as 'the Spartans and their allies'. This multi-state, supra-*polis* organisation was perhaps given some sort of formal status in or around 505 BCE, following the failed Peloponnesian attack on newly democratic Athens. Certainly it was this alliance that formed the backbone of the loyalist Greeks' resistance to the Persian invasion of 480/79. Indeed, it was precisely because Sparta was *hegemon* of 'the Peloponnesians' that Sparta was the unquestionable choice as leader of that resistance—at sea as well as by land: about half of the thirty-plus Greek cities and peoples known to have united as 'the Hellenes' were members of the Spartans' own alliance.

However, two of those Peloponnesian League allies, Mantinea and Elis, most suspiciously failed to turn up in time for the decisive land battle of Plataea in late summer 479. It is surely not wildly over-speculative to interpret that disloyal tardiness as reflecting not just caution (it was by no means certain that the Greeks would prevail) but also political disaffection. Nor does it seem excessive to suggest a connection between their putative disaffection and the fact that these two cities are the only members of the Peloponnesian League alliance known to have had a democratic government at some time during the fifth century, though unfortunately it is not known when they first acquired such a form of *politeia*. Sparta's principled opposition to democracy has already been mentioned, together with its instant interventionist reaction against the establishment of the very first democracy in a Greek *polis* at Athens in 508/7.

In fact, Sparta's opposition to the rise of democracy was one of the most potent factors inhibiting its spread in the Aegean Greek world. On more than one occasion Sparta succeeded in actually rolling back democracy's advance, most conspicuously in and after 404 at Athens and in cities of its former empire such as Samos. Sparta's preferred foreign policy objective was to surround itself and its vulnerable Helot base with a *cordon sanitaire* of cities that were its allies, and reliably allied because they were under the control of well-disposed oligarchies. Members of these subordinate regimes would be connected personally to leading Spartans, not least the two kings, through ties of ritual friendship. It therefore took exceptional circumstances for an allied Peloponnesian League city to achieve let alone maintain democracy, as Mantinea and Elis did.

Mantinea was one of the two biggest and most powerful cities of Arcadia, the upland region immediately adjoining Sparta's Laconia to the north and therefore potentially controlling Sparta's egress towards its principal Peloponnesian enemy, Argos. As was often the case in such situations, Mantinea was frequently at loggerheads with the other major Arcadian city, Tegea, which—therefore—was typically far more loyal to Sparta; this was so partly due to its greater proximity but also and not least because Sparta, after a disastrous failed attempt to 'helotize' it in the 550s, treated Tegea with exceptional respect. Conversely, Mantinea had the support and example of relatively nearby Argos in its turn to democracy. Elis, for its part, though not a major city in its own right, controlled and managed the holy site of Olympia and the Olympic Games, giving it enormous prestige throughout the Hellenic world; Sparta was keen to take advantage of this religious prestige, and its citizens were notably prominent and successful competitors in the Games. Normally, therefore, Sparta was very reluctant to intervene in internal Elean affairs. What sort of a democracy either Mantinea or Elis had cannot be ascertained, but one assumes that in both cases it would have been relatively moderate.

From the Peloponnese we move west to the region called by the ancients Great Greece (Megale Hellas, Magna Graecia), comprising southern Italy from the bay of Naples southwards. As its very name betrays—originally Neapolis, New Polis—Naples was one of the many cities, such as Syracuse, founded during the early-historical first wave of Greek permanent overseas settlement (c. 750–550). Ancient Taras, in the 'heel' of Italy (Roman Tarentum, modern Taranto—whence the tarantella) was another, but it was near-unique in being a foundation from Sparta, which practised, indeed largely invented itself through, the internal colonization of its own home territories of Laconia and Messenia rather than exporting surplus population abroad. Taras, together with its nearby predecessor Satyrium, was Sparta's one true colony, but instead of aping the political institutions of its metropolis experienced a far more normal and progressive political trajectory. True, there is a mention of a late-sixth-century Tarentine figure described as a king, but then Cyrene too, a sort of granddaughter city of Sparta's via Thera (Santorini today), had kings who were compatible with a republican constitution. (In about 550 BCE, in response to a request from Cyrene, founded c. 630 BCE, an elite Mantinean called Demonax had been sent out by his city to act as a political arbitrator at a time of troubles. Demonax's diplomatic solution was not to abolish Cyrene's kingship but to limit its powers to certain religious prerogatives, reminiscent of a Spartan king's or the 'king' Archon's at Athens, and to reassign the rest to 'the people'.) As for Aristophilidas and the Tarentine kingship, by the second quarter of the fifth century Taras had evolved into the sort of mixed constitution—a moderate oligarchy inclining to democracy—that Aristotle labelled 'polity'.

However, what interested Aristotle most about Taras' polity was its transformation into a democracy, probably in the circumstances sketched by the first-century BCE Sicilian annalistic historian Diodorus under the year 473/2. A major all-out war had broken out between the Tarentines and the Iapygians, the local native-Italic people with whom relations were typically hostile. The Iapygians reportedly mustered a huge force of 20,000, against which the Tarentines linked forces with the Greeks of Rhegium (Reggio Calabria in the toe of Italy). But they suffered a massive defeat in which, according to Aristotle, many 'notables' lost their lives. 'Notables' was a cant euphemism for the rich and powerful, so Aristotle was probably implying that in his view it was this disproportionate loss of life among the elite of Taras that tipped the balance towards full democracy.

Not far away from Taras, a new-style overseas settlement was founded in the instep of Italy under Athenian auspices in 444/3: Thouria, alternatively known as Thurii. This was not the first settlement abroad to be composed of Greeks from more than one city or indeed ethnic grouping of Greeks; Cyrene again offers a precedent. But it was apparently without precedent in being founded with a ready-made code of laws that were democratic; they had been drawn up by Protagoras (Chapter 6). It is tempting to see this as a classic case of ideological imperialism on the part of the Athenians, seeking to export political power and influence through the establishment of a tame democracy in a commercially and strategically sensitive area; but that was not at all how things panned out in practice. Aristotle tells a sorry tale of multiple political upheavals, often with unintended consequences for regime change (from aristocracy to democracy, and from democracy to *dunasteia* or collective tyranny). The fact that a political exile from Sparta with no known track record of democratic adherence (Clearidas, adviser of King Pleistoanax) was given not just asylum but citizenship at Thouria in the 440s gives pause; another political exile to benefit from Thourian generosity was the historian Herodotus of Halicarnassus.

Finally, there is the ambiguous case of Camarina, a Sicilian colony of Syracuse founded c. 600. A mid-fifth century BCE cache ('archive' seems too grand) of 143 folded lead tablets inscribed with names of citizens together with their phratries has been found here near the temple of Athena. They were at first interpreted optimistically as either jury allotment-tokens or records of payment for assembly attendance, and so as evidence of Athenian-style democracy, whether directly borrowed from Athens or not; but actually they are more likely to have had a military function, or perhaps they recorded contributions to a public fund or allocations of land or citizenship. From this evidence alone, at any rate, one could not infer the nature of Camarina's *politeia*, although the very fact of the recording of citizens' names in writing may suggest a certain opennness of governmental practice. However, from Thucydides' account of a debate at Camarina in 415 conducted in face of the Athenians' massive Sicilian expedition, it has been inferred that Camarina did by then have a democratic constitution. For his representation of the speech by the Athenian ambassador Euphemus accords very well with the sort of profile he gives to his Athenian speakers in Assembly debates such as that over Mytilene, and Euphemus' audience does seem to be an open, decision-making citizen assembly.

So much for fifth-century Greek democracy 'in credit'. The remainder of this chapter will examine the darker side of the democratic achievement, democracy 'in crisis', especially, but not solely, as that afflicted Athens. It will be viewed particularly through the unforgiving lens of Thucydides, the master historiographer of democratic Athens' decline and fall in what we—thanks largely to him—call the Peloponnesian War. Really it was an Atheno-Peloponnesian War, and it is still debatable whether it was one twenty-seven-year war or rather two lengthy wars interrupted by a longish interval of uneasy peace. Also open to question is the nature of Thucydides' own political views: on the one hand, he was a huge admirer of Pericles, and Pericles was undoubtedly a convinced ideological democrat; on the other hand, Thucydides makes a number of decidedly unflattering references to the way 'mobs' make political decisions, casts Cleon—the leading Athenian politician after Pericles—as a mere rabble-rousing demagogue, and states that the Athenians were best governed (enjoyed the best form of governance?) in his time during the non-democratic, moderately oligarchic regime known for short as 'the Five Thousand' (Chapter 7). That is no ringing endorsement of the regime of radical democracy over which Pericles presided as 'first man'.

Thucydides, moreover, was hardly unbiased. He had personally experienced the fickle wrath (as he would have seen it) of the *demos*, as coached by the abhorred Cleon, when he was exiled for committing a rather major military blunder that was by no means entirely his own fault. And yet as a contemporary observer and political commentator he is in a class by himself, placed there not least by his searing analyses of two major bouts of civil war—on Corcyra (Corfu) in 427 and at Athens in 411/10 (further below). No more objective than he, and no more of an ideological democrat, was Aristotle, yet two central books (5 and 6) of his *Politics* addressing how civil war arises in *poleis*, and suggesting how it may be either forestalled or least allowed for and healed, are a master class in political sociology. 'Civil war' could be rendered in ancient Greek as '*stasis* within a single tribe'. But *stasis* by itself would do just as well, and it served Thucydides and Aristotle particularly well, as we shall see. Today we use ancient Greek *stasis* as a loan word in English, but we use it very differently, to mean a steady state, a standing-still. For the ancient Greeks *stasis* in the political sense was a process of taking a stand, of standing apart together with one's own side against a rival or enemy grouping, and it was the very opposite of static in its often bloody application.

Athens' democracy was for the greater part of two centuries (508/7–322) quite exceptionally stable. This was despite the more or less constant presence of a potential fifth-column of diehard oligarchs, who scored great successes in 411/10 and 404/3 but were much less successful thereafter, if no less virulent in their hatred of democracy as a system; they would have agreed with the opinion attributed to Alcibiades that democracy was 'acknowledged lunacy'.

The record of Athenian democratic stability is all the more remarkable in that the very mode of decision-making and governance by mass meeting with open majority voting risked the flowing over of divided emotions and tensions into violence at least once a month in the fifth century, and several times a month in the fourth. Tension, however, was the norm, and 'private dissensions' between leading politicians and rivals for the ear and support of the masses were the inevitable cost of the democratic decision-making mode, and all the more acute in the absence of any sort of organised party-system. Allegiances were personal, and the personal at Athens was very political. Indeed, Thucydides ascribed Athens' defeat in the Peloponnesian War in significant measure precisely to such dissensions, which in his view fatally damaged the effective operation of policies decided by the Athenian Assembly.

One such personal difference set Pericles against Cimon, another Pericles against Thucydides son of Melesias. From the ostracism procedure of 443, which saw the removal of the latter, down to 430, Pericles was apparently elected General representing his tribe every year. He thus was in a position to dominate the making of Athens' foreign policy at a time when Athens had become the major imperial power of the eastern Mediterranean. This position it owed significantly to the feats on the sea of Pericles' former rival, Cimon, who had himself been ostracised in 461. Between 477 and 457 Athens had established an anti-Persian naval empire in the Aegean, incorporating its old rival Aegina and major islands such as Thasos, Lesbos, Chios, and Samos; from 457 it also, less wisely, sought to obtain and hold a land-empire, especially in neighbouring Boeotia. But 454 had brought a major setback in Egypt, and in 446/5 retrenchment was marked by the conclusion of a notionally thirty-year truce with Sparta and its allies; in fact, it lasted only fourteen.

Depending on one's view of Sparta's behaviour and aims and of the overall strategic situation in Aegean Greece, Pericles pushed Sparta into declaring war on the Athenian alliance in 432/1, either by pursuing a relentless policy of aggression or by not being prepared to compromise on contested territorial claims. Thucydides was probably under thirty in 431, but even in his maturity he remained a huge admirer of Pericles, regarding him as Athens' 'first man' and believing to the end that Pericles had always advocated the most prudent and foresighted policies for Athens, including the correct strategy for overcoming Sparta. Others disagreed, and with reason: Pericles' largely passive strategy in fact laid the Athenians open to severe loss of morale, and it is unarguable that he gravely underestimated the cost of the war, especially at sea. The foremost critic of Pericles just before and in the early years of the war was Cleon, a 'new politician' in the sense that he was from a non-aristocratic background, and from a family that had made its money in trade (a slave-worked tannery). Cleon advocated an aggressive foreign policy, and urged that Athens should take the hardest possible line on any allied disaffection or revolt such as that of the Mytilenaeans in 428/7. However, Thucydides' savage portrait of Cleon as a rabble-rousing, self-interested demagogue, which is echoed in Aristophanes' caricatural comedy *Knights* of 424, should not be taken at face value. Pericles was every bit as much of a demagogue as Cleon, and Thucydides at least was grossly inconsistent in praising Pericles for his sage policies while at the same time blaming the *demos* for taking against and indeed sacking Pericles when the policies he advocated were not working.

Probably at about the same time as *Knights* was staged, another Athenian intellectual composed the savage indictment of the democracy that has come down to us as Pseudo-Xenophon's *Athenaion Politeia*, otherwise known as the Old Oligarch (Chapter 1). The anonymous author's age is immaterial. The interest of this pamphlet in the present context is that although its author devoutly desired the overthrow of the democracy and its replacement by oligarchy, he drops not even the merest hint that such a consummation might—one day, let alone any time soon—be realised. Rather the opposite: although the author hates democracy and democrats and does not hesitate to say so, he grudgingly concedes that the *demos* knows how to promote and secure what it takes to be its own best interests, selfish and morally debased as these are. The situation in Corcyra (ancient Greek Kerkura), allied to Athens since 433, was considerably more volatile.

Among the precipitating causes of the outbreak of the Peloponnesian War—what Thucydides (1.23) called the 'grounds for complaint and differences' between the two sides—was the Corcyra affair. This was shorthand for a complex piece of diplomacy in the mid- to later 430s involving principally Corcyra, its metropolis Corinth, Corinth's alliance-leader Sparta, and Athens. On appeal from democratically governed Corcyra against alleged overbearing interference by Corinth, the Athenians agreed to conclude an alliance with Corcyra. It had to be a purely defensive alliance, so as not to be seen to contravene the terms of the Truce concluded with Sparta in 446/5. But in the naval war that broke out between Corinth and Corcyra in 433 a small squadron of Athenian warships engaged on the Corcyraean side, and the Corinthians brought this minor clash to Sparta as one of their grounds for complaint, sufficient in their view to justify Sparta's deciding to declare war on Athens. As indeed happened in 432/1. Four years later, Corinth returned certain Corcyraean prisoners of war to their homeland, but with the express aim of getting them to make a political revolution and then break Corcyra's alliance with Athens.

That, says Thucydides, was the beginning of the *stasis* on Corcyra, which he takes great pains to analyse for two main reasons: first, because it was the first such outbreak of revolutionary civil war during the Great War, and, second, because it was sufficiently representative of *stasis* as a generic type for his analysis to be paradigmatic for all the rest. Throughout his account Thucydides emphasises the passions that were indulged on both the democratic and the oligarchic sides. Lust for political power arising from greed and ambition was the main cause of such evils as sons killing their fathers or the gross violation of religious sanctuary. Much of the intellectual interest of the passage, however, turns on Thucydides' deconstruction and unmasking of a series of (so to speak) 'party' political slogans. Words and phrases that normally bore one unambiguous meaning were perverted for propagandistic purposes so as to mean almost the exact opposite, and Thucydides regarded such linguistic perversion as disastrous for Hellenic values and self-respect.

One sloganistic phrase has a peculiar significance from the point of view of democratic ideology: *isonomia politike*. As we have seen (Chapter 6), *isonomia* was for Herodotus' Persian debater Otanes 'the fairest of names'; the addition of *politike* in the Thucydides passage draws attention to the fact that the word could be used with a non-political (for example, a medical) sense. In both the Herodotus and the Thucydides passages the association of *isonomia* is with democracy, though formally 'equality under the laws' could be associated no less with oligarchy. Thucydides' point, however, is that this was a mere democratic slogan, not to be mistaken for a genuine aspiration. Really what the democrats spouting it were seeking were prizes for themselves and ascendancy over their opponents, not the best interests of the *polis* as a whole. Thucydides is, however, even-handed in his critical analysis. The Corcyrean oligarchs were in his view making a no less specious profession of their desire for 'self-restrained aristocracy'. Significantly, that phraseology of 'self-restraint' and 'moderation' would recur, again in a propagandistic context, in Thucydides' account of the globally far more important oligarchic counter-revolution at Athens in 411.

For that Thucydides is once again our principal witness (not of course an eyewitness, since he remained in exile until the end of the war); all that survives of the final Book 8 of his unfinished *History* leads up to or focuses upon this great *stasis*. An alternative account survives in the Aristotelian *Ath. Pol.*, since the events of 411 provoked one of the transformations, reversals, or upheavals to which Athens' *politeia* was in the author's view subjected; but this version is far less considered and insightful, and much more biased. Following the disaster in Sicily in 415 to 413 (described by Thucydides' Books 6–7), the Athenian masses had—typically, sneers the historian—blamed their gung-ho advisers rather than shouldered the responsibility that was theirs, since it was out of sheer ignorance and greed that they had voted for the doomed expedition in the first place. Oligarchic ideologues quickly seized their rare opportunity, before Athens could rack up any successes in the continuing naval war in the Aegean, for which the Spartans had now acquired significant Persian financial aid. Using the twin arguments that a democracy was manifestly incapable of conducting the war successfully and that the Persians could be induced to provide funds to the Athenians only if Athens became an oligarchy, they managed to have summoned an extraordinary meeting of the Assembly. This was to be held not in the safety of the Pnyx behind the city walls, but in the deme of Colonus actually outside the walls and more or less under the noses of an occupying force of Spartans under King Agis II, which had seized Decelea in 413. This meeting was therefore attended, as the oligarchs designed, only by members of the top 50 per cent or so of citizens—economically speaking, those who could equip themselves as hoplites or serve as cavalrymen, at a time when many of the poor masses were away from Athens serving with the fleet at Samos on the far eastern side of the Aegean. The outcome was predictable: in effect, the Assembly voted away its own democratic power. The way was paved for a coup, accompanied by extreme physical violence, by a shadowy group of 400 extreme oligarchs led by the oligarchic ideologue and rhetorician Antiphon.

The rule of the Four Hundred was at first a success, ideologically speaking, in that they instantly abolished the features they hated most about the democracy, such as the provision of political pay for any other than military purposes (e.g., rations for hoplites). However, as regards the conduct of the war, it was shambolic, partly because the regime was so narrowly focused, giving rise to envy and fear among more moderate anti-democrats, and partly because, despite the odds being so stacked against them, the Athenian fleet was nevertheless managing to achieve considerable success against the Spartans at sea. Moreover, the Four Hundred's attempt to spread oligarchic revolution throughout the allied cities of the empire, while themselves retaining power at Athens and conducting the war on behalf of the alliance against Sparta and Persia, backfired horribly. Oligarchic revolutions did indeed take place on a significant scale in the cities of the empire; Thucydides describes this ironically as their 'receiving moderation'. But the new oligarchies in the allied cities saw no reason to continue to bend the knee to Athens and opted for autonomy and independence (and cessation of tribute payments) instead. When the Four Hundred saw that they were about to be overthrown from within, so determined were they to cling to power that they were even prepared to sell out Athens to Sparta, as long as Sparta would guarantee them continued power as a puppet oligarchy (8.90). Small wonder, then, that this was not the regime under which Thucydides considered Athens to have been 'best governed in his time'. That accolade went rather to the regime that after some four months supplanted it. This is usually nicknamed 'the Five Thousand', though actually, since it was based on a limitation of full active political rights to the hoplites and above, excluding the *thetes* (the fourth census group, comprising the poor majority of citizens), it should really be known as the 'Nine Thousand' (or so).

This new regime ruled for about eight months. There is some room for dispute as to whether it was a moderate oligarchy—that is, represented the actual implementation of what had merely been a phoney promise by the desperate Four Hundred—or a moderate democracy, in which, although all citizens retained formal decision-making rights in the Assembly and the courts, only hoplites and above were eligible for office. My own strong inclination is towards the former view, not least because the non-democrat Thucydides so strongly endorsed it. Pronouncing the earliest known version of a 'mixed constitution' theory of governance, he approved it, he said, because it represented a 'moderate mixture' in the interests of both 'the few' (rich, mostly oligarchs) and 'the many' (poor, mostly democrats), by which I take him to have meant that the regime, in a Solonian sort of way (Chapter 3), accorded to those two groups what they intrinsically—in Thucydides' view—merited. That surely was, on balance, an oligarchy.

Another reason for accepting that interpretation is that Theramenes, who had been a member of the Four Hundred but switched on its overthrow to being a leading light of the Five Thousand, was no democrat (see further below). However, this new regime lasted only eight months and dissolved so noiselessly that one of Thucydides' continuators, Xenophon in his Greek History (*Hellenica*), does not even bother to mention its supersession and the reinstatement of the pre-411 democracy. In 410 the Athenians, besides attempting to win the continuing war with Sparta, decided to focus on making the city democratic not only in the present and for the future but also by reclaiming the city's past—a democratic past—for the *demos*. Among the measures set in train was a revision of the city's laws, a protracted process that took over a decade to complete. A leading figure in the revision was an ex-*demosios* (public slave) called Nicomachus, who was one of the at least three prominent figures to find themselves on trial for alleged religious offences in 399 (see Chapter 10).

Thucydides (8.68) had rightly noted the democracy's resilience: 'It was tough for the Athenian *demos* to cease enjoying freedom after the span of about a century since the tyrants had been overthrown'. Following the restoration of democracy the city was even able to achieve victories at sea that prompted the Spartans actively to consider treating for peace again. That resilience, however, eventually was exhausted in the spring of 404: after one last major naval reverse—at Aegospotami in the Hellespont in late 405, engineered by the cruelly brilliant Spartan Lysander—Athens was starved into total submission. On the way to that final crushing defeat in the war, the Athenians had hardly helped themselves in 406 by their conduct following a victory at sea at Arginousae in the eastern Aegean. This was another case of those personal dissensions fingered by Thucydides. It had been something of a Pyrrhic victory; many thousands of Athenian citizens had perished because the Generals (no fewer than eight of the Board were directly engaged) had failed justifiably or otherwise to rescue them from sinking hulks after the battle due to a storm. Theramenes helped to lead the attack against them, which erupted in open Assembly: all those Generals who made the mistake of being present (six out of the eight accused, including Pericles' homonymous son with Aspasia) were convicted of treason and condemned to death, illegally, by the Assembly acting as in effect a kangaroo court. The sorry tale is told—in a very slanted version and with considerable retrospective glee—by the normally pro-Spartan and pro-oligarchic Athenian exile Xenophon. The most telling moment in his account is when shouts from the floor of the Pnyx to the effect that 'It would be monstrous if the *demos* were not to be permitted to do whatever it pleases'—regardless of the laws—lead to the fateful verdict on the Generals.

What was to become of the Athenian democracy in the ungentle hands of the Spartans as represented by the fanatically pro-oligarchic Lysander? In short, it was abruptly terminated and replaced by an equally ungenteel junta of just thirty ultra-oligarchs, led by Critias. The evidence is to be found in the jejune and biased narrative of Xenophon, backed up by the also anti-democratic *Ath. Pol.*, and countered only by a speech written by the distinguished, pro-democratic metic and speechwriter Lysias in his own behalf, since he was attacking one of those members of the post-404 regime who had had his own brother murdered. It was such greed-motivated butchery that gave the new regime its nickname of the Thirty Tyrants. They were a *dunasteia* or collective tyranny, since they lacked constitutional legitimacy and ruled without reference to law properly so called. They had been imposed on the Athenians at the point of Lysander's spear, and their vicious rule was propped up by a garrison supplied by Sparta—from specially liberated members of its Helot underclass.

The Thirty Tyrants' aristocratic leader was a relative of Plato on his mother's side, and, like Plato, a political theorist with an even more pro-Spartan bent than his kinsman. Critias wrote two accounts of the *politeia* of the Spartans, one in prose, one in verse. It is not inconceivable that he had it in mind somehow to remodel Athens on Spartan lines: at any rate, the number 30 corresponded precisely to that of Sparta's senior governing body, the Gerousia, and there is mention by Lysias of 'Ephors', a markedly Spartan term of political art. Theramenes again played a double role in this ultra-oligarchic regime—until he was executed by decision of the so-called Council on Critias' orders. But it was less such internal dissension than the decision of Sparta to cease supporting the Thirty in face of mounting internal and external opposition that paved the way for its overthrow. A decisive battle took place in the Peiraeus between the 'men of the City' (the 3,000 or so citizens of the new oligarchic *polis* of Athens) and the 'men in the Peiraeus', the diehard democrats, which the latter won, killing Critias in the process. A leading role was played in the peace agreement by the eirenic Spartan king Pausanias, son of the Pleistoanax who had negotiated the peace with Athens of 421. Democracy was restored yet again, after the passage of about a year.

This restoration, however, unlike that of 410, occurred in peacetime, and, thanks to Pausanias' very special kind of non-intervention, it was brought about in circumstances that allowed the Athenians to think forward, try to learn from past mistakes, and thus prevent the recurrence of a further anti-democratic transformation. For Pausanias had compelled the Athenians to swear a mighty oath of amnesty—literally, 'not-remembering'. Excluded from its terms were the surviving members of the Thirty and their creatures in the police body known as the Eleven and the Board of Ten (including another relative of Plato, Charmides) that had ruled Peiraeus on their behalf. For all other Athenian citizens—and especially of course those who had more or less actively supported one or other kind of oligarchy between 411 and 403—there was to be an official forgetting of their past anti-democratic crimes: no politically motivated allegiance or activity entered into before 403 could now be legally or legitimately used as basis for a court action against an individual. This was probably the first general amnesty in recorded human history. But of course it was far from being a purely idealistic arrangement. Failure to comply with the amnesty's terms would bring the Spartans crashing back down on Athenians' heads. Likewise to Sparta's advantage—Pausanias was no soggy liberal—was its insistence on the recognition or at least non-suppression by the restored democracy of the ultra-oligarchic statelet of Eleusis, to which some of 'the men of the City' who had survived the decisive battle in the Peiraeus had fled. Thus did Sparta effect the political break-up of the Athenian *polis*, reversing the original unification that was attributed to founder-hero Theseus and celebrated in the annual festival of the Synoikia. I myself would also see the tomb of those Spartans who had died in the fighting around Athens in 403 as part of the Pausanias deal: it was prominently located at a junction in the state cemetery of Cerameicus, and at least the Spartans whose names were honorifically inscribed on the outside of the tomb were to be remembered favourably by the Athenians.

Among those who had signed up as one of the 3,000 citizens of the new, Thirty-directed oligarchic *polis* of Athens was Socrates. Athens had survived its crisis as a democracy, but Socrates' crisis was yet to come. He had not joined the democratic Resistance in 403, although he had not been an active supporter of the Thirty, either. He was thus initially one of those to benefit from the amnesty, or more precisely from its observance. All the extant sources, oligarchs to a man, are agreed, rather to their astonishment, that the restored democracy did as a rule observe its terms faithfully. And in 401/0 the Eleusis statelet was reabsorbed and the *polis* reunified. However, in 399 Socrates was put on trial. How, by whom, why, and with what effects we shall explore in the next chapter, together with a rather earlier trial involving the arch-oligarch of 411, Antiphon, and the later trial of Ctesiphon, a proxy for the arch-democrat politician Demosthenes. All three court cases throw exceptional light on the Athenians' very peculiar democratic practice.

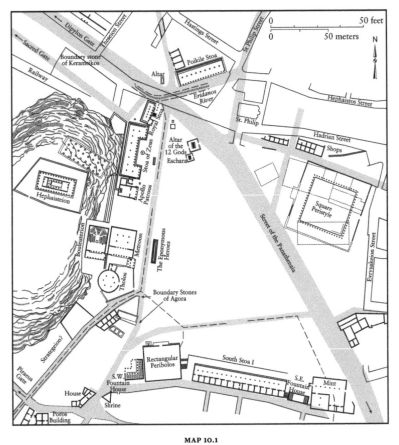

MAP 10.1

The Athenian Agora c. 400 BCE. From *The Agora Excavations*, Camp and Mauzy (2009), redrawn by George Chakvetadze.

10.

ATHENIAN DEMOCRACY IN COURT

The Trials of Demos, Socrates, and Ctesiphon

IN EARLIER CHAPTERS IT has been emphasised that the Athenian *demos* did not exercise its *kratos* only in the Assembly but also—and with equal authority—in what by 460 had come to be called the Dikasteria or People's Courts. This was the newer term for what had been known since Solon's day (Chapter 3) as the Heliaea, a term linked etymologically to a Greek word for assembly or gathering. Aristotle famously defined the citizen of a *polis* as the one who 'has a share in judgement, *krisis*, and rule or office, *arche*', making it clear that judgement included the passing of legal, courtroom judgements. The author of the Aristotelian *Ath. Pol.* anachronistically but tellingly wrote that 'when the *demos* gains control of the courts, it gains control of the constitution (*politeia*)'.

Consistently, the democratic Athenians rendered jurisdiction as democratic as it could possibly be (Chapter 7). Jurymen were chosen by lot, most of them were drawn from the *demos* in the sociological sense of the poor masses, and payment for service in the jury courts was among the first kinds of political pay to be introduced, on the proposal of Pericles in the 450s. There were no professional barristers formally in action in court, and there were no judges in the modern sense of career experts—jurymen were also at the same time judges, and there was no public prosecutor (or public prosecution service): all prosecutors in non-personal cases were volunteers. Legal procedure was more important than the letter of the law, equity more important than observing the niceties of strict legal rules of evidence and precedent, and offences were typically not precisely defined. In short, jurisdiction in democratic Athens was amateur (in both senses) and attuned as far as possible to

FIGURE 10.1
Kleroterion fragment
Greek democrats believed that the lottery was the proper way to select citizens for key public functions; in this case, the lottery machine served to choose dicasts (juror-judges) for the Athenian People's Court.
© Gianni Dagli Orti / The Art Archive at Art Resource, NY

the everyday life experience and notions of the 'average' citizen. In major political trials—in a sense all trials were political, of course—the overriding consideration for a juror was not necessarily the guilt or innocence of the defendant as charged, but rather what verdict and (where relevant) punishment would most likely further Athens' best interests as a democratic *polis*.

A key pathway therefore into not only the institutional mechanisms of the Athenians' democratic decision-making but also their democratic mindset is provided by the extant evidence for court cases between the late fifth and late fourth century. Some 150 lawcourt speeches survive, and these take us closer than do any mere narrative references to the actuality of what went on in a court. Yet these speeches usually represent only one side of a case, and do not necessarily correspond exactly to what the litigants actually said in court but rather convey the version of what was actually said that the speechwriter wished a wider audience or readership to hear or read. In the three trials that I've selected here for illustrative purposes the evidence is in the first two cases

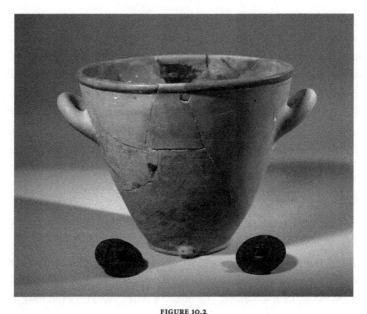

FIGURE 10.2
Water clock fragment
Greek democrats were fervent believers in strict equality; here the (reconstructed) water clock
metered out exactly equal amounts of time to rival litigants. © Getty Images: Dea/ G. Nimatallah

even worse than this, if I may put it that way: for the trial of the prominent
Athenian citizen called Demos we have just a few fragments remaining from
what was clearly a major lawcourt speech by one of the foremost speechwrit-
ers of the day, and for the trial of Socrates we are reliant mainly on two versions of his defence speech (the English 'Apology' renders the Greek *apologia*).
These were composed not by a speechwriter, let alone by Socrates himself (who
wrote hardly anything for publication and possibly did not even deliver a formal defence speech of any kind at the trial), but by two philosophically minded
followers of his, each of whom had his own—different—agenda. In the third
and final case, the trial of Ctesiphon, we do almost uniquely have written versions of speeches delivered on both sides, although not a version of the formal
defendant's speech.

It is my contention that the implications of these trials are so fundamental
and central to the understanding of the fifth- and fourth-century democracy
(or democracies) that the vagaries and deficiencies of the evidence are worth

struggling against. Each in its different way arose from a crisis of the Athenian democracy: the first two from the crisis experienced in the last fifteen years or so of the fifth century, involving a major military defeat, the third from the crisis occasioned by the catastrophic military defeat of 338. The cases, finally, throw broad beams of light upon Athenian high society and foreign policy, upon Athenian religious politics, and upon the dynamics of the rivalry for the ear and favour of the *demos* between leading politicians, for whom the current phrase was 'the orators and politically active'. What follows is a rather stream-lined account of each.

The Trial of Demos

In 422 Aristophanes had in a sense put Demos—the Athenian People as such—on trial in his drama *Wasps*. This was a comic fiction that both recognised and hilariously caricatured the centrality of courtroom behaviour to the demo-cratic process; arguably, by mercilessly satirising such behaviour it possibly also hoped to moderate it somewhat. About half a dozen years later (on my hypo-thetical chronology; the true date is not known) a very prominent Athenian citizen with the striking given name of Demos was put on trial by another prominent citizen called Erasistratus. The filiation and genealogy of Demos are well known; he was the son of the Pyrilampes who was a close associate of Pericles and who, by a second marriage to his niece (his sister's daughter), became Plato's stepfather (and thus related also by marriage to Critias, future leader of the Thirty Tyrants). The identity of the Erasistratus in question is far less certain, as there were several Athenians called Erasistratus around then, but my own view is that he is most plausibly to be identified with the Erasistratus who in 404/3 became a member of Critias' Thirty. At any rate, given the nature of high-profile Athenian political prosecutions, the prosecutor of a man of the status and stature of Demos is unlikely to have been of lower social and politi-cal standing himself. Juries may typically have been slanted in their composi-tion towards the lower end of the socio-economic spectrum, but it was the elite who often were compelled or chose to act out their personal and political rivalries before them in a kind of soap opera on the courtroom stage. This was indeed a principal field of engagement—in the hostile military sense as well as that of less antagonistic interaction—between the mass and the elite of the Athenian body politic.

Further, clinching confirmation of the high status of the affair is provided by the identity of the speechwriter hired by Demos—namely Antiphon, son of Sophilus of the deme Rhamnous, the leading ideologue of the ultra-oligarchic Four Hundred. He was executed in 411 after a public trial for high treason, but his swansong defence speech on that occasion was very highly regarded by Thucydides the historian, possibly a former pupil. Antiphon had had a long time to prepare for it, since he had been in the business of acting as a legal consultant and speechwriter for others for many years and was indeed the first such to publish versions of his speeches after the event, presumably usually in cases where his clients had been successful. On top of that, he wrote and published purely theoretical speeches—ones, that is, that could serve as templates or models for use by litigants on either side in actual cases of the offences in question, such as homicide by poisoning. It's this theoretical side of his output that lends credence to the suggestion that he is to be identified with Antiphon 'the Sophist'—that is, the author of some challenging philosophical tracts, only fragmentarily preserved, including one provocatively titled 'On Truth'.

The case brought against Demos by Erasistratus is reported to have centred upon 'the peafowl'. That is all we know; we do not know, in other words, what type of a procedure Erasistratus used, nor what it was exactly that Erasistratus was accusing Demos of doing or not doing vis-à-vis the said avians. But we do know a little about the peafowl themselves, and can infer more as to what their presence in Athens and their connection with Demos may have signified, or might have been alleged by Erasistratus to signify. Peafowl were exotic Asiatic birds of specifically Persian derivation and association, and carried a very high monetary valuation (1,000 drachmas for a breeding pair, or some three years' wages for a skilled craftsman continuously employed). The original breeding pair (or pairs) were a diplomatic gift bestowed upon Demos' father Pyrilampes by a Persian Great King, to whom he had led an official Athenian mission or embassy. Once a month, on the first day of the month, Demos' menagerie was somehow opened to any Athenian who wished to visit them, but otherwise it remained firmly off-limits. That amount of public access may not have been enough to satisfy Erasistratus, who may have argued that as the birds were really Athenian public property, Demos should not be entitled to make personal profit from possessing them (and selling eggs or birds). Another line of attack that likely lay behind the prosecution was

the accusation that Demos was somehow, if not an outright Persian sympa-
thiser ('medizer'), unduly constrained in his political activity by his family
connection to the Persian royal house. Whatever the outcome of the trial (I'd
guess Demos was found not guilty), Demos reappears still diplomatically
active deep into the 390s.

The date of the speech and trial is, as mentioned, unknown, but it has of
course to have been held not later than 411, the year of Antiphon's execution.
A possible context in or around 415 or 414 is suggested by the following circumstances: around 415/4 Athens was actively supporting the rebel satrap of
Lydia against his master the Great King; at the same time there was a general
witchhunt being conducted at Athens, prompted by two religious scandals
(mutilation of sacred images of Hermes in 415, and private profanations of
the Eleusinian Mysteries); and in 414 Aristophanes had performed his memorably colourful, escapist comedy *Birds*. On this reconstruction Erasistratus
looks to have been taking a high demagogic line against Demos, playing the
pro-democratic volunteer prosecutor on behalf of the Athenian *polis*, and
yet a decade or so later this same Erasistratus was, hypothetically, an ultra-
oligarchic member of the Thirty. Such a volte-face would have been neither
unprecedented nor entirely surprising. Peisander too had started out as a
democratic ultra before becoming a leading light of the Four Hundred. And
perhaps what started Erasistratus on his anti-democratic road, ironically
enough, was his failure in this high-profile court case, in which his opponent's brilliant defence consultant was a shadowy backroom politician of
consistently oligarchic views.

In short, the trial of Demos throws all sorts of unusual sidelights on the
Athenian democratic process in the later fifth century BCE. Aristophanes had
as it were put Demos on trial comically in his *Knights* of 424: Demos as a
character is made to look rather slow and foolish—if well-intentioned—by his
uppity and borderline crooked 'slave' politicians. But the real trial of a politician with the given name Demos, a man from the top social drawer advised
by the leading forensic consultant and speechwriter of the day, shows what
the real Athenian *demos* had to contend with if they were to carry out one of
the cardinal theoretical as well as pragmatic principles of *demokratia*, namely
making their leaders legally responsible as well as responsive to their perceived wishes and needs.

FIGURE 10.3
Demosthenes
Demosthenes (384–322 BCE) was an exact coeval of Aristotle, but whereas Aristotle was not a democrat or practical politician, Demosthenes championed democracy against Aristotle's former employer and Athens' conqueror, King Philip II of Macedon. © Vanni Archive/ Art Resource, NY

The Trial of Socrates

Our sources for this deeply resonant but ill-documented event of 399 consist primarily of Plato's *Apology of Socrates* and Xenophon's *Apology of Socrates* (but note how different they are, in argument as well as style), together with the actual terms of the original indictment. The latter are preserved by a much later, third-century CE writer, but there is no reason to think them seriously inaccurate. A savagely caricatural (we must assume) portrait of Socrates and his teachings is provided by Aristophanes in his 423 comedy *Clouds* (extant only in the revised version of c. 418, rewritten, but not for performance, after its regretted failure on the stage; it came third and last). The modern bibliography, which goes back to the later eighteenth-century Enlightenment period, is simply vast. For Socrates is one of the most famous philosophers in the Western tradition, which is not bad going for one who committed not a single word of his philosophy to writing.

Socrates was accused, before the court presided over by the 'king' Archon, of impiety, a potentially capital offence—but not only of that. He was also accused of corrupting the youth of Athens. The jurors were, as always, a random selection chosen by lot from the total panel for that year of six thousand. Their number, 501, was a usual size—too big to be easily bribable, but big enough to constitute a grouping whose opinions were reflective of the body politic as a whole. Above all, it was an amateur jury, not necessarily able to specify precisely what the principal charge of impiety denoted or connoted, but knowing an impious citizen when they saw one. They probably all of them would at least have heard of Socrates before his trial, and many of them could have seen him in action philosophising in or around the Agora. Given the jury's likely age profile, quite a few would have been old enough to have seen *Clouds* twenty-four years earlier or even to have fought with him at the siege of Potidaea between 432 and 429. Socrates himself, born in 469, was seventy in 399. All of them too would have known or soon been told that in 404/3 he had been enrolled as a citizen under the oligarchic regime of the Thirty, and that among his pupils and followers had been the late Alcibiades, convicted for impiety in 414, and the late Critias, *capo* of the Thirty.

To return to the charge sheet in more detail, Socrates was accused, first, of not duly recognising the gods and goddesses whom the *polis* of the Athenians officially recognised and worshipped, and of introducing other new divinities. To which accusation of impiety was added the second, moral-political charge that he had subverted and corrupted (literally 'destroyed') the youth of Athens. The chief prosecutor—a volunteer, since this was not a charge involving personal or familial damage—was a relatively unknown and not politically prominent poet called Meletus. But one of his two supporting prosecution speakers was Anytus, a very prominent politician indeed; he had played a conspicuous role in the restoration of democracy in 403, and it may have been he who was particularly responsible for adding the charge of corruption to that of impiety. The other supporting speaker, Lycon, is as unknown as Meletus, which suggests that these two prosecutors may have represented themselves as Athenian 'everymen' deeply offended by Socrates' alleged irreligion. The latter, they will surely have argued, had so offended the gods as to alienate their goodwill from the people and city of Athens: hence the plague of 430, the public and private impieties of 415, the utter defeat by Sparta in 404, and the horrors of civil war in 403, all signs of divine enmity in the eyes of ordinary believing Athenians.

The legal procedure employed was a public 'writ alleging impiety'. 'Impiety' would not have been defined by statute, and anyhow Athenian religion was not a matter of doctrine and dogma but rather of customary values and above all conventional behaviour; that meant especially participation in collective public worship at, for example, the Great Dionysia and Panathenaea festivals (Chapter 8). Hence the verb used for not 'duly recognising' (*nomizein*) the city's gods and goddesses has the same etymological root as *nomos* in both its sense of 'law' and its sense of 'customary practice'. Xenophon's Socrates protests vigorously that he *had* participated adequately and conventionally enough in such rituals, but Plato's Socrates in the *Apology* and elsewhere in Plato's works suggests that even if his overt religious practice had been conventional, the spirit in which he'd conducted it was not at all conventional. Besides, there was the matter of Socrates' own personal 'little supernatural power' (*daimonion*), which he not only did not disavow but seems to have been rather proud of. For he claimed that this inner voice, a sort of 'hotline' to the divine, only ever told him when *not* to do something. But that would have done nothing to reassure the jury of his religious normality or to combat his popular image, relentlessly exploited by Aristophanes, as a batty old fellow with some very odd and potentially very dangerous religious ideas. Ordinarily, perhaps, that wouldn't have mattered all that much—but when the gods seemed to have turned against Athens so violently, any unconventional religious attitudes might well have been taken as jeopardising the entire community and therefore in need of official and public purgation.

Likewise any unconventional religious behaviour, such as the alleged introduction of other new divinities. There was nothing in itself impious in introducing new divinities—so long as the introduction was done publicly and officially through the proper democratic channels, by the *demos* itself; for then the divinities in question (Asclepius, Bendis, Pan, etc., all fifth-century additions) would, despite their varied origins and natures, all end up in the recognised Athenian pantheon, and so long as the divinities were commonly recognised divine beings or powers. But for Socrates to introduce by himself his own private divinities for his personal, not communal, benefit: that, even if it was not necessarily illegal, contravened Athenian democratic custom and convention. 'Other' here means the other of two, polar opposite categories of divinities, the good and the bad: Socrates' were of course 'bad'—antisocial at best, positively harmful to the citizen community at worst. Greeks had more than one word for 'new'; Meletus' choice of *kaina*, 'brand-new', carried the connotation of dangerously newfangled. Since Athenian religion overall was an 'ancestral' affair, characterised by tradition and conformity, such novelty was by definition a bad thing. Finally, there are the 'divinities' (*daimonia*): by using the plural, the prosecutors wanted not just to refer to Socrates' inner voice but to draw a contrast between the host of gods and goddesses that the city officially recognised and worshipped, the *theoi*, and the inferior 'demons' that allegedly were Socrates' preferred religious currency.

To me that adds up to a very powerful religious indictment, even if the prosecution were not obliged to spell out precisely how it counted as impiety, and it explains why the religious charge comes first and is the more fully elaborated. Many scholars, however, believe that the second charge—corrupting the youth—was as it were the 'real' one, but that it could not be spelled out because it would have violated the terms of the Amnesty sworn in 403 (Chapter 9). Undoubtedly, by 'the youth' the prosecution (especially Anytus?) had in mind very specifically two Athenian youths whom Socrates had somehow mentored: Critias (born about ten years after Socrates) and Alcibiades (born about 450). Each of them had flagrantly pro-Spartan and anti-democratic track records; Alcibiades, moreover, had actually been convicted of sacrilege, and Critias was debited with composing inflammatory, anti-conventional religious drama. And some fifty-five years later, in 345 BCE, the leading politician Aeschines bluntly stated in a major political trial speech: 'You put to death Socrates the Sophist who taught Alcibiades and Critias'. But instead of this being the real charge, I would suggest rather that it was added on, to convince those jurymen who may not have been entirely clear what impiety was or how precisely Socrates was guilty of it, but were quite clear that Socrates had been complicit with traitors and enemies of the democracy.

Finally, there is the issue of the penalty imposed. Since this was technically a lawsuit without an automatic, fixed penalty, the jury was required to vote twice, first on 'guilty' or 'not guilty', and second (after further arguments or pleas by prosecution and defence) on the penalty. Voting was done by secret ballot—jurors placed one of two bronze ballots (one for 'guilty', the other for 'not guilty') in a receptacle in such a way that it could not be seen which of the two had been deposited. It turned out that more of the 501 jurors voted for the death penalty demanded inevitably by the prosecution than had voted Socrates guilty in the first place: a possible breakdown for the first round is 281 versus 220, since it was said that just 30 votes going the other way would have given Socrates a majority for acquittal, and then 321 to 180 for the second round. What had gone so wrong for Socrates? His claim that, so far from being guilty as charged and therefore a public menace, he was in fact a public benefactor, indeed a kind of public hero who deserved to be honoured in something like the manner and style in which victors in the Olympic games were honoured (free meals in the City Hall, reserved seats at the theatre, etc.), will not have endeared him to some of the jurors; to others the size of the fine that he eventually did volunteer to pay—half a talent—will not have seemed either adequate, given that he had very rich friends such as Crito, or proportionate to his monstrous crimes.

All the same, Socrates did not absolutely have to die. I put it that way because probably the vast majority of non-specialist observers of the trial and its outcome, following Plato's lead, see Socrates' enforced death as a major and indelible blot on Athenian democracy's record. For example, for the British nineteenth-century philosopher and campaigner J. S. Mill, who was otherwise normally prepared to defend the democracy against its anti-democratic critics, it represented one of his greatest bugbears, the tyranny of the majority, in unforgivable action. For I. F. Stone, the twentieth-century contrarian and activist, the Athenian democratic jury's crime was to have broken the democracy's own basic principle of freedom of political speech. To them I rejoin that the fact of the trial and the manner of its proceeding were both entirely democratic (there was no such principle as Stone posited), and entirely 'just', according to the Athenians' democratic notions of religion, politics, and justice—which are not ours, and that, as regards the death of Socrates (self-administered; technically, he was not executed, as he is usually said to have been), it need not have happened—if, as I believe many convicting jurors will have expected would be the case, Socrates had gone into permanent exile with the help of his devoted and very wealthy friends. The devoted Plato in his *Crito* dialogue makes his Socrates argue that the very laws of Athens required him not to so flee, but few if any of the jurors would have seen Socrates as quite such an unquestioningly obedient servant of Athens' democratic laws. If therefore Socrates was a martyr to freedom of religious thought and political action, he was very much a voluntary martyr. And the Athenian *demos*, as represented by the jury at the trial of Socrates, should be found 'not guilty' of undemocratic activities.

The Trial of Ctesiphon

Little is known of the Athenian minor politician Ctesiphon, but a great deal is known of his trial, which originated from his proposal of a crown for Demosthenes in 336, although the trial itself was postponed until 330. This trial takes us into the territory covered more fully in Chapter 12, but the legal procedure involved was in existence and operation by at latest 415 BCE, and the manner of its application in 330 illuminates not only the form of democracy then enjoyed by the Athenians but the entire nature of what was understood by *demokratia* ever since the People had been allowed to exercise its power (*kratos*) through the People's jury courts as well as through the Assembly, that is, since the 450s BCE.

The Crown Affair of the 330s arose because Ctesiphon's proposal in the Assembly of a crown for Demosthenes in 336, though passed, had then been blocked by Aeschines' lodging of a writ alleging an unconstitutional proposal. The symbolic award of a crown was the highest civilian honour available in democratic Athens. The proposal was made on the basis of Demosthenes' entire career to date (since the 350s), not—obviously—to crown the total failure of the policy he had advocated in the recent past against Macedon; it also was intended to signal to Macedon and to engender among the Athenians the strongest possible spirit of democratic defiance. Since the 338 Chaeronea defeat, Thebes and other major Greek cities may have had their democratic constitutions abrogated and Macedonian garrisons imposed to prop up the replacement oligarchies, but Athens—still a democracy, still without a garrison—was not going to bend the knee to the new superpower. So what was at stake in the case was not just the continuing personal rivalry between Demosthenes and Aeschines, but also the dominant issue of Greek foreign policy of the day and in a sense the very essence of the Athenian democracy: who ruled?

The unconstitutional proposal writ procedure is first attested in 415, the year after the last attested (and failed) ostracism was held. That conjunction cannot have been merely a coincidence. In the fourth century the procedure became the weapon of choice for rival demagogues or politicians to attack each other with, hence Aeschines' automatic resort to it in 336. But for whatever reason, the trial of Ctesiphon on that charge was postponed and not reactivated until 330, following the crushing of Spartan king Agis III's rebellion against Alexander the Great's Macedon (from which Athens had wisely stayed aloof). Ctesiphon was the official defendant in the trial, but he in effect handed his defence over to Demosthenes, acting in the capacity of supporting advocate. So powerful and so effective was Demosthenes' crown oration (a lavish version of which he published, as, less understandably, Aeschines had published a version of his prosecution speech) that Aeschines failed to win even one-fifth of the jurors' votes.

All such prosecutions were high-stakes, high-risk political manoeuvres. But for Aeschines this defeat was so complete and so final that, his career in shreds and tatters, he went into permanent exile, first on Rhodes and then on Samos, both islands very far from Athens. The Greeks had a rather gloomy proverbial saying 'look to the end': this meant that so long as you ended your career, or your life, well, then your career and life would be adjudged both retrospectively and prospectively to have been a success. If the reverse occurred, however, then the reverse view operated—regardless of how many or how great were the earlier successes one might have achieved. Aeschines certainly had achieved great successes. Not least of them was his successful prosecution in 345 of another supporter of Demosthenes, Timarchus, which he followed up in 343 with a successful defence against Demosthenes' prosecution of him for malfeasance during a diplomatic mission to Philip in 346 on which they had served as fellow ambassadors. But in 330 the jury deemed otherwise—indeed, resoundingly so. Aeschines, as noted, did not even achieve a certain required minimum (one-fifth) of the votes, and therefore had to pay a large fine—financial injury heaped upon political insult.

III

11.

GREEK DEMOCRACY IN CREDIT

AND CRISIS II

The Golden Age of Greek Democracy (c. 375–350) and Its Critics

I OPEN THIS ACT OF our democratic drama with a couple of seeming paradoxes. First, the golden age of ancient Greek democracy that I have in mind is not the age of Pericles or any other portion of the fifth century BCE, before the temporary termination of Athens' democracy and empire in 404. It falls rather in the second quarter (more or less) of the succeeding fourth century. This century—an accidental product of the BCE/CE system of chronography devised in the sixth century—is often viewed erroneously as a time of decline from a supposed fifth-century peak. In fact, although it did undoubtedly witness the general and near-universal suppression and supersession of democracy in the Greek world by one or other form of monarchy, that was not before democracy had genuinely peaked. Second paradox: Sparta, the city that refused to countenance at home what counted for the ancient Greeks as *demokratia* and that dedicated itself abroad to supporting oligarchies and forestalling or eliminating democracies, nevertheless as its power waned provoked and fostered its spread, including in important Greek cities that had hitherto managed to get by without benefit of democracy.

In this chapter we shall attempt both to do justice to Sparta's own unique, alternative political system and to chart the rise of democracy as a global phenomenon of the fourth-century Greek world. But first it is well to recall that

FIGURE. 11.1
Model of Athenian Acropolis c. 400
The 'High City' of Athens had been the political and religious centre of the region since time immemorial,
but in the fifth century, following the Persian sack (480 and 479 BCE), it was rebuilt, reconfigured, and
embellished to an extraordinary degree. Through the monumental entrance way (Propylaea) the visitor
was confronted by a plethora of statuary and minor shrines, above which towered the great Parthenon
and Erechtheum temples, both dedicated to the city's patron Athena. With permission of the Royal
Ontario Museum © ROM.

within the period to be covered here there was born and grew to maturity one
of the great innovating intellectual geniuses of the ancient—or indeed any—
world, a 'giant thinker', as one of his most devoted followers (Karl Marx) aptly
called him: Aristotle, son of Nicomachus of Stageira (or Stagirus) in northern
Greece (384–322). In about 335 Aristotle founded at Athens his philosophical school known to us as the Lyceum, and it was exclusively for students of
this school that the work that we call the *Politics* was produced. Later scholars
divided the work as a whole into eight books, but it is a mark of its rawness and
the occasional inconsistency due to its origin in lecture notes that the ordering
of the books is disputed. Mine follows the majority view.

Book 1: what is the (nature of the) *polis*, and who are its necessary constituents. Book 2: ideal *poleis*, whether actual (e.g., Sparta) or imagined
(e.g., Plato's *Republic*), that had been proposed as models but which Aristotle
finds variously flawed. Book 3: what is a citizen? Aristotle's own definition of

the *polites*, the adult, free male *polis* member or citizen, as he who actively shares and participates in judgment, including legal judgment, and ruling, was by his own admission better suited to defining the citizen of a democracy than of an oligarchy. Book 4: still very theoretical, setting out typologies of regimes. Democracy was not itself one single thing; rather, it could be further analysed into sub-species, of which the Athenian democracy of his day was taken to be one of the few to represent the last or most extreme version. Books 5 and 6: the mainly empirical books, either somehow based on or related to the 158 *Politeiai* compiled by him and his students, of which only the *Athenaion Politeia* (*Ath. Pol.*) survives as such. Book 5 focuses on how *staseis* (political revolutions or other major disturbances) arise and how they may be avoided; Book 6 looks at the varieties of democracy and oligarchy, again with an eye to how they may best be conserved and preserved. Books 7 and 8: an incomplete sketch of Aristotle's own ideal utopia, to which we shall return at the end of this chapter.

Most golden-age Greek democracies were less extreme, more moderate, than the Athenian. Sparta, on the other hand, was not a democracy at all, in the accepted political-constitutional sense; but what exactly it was posed a real problem of classification. Aristotle's account in Book 2 well reflects the difficulty that ancient analysts had in assigning Sparta to any one defined constitutional form. The explanation for that lies in Sparta's achievement of a stable constitutional form very early on, perhaps earlier indeed than any other Greek city, and thus well before democracy had been invented either as an institutional practice or as an analytical category. Since the Spartan polity seemed to possess monarchical (or at least kingly), oligarchical-aristocratic and democratic features, one vaguely respectable escape route touted by Aristotle among others was to dub its *politeia* 'mixed'. Most commentators, however, saw it as some form of aristocracy or oligarchy. Xenophon was alone in speaking of it as a 'kingship'. Those who were prepared to bite the bullet and call it a democracy significantly did not do so on grounds of the city's strictly political, decision-making institutions, but because of two cardinal social institutions: the common, compulsory, and centrally imposed upbringing, successful passage through which was a requirement for attaining citizenship; and the common dining-messes, membership of which was a requirement for gaining and retaining citizenship status.

Taken politically, however, Sparta's *politeia* failed the democratic tests across the board: all offices, including therefore the most powerful, were either elective (none was allotted) or hereditary (the kingship). The chief executive office of the Ephorate (a board of five) was open to all Spartans and annual, whereas the Gerousia (the Senate, twenty-eight members plus the two kings *ex officio*) was probably restricted to members of a few elite families and election was for life. Neither elections nor (normally) other modes of public collective decision-making, however, were conducted on the basis of absolute political equality of all citizens—that is, through application of the one citizen, one vote principle. The usual method of voting was by shouting, and shouts were collectively guesstimated rather than individually counted; obviously, individuals had naturally differing strengths of voice. The one attested use of voting by division, as opposed to by shouting, in the Assembly was resorted to in 432 only as a last-minute expedient by a unilateral decision of the elected Ephor presiding over the meeting, in order to secure the largest possible majority for a decision to go to war with Athens despite the opposing advice of the senior king. The Gerousia enjoyed the right of initiative and preliminary deliberation, in effect a prior veto over the formal decision-making by the Assembly; moreover, if the Assembly's mood seemed to them to be taking an unwelcome turn, they were entitled to dismiss it or even override its decision. There were no written laws, and no popular judiciary; the Ephors, who were not accountable by means of regular popular audit, and not therefore responsible to the People (*damos*), interpreted and applied the laws as they saw fit. Conjointly with the Gerousia they served as a supreme court, having the power even to try and convict kings, who therefore were accountable—but not directly to the People (see further below). In short, *kratos* for the Spartan *damos* as apparently specified in a probably authentic text known as the Great Rhetra (seventh century?) did not equate to and could not possibly have equated to fifth- and fourth-century style *demokratia*.

The Spartans themselves seem to have referred to their mode of self-governance as *eunomia*, an archaic term meaning something like 'lawful government' or 'submission to the right kind of laws'. However exactly one would wish to characterise it, though, abroad the Spartans consistently and consciously championed more or less reactionary oligarchy—even if they had to impose it by force or threat of force, and even when imposing it meant, as we shall see, that they had to break their own religious oath. Given the Spartans' extreme and normally inflexible religiosity, their willingness to make an exception in this type of case is really very revealing indeed. In what follows we shall first examine Sparta's relations with a series of mainland Greek cities, most allies or former allies, in which the issue of democracy versus oligarchy played a—or the—major role.

Having crushed the Athenians and dismantled their empire in 404, if only thanks to very extensive financial aid from Persia, the Spartans enthusiastically set about placing their broad feet into the Athenians' imperial shoes. Their new Aegean empire, however, was to be one of subordinate oligarchies and indeed, to begin with, 'dynasties'—extreme and narrowly based oligarchic juntas, such as that of the Thirty at Athens. However, assuming Athens' liberationist imperial rhetoric and acquisitive imperial ambitions quickly landed Sparta on the horns of a dilemma. Included among the many subjects of Persia in 404 were Greeks, the Greeks of 'Asia'—the very Greeks whose freedom from Persia the Athenian empire had ostensibly been set up and maintained to deliver, and whose liberty the Spartans had themselves already once sacrificed in 412/1 in return for vital and abundant Persian cash. By the early 390s Sparta had reversed its friendship with Persia and was fighting on land in Asia on behalf of Greek freedom, and it had abandoned the dynasties idea in favour of supporting more conventional oligarchies.

But even that policy reversal was no longer sufficient by the mid-390s to maintain the loyalty of two oligarchies actually within Sparta's own Peloponnesian League alliance: Corinth and the Boeotians, that is, the Boeotian federal state dominated by Thebes. Both had been disaffected during the Peloponnesian War, and Corinth had indeed temporarily abandoned Sparta in 420 for an alliance with Sparta's perennial enemy Argos, whereas the Boeotians had remained loyal to Sparta precisely because they considered Sparta would be more favourable to their oligarchy than would the Argive democracy. But in 395 the Boeotians and Corinthians jointly revolted from Sparta, having entered into a quadruple alliance with Athens and Argos, and thereby initiated the so-called Corinthian War—actually, a war that was fought between 395 and 386 on the sea as well as the land and not only around the Isthmus of Corinth, but throughout the Aegean.

As in the Peloponnesian War, so in the Corinthian War Sparta eventually won, but only by again going cap in hand to Persia, and in this case the collateral damage caused by the war was considerably more devastating for Sparta. For a start, the alliance of Corinth with Argos in 395 represented a geopolitical catastrophe: not only was Sparta now deprived of its major naval ally but its freedom of movement by land into and out of the Peloponnese was virtually terminated. Worse was to come in the shape of the so-called Union of Corinth and Argos in 393/2, one of the more remarkable political experiments of the entire *polis* era of ancient Greek history. An extreme outbreak of *stasis* in Corinth brought the bloody massacre of the pro-Spartan oligarchs running the city (as their predecessors had done ever since it had first allied with Sparta, by 525 at the latest). Corinth, now democratically governed, entered into a pact with long-since-democratic Argos. The boundary stones marking the common frontier between the territories of the two *poleis* were symbolically removed, and thenceforth formerly Corinthian citizens could exercise the rights of Argive citizenship within the *polis* territory of Argos, and Argive citizens vice versa within the territory of Corinth. The Spartans, in kneejerk response, led on ferociously by the stubbornly anti-democratic King Agesilaus II, did all they possibly could to break the Union by main force; in 390, however, they suffered an unprecedented disaster on land near Lechaeum, one of Corinth's two main ports. It was not until the Spartans had performed yet another diplomatic somersault in 388/7, securing the renewed Persian funding that enabled them to enhance their efforts at sea under the admiralty of Antalcidas among others, that the tide of war turned decisively in their favour.

Under Agesilaus' co-king Agesipolis, the Spartans had invaded the territory of Argos in 388, but been forced to withdraw without inflicting major damage. In 387/6, however, the mere threat of renewed Spartan force with the backing of the Spartans' renewed diplomatic agreement with Persia was sufficient to compel the break-up of the Union of Corinth and Argos and to foster the re-establishment in the former of a pro-Spartan oligarchy, while Argos remained more genuinely autonomous and democratic. A threat of force was likewise enough to influence the Boeotians, still under a moderately oligarchic regime, to break off their alliance with the Athenians and return to the Peloponnesian League fold alongside Corinth. There was then concluded, at Sparta's instigation, a diplomatic instrument known alternatively as the King's

Peace or the Peace of Antalcidas in 386—the king in question being Persian Great King Artaxerxes II, and Antalcidas being the Spartan who acted as the chief negotiator on the Greeks' side. When the Spartans were accused of (again) betraying Greek freedom—specifically that of the Asiatic Greeks—and so being guilty of 'medism', Agesilaus is said to have replied with a typically laconic 'apophthegm' to the effect that it was not the case that the Spartans had medized but rather that the Medes (Persians) had 'lakonized' (turned pro-Spartan)—so clearly were the Spartans the chief beneficiaries of this first 'common' peace. It was common in the sense that all relevantly situated cities were deemed to be subject to its terms whether or not they'd positively signed up to them. But yet even that restoration of the status quo obtaining vis-à-vis the Boeotians down to 395 did not satisfy by any means all in the upper reaches of Spartan policymaking, as we shall see.

First, however, we must return to consider the post-Peloponnesian War fate of the two Peloponnesian League allies that had become democracies (relatively moderate, we assume) as long ago as the first half of the fifth century: Elis and Mantinea (see Chapter 9). Elis was not only a notionally autonomous member of the Peloponnesian League but also the city that managed the Panhellenic—all, and only-Greek—Olympic Games every four years and permanently oversaw the religious structures and observances on the site of Olympia, including an oracular shrine of Zeus. In 420, the first Olympic year after the temporary cessation of hostilities in the Peloponnesian War (the Peace of Nicias, concluded in spring 421), Elis had exercised its supervisory authority to ban all Spartans from competing in the Games. There were various reasons for Elis' disaffection from Sparta, which went as far as the Eleans seceding from the Peloponnesian League, but it was their Olympic ban on Spartans that struck the deepest psychological blow, not least because the Games were in essence a religious festival. The Spartans' revenge on Elis was necessarily long postponed until after the Peloponnesian War had been won, but all the more severe when it did eventually fall in 401/0. In two successive summer campaign seasons, Agesilaus' older half-brother Agis II led major punitive expeditions against Elis that not only inflicted huge economic damage but also terminated the democracy and replaced it with a narrow oligarchy headed by men personally connected to the king. Agis then died and was succeeded, controversially, by Agesilaus, thanks to crucial support from Lysander (the victor of Aegospotami).

The case of Mantinea was rather different, and rather more difficult for Sparta. It was a city of Arcadia, but traditionally it was at odds with the other major city of that region, Tegea in the far south (which typically had maintained cordial relations with Sparta since the mid-sixth century); uncomfortably for Sparta, it was located much nearer to Argos. During and after the Peloponnesian War, Mantinea had been a less than enthusiastic ally of Sparta, despite—or because of—a separate thirty-year treaty concluded in 417. Presumably the Spartans had sought to tie down the Mantineans by treaty in the wake of their victory over the Athenians at the battle of Mantinea the previous year, so as to pre-empt the kind of insolence and insubordination they had suffered from Elis in 420. A further complicating factor was the residence in Mantinea since 395 of the exiled Spartan king Pausanias.

Sparta's legal system was in many ways rather unpolished; as mentioned, there was no popular judiciary, and the chief judicial magistrates were also the state's chief executive officers, the Ephors, who exercised legal judgment without the constraint either of written laws or of formal legal precedent. When sitting in judgment upon a king, they sat together with the other twenty-nine members of the Gerousia, forming a supreme constitutional court of sorts. In 403 that supreme court had acquitted Pausanias of the charge, levelled by his fellow king Agis, of un-Spartan activities: for being in effect soft not just on the Athenian democrats in the Peiraeus but even on democracy as such, since he had overseen the democratic restoration at Athens in the teeth of Spartan opposition from above all the fanatically pro-oligarchic Lysander. In 395 supporters of the late Agis and of Lysander, including pre-eminently Agesilaus (whose vote would have had to be delivered by a proxy, since he was away campaigning in Asia at the time), saw their chance to wreak their revenge at last upon Pausanias, and he was put on trial again, on exactly the same charge as in 403—Sparta's legal system countenanced double jeopardy in such cases of alleged high crimes and misdemeanours. This time he was found guilty and, rather than have him executed (which would have raised delicate religious issues, since Spartan kings were to a degree sacrosanct), the Spartans banished him *sine die* (as indeed they had banished his father, Pleistoanax, half a century before in 445). Pausanias' decision to spend his exile at Mantinea was not without political calculation, although whether it was influenced by any ideological sympathy for democracy—as opposed to principled respect for the genuine autonomy of Sparta's allies as laid down by sworn treaty agreement—cannot be determined.

At all events, Pausanias was very visibly present in 385 when, under cover of the King's Peace, the Spartans led by his son and successor Agesipolis I set out to punish Mantinea for its disloyalty—and democracy—in the most strongly political way imaginable. That is to say, they effected a break-up of the *polis* of Mantinea as such, which was decomposed into its original five villages. That was not the first such break-up of another city carried out by Sparta: between 403 and 401 they had hived off the deme of Eleusis from the rest of the *polis* of Athens and separately recognised it as an oligarchic statelet within the borders of Attica. But this was far more drastic and comprehensive. In place of the overall democracy of the unified state, each of the Mantinean villages was now ruled by an aristocratic oligarchy, and the walls built around the political centre were symbolically dismantled. Xenophon with superb hypocrisy says that the major Mantinean property owners were delighted with the new arrangement, since it enabled them to live closer to the estates from which they drew their wealth. In practice, this situation was to last for only fifteen years, well under a generation: following Sparta's defeat at Leuctra in 371 there was a general rebellion against Sparta in the Peloponnese, and in 370 both democracy and central city walls were restored to the once more autonomous *polis* of the Mantineans.

Sparta's unhappy experience with democratic Mantinea was partially replicated with nearby Phleious, a city important not so much for itself as for its location: its wide plain served as a convenient muster-ground for Peloponnesian League armies. It was probably in the later 390s that, like Corinth, Phleious had first turned democratic. In 381, following their interventions in Mantinea and Thebes, the Spartans at the instigation of Agesilaus responded positively to a plea from a small group of oligarchic Phleiasian exiles. Phleious was placed under siege for some twenty months between 381 and 379, until it was finally starved into surrender. The oligarchs were restored not just to their city and estates but to political power, with fervent Spartan ideological support orchestrated by Agesilaus in person. But even Xenophon felt obliged in retrospect to include in his *Hellenica* narrative a remarkable exchange of opinions taking place within the Spartan siege army: 'We are making ourselves hated', so some Spartans were allegedly moved to observe, 'by a city of 5,000 men'.

The size of the democratic citizen body of Phleious was a doubly relevant argument. Sparta's own citizen body was by this time reduced to only about 2,500 to 3,000. But for Agesilaus it was not the size of Phleious' citizen body that most motivated him but the fact that it was a disloyal democracy. He therefore gave every support and comfort to the handful of exiled oligarchs, encouraging them to behave as much as possible like Spartans in order to win the besieging Spartans' respect—a tactic that proved by no means wholly successful. In another work of Xenophon, his posthumous encomium of the king known simply as the *Agesilaus*, this irredentist, politically retrograde attitude of Agesilaus is given a wholly positive, moralistic spin: regardless of its political dubiety, it was for his eulogist a classic example of Agesilaus' virtue of love for his close political comrades. That paid practical political dividends in the form of the passionate loyalty shown thereafter to Sparta by oligarchic Phleious. In particular, the city was especially energetic in the 370s in supporting Sparta against democratic Thebes, and remained unswervingly loyal even after the disaster of Leuctra in 371 and the dissolution of the Peloponnesian League in the mid-360s. For that conspicuous loyalty, it earned Xenophon's highest praise.

So we come to focus on Thebes, the major player in mainland Greek politics after 404 along with (and often locked in a fateful triangle with) Sparta and Athens. Thebes had been allied to Sparta since the late sixth century, and, as the leading city of the oligarchic Boeotian federal state (formed in 447 following the liberation of Boeotia from Athenian control), it remained loyal—just—to Sparta throughout the Peloponnesian War. But in 404 Thebes claimed to be exceptionally annoyed that Sparta had not physically annihilated Athens, and in 403, though still oligarchic, it had supported the restoration of democracy at Athens, precisely so that Sparta could no longer use a tamed oligarchic Athens as a catspaw against itself. In 395, when still oligarchic, Thebes and the Boeotians finally did revolt from Sparta to join a quadruple alliance with Athens, Argos, and Corinth. In 386, therefore, it was a principal target of Sparta's vengeful resentment, and a principal motive for Sparta's conclusion of and swearing to the terms of the King's Peace was to keep Thebes in what Agesilaus—allegedly a Thebes-hater—in what he considered its proper, subordinate place.

The peace's autonomy clause ostensibly guaranteed to all cities freedom from external interference or control, but it was more than once breached by Sparta, and most blatantly of all in the case of Thebes in 382. Sparta then imposed on moderately oligarchic Thebes—as it had on formerly democratic Athens in 404—a junta of extreme pro-Spartan oligarchs backed up by a Spartan garrison (located on the city's commanding acropolis, the Cadmea). Not only was this intervention grossly illegal, however, but it constituted also a sacrilegious violation of the oaths underpinning the King's Peace. The normally pro-Spartan but also exceptionally pious Xenophon was so horrified that, in retrospect, he saw this particular violation of the peace as the beginning of the end of the domination or empire that Sparta had exercised over the Aegean Greek world for most of the period from 404. For it was through Thebes that the hand of divine retribution, as he saw it, was to be wielded against Sparta eleven years later, at and after the Battle of Leuctra in 371.

However—and it is a very big however—the *politeia* under which Thebes was ruled in 371 was not the *politeia* of 382 and the immediately following years, or even the far more moderately oligarchic one of 447–382: for early in 378, for the first time ever, and with significant Athenian encouragement, inspiration, and physical assistance, Thebes had become a *demokratia*, following its liberation from Spartan control by a small band of politically motivated exiles led by Pelopidas. Not only Thebes but also the Boeotians (Xen. *Hell.* 5.4.46), that is the federal state as a whole, went democratic: central, federal finances and the increasingly efficient federal army (as commanded by Gorgidas and the great Epaminondas as well as Pelopidas) were now to be managed democratically, ultimately under the jurisdiction of the democratic federal Assembly. Full active and participatory citizenship was extended below the level of the cavalry and hoplites to the broader *demos*, whereas under the former oligarchic regimes the exercise of a craft or the practice of commercial exchange in the marketplace had been sufficient to disqualify a Theban and most Boeotians from active citizen privileges.

So the Boeotians and Thebans continued, constitutionally speaking, despite a major diplomatic falling-out with Athens (which actually allied with Sparta against a rampant Thebes between 371 and 362), until the democratic city made the irretrievable and ultimately fatal mistake of antagonising the rising monarchical power of Macedon. In the 360s, at the time of its shortlived hegemony, Thebes could get away with holding a younger brother of the Macedonian king as a hostage in Thebes for three years (probably 368–365). But when that brother became Philip II, king of Macedon, in 359 and rolled over all southern Greece, including Thebes and its renewed ally Athens, on the battlefield of Chaeronea in Boeotia in 338, Philip took a leaf out of Sparta's book: he terminated the Thebans' democracy, replaced it with an oligarchy, and installed a garrison to guarantee the new order. When nevertheless Thebes rose up in revolt against Philip's son and successor Alexander III, that was considered a step too far, and in 335 Alexander ordered to be done to Thebes what Thebans had wanted done to Athens in 404: physical annihilation.

Little or nothing of that unhappy demarche could have been predicted in the newly democratised Thebes of 378. Indeed, in that year Thebes was so gung-ho and on such good terms with Athens that it consented to join, as one of six founder members, a new and fundamentally anti-Spartan alliance headed up by Athens, the Second Athenian League, even though it was a basically maritime organisation. Alongside those two stood the island-city of Rhodes (founded only at the end of the fifth century), Byzantium (later Constantinople), Methymna (one of the five cities of Lesbos, already democratic and uniquely loyal to Athens back in 427), and Chios, another east Aegean island-city. Boeotia does have a coastline (including Aulis of Homeric fame), but inland Thebes was hardly less landlubbing than inland Sparta. The other five founder allies were significantly naval, and all were democracies. Rhodes, largely because of its strategic location, was the site of fierce ideological internal battles and political reversals both at the end of the Peloponnesian War and in the early fourth century. Of Byzantium's internal politics little is known, but its strategic situation at the mouth of the Bosporus made it a vital asset to Athens and a key prize in the struggle for Mediterranean supremacy between Athens and Sparta. Methymna had been a democracy already in the later fifth century, when as noted it alone had stood aloof from the revolt of 427 against Athens of the other four Lesbian cities led by then oligarchic Mytilene. But Chios, like Thebes, had never been a democracy until the early fourth century; indeed, Thucydides had singled it out for praise as a city that conducted its oligarchy with exemplary sober moderation (8.5–6, 9, 14, esp. 24), and it was as a ship-contributing oligarchy that it had revolted from Athens' alliance in 411, thereby contributing significantly to Athens' naval embarrassment in the eastern Aegean. Yet when it first made alliance again with Athens, in 384— the year after the break-up of Mantinea, at a time when Sparta was blatantly exploiting its position within the framework of the King's Peace to drive its expansionist and reactionary oligarchic agenda—Chios had by then become a democracy, as it was still in 378.

The new Athenian-dominated League shows interesting differences from its predecessor of almost exactly a century earlier, the Delian League founded in winter 478/7. For a start, it was certainly bicameral: that is, any decision made by the Athenian Assembly had formally to be ratified by the Congress of the allies' delegates, within which Athens did not have a vote. Secondly, the Athenians felt obliged, in light of the multiple allied revolts of the fifth century, to publish early on a binding prospectus of the terms on which the alliance was made; in particular, this so-called charter spelled out the terms and conditions by which the Athenians bound themselves not to repeat the errors or transgressions of the fifth-century empire. Above all, apart from the formal ratification proce- dure already mentioned, the Athenians—both collectively and individually— were forbidden to own or by any other means directly or indirectly to exploit lands belonging to allies. A guarantee of political autonomy formally precluded the imposition of democracy upon any allied city. The Athenians also believed it politic not to impose again on its allies a fixed money 'tribute', but rather to solicit from them supposedly voluntary 'contributions'.

At first, all went swimmingly: the number of allies soon swelled to seventy- five, many of which would have been democracies, if of a more moderate kind than that of Athens. This development made a major contribution towards mak- ing the second quarter of the fourth century BCE the golden age of ancient Greek democracy. (It was not the sole cause, of course: for example, Locri Epizephyrii in Magna Graecia developed its democracy independently.) However, it was not all that long before the first cracks in and breaches of the League charter appeared. Allies found themselves summoned before Athenian law courts, contributions proved after all not to be entirely voluntary, and radical differences of foreign policy goals emerged between Athens and major allies to ultimately fatal effect. After 371, to take a conspicuous instance, Athens so feared the rise in main- land influence of its fellow founder member Thebes that it allied separately with Sparta—against whom, ostensibly, the League had been established. From 368, moreover, Athens displayed an almost monomaniacal passion to regain control over its original foundation of Amphipolis (founded 437, lost to Sparta in 424, and never recovered), thereby placing an intolerable burden on allies for whom the restitution of Amphipolis to Athens was far from a pressingly immediate priority. In 357–355, finally, major defections from Athens were led by two other founder members, Chios and Byzantium, who received important financial as well as moral support from a Carian governor in Persian service (Mausolus of Halicarnassus). The resulting Social (allied) War was an emphatic defeat for Athens—and the end of Athens' ability to advocate let alone enforce its wishes through naval power. By 355, too, Athens had not only Mausolus to contend with in Asia, but a nearer and more deadly adversary in Europe—one that not only succeeded in gaining control of Amphipolis for himself but also threatened Athens' very lifeline of imported grain from the Black Sea. That enemy was the former Theban hostage Philip II of Macedon, and it was his kingdom that was to decide the fate not just of Athens' power abroad, but (as we shall see in Chapter 14) of its very democracy at home.

Finally, there is Argos, the next most important democracy in mainland Greece after Athens. It had become a democracy early in the fifth century and remained such, with periodic oligarchic interruptions, thereafter. Because it was always anti-Spartan, it was always potentially open to alliance with fellow democratic Athens, and the two cities duly became allied first in the late 460s, a critical moment in the history of Athens' democracy. In his *Oresteia* trilogy of 458 the patriotic tragedian Aeschylus significantly transferred the seat of King Agamemnon from the traditional Mycenae to Argos—in part but only in part, because in hard contemporary reality Argos had physically destroyed little Mycenae in the early 460s. During the Peloponnesian War (broadly interpreted to include the interim period of phony peace from 421 to 414) Argos experienced some switching between democratic and oligarchic regimes but remained solidly democratic in the fourth century, when, as noted above, it joined with Athens in a quadruple alliance against Sparta in 395. Defeat of Argos by Sparta in the Corinthian War did not lead to the termination of its democracy—as was the case for Corinth—but Sparta did put an end in 386 to the remarkable political 'union' (isopolity) of Argos with Corinth. As is usually the case with all Greek internal politics, very little is known in detail of the workings of the Argive democracy between the early fifth and the early fourth century. But quite recently a major archaeological discovery has thrown a flood of new light on at least one aspect of them: public finance.

A hoard of some 150 inscribed bronze tablets has been unearthed, almost all of them official records of the political-cum-religious organizations dealing with sacred funds of Hera (the city's patron goddess) and Athena (to whom the state treasury was devoted). This is a veritable treasure trove of financial transactions: rents, leases, sales of confiscated property, interest paid out on loans, spoils of war, fines and penalties of many sorts, proceeds from the sale of hides of public sacrificial victims, even bribes from Persians (to support anti-Spartan activity). Expenditures were made on war, on the Heraea (Hera's annual festival, including athletic games), on the manufacture of cult objects, on construction works on Hera's temple and the hippodrome (a horse race course), on roads, on expenses for cults, on the salaries of workmen, and—not least—on the inscribing of the records. Many of the sums are very large: for example, one of 217,373 silver drachmas (c. 720 skilled man-years of pay), or unworked gold weighing 700 drachmas (on the Euboic standard); there is possibly record even of gold dust. Most officials served only a six-month term, to ensure observance of the democratic principle of rotation of office and prevent undue access to such temptingly large sums. Democratic too, in ideology, were the inscription of the records on non-perishable materials and their public display.

However, democratic Argos, like democratic Corcyra in 427, also exemplifies to an unfortunate degree the downside of Greek-style politics: in-your-face, black-white, zero-sum. In 370 there occurred the notorious clubbing to death of some 1,200 to 1,500 oligarchs by democratic thugs (Diodorus 15.58). That was exactly the sort of fanatical, extremist behaviour that the moderate non-democrat Aristotle would deplore in his *Politics* and offer sage advice on how best to avoid or pre-empt. It was also just the sort of behaviour that led dedicated opponents of Greek democracy to conjure up imagined 'ideal' polities that were as far removed from the actualities of democracy—as they perceived them—as they could possibly be. One such dedicated opponent stands head and shoulders above all other political theorists, not least in this regard: Plato of Athens (c. 428–347). Bitter personal experience, both as a relative of leading figures in the regime of the Thirty and as a devoted disciple of Socrates (Chapter 10), seems to have led to his decision to withdraw more or less completely from active, public participation in the politics of his native Athens, which for all but one or two of his eighty-odd years was governed democratically.

This is not necessarily, however, the same as saying that Plato abandoned all political ambition, and there is indeed a case for arguing that he aimed—through the pupils he educated at his Academy (named after its location within a public Athenian gymnasium)—to influence indirectly the politics not so much of Athens, but of other Greek cities as far afield as the Black Sea area and Sicily. His two most famous works of political thought and theory, both written in dialogue form, are the *Republic* (c. 375) and the *Laws* (c. 350, a work of his last years). 'Republic' is actually just the English form of the shortened Latin translation, *Res Publica*, of the work's original Greek title, *Politeia or On Justice*. It is not a work of 'republican' in the sense of anti-monarchical political theorizing. The *Laws* is more aptly so titled, since the three interlocutors—a Cretan, a Spartan, and an anonymous Athenian (a sort of Plato surrogate)—do manage to thrash out a legislative programme for a brand-new city called Magnesia that they intend to found somewhere inland on the large island of Crete. Islands have often been found good to think with by utopiographers—consider Thomas More's eponymous 'Utopia' of 1516, a neologism that translates roughly as 'nowhere place'. By contrast, the ideal city sketched in the *Republic* by Socrates and his interlocutors is given the positive name 'fair, fine or beautiful City' (Callipolis; see Chapter 6), although it is not at all clear that there was any serious intention of converting the fair city they theoretically conceive or imagine into a material reality anywhere on earth.

Aristotle, Plato's most distinguished pupil at the Academy (where he was a student for a score of years, from 367 to 347), had very serious disagreements both theoretical and pragmatic with Plato's Callipolis—differences of opinion which he aired vigorously in the second book of his *Politics*. But he shared with his mentor and master a preoccupation with the besetting political evil, as they both saw it, of *stasis*. As noted, especially in Books 5 and 6 of the *Politics* Aristotle adumbrated possible antidotes or preferably preventatives for this disease of the body politic. In Books 7 and 8, he even tentatively began to sketch out the lineaments of his own ideal ideal city, the city 'to be prayed for', as he put it. But his head lay far more in the theoretical construction and practical implementation of less idealistic and much more immediately realisable cities, and to the constitution of these he gave the name 'politeia'—the same as the title of Plato's major theoretical work.

That, however, was all they had in common. For whereas Aristotle's politeia was a mixed regime, drawing upon what he considered the morally best and most practically workable elements of actually existing democratic or oligarchic constitutions, Plato's politeia presupposed an intellectualist *tabula rasa*, a back-to-the-drawing-board blueprint and a brand-new start. Plato, to be fair, could be as hard-headedly empirical as Aristotle when he wanted to be: a city run by oligarchs, he has his Socrates bluntly assert, was not one city but two—a city of the rich and a city of the poor, ranged in deadly opposition to each other. But when it came to proposing a solution to the current political evils of the Greek world in c. 375—roughly the date of the lethal Argive clubbing (above)—he took off into a flight of fantasy: it is only, he has his Socrates affirm, if existing rulers of cities become philosophers, or if philosophers become rulers, that will there be an end to our present troubles. By 'philosophers' he meant Platonic-style philosophers, who alone thanks to their natural gifts and exceptional education would have access to knowledge (properly so called) of truth and goodness and therefore would alone be able to apply that knowledge to the mundane business of political governance; and for 'rulers' (by which he clearly meant oligarchs or even tyrant rulers, rather than leading democratic politicians) he did not scruple to substitute 'kings', an archaic and antiquated notion that any self-respecting Greek republican or democrat would have felt the Greek city should have grown out of many moons ago.

In case any of his as yet unconverted readers might still be in any doubt as to his (Plato's, not just those of his Socrates) views on Greek political actualities, as opposed to his ideal solution or remedy of them, in Book 8 of the *Republic* he composed an ideal-typical rake's progress to illustrate how as he saw it constitutions first decay internally and then decline successively from one better form to a worse. Finally, almost at the very bottom of the moral-political slide, after aristocracy, timarchy, or timocracy (rule according to 'honour', that is, a combination of birth and wealth) and oligarchy, and only just before tyranny, Plato locates democracy and the corresponding character type, democratic man. Under democracy, it is alleged—or rather charged—that liberty is mistaken for licence, unequals are treated equally, and democrats teem with inappropriate pleasures and appetites and are governed by unnecessary desires. Why, under democracy even donkeys (not the most highly respected members of the animal kingdom) assume airs and get puffed up!

The *Laws*, a work of Plato's extreme old age, was a very different intellectual animal from the *Republic*. Ostensibly, it was a far more down-to-earth and indeed rather tediously mundane project of political instauration, but it also contained some rather remarkably reactionary (the stigmatization of homosexual eros as 'unnatural') as well as no less remarkably revolutionary (formal advocacy of a kind of fundamentalist theocracy equipped with a most unpleasant punitive apparatus to deal peremptorily with any hint of atheism) nostrums. By the time Plato died in 347, however, he was far from alone at Athens in raising a critical voice against democracy in terms both of general principle and of applied practice. But it is very noticeable that, unlike the criticism of the later fifth century as practised by Antiphon and his kind, anti-democratic sentiment could no longer be expressed openly as such. Rather, it had to be wrapped up: as it was most blatantly in the voluminous pamphleteering of the long-lived Isocrates (438–336), as a call for a return to the 'better', older kind of democracy that had supposedly been abandoned. In this regard Isocrates' *Areopagiticus* of c. 355 BCE is paradigmatic, harking back as it does to the supposedly good old days when the Areopagus set the tone.

Certainly, by 347 the democracy was not faring at all well in foreign policy terms, as we shall see in more detail in the next chapter, and at home the cost of that failure could be measured in such practical terms as the occasional temporary drying-up of public funds to pay jurors or, conversely, the need to introduce a public subsidy (the theoric fund) to enable the poorest Athenians to attend state theatre festivals. Yet the time of Plato's death is also, paradoxically, the ushering-in of—for us—easily the best documented of all the periods or epochs of democracy at Athens, roughly from 350 to its demise in 322/1. The next chapter will therefore seek to do some sort of justice to that fact. The scare quotes around 'age of Lycurgus' in its title are intended both to challenge the validity of any such evaluation of an epoch's significance in terms of a single personality's allegedly decisive impact, and to draw attention to the circumstance that though the Lycurgus in question lived through most of that period, he did not rise to prominence until about halfway through it and even thereafter was constantly having to contend with Athenian democratic politicians of a very different stamp.

12.

ATHENIAN DEMOCRACY AT WORK

IN THE 'AGE OF LYCURGUS'

A RATIONALE FOR SPEAKING OF an 'age of Lycurgus' has just been briefly set out. But Lycurgus himself, who was born in c. 390 into a family of the highest priestly aristocracy and died in 323, might well have thought that for much of his adult lifetime he was living through the age of Demosthenes. The latter was his close contemporary (b. 384, d. 322 BCE) and more widely famous, but also far lowlier-born: Demosthenes' father, also called Demosthenes, was in manufacturing. The politician Demosthenes, however, once celebrated unambivalently as a patriotic hero, is by far the more controversial figure of the two, not least because his long career as a professional politician manifestly ended, unlike that of Lycurgus, in failure as well as death. Demosthenes, however, was not merely a proudly self-proclaimed patriot, standing firm and tirelessly rallying his fellow countrymen and citizens against above all the kingdom of Macedon as led successively by Philip II (r. 359–336) and his son Alexander III, posthumously styled 'the Great' (r. 336–323). He was equally proudly a democratic patriot, or patriotic democrat, living magnificently up to his given name meaning 'strength of—or for—the People'.

To put Lycurgus'—and Demosthenes'—achievements in broader context, I start this chapter with a very brief historical retrospect of Athens' recent political history: from the restoration of its democracy in 403 and the reunification of the *polis* territory in 401, to the decisive defeat at Chaeronea in 338. Perhaps somewhat surprisingly, this last resounding defeat did not terminate the career of Demosthenes. But it certainly did set the stage for the emergence of Lycurgus to pre-eminence and provided the essential backdrop to his overseeing for a dozen or so years the recovery of Athens' economic, political, and even spiritual fortunes. But was the revived 'Lycurgan' democracy a different kind of Athenian democracy? If so, it would have been Athens' third or fourth, and not necessarily its last (see Chapter 14).

The restored democracy of 403 took a long time to regain an internal political equilibrium before it attempted once more to throw its (much reduced) weight around in the Aegean sphere. The trial of Socrates in 399 (Chapter 10) well illustrates the kinds of enduring tensions that the civil strife of 404/3 engendered. In the mid-390s through ex-general Conon Persian funds were channelled to Athens rather than Sparta to finance the rebuilding of Athens' city walls and those of the Peiraeus, and in the late 390s the first green shoots of a naval resurgence under the leadership of civil war hero Thrasyboulus became evident. But as in 405/4 so again in 387/6 the Spartans, thanks to renewed Persian financial support, achieved naval control of the Hellespont and so a stranglehold on Athens' jugular. It was through the Hellespont waterway that the literally vital bread wheat flowed to Athens annually from the grainlands of today's south Russia, Crimea, and Ukraine. Athens, along with its other three main allies (Argos, Corinth, the Boeotians), soon found itself forced to submit to the terms of the King's Peace. But the treaty might just as well have been named after Spartan king Agesilaus II (r. c. 400–359), since it was he who most energetically applied his interpretation of the peace terms throughout mainland Greece in what he took to be Sparta's best interests.

It was against this domineering, expansionist, imperialist Sparta of Agesilaus that in 378 Athens founded a new multi-state Greek military and political alliance, the Second Athenian League. This proved an instant hit, and by 375 the League could count some seventy-five adherents and some notable naval successes. It even managed to include among its founders a newly democratized Thebes, which in turn led a newly democratized and militarily enhanced Boeotian federal state. In 371, however, Thebes crushed Sparta and its allies at the Battle of Leuctra; and although that spelled the beginning of the end of Sparta as a great power, the Thebans' emergence also so frightened Athens that it actually allied itself again with Sparta. Not that landlubbing Sparta could ever have been much use as an ally to the Athenians in what from 368 became their obsessively overriding foreign policy objective. This was to recover by sea Amphipolis in northern Greece, a strategically located and materially well endowed city that the Athenians had themselves founded in 437 but had lost—permanently as it turned out—in 424. Allies of Athens in the Second Athenian League who thought they had signed up to a mutual defence force aimed at choking off Sparta and ensuring observance of the autonomy clause of the peace of 386 increasingly questioned why their manpower and financial contributions were being devoted to—or wasted on—such a peculiarly and divisively Athenian objective as Amphipolis.

As for the Athenians themselves, public funds became on occasion sufficiently short for jury service, a cardinal feature of their democracy since the 450s, to be temporarily suspended. *Pari passu* the pressure on the resources of the richest few Athenians and metics who were obliged by law to perform 'liturgies' (literally, public service, a kind of super-taxation) increased to boiling point. There were two kinds of liturgy: military or rather naval, that is the equipping and commanding of a trireme warship for a year; and festival—that is, the funding of various aspects of the great annual festivals, the Dionysia and Panathenaea, above all (see Chapter 8). There might be over one hundred liturgies to be performed in any one year. Already in the latter stages of the Peloponnesian War liturgists had found it necessary to double up as trierarchs; from 378, to fund the Second Athenian League, taxpayers had been organised into larger boards (symmories). But even this potentially more equitable and efficient system occasioned lawsuits in which Athenian jurors were called to adjudicate the rival claims of their super-rich and not necessarily very democratic fellow citizens.

Between 371 and 362 Thebes developed an ascendancy over mainland Greek affairs, to such an extent that for three years the future King Philip II of Macedon was held in Thebes as hostage for his state's good behaviour. In 362 at the (Second) Battle of Mantinea, Thebes and the other Boeotians defeated the combined forces of Athens and Sparta. But instead of confirming Thebes' ascendancy the battle produced only 'greater confusion in Greece than before' (Xenophon's despairing final comment at the end of his *Hellenica*). Clarity of interstate relations was in fact not to be achieved until the establishment of a far more steely Macedonian hegemony.

From 359 and more especially 357 the kingdom of Macedon under Philip II became Athens' main foreign policy preoccupation; it was symbolic of the new balance of power that in 357 he outwitted and outfought the Athenians by grabbing hold of Amphipolis. As ever, his timing was superb. For in that same year there broke out within the decaying remnant of the Second Athenian League a revolt known as the Social (that is, allied) War; this was led by democratic Chios (a founder-member of the League) and Byzantium, and was crucially aided by Maussolus of Caria, a Persian local governor who had adopted the mainly Greek city of Halicarnassus as his new capital. Athens' defeat in the Social War in 355 ended its claims to be a great naval—or indeed any kind—of power. Failure at sea provoked both Isocrates' conservative political tract known as the *Areopagiticus* (Chapter 11) and Xenophon's rather radical pamphlet titled *Poroi*, devoted to ways and means of increasing public revenues. The Athenian democracy was in a rather parlous condition.

This was hardly the most auspicious moment for the thirty-year-old Demosthenes to make his political debut, but it is not at all surprising that he should have done so under the wing of a conservative, managerial technocrat such as Euboulus, who was more concerned about restoring and conserving Athens' public finances than promoting or pursuing any particularly democratic agenda. Demosthenes, however, increasingly took issue with his mentor over what he considered the paramount need for Athens to take on Philip in his own northern backyard, rather than wait and watch as he spread his tentacles—and complaisant oligarchies or even tyrannies—ever further south. It was in 352 that Demosthenes appears to have experienced an ideological quasi-conversion and moved sharply to the left, and it was over Demosthenes' policy of appropriating the Theoric (religious festival) Fund for military purposes that he broke decisively with Euboulus. Not long afterwards an image of the personified Demos began to be depicted on Athenian document reliefs, a sign both of increased professionalism and of the democracy's growing self-consciousness.

Thereafter Demosthenes persistently argued to a not always suitably responsive Athenian public that the ascendancy of Philip over mainland Greece and in particular Athens would mean the end of Athens' democracy. For Philip was much more likely, in the manner of so many ancient autocrats and imperial powers, to favour oligarchy or even tyranny over any form of democracy, however moderate, in the states subjected to his rule. In general, indeed, he did—but not, as it turned out, at Athens. Demosthenes championed equally democracy at home and a vigorous anti-Philip policy abroad. Matters came to a head first in 349/8 over the defence of Olynthus, leader of a revived Chalcidian federation, whose independence Philip menaced. But despite Demosthenes' best rhetorical efforts, Athens sent too little aid to Olynthus, and too late. In 348 Philip annihilated Olynthus, along with other Chalcidian towns and cities including Aristotle's native Stageira; many Chalcidian Greeks were either killed or sold into slavery abroad. Philip's message was clear: submit to me, or else. Two years later, after instigating further military successes for himself and setbacks or worse for Athens, Philip was able to negotiate Athens cannily into accepting peace terms (the Peace of Philocrates), which it really had no option but to accede to, but out of which, encouraged by Demosthenes, it attempted unsuccessfully to wriggle.

A clear sign of the internal pressure being felt at Athens was the decision in 346/5 to review and revise all the citizen rolls held by the demes under their elected or allotted demarchs ('mayors'). Some quite prominent heads rolled as personal as well as political scores were settled, including that of a man who had himself been a demarch of his deme (Halimous) and applied to Demosthenes for a speech in appeal against his fellow demesmen's decision to strike him off (on grounds of his either slave or foreign parentage). As usual, we don't know the outcome of his case, but the stakes were as high as they possibly could be: had he failed to convince the central jury court, he would have been sold abroad beyond the boundary of Attica into slavery.

The stakes between Demosthenes and his principal opponent Aeschines, a former actor, were in their way just as high. Political careers were on the line as well as rival policies. Whereas Demosthenes thought the Peace of Philocrates should simply be abrogated, even though he like Aeschines had played a direct part in negotiating it, Aeschines argued that the Athenians had little or no chance of striking an improved deal with Philip, and should therefore make the best of a bad job; in Aeschines' deeply biased view Demosthenes was merely a self-serving scaremonger. At first Aeschines got the better of the tussle, especially in the lawcourts, but from 343 the tide began to turn—decisively—in Demosthenes' favour. In 339 Demosthenes, as diplomatic representative of Thebes at Athens, engineered a historic rapprochement with that city, thereby recombining Athens' strength at sea with the Thebans' undoubted strength in warfare on land. But in 338, at the Battle of Chaeroneia fought by land on Boeotian soil, the combined cavalry and heavy infantry forces of Philip and his son Alexander and their well-rehearsed tactics proved far too strong for the central Greek coalition. The resounding Macedonian victory left Philip master of all mainland Greece and with his eyes now turned to the east, firmly set on Persian conquest.

Symbolically, Philip dispatched his eighteen-year-old son and heir apparent Alexander with an honour guard to accompany home the ashes of the Athenian dead. This was the only time that Alexander would visit the city where his former tutor Aristotle would soon establish his own institute for advanced learning. But it was by no means the last time that Alexander would have important political dealings with Athens. Possibly for purely pragmatic reasons (divide and rule), but possibly also partly for sentimental ones, Philip did not in fact—as Demosthenes had long been predicting—wreak political havoc on Athens by terminating its democracy and imposing a Macedonian garrison. But that is exactly what he did do to Thebes. On the other hand, Athens was no less subordinate or even subject to Philip under the terms of the global post-Chaeronea settlement. All mainland Greece for the first and almost the last time in ancient Greek history was unified politically within the framework of what is known as the League of Corinth (from the location of the oath-swearing).

The League was an offensive and defensive military alliance, with Philip as its appointed 'leader'; and the first decision of the League's Greek delegates was to declare war on Persia and make Philip the prospective commander-in-chief of a Hellenic military force for the invasion, conquest, and occupation of at least some part of the Persian empire's Asiatic domains. Combined with this traditional military instrument was a peace optimistically dubbed 'common', in the sense that all Greek cities were deemed by fiat to be a party to it whether or not they actually swore the relevant oaths, and bound thereby to observe non-aggression amongst themselves. However, unlike under the terms of the first such common peace, the King's Peace or Peace of Antalcidas, there was no pretence made by Philip that it was intended to guarantee any sort of autonomy. Greek cities were forbidden to engage in internal civil war and forbidden specifically to cancel debts, redistribute land, or free slaves for political purposes—all these prohibitions being gross violations of 'autonomy' as that had conventionally been understood, even if in practice honoured too often only in the breach.

Over the next fifteen or so years the Athenian democracy experienced first crisis and then renewal, followed by renewed crisis—and finally disaster.

Although Athens did not in fact suffer Philip's direct and directly reaction-ary political interference in the manner Demosthenes had predicted, most Athenians nevertheless feared that it would or could. That explains the passage in early summer 336 of a law (not merely a decree of the Assembly, but a law ratified under the special procedure of legislation introduced after 403/2) on tyranny (Chapter 1). This was a classic democratic move, ideologically speak-ing, in the sense that the founding myth of the original democracy of 508/7 was that of the (two) Tyrannicides. Democrats, insofar as they embraced any particular theory of democracy, liked to represent democracy as the antithesis of tyranny, just as conversely anti-democrats were prone to represent democ-racy as either itself a form of tyranny (of the masses or mob) or a political form peculiarly liable to give rise to one-man tyranny. But the law of 337/6 served a further cardinal ideological purpose and function, which was to smack down the political pretensions of the Areopagus council. A key part of the second wave of democratic reform promoted by Ephialtes in the late 460s had been the stripping of the oldest and most august Athenian council of any real power. But one plausible reading of the anti-tyranny law would suggest that perhaps since 346 and certainly since 338 this body of ex-officials had been undergoing some sort of political renaissance. Possibly, as in the wake of the Sicilian disaster of 413, conservative voices were being heard to the effect that in the parlous politi-cal circumstances major affairs of state should be entrusted once more to the reliable management of the experienced ex-Archons who were life-members of the Areopagus, rather than to the ephemeral unwisdom of the Assembly and People's lawcourts.

Enter Lycurgus, born c. 390 into the aristocratic patriline of the Boutadae, who had taken to styling themselves '*Eteo*boutadae', or *genuine* descendants of the patriarch Boutas. The Boutadae family had given their name to the deme into which they were hereditarily inscribed from 508/7. It was also their pecu-liar privilege to supply the lifetime holders of two exceptionally important priestly offices, one male, one female: those of Poseidon Erechtheus and Athena Polias. This was in apparent contradiction of the egalitarian, anti-aristocratic spirit of much democratic legislation regarding citizen privileges, but corre-sponded to the conservatism that dominated traditional religious observance. If Lycurgus did indeed attend Plato's Academy as a youth, it would not have been utterly extraordinary if he had turned out to be at most a lukewarm supporter of democracy (in any shape or form); more predictably, he might well have been a crypto-oligarch of a similar stripe to Isocrates, say, or even an outright anti-democrat as Plato (at any rate in theory) was. As it was, Lycurgus proved a key enabler of more or less steady-as-she-goes democratic functioning over an extended period, and a patriot and moral rearmer besides, in an era when anything much more positively or aggressively democratic was rendered inoperable by the exigent power of the all-conquering and systematically anti-democratic kingdom of Macedon.

Discussion and evaluation of Lycurgus' achievement may be conducted under three broad and somewhat overlapping rubrics: economics, moral re-armament, and civic religion. Underpinning all was a massive increase of Athens' external and internal revenues to a round figure of (allegedly) 1,200 talents per annum. The size of that increase may be appreciated by noting that in a world not polluted by hyper-inflation, it roughly equated to the total annual revenue of Athens during the third quarter of the fifth century almost exactly a century earlier, when Athens' empire was at its peak—before the Peloponnesian War and allied defections took their severe toll. Lycurgus was somehow elected, in about May 336, as a kind of super-treasurer (chancellor of the exchequer in British terms, perhaps, or secretary of state for finance). This was for a four-year term, which was twice renewed by proxy, making an effective total of a dozen years from 336 to 324. There was a minor and inexact precedent for his position and role in the career of Euboulus in the 350s and 340s, when Athenians showed a new willingness to entrust their fortunes to a financial technocrat—subject of course to the usual democratic protocols of audit and accountability. But actually a closer parallel if not precedent for his position was provided already in the fifth century by Pericles, who besides his Generalships and promotion of democratic legislation also took great care to get himself appointed to positions of major financial responsibility, such as membership of the board of commissioners for oversight of the Parthenon's construction.

On Lycurgus' watch, if we may so call it, a whole slew of legal measures, both of the carrot and of the stick variety, were introduced and implemented; they were taken with a particular eye to ensuring the regular and affordable supply of imported grain, especially bread-wheat from the northern shore of the Black Sea (and to a smaller extent elsewhere). We learn from the Pseudo-Aristotelian *Ath. Pol.* that the grain supply was one of those utterly fundamental political issues that by law *had* to be discussed at what had since some time after 350 become designated the principal Assembly meeting out of the four stated meetings held each civic month (forty meetings minimum altogether per annum). For attendance at every principal meeting a premium fee of 1.5 drachmas instead of the regular 1 drachma was paid to attenders, which presumably ensured a higher turnout than the average, and in particular guaranteed the attendance of the 6,000 at two consecutive meetings that counted as the quorum for the passage of a law such as that on tyranny discussed above.

The grain supply was overwhelmingly conducted by non-Athenian and not necessarily Greek traders, and financed by Athenian, resident alien, or even slave bankers. To facilitate the supply, a variety of measures were passed compelling traders legally resident in Athens to import grain first to Peiraeus. On the other side, new judicial and courtroom procedures were introduced to speed up the resolution of any commercial lawsuits involving traders or financiers, and special officials were appointed to operate in the Peiraeus both to ensure that the legally imposed import-export taxes and harbour dues were paid and to forestall or mediate any such potentially litigated conflicts before they became subject to time-consuming and expensive courtroom manoeuvres. Since Athens—like many Greek cities of the eastern Mediterranean—seems to have suffered more than one severe grain shortage during Lycurgus' terms of office, it is clear that not even this financial wizard could simply wave a magic wand to counter a combination of natural harvest failures and human profiteering or tax avoidance. One modern scholar has even spoken of a 'hidden economy', a black economy that Lycurgus was powerless to overcome.

Sometimes, therefore, the Athenians, so far from acting coercively, went above and beyond the strictly necessary minimum of encouragement to foreign non-residents by permitting the establishment of permanent non-Greek religious cults on Athenian soil—again, predictably, within the Peiraeus, which functioned both as a regular Athenian deme and as an international emporium, indeed the largest such centre in the entire Mediterranean. Thus Phoenicians from Citium on Cyprus were in 333/2 expressly permitted a sacred cult-space to worship their goddess Aphrodite (Astarte) on exactly the same terms as had previously been granted to Egyptians desiring to worship their goddess Isis. Individual foreigners—that is, foreigners with sufficient disposable income—were also encouraged to make voluntary contributions to help increase Athens' public income, and depending on one's point of view relieve the burden on state finances. In return, they might be offered honour, that is symbolic public esteem, or indeed honours, including even honorary Athenian citizenship.

Under the heading of what I've called anachronistically 'moral re-armament' I place a measure not directly credited to Lycurgus, but so completely in tune with his outlook that I am in no doubt that he was a major supporter if not instigator of it. By coincidence (or not), the Athenian Lycurgus shared a name with an even more famous Spartan Lycurgus, around whom—if indeed there was a real person there to begin with—there grew a dense encrustation of fable and myth. But if the Spartan Lycurgus was (very probably) not a real mortal man, the Spartan poet Tyrtaeus certainly was, and in his one extent forensic oration Lycurgus quotes his martial elegy extensively. The aim of that speech was a prosecution for flight from the battlefield, for desertion and cowardice—the exact opposite of the qualities hymned and advocated by Tyrtaeus. Exactly the same martial and patriotic sentiment as prompted that prosecution speech animated also a measure of paramilitary reform that was passed in 336/5. The formal institutionalization of the Ephebeia or Ephebate, a kind of national service, was credited to one Epicrates, but that he was a lieutenant of Lycurgus and a coadjutant of his programme I have no doubt.

Ephebos means 'on the threshold of manhood', and Athenian ephebes were 18- and 19-year-olds, technically adult (having come of age at 18) but not yet fully empowered as Athenian citizens. It is not quite clear whether all Athenian young adults were required or at least encouraged to enrol as ephebes—or perhaps rather to be enrolled by their father or another male ascendant—or whether it was only those whose family was of hoplite status or above who did so, but roughly the top one-third or so, economically speaking did so. What is clear is that a great deal of official energy and ideological investment was put into this new initiative. Lists of ephebes began to be inscribed on stone or bronze and published, in the accepted democratic mode of publicity, from the mid-330s on, in a wide variety of styles and formats. The Aristotelian *Ath. Pol.*, composed in the late 330s and early 320s, significantly devotes a good deal of space to the new institution and the mode of its recruitment. At the age of eighteen, new citizens who successfully withstood the scrutiny of the demarch and his assistants had their names entered on the official lists of their respective demes. The 139 or 140 demes were aggregated via the *trittys* system into ten tribes, and it was the tribes which each selected three citizens aged over forty to serve for the year as supervisors (literally 'orderers') of the new ephebes; but it was the Assembly which appointed the overall director of the Ephebeia for that year.

Service in the Ephebeia extended over two years. During the first year, after being led by their officers around the sacred precincts of Attica, ephebes were detailed to perform guard duty in the Peiraeus. There they learned proficiency in the use of the bow, the javelin, and the catapult while clad in armour. A sum of money was made available for their provision from state funds, which were managed by the superior officer. At the beginning of their second year the emphasis shifted firmly from light-armed skirmishing to training for heavy-infantry hoplite fighting. A full suit of hoplite armour was provided for each ephebe from public funds, and it was while wearing this that he swore a solemn oath. Lycurgus in the *Against Leocrates* summarises the Ephebic Oath in a manner that suited the case he was making: the ephebes, he says, swore not to bring reproach on their hallowed arms and not to leave their place in the hoplite ranks, but to defend their native land and hand it down to their children a better country than when they received it. Other literary sources of much later periods give fuller versions or quote clauses not otherwise attested, but in 1932 a remarkable inscribed stele turned up at modern Menidhi (ancient, and since so renamed, Acharnae), which combined a version of the Ephebic Oath with a supposed Oath of Plataea (see Chapter 1).

The Ephebic Oath has various points of immediate—330s BCE and later—cultural importance. For example, it assumes that responsibility for the defence of the fatherland is implied in citizenship. It is a duty on a par with that of supporting the laws of the land; as an Athenian citizen, one can no more be relieved from the one than from the other. The significance of the Plataea Oath cannot be read quite so straightforwardly off the surface of the stele as it were. For as well as having an immediate contemporary relevance to the post-Chaeronea crisis of the Athenian military and polity, it also has its place in a much longer-run series of ideological conflicts between Sparta and Athens over which of the two was really the most responsible for defeating the Persians in 480–479 and thereby freeing mainland Greece. Actually, both had won crucial victories, but the Athenians were not satisfied with claiming Salamis; they wanted their piece of the Spartans' Plataea victory too. Hence the linkage on the Acharnae stele of the Ephebic and Plataea Oaths: back to the future.

From moral re-armament I move finally to some of the most important measures Lycurgus took to buttress or enhance Athenian civic religion. The All-Athenian Panathenaea festival officially celebrated each year the birthday of the city's patron goddess (Chapter 8). As reorganized in 566/5, it was held with especially great pomp and magnificence every fourth year, under the rubric of the Great Panathenaea. In the other three 'ordinary' years it was the Little Panathenaea that was celebrated, and in c. 335 new financial arrangements for managing the animal sacrifices at the latter were introduced by a measure that was at once a decree of the Assembly and a law. What exactly was new about the sacrifices or their funding is unclear; the officials concerned were at any rate traditional enough: the public auctioneers, the overseeing treasurers for the festival as a whole, and lesser accountants. But it is noticeable that the sacrifices were to be offered not only to Athena Polias but also to two other Athenas, Hygieia (of health) and Nike (victory). In the later 330s and early 320s Athens' economic circumstances were not the rosiest, and there was a particular problem with the supply of overseas grain, so health no doubt deteriorated among the poorest sections of the Athenian citizen masses. Victory would have been a fine thing at any time, but rarely more so than in the wake of the Chaeronea disaster. Another innovation (so it seems) was more political than religious or economic. The distribution of the sacrificial meat was not to be equal among all citizen participants: the fifty 'presidents' of the Council of 500's presiding tribe were to receive the largest number (five) of portions each. This looks a quite minor but nonetheless noticeable derogation from strict democratic principle, in favour of those Athenians who happened to be holding an annual office.

Likewise significant is the beginning of a marked shift away from the old democratic liturgy system for the public financing of festivals and the warfleet in favour of voluntary donations by the wealthy. Under the liturgy system, which persisted, even non-citizen metics might be liable for some burdens, but in the 330s Eudemus, a metic originally from Plataea, made a voluntary gift of 1,000 yoke of oxen 'towards the making of the stadium and the Panathenaic theatre'. (Probably the stonecutter misplaced 'Panathenaic', and what he should have carved was 'towards the making of the Panathenaic stadium and the theatre'). It was in this stadium that the four-yearly Panathenaic Games took place. The theatre in question was the theatre of Dionysus used for the annual Lenaea and Great/City Dionysia play-festivals (Chapter 8). Archaeologically, the building of Athens' first stone theatre belongs exactly to this period c. 330; and to be associated with that permanent monumentalisation is Lycurgus' commissioning of official texts of all the extant tragedies of the three great classic playwrights of the fifth century BCE, Aeschylus, Sophocles, and Euripides. At a time when tragedy was being performed from Sicily to as far east as India, the Greek world needed to be reminded of Athens' priority. But it was now a theatre of heritage more than a theatre of vitally critical reflexivity and creativity. Back to the future, once again.

Those are two particular instances of Lycurgus' general concern to reestablish major public cults and festivals on a sound financial basis and to provide for their continuation in perpetuity. The old liturgic system of financing them was, as mentioned, still in operation, and there was nothing new by then in a winning impresario erecting a prominent choregic monument. But the particular splendour and durability of that commissioned by Lysicrates, which is still very visible in Athens even today, must be somehow connected with 'the urgency of the Lycurgan theatre programme and its efforts to ensure that tragedy be recognised as uniquely, autochthonously Athenian' (Hanink 2014: 194). The increasing emphasis on private donation, already noticed above, could no doubt be explained or explained away as due to the exigencies of the economic crisis, but it will likely also have had a somewhat negative symbolic effect on the self-perception of the *demos*. It's not purely coincidental, I believe, that in the 320s and 310s the instances of public inscriptions recording commendations and rewards of individuals for their services to deme or tribe multiply. The language used for the grounds of the awards—'moral excellence' and 'desire for honour'—was carefully non-commercial and non-mercenary, but the bottom line was strictly financial. The next step on the road to disengaging or diminishing democratic political control over the public deployment of private wealth is spelled out presciently by Aristotle: linking of the payment of liturgies to office-holding, and this move is explicitly characterised as oligarchic. It became the characteristic method of financing public projects in the succeeding Hellenistic era (Chapter 14).

That move was not, however, taken by Athens under Lycurgus, whose profile remained correctly democratic. Indeed, in 331 or 330 Lycurgus undertook a thoroughly democratic prosecution of Leocrates (see above). Following the Chaeronea debacle Leocrates had been in self-imposed exile on the island of

Rhodes and at Megara for seven or eight years, but had judged the interval sufficient to permit him to return to his native land in peace if not with honour and, when prosecuted, for the judges to take a lenient view of his less than glorious battlefield behaviour. That judgment proved correct, but only just: he was acquitted, but by only one vote, leaving Lycurgus the moral victor. Our final estimate of Lycurgus' importance and effectiveness is complicated, but the moral-political balance is surely more in the black than red. On the question whether Athens under his management became a qualitatively different sort of democracy, or just less democratic, my answer would again, on balance, favour the latter reading.

Shortly thereafter, another, far more major political trial took place, the trial of Ctesiphon in the matter of the crown (dealt with already in Chapter 10). The principal object—and beneficiary—of that trial was not Ctesiphon but Demosthenes, and Demosthenes' total triumph over Aeschines in court that day left him free to enjoy for a further half-dozen years the respect bordering on adulation that his democratic defiance of autocratic Macedon commanded. It was Macedon, however, that was in a position to call the shots, and Athens' external powerlessness was only aggravated by the series of quite severe problems over its grain supply in the early 320s.

The end of Athenian democracy in its Demosthenic or Lycurgan form came all too soon. It was precipitated in 324, the year before Lycurgus died, by the Harpalus Affair. Since Chaeroneia, Athens had not dared, even though some Athenians had wished, to confront the military might of Macedon directly. In 331 or 330, most notably, Athens had stayed conspicuously aloof from a revolt led by Agis III, the failure of which was probably foredoomed in any case but was rendered virtually certain by Athens' absence. Rather than engage others militarily abroad, Athenians preferred to engage each other politically at home—on the same Macedonian issue, but over a much broader canvas. But in 324 Harpalus, a boyhood friend of Alexander and ex-treasurer of his vast empire, defected to Athens with the enormous sum of 5,000 talents—quite enough to give those who favoured direct anti-Macedonian military action the edge in policy determination. However, these anti-Macedonian stalwarts soon fell out amongst themselves, reminding us of Thucydides' harsh judgment (2.65) on the 'successors' of Pericles for pursuing private feuds to the detriment of Athens' best interests. Thus Hyperides, a long-time supporter of Demosthenes, turned viciously against him, and Demosthenes was found guilty of peculating some of Harpalus' money and fined the great sum of 50 talents (recalling Miltiades' fine in 489 BCE). He went into exile, was recalled, but fell out again with his rivals in Athens. In 322, anticipating a Macedonian death squad sent after him following Athens' failed revolt, Demosthenes poisoned himself fatally on Calaureia (the modern island of Poros). He was aged sixty-two and had spent more than half his life in frontline democratic politics.

Rather than for fighting Macedon in person, the Athenians had at first used Harpalus' money to pay mercenaries to do their fighting for them—under an Athenian commander such as Leosthenes, who had been strategically based for recruitment purposes at Taenarum on the southern tip of Laconia since 325. But the death of Alexander at Babylon in June 323 was the long-awaited signal for Athenians to do what Demosthenes had been urging them since the late 350s, to 'serve in person'—though they continued to employ large numbers of mercenaries as well—and to do so in their vast fleet of trireme warships as well as by land, for the first time since 355. The resulting showdown with Macedon was of such a scale, involving some twenty states in all, as to earn it the title of the Hellenic War. But defeat at the hands of Macedonian regent Antipater both at sea (off Amorgos in the Cyclades) and by land (at Crannon in Thessaly) left democratic Athens vulnerable to Macedon's final solution.

The end of the line for the old-style Athenian democracy came in 321. Antipater's key move was the imposition of a minimum wealth qualification for the holding of Athenian citizenship: 2,000 drachmas or some three years' continuous skilled labour wages. Any sort of financial qualification for citizenship was in and of itself an oligarchic move, but Antipater's census knocked more than one-third of the Athenian citizen body off the registers at a stroke— about the same proportion as had been carried off by the non-human agency of plague a century earlier. How many exactly were disfranchised is uncertain. Diodorus and Plutarch agree that the reduced citizen total was of the order of 9,000 in round figures (roughly the same as Sparta's in 480, but only one-fifth or so of Athens' fifth-century peak); but whereas Diodorus says 22,000 were struck from a previous round total of 31,000, Plutarch says 12,000 were struck from 21,000. Democracy—or at least the name and shadow—was not yet finally dead at Athens, or elsewhere in the ancient Greek world, but it had been dealt a mortal blow.

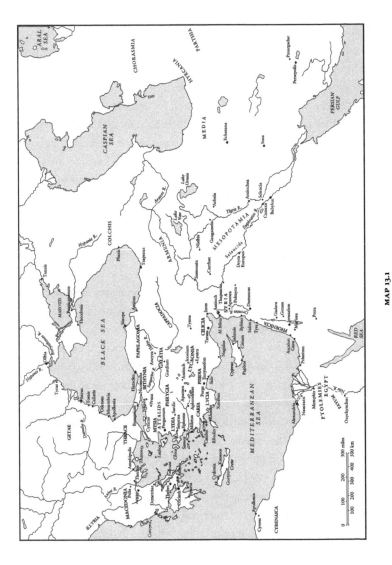

MAP 13.1

Hellenistic World. From Pomeroy, *Ancient Greece: A Political, Social, and Cultural History* (1998).

13.

THE STRANGE DEATH OF CLASSICAL

GREEK DEMOCRACY

A Retrospect

ONE OF THE MAIN objectives of this book is to demonstrate that there was no such thing as ancient Greek democracy—no one *single* thing, that is. Rather, as Aristotle (Chapter 6) had indicated, there were several, often very different forms of ancient Greek democracy. Athens alone had at least three down to 322/1 (see further below), and was to have at least one more thereafter (Chapter 15). Moreover, democracy as a genre of political self-rule waxed and waned in the ancient Greek world. Most non-specialists and many specialists imagine that the so-called Periclean age—roughly the second half of the fifth century—was also the golden age of democracy. In fact, it was only in what we call the fourth century, especially its second quarter, that democracy came into its own to such a degree that Aristotle could speak of most Greek cities in his day (330s–320s) having a *politeia* of either a democratic or an oligarchic type.

We might begin this brief retrospect on Classical Greek—not just Athenian—democracy by asking how significant were the differences between fourth-century, post-403 BCE Athenian democracy and its fifth-century predecessor or predecessors? There are those scholars who emphasise the post-403 break as a marker of qualitative and not merely quantitative distinction, whereas others emphasise continuity over change. I would not myself pose the interpretative choice as between *Vollendung* (completion, perfection) and *Verfall* (decay, decline), as one German symposium did. But both

FIGURE 13.1
Alexander the Great as Pharaoh
Alexander III of Macedon (356–323 BCE), posthumously termed 'the Great', both conquered the Persian
Empire and went to great pains to have himself recognised as the legitimate successor of the Achaemenid
sovereigns. Hence in Egypt he became Pharaoh and had himself depicted as such, as here on the Great
Temple of Amun at Luxor, standing before the Egyptian god Min. © Print Collector, Getty Images

'fourth-century' democracy and 'fifth-century democracy' are in their way
rather contentious terms. Highly respected colleagues contend that democracy properly so called came into being at Athens only with the reforms of
Ephialtes (and Pericles) in 462/1, even though clearly some democratic institutions (e.g., ostracism) were already in existence before then and remained
in force thereafter. I am myself in no doubt that the reforms instituted under
the name and perhaps also the aegis of Cleisthenes in and after 508/7 made
of Athens' polity an early, indeed the earliest known, form of *demokratia*. But
even I am bound to concede that the word *demokratia*—which is not explicitly attested until the 420s—was not invented until some time after 508/7,
although almost certainly before 462/1. Then there are those colleagues who
would argue that 'Lycurgan' democracy (336–322/1) was qualitatively different again from the democracy of 403–336, but I—for the reasons given in the
previous chapter—am not among them.

No one, however, disputes that in 411 and again in 404 democracy of whatever sort was terminated at Athens, on the first occasion through internal revolution, and on the second through external, Persian-financed Spartan compulsion. But was the half-century of Athenian *demokratia* of 462/1 to 411 itself an uncomplicated, uniform thing? A famous passage of Thucydides, admittedly a far from non-partisan observer, even casts doubt on the propriety or accuracy of applying 'demokratia' to the period of the ascendancy of Pericles. What really counted in practical terms, he seems to be claiming, was not the formal *kratos* of the *demos*, but the 'rule' of Athens' 'first man', Pericles. And that was so even though he puts the very term *demokratia* into the mouth of his Pericles in the funeral oration. Besides, not even the *arche* of Pericles was for Thucydides the 'best' mode of governance Athens experienced during his own lifetime. That accolade he bestowed instead upon the regime of the Five Thousand, which for eight months in 411/10 succeeded the narrow oligarchy of the Four Hundred: for that regime in his view constituted a 'moderate blending in the interests both of the Few and of the Many'. Thucydides, in other words, was no ideological democrat, predictably enough, but he was no dyed-in-the-wool oligarch either; in fact, he is the earliest exponent on record of a 'mixed constitution' theory. In that respect he anticipated the further refinements made by Aristotle (Chapter 11) and later by Polybius (Chapter 15).

Thucydides had personal reasons for seeing democracy, and Pericles, as he did. But even before the counter-revolution of 411, there is at least one major indication that the Ephialtic-Periclean democracy was under strain and undergoing significant modification. From 431 Athens was engaged on and off for twenty-seven years, a whole generation, in the near-equivalent of a world war with Sparta and its allies. Such were the divisions of personality and policy among the leading Athenian politicians that for the first time since 443 the supposedly air-clearing device of ostracism was once again called into play by the Athenian Assembly, probably in 416. But on this occasion it failed to have the desired effect: neither of the two main protagonists was ostracised, and in the same year that Athens embarked on its disastrous Sicilian adventure, 415, a new form of judicial procedure is first attested (though it may have been introduced and practised before then): the 'writ alleging an unconstitutional proposal'. This proved not only to be innovative judicially, but also to offer scope for a new mode of intestine political warfare between the leading democratic politicians.

As a writ, this new procedure was public, not private; it was the kind that 'anyone who wished'—any citizen, whether holding an office or not—might bring. In practice, as surely by design, it was only certain Athenians who would even contemplate bringing such a suit against others of the same stripe: that is, members of the small, informal group known later as the orators and politicians, or more abusively as demagogues—in other words, professional politicians. These were citizens who had the nous, the leisure, and the wealth to devote themselves to politics, to stand up and be counted, and, given the nature of Athenian democratic politics, to above all step up regularly to the speaker's platform on the Pnyx to advocate or oppose a particular policy line, or launch a prosecution of a major political rival. The introduction of this new, political lawsuit among other things satisfied a felt need for a legal means of preventing the Assembly from taking any policy decision irrevocably. The best way of achieving that goal, it was thought, was to be able to review an Assembly decision (taken by a majority vote of the 5,000 or 6,000 or more attendees) in a people's jury court (staffed normally by 501 jurors).

For the principals this was an extremely high-stakes, high-risk kind of action; how high-risk is amply shown by the experience of Aeschines in 330 (Chapter 10). But how embedded in normal democratic practice it had soon become is demonstrated by the way that in 411 the 400 oligarchs instantly suspended it, as an essential ingredient of their anti-democratic, counter-revolutionary platform; and in 404 the ultra-oligarchic Thirty abolished it. Further corroboration comes from the anecdotal evidence that one Aristophon was prosecuted under this procedure no fewer than seventy-five times, and yet never once successfully. The restored, post-403 democracy clearly felt that it could not do without the writ against unconstitutional proposals, even though other changes were introduced that tended in the same direction of controlling the actual amount of the Assembly's *kratos*.

After the turbulent, bloodstained, and deeply divisive oligarchic interludes, the Athenians decisively re-embraced democracy in 403. They represented it, quite unhistorically, as their 'ancestral constitution' and ascribed its foundation no less erroneously to Solon, if not to mythical king Theseus. According to the author of the Aristotelian *Athenaiōn Politeia*, writing in the earlier 320s, with the restoration of democracy in 403/2 the Athenian constitution underwent the last of its eleven 'transformations'. That is arguable (in both senses). But what should one make of that author's further claim that the polity thereafter continued 'increasing the power of the masses'? Let us begin by rehearsing some of the indisputable differences between fifth- and fourth-century democracy, apart from the increased frequency of resort to the writ against unconstitutional proposals and the total eschewal of the ostracism procedure. These include the re-codification of Athens' laws, a process initiated in 410, after a restoration of democracy, but completed only in 399 (after another democratic restoration); a formal distinction drawn between a law and a decree, so that after 403 the Assembly as such no longer legislated; the introduction in the 390s of a payment for Assembly attendance; and an increase in the number of stated meetings of the Assembly each civil month from perhaps as few as one per month to, by 350, four per month. Are these changes significant, and, if so, how (and to what extent)?

A maximalist modern view of the law versus decree separation and distinction coupled with the completed codification holds that it was only after 399 that 'rule of law'—as opposed to *kratos* of *demos*—was established. But this is to commit anachronism. The laws had always ruled Athenians, but it had always been Athenians who made their laws and who, because laws by definition are general, interpreted and applied them—democratically, with interruptions, after 508/7. It has also been argued that after 403 Athens passed from a regime of 'popular sovereignty' to one of 'the Sovereignty of the Law'. But 'sovereignty' is also a dangerously anachronistic notion, and drawing a distinction between the 'immediate' sovereignty wielded by the Assembly and the 'ultimate' sovereignty that resided with the People's *dikasteria* does not help. Just as there was no modern notion of the separation of powers in the Classical Athenian democratic *polis*, and no Supreme Court, so sovereignty is a concept best reserved for post-ancient States. The *demos* 'ruled', exercising its unique *kratos*, in the fourth century BCE no less than in the fifth; it just did so differently.

But suppose one were to apply a quantitative as opposed to qualitative criterion to the argument, then one would have to award the victory to the fourth-century democracy. The Athenian citizen body after 400 BCE, even if we go with the higher figure of 31,000 rather than 22,000 in 322/1, was appreciably smaller than it had been in the fifth century, when at its height in c. 430 it may have numbered as many as between 50,000 and 60,000. Yet in the fourth century that smaller body had to—legally was obligated to—field a quorum of 6,000 at two successive Assembly meetings, in order, for example, to begin the process of enacting a Law or to confer the privilege of citizenship. The introduction of Assembly pay in the 390s, therefore, modest though it was, may be construed not only as a form of disguised poor relief but also as a necessary incentive to persuade ordinary citizens to attend. Aristophanes' satirical comedy of c. 392/1, *Women Attending the Assembly*, confirms the current interest in the matter, and by 350 citizens were being invited to an Assembly meeting every nine days or so. And attend they did, in numbers—or so one is bound to infer from the archaeologically established fact that in the 330s or 320s under the Lycurgan dispensation (Chapter 12) the seating area of the Pnyx assembly space was significantly enlarged.

A smaller citizen body after the ravages of the Peloponnesian War meant also a smaller pool from which to draw members of the Council of 500, whose service was restricted to a maximum of two annual—and not consecutive—terms per fully adult lifetime (thirty years old and above). Most Athenians will have had to serve on the Council in the fourth century simply in order to fill the set deme and tribal quotas. There were no such temporal restrictions imposed on the holding of other offices, most of which were sortitive, and one can well imagine that the formal property restriction imposed on the holding of the Archonship (thetes remained formally barred) was often or even normally relaxed. Nor was there any temporal or status restriction on recruitment to the panel of 6,000 citizens selected annually by lot to serve as jurors. The restriction in that case affected rather the supply of publicly funded cash due to them as both an honorific token of public esteem and a material civic benefit.

In that quantitative sense, then, one might perhaps want to agree with the *Ath. Pol.* writer that the power of the masses was, on the whole, increasing after 403. But there are one or two telling signs that within that period of seventy or so years, and especially during the Lycurgan era, the democracy was changing significantly in its spirit: that it was becoming more 'managed' or managerial, more top-down, less spontaneously co-operative and egalitarian. One issue was the Athenian equivalent of a 'guns before butter' debate: should any surplus of public funds, if there should happen to be one, go towards swelling the Military Fund or the Festival Fund? Another issue was more generic: to the extent that the Athenians understood or wished to understand the notion of a state budget, how should the apportionment be managed, or, more to the point, by whom? Twice the *demos* leaned sharply towards increasing individual executive responsibility by appointing through election the equivalent of a chief finance minister—Euboulus in the 350s and 340s, Lycurgus in the 330s and 320s. But even so they in no way sacrificed the fundamental democratic principle that all elected (and sortitive) officials were responsible to the People, either directly through the Assembly and Courts or indirectly through the regular audit carried out in the *demos*' name by the Council of 500. On the other hand, the creation of a new elective office of water commissioner that was neither financial nor military, and the weakening of the old compulsory liturgy system in favour of the voluntary method of private donation for the raising of large sums of public money from private wealthy individuals at short notice, were both signs of the times and in retrospect pointers to a non-democratic future.

To conclude this chapter, I widen the angle of vision from democratic Athens to democracy in the Hellenic world generally, and—even more widely—to the condition of the Greek *polis* as such on the threshold (as we with 20:20 hindsight can see clearly) of losing its prized independence to a small handful of mega-state, multi-state territorial monarchies in the new—post-Classical, Hellenistic—epoch. Democracy, as mentioned, expanded its reach in the fourth century, but more could also mean worse—or at least no better. Probably one of the reasons why Thucydides favoured a mixed constitution at Athens, and certainly the overriding reason for Aristotle's promoting it as the best practicable kind of polity, was that it offered some sort of solution to or even a preventative of the worst kind of political *stasis*—outright civil war. Over twelve months between 404 and 403 the Athenian Thirty are reckoned to have murdered some 1,200 to 1,500 citizens and metics. In 370 the democrats of Argos clubbed to death in a very much shorter space of time roughly the same number of their oligarchic opponents. Although both those cases are extreme instances, there's no denying that lower-level *stasis*—involving at best threats if not the actual execution of redistribution of land and cancellations of debts, and sometimes also the freeing of slaves for the purpose of fomenting or prosecuting civil war—was more or less endemic in the Greek *polis*-world, to such an extent that one of Philip of Macedon's first moves upon attaining the mastery of the Aegean was to outlaw such measures in the cities he now held in subjection.

But did such a scenario amount to 'the crisis of the Greek city', a formulation that once attained currency especially in the Soviet-dominated East Germany of the 1970s? Alexander the Great, when he literally laid the foundations for Alexandria in Egypt in 332, certainly believed not only that the Greek city was not in crisis but also that it had a future, though not a democratic one. He would have rejected with contumely the modern notion that for ideological as well as economic and political reasons it was merely an evolutionary dead-end. If it was indeed dying, it had an awful lot of dying left in it.

Rather more fruitfully interesting, I suggest, is the way in which the question of a possible fourth-century failure has been posed and framed by A.N.W. Saunders. He canvassed five ways in which the fourth century (itself of course an artificial chronographic construct) might be considered to have failed: (i) political, in the literal sense: it was individual *poleis* or alliances of them that failed militarily against the non-*polis* kingdom of Macedon; (ii) ethnic, in the sense that Greeks failed to achieve Hellenic unity, despite rising economic prosperity; (iii) social, because the better-off citizens failed either to maintain or to extend democracy; (iv) cultural, because continued reliance on slave labour precluded scientific innovation; and finally (v) psychological, inasmuch as the clinging to the past represented a failure of nerve.

One can query the precise formulation in each case; for example, Hellenistic civilisation (to be discussed in the next chapter) was no less dependent on slave labour but yet it generated massive scientific innovation, at any rate on the theoretical plane; and 'Hellenic unity'—with the one giant and only partial exception of 480–479—was always an aspiration rather than a practical reality. But at least the third type of alleged failure (social) does bear directly on the problematic of this book, and poses a challenge to any simplistic paean to the Greeks' democratic achievement. Even so, taking the long-run view, I remain more favourably impressed by the latter achievement than otherwise, and comfort myself with the parting thought that the giant thinker of the age, Aristotle, ended up by offering a definition of active citizenship and a pragmatic version of an ideal mixed constitution that were at least democratically inflected and inclined.

IV

14.

HELLENISTIC DEMOCRACY?

Democracy in Deficit c. 323–86 BCE

A.H.M. JONES, ONE OF the greatest of ancient historians, specialised in the Later Roman Empire, but in his many excellent publications he covered more or less all the ancient Graeco-Roman world, including the Athenian democracy. In an article on the Greeks under the Roman empire he wrote: 'The predominant form of constitution in the Hellenistic age was democratic, and the kings imposed their control more by means of governors and garrisons than by constitutional restrictions on democratic liberty'. How paradoxical is that—democracy and democratic liberty, but controlled by kings who imposed governors and garrisons? But this paradox nicely captures the fact that the Hellenistic age, of which Jones also gave an admirable summary account, was in global-historical terms a transitional era between the world of the more or less independent Greek *polis* and the world of the Roman Empire. The hinge between them was formed by the conquests of Alexander the Great of Macedon (r. 336–323), and the brutal carving up of his hypertrophied and short-lived empire among a number of Successor kingdoms.

The Hellenistic era is usually taken to run in full from the death of Alexander the Great at Babylon in 323 to the fall of the Ptolemaic kingdom of Egypt to the Romans in 30 BCE. The term 'Hellenistic' existed already with a different, linguistic meaning, but it was first used to designate a historical epoch by the nineteenth-century German historian Johann-Gustav Droysen (1808–1884). He so labelled it because its culture was no longer entirely (or purely) Hellenic but represented a significant mixture or even fusion between Greek and (oriental) non-Greek. To the mystical Droysen, moreover, the creation of such a culture was part of a far grander, divine scheme for the history of humanity: the spread of Hellenism to the Holy Land of Palestine enabled the creation and diffusion of Christianity as an original Greek–Jewish palimpsest with the catholic (universal) potential to spread globally from within the Hellenised, eastern portion of the Roman empire. Paul (born Saul) of Tarsus in southeast Anatolia was a Roman citizen as well as an orthodox Jew by birth and upbringing; the first Christians (probably first so labelled in the new, Hellenistic Greek city of Antioch in Syria) took their name from *Khristos*, the Greek translation of the Hebrew word Messiah or 'the anointed one'. They compiled and read their New Testament in common dialect (*koine*) Greek. Their Old Testament was the Hebrew Bible as already translated into Greek in Ptolemaic Alexandria in the third century. The Letters attributed to Paul and included in the canonical New Testament reached out to early Christian communities as far afield as Rome in Italy, Corinth and Philippi in Greece, and Colossae in Asia Minor.

Few if any modern scholars of the Hellenistic age and world have shared Droysen's apocalyptic vision, and there is great and continuing confusion and dispute over the extent to which Hellenistic culture was a genuine mixture or fusion, or whether Hellenism was ever anything more than an administrative superstructure and thin veneer lightly spread over still vibrant—and resistant— native cultures. We need not trouble ourselves with such deeply contested matters here. Instead, we shall try to gain some understanding of what democracy may actually have meant in both theory and practice in a world dominated by kings or other kinds of monarch not necessarily so labelled. In what sense, and how, did it come to be the 'predominant form of constitution in the Hellenistic age'? A remarkable flurry of recent work on Hellenistic democracy has led some scholars to speak even of a 'rehabilitation of the post-classical Greek cities', and that surely requires our reinvestigation. For once, and for the first time in democracy's life, Athens need not take centre stage, and, despite its redoubtable democratic tradition and continued democratic will, Athens will be considered only at the end rather than the beginning of this chapter. For once, too, epigraphic sources will occupy as important a place as the literary.

Alexander the Great succeeded his murdered father Philip II of Macedon in 336. Already Philip's anti-Persian campaign in Asia was underway, but the expedition's precise limits, both political and geographical, remained unclear—beyond the aims of establishing Philip's credentials as a pukka Greek champion and expanding his power and glory, at least in his own eyes. Alexander was the only obvious or conceivable Macedonian heir apparent, but lately he had fallen out with his father and been bypassed by him entirely for the Persian campaign. He seized the opportunity of his father's assassination to reconfigure it in his own image on the grandest possible scale. The mere conquest of Asia Minor—and the incidental liberation of the Asiatic Greek cities from Persian suzerainty—were nowhere near ambitious enough goals for the twenty-year-old prodigy. Irritatingly, it required as much as two years for Alexander to wrap up Greek and Balkan affairs and permit him, with his backyard secure, to join the advance force in northwest Anatolia. But any old-fashioned or nostalgic Greeks who imagined that the death of Philip might mean the rebirth of genuine freedom and autonomy for the Greek cities within his purview would have been very quickly disabused. In 335 Alexander ruthlessly ordered the political emasculation and physical annihilation, with the exception of some religious or otherwise symbolic locations, of the rebel city of Thebes. The Macedonians' anti-Persian expedition in Asia was ostensibly cast in the mould of a panhellenic Greek 'crusade' of liberation. But loyalty and security, at any rate to begin with, mattered far more to Alexander than Hellenic purity or even identity; the precise form of constitution he permitted to or enforced upon his Greek subjects was a matter pre-eminently of tactics rather than ideology.

Thus in 334, after he had crossed over the Hellespont into Asia and had won at the Granicus river the first of his set-piece victories, he proceeded south along the Anatolian coast as far as the major Greek city of Ephesus in Ionia. Here, according to Arrian (author of our best extant narrative account, even though composed in the second century CE), he set up a democracy to replace the pro-Persian or at least complaisant oligarchy. But at the same time he sensibly took steps to prevent the empowered *demos* from wreaking its revenge on the innocent as well as on their oligarchic enemies. Furthermore, he made a general declaration of support for democracies in all the former Persia-subjected Greek cities, including the offshore islands; an illustration is provided by a much later document preserving a letter (really an imperial rescript) of Alexander to the island-city of Chios. Chios had been in a condition of *stasis* between oligarchs and democrats since 336, and Alexander weighed in on the side of democracy.

This does not mean, however, that Alexander, a hereditary Macedonian monarch and autocrat, was in any sense a convert to democracy on principle. It was simply that he had opportunistically found a simple way of diverting the Asiatic Greek cities from their Persian allegiance to allegiance to him, by overthrowing the oligarchs' regimes and promoting the cause of their internal, anti-Persian democrat opponents. If we look forward to 324, by which time Alexander had completed the conquest of the old Persian empire and started to give serious thought to how he would govern his new empire, we see a dramatically altered picture. To coincide with the Olympic Games of that year, he sent back to Greece from Asia a peremptory diktat known as the Exiles Decree, ordering the Greeks to receive back any exiles and restore their property rights to them. His overriding motivation was to rid himself of a massive surplus of mercenary troops, but the solution he adopted shows how much—or rather how little—respect he had for the autonomy, let alone the democratic governance, of Greek cities. Contemporary documentary evidence from, for example, Tegea in Arcadia in mainland Greece gives an inkling of the kind of political, economic, and social problems and turmoil that the decree so far from resolving instead caused.

Following Alexander's death at Babylon there ensued a half-century of bloodstained struggles between a handful of major warlords, each contending for their piece of Alexander's empire. The upshot was broadly a tripartite division of the spoils between the Antigonids of old Greece based at Pella in Macedonia, the Ptolemies of Egypt ruling from Alexander's new foundation of Alexandria, and the Seleucids of Asia who ruled from their (also new) twin capitals of Seleuceia on the Tigris (in Iraq today), and Antioch on the Orontes in Syria. All chose to style themselves as kings, a throwback to Homeric or indeed pre-Homeric times. Other, lesser dynasts or dynasties rose and fell, the most durable proving to be the kingdom (naturally) of the Attalids based on the old Greek city of Pergamum in northwest Asia Minor. But it was the Seleucids who managed to grab and hold the largest chunk, essentially most of what Alexander had briefly ruled in Asia.

In the 270s to 260s a Seleucid king speaks of democracy existing at Lysimacheia, capital of another minor and short-lived dynasty in the Hellespont region; but in another text relating to 278 BCE the Seleucids are said to be

FIGURE 14.1
Tyche, Roman bronze
Fortune (or Chance) was worshipped as a goddess in ancient Greece, by individuals as well as by cities, and never more fervently or widely than during the politically unstable Hellenistic epoch (c. 323–30 BCE). Image copyright © The Metropolitan Museum of Art. Image source: Art Resource, NY

'eager to deprive cities of democracy'. The latter was nearer the mark and the monarchic norm. Earlier, in 313/2, there was talk of a restoration of democracy at Miletus by Antigonus the One-Eyed, one of Alexander's premier generals and ultimate progenitor of the Antigonid dynasty. But this is to be interpreted in exactly the same way as his old sovereign's general proclamation of democracies in the same region in 334: it was merely a manoeuvre to confound his enemy, who in this case happened to be another Macedonian dynast, and a convenient buzzword, to go with the oft-proclaimed slogan of the 'freedom' of Greeks. Nevertheless, Miletus (together with Didyma) is one of four examples of Hellenistic democracies offered in a book with the subtitle 'Freedom, Independence and Political Procedures in Some East Greek States'; the other three are Ionian Iasus, Calymna in Caria, and the offshore island-city of Cos. What exactly, then, does that democracy amount to? Was it anything more than the absence of direct rule by a monarch, as for example at the city of

Chersonesus in Crimea in 155 BCE—a city that had earlier had some form of democratic constitution?

In the late fifth and early fourth centuries Miletus had had a democratic constitution modelled after that of Athens, involving demes and tribes. After experiencing bouts of tyranny in the late fourth century and again in 259/8, it is said (by Carlsson) to have had its freedom, autonomy—and democracy—restored. A number of inscribed decrees of the Hellenistic period are extant, which probably represent two temporally and politically distinct decision-making procedures. Down to the 280s, named individuals propose decrees, mainly regarding domestic matters, the enactment formula of which mentions the Council and the People (in Assembly). From the 280s officials called Epistatai (presidents, overseers) regularly propose decrees of which the enactment formula mentions only the People, though that may be because the Epistatai are a committee of the Council. But who became members of the Council, and how? And how much independence, let alone initiative, did the People really have? Two points seem decisive against the notion that this was democracy in any late fifth- or early fourth-century sense. First, where the mode of appointment of officials is known, it is election (not the quintessentially democratic lottery), and the eponymous official bore the alternative, suspiciously undemocratic title of 'wreath-bearer', the regular title of an official sponsoring a festival liturgy in Hellenistic Greece, and 'arbitrator', one who is given sole power to resolve conflicts. Second, there is no evidence in any decree of a genuine amendment, which suggests there was little or no actual discussion in the Assembly. If that counted as democracy for the citizens who composed the *demos*, it seems a very restricted exercise of *kratos* at home, and it seems that as regards the determination of foreign policy, the best and most that could be hoped for was to keep on good terms with the real power-brokers, the kings.

However, there is a promising case of genuine democratic sentiment still existing in the old sense into the third century at Ionian Erythrae. Some time after 300, perhaps as late as 280, the Council and the Demos passed two decrees, which they had inscribed on stone, reaffirming the—by implication democratic—principle of anti-oligarchic tyrant-slaying. The key phrase runs thus:

> Since the oligarchs removed the sword from the . . . statue of Philites the
> tyrant-slayer . . . be it resolved by the People . . . that the statue be restored
> as it was before . . .

This is one of six instances of anti-tyrant or pro-tyrant-slaying legislation,
running from the decree of Demophantus passed at Athens in 410 to a decree
of Ilium (Troy) and roughly contemporaneous with the Erythrae decrees, that
have been studied innovatively by David Teegarden (2013a). In the turmoil
ensuing after Alexander's liberation of Greek cities such as Erythrae and his
subsequent conquest of the Persian empire, a patriotic and anti-oligarchic citizen of Erythrae named Philites had slain a possibly pro-Persian and certainly
anti-democratic tyrant. For that deed he had been rewarded by the city with
a bronze statue depicting him carrying the sword of freedom. Subsequently
oligarchs had regained control of the city, and, in a public demonstration of
their ideology, 'removed the sword' from the effigy. It was a restored popular
regime, which may well have called itself a democracy, that passed the decree
quoted above.

The decree continues:

> let the Examiners in office contract out the work,
> . . . let the monthly treasurer serve their needs, and let the
> Superintendents of the Agora take care that the statue be free from
> patina and crowned always on the first day of the month and on the
> other holidays.

A second decree inscribed on the same marble stele then deals with how
the maintenance should be paid for, and especially how the crowns should be
financed—we remember how important crowns were in the Athenian democracy from the crown case pitting Demosthenes against Aeschines (Chapter 10).
It has rightly been observed by John Ma that this was 'the public enactment of
democratic values of accountability and transparency, in contrast to the oligarchical secrecy'. It was also—and this is Ma's major theme—an example of
the deliberate creation of social memory, reaffirming (democratic) identity in
the present and passing it on to the future. All the same, it seems to me a big

stretch from there to Teegarden's claim that such anti-tyranny measures helped make viable a democratic revolution in Asia Minor ushered in by Alexander the Great. Rather, Erythrae seems to be the proverbial rule-proving, democratic exception.

Moving south from Erythrae we come to the island and city of Rhodes, one of the very few able to do more than pay lip service to their autonomy and independence from Hellenistic kings and (later) even from the Romans. The Rhodians described their constitution as a democracy. Yet as the Greek geographer and historian Strabo wrote towards the end of the first century BCE: 'The Rhodians care for the common people (*demos*), although they do not live under a democracy; they wish nonetheless to maintain the goodwill of the mass of the poor'. So who was right? A good case has been made for a non-democratic mode of rule by a (ruthless, opportunistic) naval aristocracy involved in trade, who kept the *demos* out of power but yet were willing to share with it some of the spoils of trade and piracy.

In mainland Greece the big new political development was the rise of federal States with continental ambitions. The two largest were the Achaean League, a new foundation of the early third century, and the Aetolian, an older body attested at least since the late fifth or early fourth century but newly galvanised. The logic behind their instigation was simple: the need for units larger than individual, atomised *poleis* to resist the potential for unwelcome intervention by their imperial overlords in Macedon. The principle of ethnic homogeneity was the same that underlay the much earlier federal states of the Boeotians (from the late sixth century) and the Arcadians (intermittently from the early fifth century, Sparta permitting). But the coming of democracy to such federal states was a phenomenon only of the fourth century, most notably in Boeotia (from 378: Chapter 11). Jakob Larsen, the great expert of an earlier generation on ancient Greek federalism, spoke of democracy as well as 'representation' in Hellenistic federalism, but at least as far as the two largest and most important federations were concerned that seems mightily over-optimistic, at best a case of loose usage.

The major source on these two federal states, as indeed on all Hellenistic Greek history from 220 to 145, is the Greek Polybius (born c. 210–200, died c. 120). He came from from Megalopolis in Arcadia, a city that was founded in 368 as an anti-Spartan bulwark and served as the capital of the then

Arcadian federal state. The remains of its simply huge theatre, the largest in the Peloponnese, which hosted federal gatherings, are still impressive to this day. Polybius is also the prime witness to one key aspect of the subject of our next chapter, so further detailed discussion of him and his political views will be deferred until then. But to prolong the suspense no further, it can safely be said that he was no democrat—in any Aristotelian sense. One egregious example of his general historiographical principle that it is permissible to exempt patriotism from the general requirement of objectivity and impartiality concerns the Achaean League, of which his native Megalopolis was a key member: 'No political system can be found anywhere in the world which favours more the principles of equality, freedom of speech and true democracy than that of the Achaeans'. It is not merely coincidental that the birth and growth of the Achaean League federal state, control of which was safely in the hands of wealthy or aristocratic landowning elites such as Polybius, coincided with a growing economic immiseration of the poor citizen masses and a consequent loss by the elite of those poor masses' goodwill. The late-third-century Cynic poet Cercidas, who moralised against the increasingly uneven distribution of wealth, did not just happen to be a citizen of Megalopolis.

So great indeed was the distress of poor citizens in the Peloponnese generally that in the third quarter of the third century they found a most unlikely champion—or at least a powerful political personality willing and able to exploit that distress for his own political ends. Sparta had ceased to be a great power, or indeed any sort of power, in the 360s; the loss of over half its *polis* territory with the liberation of the Messenian Helots and the foundation of Messene reduced it for over a century to the lowly status of a mere Peloponnesian squabbler. Part of Sparta's problem, already signalled as such in an abortive internal coup of about 400 BCE (the 'conspiracy of Cinadon') was the gross and growing inequality between rich and poor Spartans. But it was not until 244 BCE that the poor and dispossessed—and often declassed—Spartans found a leader who not only wished to but was seemingly in a position to do something to rectify their grievances. That leader was Eurypontid King Agis IV, who came to the throne in 244 and announced what elsewhere in the Greek world would have counted as a radical programme of economic transformation: a combination of a cancellation of all debts with a redistribution of private landed property. Had it been implemented, it would have amounted to a political revolution. But although he made some headway with the former, and written deeds recording debts were symbolically burned, his touch in foreign affairs was less adroit, and in 241 he was assassinated.

However, Cleomenes III, a king from the other (Agiad) royal house, married Agis' doughty widow Agiatis, and with her support and that of her wealthy family he carried on in 235 where the reformist Agis had been compelled to leave off; indeed, he advanced for some considerable distance beyond that. Not only were further debts cancelled, but some land was redistributed—and not only to poor Spartans but also to non-Spartans, including both Perieoeci and mercenaries and even ex-Helots. It should be noted, though, that the 6,000 Laconian Helots Cleomenes liberated had to buy their freedom, and that they were liberated chiefly to bulk up Sparta's new-model, Macedonian-style army. Nevertheless, the nature and scale of the reforms justify our talking of a Spartan 'revolution', even if it was in no sense a democratic one.

All the same, Cleomenes' posture frightened in particular the leaders of the Achaean League. That, together with Cleomenes' savaging of Megalopolis in 223, unfortunately presaged the League's eventual revenge on Sparta, which was exacted during the first half of the second century. First, the internal reforms were annulled, and then a tamed Sparta was itself incorporated as a subordinate League member, spelling the end of its long cherished autonomy and independence, after the passage of some 800 years. That is not to mention the role of Nabis, self-styled king of Sparta but actually more of a tyrant, who between 207 and 192 tried both to reanimate Cleomenes' reforms at home and to contend with both the major Greek Leagues and with the nascent power in mainland Greece of Rome. That he failed ultimately both at home and abroad was no real disgrace—or surprise, even if he left his mark on Sparta socio-economically by liberating most of the remaining Helots.

However, although Cleomenes may be held to have accomplished a social and economic revolution at Sparta, he cannot be said to have accomplished also a political revolution that might conceivably be described as in any way democratic: the initiative had come from the top, and Cleomenes' renewed and reshaped Spartan citizenry were in no wise empowered democratically. Moreover, by placing his brother on the Eurypontid throne and thereby abolishing the dyarchy that had on the whole served Sparta very well for those eight centuries, Cleomenes had turned himself into something much more like a Hellenistic dynast. His dealings with Ptolemy III support that reading, and it was perhaps not wholly inappropriate that in 219 he died, not in his bed in Sparta nor on a foreign battlefield, but in a street brawl in Alexandria. He had fled there for refuge following Sparta's terminal defeat in battle in 222, at Sellasia, just north of Sparta, a humiliating loss inflicted by the suzerain of Greece, Antigonus III Doson.

Finally, we turn to consider the state of Athens following the enforced termination of the Lycurgan democracy by the Macedonian superpower in 322/1 (Chapter 12). The work of Peter Rhodes, an excellent scholar of Athens in particular and of Greek political institutions more generally, seems to me to illustrate very well the difficulties and doubts surrounding this issue. On one hand, Rhodes thinks the term 'democracy' can be applied to post-322/1 Athens, as in his heading 'Democracy Restored, 287', which refers to a revolt against Macedon led by Callias (to whom we shall return below). On the other hand, in a later article Rhodes properly lays down a more stringent criterion: a true democracy not only has a paper democratic structure but functions democratically, that is, with a 'significant degree' of participation by the *demos* at all levels. Yet in the conclusion to that same article he seems to backtrack and on the whole stresses continuity over discontinuity, even while conceding that Hellenistic Athens was 'perceptibly different' from Classical both in the greater passivity of the Assembly and in the larger participation by rich citizens.

Arguments and evidence can be brought in favour of several positions and shades of interpretation. Take for example the final four years or so of the immensely long career of Phocion, born in 402 BCE and elected general no fewer than forty-five times. (Plutarch thought him worthy of a *Life*.) Between the termination of the democracy and imposition of a Macedonian garrison in 322/1 and his official condemnation to death in 318, he was the virtual ruler of subjected Athens and conducted relations with Macedon in what he took to be the Athenians' best interests. Without question he acted as Macedon's agent with great moderation and personal honesty, but he nevertheless did act as Macedon's agent, and thus suffered doubly both from a change of personnel at the helm of Macedon's affairs and from the deep resentment that his far from totally democratic outlook and apparent complicity with Macedon aroused among ordinary Athenians. He was forced to take the hemlock, and so died the death of an earlier philosopher.

On the other hand, the sheer ubiquity of democratic discourse as late as the 270s argues the other way. This was even the case when, between 317 and 307, Athens was under the thumb of the philosophic Demetrius of Phaleron, a former associate of Phocion, who reportedly commented that he did not destroy democracy, but corrected it. A protégé of Cassander (son of Antipater), Demetrius was definitely not democratic. In what legal capacity exactly he governed Athens is unclear: was it as overseer, general, or lawgiver? Whatever the terminology, he was de facto a tyrant and, to borrow a much more recent term, a 'quisling'. Under his regime the property qualification for citizenship imposed by Antipater was halved (from 2,000 to 1,000 drachmas), but it was still retained, and under him too Athens was subjected to its first ever census, something the democracy had felt able to do without. The distinguished comic poet Menander, a former pupil of Theophrastus at Aristotle's Lyceum institute, was said to be an intimate of Demetrius. If so, it may be instructive to note that in Menander's *Hero*, set contemporaneously in the deme of Ptelea, a brother and sister are represented as working off a debt, and so suffering a form of debt bondage (the sister is referred to by her lover as 'a kind of slave'). Debt bondage had been outlawed for Athenians by Solon in c. 600 BCE, and the equation of personal freedom with citizenship and democratic entitlement had been an unquestioned datum of the old Athenian democracy.

On the other hand, the philosopher in Demetrius, harking back perhaps to the pre-democratic Solon, did introduce sumptuary legislation regarding funeral expenditure as a curb on the excesses of the rich and perhaps as a sop to democratic sentiment among the poor. Yet during Demetrius' decade in control the Assembly was mostly inactive, the writ against unconstitutional proposals was dropped, and the liturgy system was ended, thereby undermining one of the crucial economic bases of a functioning democracy properly so called. The Ephebeia, on the other hand, grew to be one of Athens' most important social institutions, and progressively—or rather regressively—more and more the preserve of a social and indeed no longer entirely Athenian elite.

Demetrius of Phaleron was replaced as Athens' ruler by Demetrius of Macedon, later nicknamed 'the Besieger'. To him were voted quite extravagant as well as quite unprecedented honours. Two new Athenian tribes were invented to add to the existing Cleisthenic ten, and they were named honorifically for Demetrius and his father Antigonus the One-Eyed, who moreover were worshipped as gods in their lifetime. Lifetime worship of rulers as gods was by then nothing new. It went back as far as the late fifth century BCE on Samos (for Lysander) and had become standardised under Alexander and his successors: in 305 the latter had all, whether royal by birth or not (most of them not), unilaterally declared themselves to be kings and therefore owed the kind of divine worship that now standardly went with that title.

A further devaluation of the old democratic norms was the erection of statues of Antigonus and Demetrius in the Athenian Agora, next to those of the Tyrannicides (Harmodius and Aristogeiton). How were the mighty set up on a pedestal! Besides, at the most direct practical level, interference in Athens' institutions by these 'royal' overlords severely pre-empted any genuinely democratic practice. For example, by means of so-called royal letters Demetrius was able to override the authority of the Athenian courts and Assembly. Perhaps the crowning inglory came when he infamously secured for himself, via a proposal of the sycophantic Stratocles, a fast-track induction into the Greater Mysteries of Eleusis, flagrantly disregarding the prior requirement of initiation into the Lesser Mysteries of Agrae. For this gross violation of custom and precedent Stratocles was mocked by the Athenian comic poet Philippides (for 'squeezing the whole year into one month', or words to that effect), but such feeble mockery was the limit of the Athenians' ability to resist the dictates of their Macedonian suzerain.

Between about 300 and perhaps 295 there occurred an obscure 'tyranny of Lachares'; whatever exactly that meant in practice, it symbolised the continuing erosion of the old, largely *stasis*-free Classical democracy. But sparks of that ancient regime were not yet quite altogether dead. In particular in 287, as mentioned, an Athenian revolt against Macedon was led by Callias of the deme Sphettus. Then, as the much later (270/69) decree in his honour put it, 'the revolution of the *demos* took place', and Callias is roundly praised for protecting the democracy. However, there would appear to have been a considerable disconnect here between ideology and actuality, since Callias had served as governor of Halicarnassus in the interests of King Ptolemy II of Egypt, who is not known to have been pro-democratic.

It is in the same, almost purely gestural sense that other similar democratic sparks should probably also be interpreted: the honouring of Euphron of Sicyon in 318/7 during a brief democratic interlude between Phocion's and Demetrius of Phaleron's primacy; the liberation of Athens from the latter in 307; and the erection in the Agora of a statue to the great democrat of yore, Demosthenes, in 280/79. And then there is the alliance that Athens concluded, in some desperation, to fight the so-called Chremonidean War together with a toothless Sparta under King Areus between 268/7 and 265/4. According to the (Callias) decree, this was decided upon 'by the Demos', but there is no mention of the old democratic formula 'by the Council and Demos'. This seems to me to bespeak at least the near-terminal atrophying of the old genuinely democratic institutions.

So I move on rapidly to what may perhaps be considered the ancient Athenians' last act of political revolution: their defiance not of any Greek dynast but of imperialist Rome, between 88 and 86 BCE. The sources—non-Athenian, pro-Roman, by no means democratic—are of course deeply unsatisfactory. So we have to be wary when we find the two most prominent anti-Roman leaders—Aristion and Athenion—both labelled as 'tyrants'. However, it is possible that their revolution consisted in rebelling against not only the lack of freedom imposed by Rome but also the sort of non- or anti-democratic constitution that the Romans consistently favoured and promoted throughout their empire (Chapter 15). In any event, the Athenians' rebellion was quite quickly crushed, and savagely so, by the Roman noble Lucius Cornelius Sulla surnamed Felix ('Lucky'); just five years later Sulla had himself appointed as Dictator of Rome and thereby sealed the fate of the 'free' Roman Republic—however precisely that should be understood in constitutional terms (the subject of our next chapter).

To conclude: the life of democracy in the Hellenistic period presents much scope for interpretative confusion. Although the *polis*-form as such retained its legitimacy and vitality, the constitutional trend in political actuality was firmly towards various shades of oligarchy. But for agit-prop and self-reassurance reasons, *demokratia* came to be used standardly in the Hellenistic Greek *poleis* both new and old as a slogan both for republic—that is, not monarchy or tyranny (see further Chapter 15)—and independence (from the relevant great power or powers). The new emphasis here, promoted by the empowered oligarchic rulers, was on *demos* as 'People', not *demos* as the mass of the poor citizens, and on independence from direct foreign rule. That is what is meant (and all that can be meant) by talking of 'free' Hellenistic Greek *poleis*. Overall, the condition of this Hellenistic mode of democracy was one of some durability, no doubt, but far more one of decline from an earlier, full-blooded political mode. Hellenistic *demokratia*, lacking to a greater or lesser degree the key qualitative defining elements of freedom, both internal and external, and political, civic equality, simply could not have been anything much like *demokratia* even in the most moderate of the variant forms identified by Aristotle in his *Politics* as recently as the later 330s or early 320s. Any usage of the term *demokratia* in such a historical context must necessarily have involved some devaluation, if not actual degradation, of that word's original force and meaning.

15.

THE ROMAN REPUBLIC

A Sort of Democracy?

IN THIS CHAPTER I SHALL be examining, first, the ancient Greek view (as expressed by the contemporary historian Polybius) that Rome's Republican constitution in the Middle Republican era (287–133 BCE) was a mixed polity, including a strong component of democracy. In the second part I shall assess the modern view (associated especially with F. Millar) that both in the Middle and in the Late Republic (133–27 BCE) the Roman Republic was a kind of democracy.

Our English word 'republic' is derived from the Latin *respublica*, itself a compound of two words: *res* ('thing') and *publica* ('of or belonging to the *Populus*', 'People'); crudely translated, they mean 'the People's thing'. By 'People' was understood the entirety of the Roman citizen population who were entered on the lists held by the most senior elected officials called Censors. In military terms, they were a combination of those citizens who possessed a certain minimum of property and were therefore liable for compulsory service, and those who owned or possessed less than that stipulated minimum. There were five levels of property-owning citizens, quantitatively graded; probably already by 200 BCE they were outnumbered by the propertyless. How those gradations were cashed out in political practice will be explored below (esp. the second part of this chapter on the Millar Thesis).

As in English, so in Latin, republic connoted in essence a political system characterised by the absence of a monarch; or, in the case of Rome's Republic, the conscious rejection and subsequent scrupulous avoidance of a king (*rex*).

The birth of the Republic coincided with the termination of a prolonged—and considerably mythicized—period of monarchy that began traditionally in 753 BCE with Romulus and ended in 509, when Rome's last king, ethnically non-Roman, was ejected. In conventional chronology the period from 509 to 287 is referred to as the Early Republic; the traditional chronography of the Middle and Late Republican eras is set out in the opening paragraph above.

Actually, there was no Roman Republican constitution, formally speaking— the Latin word *constitutio* means something quite different. But the term 'constitution' is hard to avoid, and how best it should be defined and understood is a vitally important question for our history of the life of democracy in all sorts of ways, and at many different periods, for at least three reasons: first, because by 30 BCE the Romans' empire had engulfed all the old Hellenistic Greek world; second, because in the process of empire-building Rome had of set purpose endeavoured to stamp out all traces of the old Greek democratic institutions and spirit; and, third, because even long after Antiquity it was Roman law and customs and Roman political conceptions that set the tone for all civic and political life in Europe until the late eighteenth century and even beyond (Chapters 18 and 19).

The issue of Republican Rome's relation to democracy is complicated by the geopolitical fact of empire in another, crucial way. Although Rome of the Republican era was a kind of *polis* in a Greek sense and importantly retained *polis*-type political institutions of direct participatory self-governance, spatially Rome also grew to become an imperial power of unprecedented scope in Mediterranean terms and extended its citizenship or variant versions of it way beyond the normal or normative bounds of any *polis* that Aristotle might have recognised. For him, a *polis* of more than 10,000 adult male citizens already exceeded a desirable limit, but the number of Roman citizens formally enrolled on the census lists in the Late Republic amounted to tens of thousands. And already by the middle of the second century BCE there were Roman citizens permanently settled as far afield as Greece and Asia Minor.

That extra-Italian imperial growth—initially between about 220 and 145 BCE—was taken as his subject by Greece's next major historian after Thucydides, Polybius of Megalopolis (c. 210–200 to 120 BCE); it is with his life and life's work, and their wider historical contexts, that I shall begin this chapter. As Herodotus and Thucydides had done, he too set out by posing to himself the biggest possible historical questions: why, and how, had Rome managed this unique feat of imperial growth? What was it about Rome that had made it possible, or even inevitable? And he gave a quintessentially Greek—that is, political-constitutional—answer, as we shall see.

Polybius' Roman Constitution

Between 264 and 241 BCE Rome and its allies waged against Carthage (in modern Tunisia) the First Punic War (of three). As with 'Peloponnesian War', the very terminology privileges one side's viewpoint: this was a war of the Romans against the Carthaginians (*Poeni* in Latin, adjective *Punicus*, hence 'Punic'). The Greeks, especially but not only those of Sicily, were all too familiar with this vigorous people; Aristotle had even written about their political system. But the Romans, clashing initially over control of the strait of Messina, came to regard them as a threat to be eliminated utterly. Polybius glanced back at the First Punic War but reserved his special attention for the Second War of 218–201. It was during this conflict that Rome experienced one of its most crushing ever defeats, at Cannae, in 216, and it was this and Rome's recovery from it that prompted Polybius' detailed comparative reflections on the political arrangements of the Romans' Middle Republic.

In between those wars, however, the city of his birth, Megalopolis in Arcadia, had become embroiled in a struggle for Peloponnesian domination between the Achaean League and Sparta, and had suffered severe destruction at the hands of Cleomenes III in 223 (Chapter 14). Whence arose Polybius' undying hatred of Sparta; his perhaps instinctive patriotism was further fanned by the accidental circumstance of his birth to Lycortas, a high executive officer within the Achaean League. This patriotic stance was to leave a powerful mark on Polybius' historiography. On condition that historians told the facts straight, he argued, it was in principle perfectly all right for them to make concessions to patriotism in interpreting them.

Responsibility for the outbreak of the Second Punic War is not quite such a complicated question as that for the Peloponnesian War—let alone the First World War. The initiative on the Carthaginian side was seized by one Hannibal Barca, who availed himself of Carthage's possessions and connections in eastern Spain as a springboard to launch an elephant-assisted invasion of northern Italy via the Alps in 218/7. The high tidemark of Hannibal's campaign was reached quite early on, with his stunning victory over Rome's legions at Cannae in 216. Further successes followed, but the initiative passed to Rome, which took the fight from Italy first to Spain and then to Carthage's own North African backyard, where Scipio (later dubbed 'Africanus') routed Hannibal at Zama in 202.

Such was the impact of Cannae on the consciousness of Polybius that he took Rome's recovery from that catastrophic defeat as the starting point of his 'universal' history, for two main reasons. First, it was from the nadir of 216 that the Roman Republic in its Middle phase rose to conquer and by 146 rule the whole known world; that is, much of the central and eastern Mediterranean. Second, although Polybius was careful not to claim that he was the first to attempt to write a universal history, he did claim that he had written the first truly universal history. For, from 217 onwards, the affairs of Italy and Africa had become 'intertwined' with those of Greece and Asia, and that 'intertwining' was coupled with—indeed crucially effected through—Rome's rise to universal domination. But what factor or factors had most enabled Rome so to rise and conquer? Its *politeia*, was Polybius' emphatic answer. We shall return to analyse this conception in some detail, after concluding a brief resume of his extraordinary life and times.

Polybius was born around 200 BCE, perhaps even as early as 210, to Lycortas. Rome's interest in and intervention in mainland Greek affairs went back by then some two to three decades, but the stakes were raised during the Second Punic War by Philip V of Macedon's decision in 215 to ally with Rome's enemy Hannibal of Carthage. By 200 the threat of Hannibal had been expunged, so the Senate, Rome's elected governing body, decided to overthrow Philip, which they achieved through winning the Second Macedonian War, in which the Achaean League of Polybius' father allied itself opportunistically to Rome. In 196, in the person of ex-consul Titus Quinctius Flamininus, Rome—following Hellenistic Greek power-political precedent—proclaimed the 'freedom' of Greece. By which was meant freedom for Greeks from any (other) Greek dynast such as the king of Macedon, but very much less than total freedom from any outside power whatsoever. This was not in any sense an act or even gesture of philhellenism. Actually, Rome took it upon itself to become the arbiter of Greek freedom and within a mere couple of generations to destroy any genuine Greek political freedom utterly, and for good.

Between 195 and 192 Rome and its Achaean League allies next set about over-throwing Nabis, who had ruled Sparta since 207 as a tyrant but called himself king and who, somewhat like Cleomenes III, was causing considerable disruption and nuisance (to major property owners) by his socio-economic interventions elsewhere in the Peloponnese, especially at Argos. The death of Nabis meant also the end of Sparta's control of Laconia and indeed the effective end of old Sparta, both externally (with the loss of all remaining vestiges of independence) and internally (with the end of what remained of the famously Spartan socio-economic and cultural-educational regime). The Achaean League, within which Sparta was forcibly enrolled, was the main immediate gainer, but its influence proved transitory, and nine years later Philopoemen of Megalopolis, the strong man of the League, died without leaving any comparably effective successor. Polybius' later eulogy of Philopoemen was also a kind of memorial of the League itself. In 181, still only twenty or little more, Polybius himself was chosen as an ambassador of the League to the Ptolemaic king, but did not actually visit Alexandria.

In 172 war broke out once more between Rome and Macedon, this time under King Perseus. Again, predictably enough, Rome emerged victorious from this Third Macedonian War, in the course of which Polybius held high office as the Achaean League's Cavalry Commander in 170–169. In retrospect, however, Rome felt that the League's support had been less wholehearted or effective than it ought to have been, and prospectively took the view that the League's continued existence might constitute a threat to its domination of the Greek peninsula south of Macedon. Thus it was that in 167 Polybius found himself included among the 1,000 high-ranking Achaeans forcibly transported as hostages to Rome and Italy. Polybius, however, fell on his feet, in that he was entrusted to the supervision of the Younger Scipio (b. 185) and, being some fifteen to twenty years his senior, became his spiritual mentor. As he had for Philopoemen, Polybius delivered a powerful posthumous eulogy for Scipio. But much water had flowed under several bridges between 167 and Scipio's demise in 129.

Finally, in 150, Polybius was officially permitted to return home to Megalopolis. But was that all there was to it—a simple release? Or was there a covert condition, one that Polybius was quite content to fulfil, namely to act as Rome's agent in what would prove the exceptionally contentious political circumstances of the next quinquennium? At all events, in 149 Rome decided to move to its endgame with Carthage. The Third Punic War broke out, and Carthage was indeed destroyed, as the influential Senator Cato (the Elder) had long preached it should be. And it was not just destroyed as a military-economic power and rival of Rome, but literally: physically it was utterly annihilated, as Olynthus had been by Philip II and Thebes by Alexander. The agent of the enforcement of Rome's inexorable will over Carthage was none other than the Younger Scipio, Polybius' mentee of two decades earlier, and among Scipio's entourage at Carthage to witness its torching and erasing was Polybius himself.

Meanwhile back in old Greece, Rome had defeated Macedon yet again in 147 and this time decided formally to annex the former kingdom and place it under direct rule as yet another overseas province of the expanding Roman Empire. The prospect of such permanent Roman involvement in the Greek peninsula was one of the main exciting causes of another Greek rebellion against Rome, this time in southern Greece by the only apparently tamed Achaean League. Here powerful social and economic as well as political motives were at work; the Achaeans' proclamation of the sort of political goals that Rome abhorred, including the restoration of democracy in some sense, was deemed sufficient to justify the Senate's decision to mete out to southern Greece a version of the punishment accorded to faithless Carthage. Under Lucius Mummius, Rome inflicted on Corinth in 146 a destruction and plundering only marginally less vehement than those dealt out almost simultaneously to Carthage. Polybius, after voyaging west along the coasts of North Africa and southern Portugal, actually managed to return to Greece in time to witness the sack of Corinth.

Macedon in 147 had been made a full Roman province with a governor and garrison under the name and title of Macedonia. Greece south of Macedonia was not given equivalent status in 146, but rather that of a dependent protectorate; full provincial status was not to be imposed until 27 BCE. However, the region was given a new name, Achaea, adding insult to the injury inflicted by dissolving the Achaean League in 145. Who was to play the key role of mediator between Rome and the mainland Greeks in this awkward moment of political transition? The role fell to—or rather was eagerly assumed by—Polybius, who thus crucially helped determine the new subject status of the Peloponnesian cities, including his own Megalopolis.

Polybius had begun to compose his *History* as an exile and hostage in Italy and Rome after 167, intending that to be its terminal date. But in light of the momentous events of 146/5 he decided to continue his massive work that far, even though in his own words those two added decades were a period of 'confusion and upheaval'—an ominous phrase recalling Xenophon's concluding comment in the *Hellenica* upon the state of Greece in 362 BCE. The prolongation, it need hardly be added, also enabled Polybius to give what he considered to be a fitting account of his part in the fashioning of the new, and emphatically not democratic, order.

Nothing subsequently in Polybius' life could possibly equal the thrills and spills of 167–145. In about 140 he travelled to Egypt, Syria, and Cilicia in southwest Turkey. In 133, aged by then 70 or so, he was once again present at the sack of a major enemy city (his enemy now as well as Rome's), Numantia in Spain, thereby putting into practice his historiographical nostrum that the historian must ideally be an eyewitness of historic events. In 129 the death of the Younger Scipio removed Polybius' principal connection to the inner Roman Republican political elite. Within a decade, he himself died, after a fall from a horse.

Of the forty original books of Polybius' *History* only the first five have survived more or less complete, together with most of Book 6, which focuses on Rome's *politeia*. What is left of Books 7 through 40 are just fragments, a polite term for more or less accurate quotations by later writers, few of whom shared either Polybius' historiographical ambitions or his critical intelligence. Of the fragmentary portion the most interesting, historiographically speaking, is Book 12, an exercise in how to write—and how not to write—history. This was directed chiefly against the Sicilian Timaeus of Tauromenium, who was targeted not least for his gall in attempting universal history, but also against Phylarchus of Athens: his crimes were partly formal-stylistic (he indulged in an inappropriately tragic style of history-writing) and partly ideological (he was far too partial towards Sparta for Polybius' Achaean tastes). How then, in Polybius' view, should history be written? One must get the facts, including the facts of impactful speeches, correct and report them accurately—in this, he was heir to Thucydides. But true history properly so called is about causation and causality—in that he was heir ultimately to Herodotus as well as Thucydides, although he engaged more explicitly and philosophically than either with different causal concepts. Like Thucydides again, he believed the historian was in the business of prediction, for the benefit of present and future statesmen. Polybius therefore wrote what he called 'pragmatic' (or 'transactional') history, a history of *praxeis* ('deeds') composed for practical purposes and avoiding mere entertainment. Once more, Thucydides rather than Herodotus was his master here.

The other historiographical quirk of Polybius—besides the patriotic concession noted above—was a firm belief in the efficacy of something he called rather confusingly 'chance' or 'fortune' (*tyche*). The confusion arises partly because Tyche was widely worshipped in Hellenistic Greece as a personified goddess, and in some cities as a patron goddess almost on a par with Athena Polias of Classical Athens. This development reflected the troubled times, in which citizens of Greek *poleis* increasingly felt not only that they were pawns in some larger, inter-dynastic political game being played out over their heads on a regional scale, but also that they were ever less in command of their own personal as well as political destinies. Polybius, however, used *tyche* both to mean chance or fortune in the sense of sheer, random caprice (the Thucydidean usage) and to refer to a higher, overarching Providence—which somehow ordained what had to happen by an inner necessity, human or divine. Hence, for example, he explicitly stated that the rise of Rome was *not* due to mere chance.

To understand Polybius' take on the Roman Middle Republican constitution, all Book 6 is relevant, but the chapters specifically devoted to Rome are 11–18 and 43–57. The key to explaining Rome's survival and rise lay for Polybius, as noted above, in its *politeia*; or rather in Polybius' understanding of the Romans' *politeia*, which was no doubt heavily influenced by the Younger Scipio and his cronies. For it was 'at its best and most perfect form' in c. 216 (the date of the Romans' catastrophic defeat at Cannae). Its perfected excellence was a mixture of elements of monarchy, oligarchy and aristocracy, and ... democracy. The monarchic element was represented by the consuls, although there were two of them at any one time and their power was restricted, at least at home within the city of Rome, by the Senate as well as by the office's collegiality (cf. the Spartan dual kingship). The aristocratic element was the Senate, Senators being deemed 'best' in terms of their wealth as well as their birth. The democratic element was represented by 'the Roman People', *Populus Romanus*—in Greek, the *demos*. The whole was deemed to be 'fairly and suitably ordered', that is, in a state of equilibrium.

The notion of mixture was not in itself original to Polybius. Thucydides had applied an early version of it to the regime of the 5,000 oligarchs at Athens in 411/10. But Thucydides had envisaged it as involving only two elements: the mutually exclusive and antagonistic groups of the few (rich) and the many (poor) citizens, and his mixture is best understood metaphorically as being of the 'pudding' kind. That is, when those two ingredients were combined, they constituted a qualitatively new political entity. Aristotle had drawn likewise on a formally similar pudding version of the mixed constitution, especially in his presentation of his best workable form of polity, which he called *politeia* (Chapter 11). And in this he seems to have been followed by Dicaearchus of Messana in his lost *Tripolitikos*, who like Aristotle looked to Sparta for exemplification. But Polybius' usage is, as we shall see, better understood rather in terms of a 'seesaw' or checks and balances model, and that is certainly how it was taken by the American Founding Fathers when drawing inspiration for their own constitution.

The major interpretative issues are these: first, did Polybius correctly identify the three main constitutional elements or forces at work in the Roman Republican polity, and their mutual relation? Second, even supposing that he did, was the resultant of those forces actually best understood in terms of a more or less harmonious mixture, or was it rather the case that one or other of the three so dominated the others as to give the constitution its characteristic shape and tone? It has been argued that Polybius' take on the Roman *politeia* was original to him, and original because he applied Greek categories of analysis and classification. That may be so, but that does not of itself guarantee either its accuracy or its point. It could equally be argued that Polybius got Rome's constitution seriously wrong precisely because he tried to apply Greek categories to alien Roman institutions. To which I would add that whether he got it right or not, Polybius' motives and influences were personal and ideological as well as disinterestedly intellectual.

The particular focus of our interest must be on the third, supposedly democratic component. That there was an essential popular dimension to Roman Republican self-governance and decision-making there can be no doubt. The Roman Republic, like democratic Athens, represented itself to itself ideologically as anti-tyranny and as naturally opposed especially to any political actors who called themselves or could be tarred with the label of kings. A standard conservative ploy directed against a radical or even just reformist Roman politician, such as Spurius Maelius, was to accuse him of aiming for kingship. That mythological imaginary at least looks popular, even demotic. So too it was officially and formally the Roman People who passed laws, elected officials, and declared war or peace. From 287 BCE on (the start date of the Middle Republic), the Council of the Plebs, representing the overwhelming majority of citizens, could also pass laws binding on all citizens, patricians as well as plebeians, and the fundamental citizen's right of appeal against an official's action was to a People's jury court.

However, against that demotic complexion and ideology of the Roman Republic must be set a whole raft of counter-indications. The short acronymic formula for the Roman Republican state was SPQR (Senatus Populus Que Romanus); 'Senate and Roman People' in that order, not PRSQ, 'Roman People and Senate'. The Senate, which consisted of all current magistrates above the level of quaestor and ex-magistrates in good moral and economic standing (eligibility was based upon a very high property qualification), had effective initiative and control in matters of public finance and foreign policy. The board of ten Tribunes of the Plebs, who were elected only by plebeian voters, were not technically magistrates (and so not Senators), and not at all the functional equivalent of Greek *demagogoi*. After 287, they were typically not radical anti-Senate populist politicians but ambitious plebeians on the first rung of the governmental ladder that would eventually lead, they hoped, to membership of an increasingly conservative and reactionary Senate. Tribunes had a veto on all legislation, but custom and precedent demanded that any legislative proposal be vetted in advance by the Senate, and key Senatorial players could even use one Tribune to veto another Tribune, as was done in an attempt to block the too radical reforms of Tiberius Gracchus in 133. The popular tribunals and law-courts were in practice all staffed by the rich few citizens; they were not People's courts staffed by allotted jurors of generally low economic means and humble social status, as in democratic Athens.

All magistrates and the Tribunes were elected; there was no place for the democratic machinery of the lot in the Roman electoral system. Moreover, voting both in elections to the highest magistracies and in legislation and treaty-making was conducted by group vote; in other words, there was no doctrine or practice in Republican Rome of the democratic one citizen, one vote formula, and the group vote method systematically favoured the rich few. Indeed, the very principle of the assembly that elected the top magistrates (censors, consuls, and praetors) was timocratic—that is, voting eligibility and power depended on one's property qualification, something fundamentally anti-democratic in democratic Greek eyes. Any Roman politicians who entertained some notion of introducing genuinely democratic (Greek) ideas into the Roman Republic's governance—one thinks especially of the Tribune Gaius Gracchus, brother of Tiberius, in 123 and 122 BCE—tended to be bumped off: illegally, of course, although their murders were legitimated retrospectively by a Senate-dominated court. In its foreign relations, it is hugely telling that in its dealings with old Greece, Rome always supported oligarchies, rather as the Spartans had done, and despised the masses and their political ambitions. Rome's foreign policy both before and after Polybius' day systematically favoured the rich few against the poor many in the Greek cities.

In other words, not only does the Greek term *demos* (in any of its senses) not correspond to Latin Populus, but Polybius also rather grossly overestimated the force and power of the Roman Populus—in relation, in particular, to the Senate. For the Roman Republic to qualify as any sort of *demokratia*, in any sense other than that of not-monarchy, there were simply too many checks and balances on the initiative and power of ordinary citizens, and far too much power in the hands of what the first-century BCE Roman historian Sallust called the 'the few potentates'.

Polybius did not, however, examine Rome's *politeia* solely or simply on its own internal political terms. He also compared it to a variety of foreign constitutions, both actual and ideal, always to the advantage of Rome, and in terms that reveal his own anti-democratic prejudices: to Thebes and Athens (6.43–4: neither of those was any good, because there 'the masses take all decisions according to their random impulses'); to Crete (6.46–7), Plato's *Republic* (6.47), Sparta (6.48–50), and Carthage (6.51–2). Such comparisons led Polybius into dwelling more on the superiority of Rome (6.52–6), a position that he summarised at 6.57. Moreover, he applied a further, cultural criterion, judging the 'true form and quality' of all polities on the basis of 'two basic elements', customs and laws (47.1). It was in accordance with this criterion that he opined that 'the sphere in which the Roman commonwealth seems to me to show its superiority most decisively is in that of religious belief', since it is 'superstition which holds the Roman state together'. By that he meant that the Roman governing elite exploited religious awe in order to keep the masses—'always fickle, filled with lawless desires, unreasoning anger and violent passions'—in subjection.

So, the cat is out of the bag: the alleged superiority of Rome's *politeia*, according to Polybius, did not only—or mainly—reside in its superior governmental process. It is therefore telling, too, that Polybius is the earliest writer on record to introduce into political discussion the derogatory term *okhlokratia*—mobocracy, mob rule. Not even Thucydides or Plato had gone so far. Thucydides, it is true, had spoken no less derogatorily of the 'naval crowd or mob' among the Athenian citizen body, and Plato in the *Laws* had made his surrogate Athenian interlocutor sneer at spectator-ocracy—the power of the theatre crowd; not even they, however, had derided Athenian *demokratia* as mere mob rule.

Polybius, in short, grossly misprised and overestimated the popular element in Rome's *politeia*. And a further objection to his mixed constitution analysis may be levelled on the more general ground that no version of mixed constitution theory could offer a plausible analysis or explanation of how the Republic actually operated. That seems to have been the view of Roman historian and leading Senator Tacitus, writing under the Roman imperial system of the early second century CE. In his persona as a historian of his own and earlier post-Republican times he was ostensibly critical of the domination of one man, since it denied to the Senate the freedom that had been its characteristic feature under the old Republic. But had he thought that the Republic had been a mixed constitution, he would surely not have rubbished that notion as he did: as a system more easily praised than realised, and, even if realised, incapable of lasting. Nevertheless, in the longer run Polybius' view did achieve great success. Renaissance and later scholars also saw Rome either as a democracy or as a mixed constitution. But should we agree with them? Or was it rather an aristocratic-oligarchic republic with important popular elements, if more so in ideology than in practice?

The Millar Thesis

From 146 and more especially 133 BCE that Republic was placed, for reasons that lie beyond our concerns here, under increasingly intolerable strain, signalled by one major outbreak of civil war in the 80s, before it collapsed amid another, even greater and more prolonged bout in the 40s and 30s. So unstable indeed was the Late Republic that one distinguished modern analyst refused even to dignify its proceedings with the title of 'politics'. That is surely to go too far at one extreme. But what are we to make of another distinguished modern scholar, who has been conspicuously persistent in taking a line on the Middle and Late Republican constitution almost diametrically the opposite of mine? 'Polybius was right ... the Roman Republic exhibited strongly democratic characteristics, which became more predominant over the last century or more of its existence as a Republic', according to Fergus Millar. And there are others who, without going so far as to claim that the Roman Republic was a democracy in the classical Greek sense of *demokratia*, follow Millar's lead in emphasising much more the democratic aspects of the Republic, since the power of the people (or People) underpinned the political process. It is necessary therefore to re-examine the question from this modern, not only from an ancient, point of view.

If his views may be shortly summarised, Millar has advanced the following four major arguments in favour of his democracy thesis: (i) rules for acquiring and maintaining citizenship status at Rome were inclusive; even ex-slave citizens (if duly manumitted by Roman citizen masters) had the public voting rights as well as private (legal) rights of citizens; (ii) there was no property-qualification for voting—a democratic feature, according to Aristotle in his discussion of the Greek *polis*; moreover, the secret ballot was introduced in the later second century BCE, an advance on typical Greek procedure; (iii) Greek-style democracy or government by mass meeting was at best an exercise in competitive rhetoric, at its worst mere demagoguery—a point criticized by Aristotle, whereas the Roman system of decision-making avoided the latter, and produced master rhetorician Cicero into the bargain; and (iv) the Roman Populus really did possess *potentia* (the most general Latin term for 'power', equivalent to Greek *dunamis*). It took the final decisions on peace and war, it elected to the highest as well as the lowest magistracies, it passed laws.

Against those arguments and claims I would offer the following counter-arguments and counter-claims, which in my submission are both individually and collectively what Protagoras would have called 'knockdown arguments'. Some of them apply no less forcefully to Millar's case than to Polybius' (above).

i.   Rome both was, and importantly was not, a citizen-state in the
full Aristotelian Greek sense of *polis*. True, Roman citizenship was
inclusive and the Romans were generous with it, whereas Greeks
were comparatively mean with theirs, but how many of those tens of
thousands of Roman citizens enrolled on the census lists actually were
in a position to turn up and be present in Rome, even if they wished to,
to hear the arguments, and vote in person, let alone 'know each other',
as Aristotle's view of citizenship required? Size is not everything, but
often it is something, and in this case the Roman *populus* dwarfed the
demos of even the largest Greek *poleis* of antiquity, both in its ever-
increasing absolute size and in its geographical spread. As Aristotle had
famously argued: 'There is a due measure of size for *poleis* as for living
creatures, plants and tools'. His own maximum was set at 10,000.

ii. There was indeed no property qualification for exercising one's vote
at Rome, but individuals' votes did not all count equally, not by a long
chalk. The assembly that elected the highest magistrates was quite
blatantly oligarchic: each of the 193 voting 'centuries' was allocated
one vote, a group vote, but 88 out of the 193 centuries were allocated
to Class I (out of the five property-census groups), and there were
many fewer citizens in each of the richer than in the poorer centuries;
to cap it all, almost ludicrously, to a Greek democrat, all the many
propertyless were crowded into just one century. Besides, bribery and
corruption flourished at both election and legislation times, despite
the series of clearly grossly ineffectual anti-bribery laws that were
passed. Introduction of the secret ballot in the 130s, a practical rather
than ideologically principled measure, seems to have made little or no
difference.

iii. Demagoguery was indeed an occupational and structural hazard
of the Greek 'government by mass meeting' form of democratic
decision-making, but *demagogoi* were a structural feature of the
Athenian democracy, enabling it to function at all. They operated,
moreover, in Assemblies that were held regularly and that themselves
made the binding decisions; whereas at Rome the nearest thing to an
Athenian-style Assembly meeting was a talking-shop (*contio*), which
could be convened (and likewise dissolved) only by a magistrate, and

which itself decided nothing. At Rome there was no decision-taking government by mass meeting. The other main voting assembly was that of the thirty-five tribes—four urban in the city of Rome, the rest rural. This was more or less identical to the Council of the Plebs, which since 287 had had the power to legislate as well as elect the ten annual Tribunes. But there was no regular public debate preceding and informing a vote, and although each tribe (like each century) had one group vote, the distribution of voters and votes did not reflect fairly and proportionately the composition or distribution of voters. Most glaringly, all ex-slave citizens, no matter where they lived, were all automatically crammed into the four urban tribes, thereby effectively minimising or nullifying their objectively increasing numerical weight.

In part precisely because of these built-in inequalities and unfairnesses, a Roman Republican version of demagogues did appear on the scene with increasing frequency from the mid-second century on, and they championed the claims of the Council of the Plebs to be Rome's true governing body. But these politicians were not a structurally organic element of the decision-making process, and they were predictably viewed by the dominant members of the Senatorial elite as a potent threat to their own continued rule—and, by variously illegal means, eliminated: the Gracchi brothers (133, 121 BCE), Saturninus (100), Drusus (91), Sulpicius (88), and Clodius (52), all Tribunes of the Plebs, were all murdered. There developed, moreover, in the city of Rome, as there was not ever at Athens under the democracy, a genuine mob, and the very existence and significant political role of this mob are among the most telling counterarguments against the view that the Roman Republic is in any useful sense to be considered democratic. For the mob was composed of Roman citizens and, thanks to its organised mass violence, it did actually make a difference to the governance of Rome by affecting both appointments to major commands and the passage of laws. The mob owed its existence to social, political, and constitutional factors: social, because the Roman urban poor lived in grindingly horrible conditions; political, because many members of the mob were ex-slave citizens, who (as noted above) had not been granted equality of representation and recognition when admitted to the body politic; and constitutional, because the (Polybian-style) checks and balances were both too many and operated too much against the interests of the poor majority of citizens, both economically and politically.

iv. There was no democracy versus oligarchy split in Roman Republican politics of the last two centuries BCE, but politics did have an ideological content, amply attested in contemporary sources such as Cicero, and tension between the respective interests of the many and the few was fairly constant (Wiseman 2002: 302, cf. 296). It was, as Sallust observed in his monograph on the disaffected noble Catiline's alleged conspiracy (*Bellum Catilinae* 20.7), the 'few potentates' who really ruled in Rome, and they did so through the Senate, which set the terms on which the Roman People participated in politics. The Populus could, at most, decide between rival potentates and programmes, between the self-styled 'optimate' ('best') and 'People's' causes. But they lacked any powers of initiative and especially any regular, legal way of holding the magistrates to account, of making them accountable to the electorate; that was a key, indispensable feature of an ancient Greek democracy, as Herodotus' Otanes had correctly observed (Chapter 6). Above all, perhaps, in Republican Rome there was no equivalent of the People's jury courts through which the *demos* of Athens had crucially exercised its *kratos*.

v. I have left to the end a linguistic trump card. By the first century BCE the standard acceptation of the Greek word *demokratia* was as an internally self-governing republic (see Chapter 14). Yet Cicero, who knew Greek, Greeks, Greek political thought, and the Greek world very well, was strenuously careful in one of his major works of political analysis, the *De re publica*, to avoid using the D-(*demokratia*) word at all—even when what he was referring to was old-style, pre-Hellenistic Greek democracy. Instead, he used either 'liber populus' ('free People') or just 'populus'; where he wanted to refer to a state in which the people are all-powerful, he used 'civitas popularis'. Cicero himself, of course, was no demagogue—heaven forfend. Despite making some gestures in the early stages of his career towards seeking greater accountability of the ruling elite, he became a staunch devotee and advocate of the 'optimate' and not the *popularis* cause in the prolonged and vicious civil war that brought the Republic crashing down. It is telling that no Roman Thucydides stepped forward to describe or analyse this classic case of *stasis*.

In conclusion: it is no easy matter to classify and evaluate the nature and quality of the Roman Republican system in and after Polybius' day. It was sui generis. But Millar's pro-democratic interpretation seems to me equally as unbalanced and misguided as Polybius' mixed constitution view. At all events, in due course and after much civil bloodshed the Republic was overthrown and replaced, as we shall see in the next chapter, by a de facto autocracy—whatever smokescreen of official Republicanism might be assiduously ejected by Rome's first emperor, Augustus.

16.

DEMOCRACY DENIED

The Roman and Early Byzantine Empires

A PASSAGE OF THE JEWISH historian Josephus' *Jewish Antiquities*, composed towards the end of the first century CE, is perhaps the earliest text by an author writing in Greek to refer to the Roman Republic as a *demokratia*. The passage exemplifies the earlier of the two main phases in the devaluation of the word's original force: from dictatorship of the proletariat, as it were (see the prologue), to its being 'used for almost any type of constitutional, republican government, however oligarchic'. That earlier phase of usage was the subject of the previous two chapters. The later phase is the subject of this. From the mid-second century CE onwards, towards the end of what is sometimes known as the Antonine age (96–180), the term *demokratia* could actually be applied to the Roman Empire. By the latter is meant the political regime that did not only succeed the Republic, but was also starkly different from it, if not opposite to it.

To appreciate the full force of that calamitous verbal collapse, we must first try to limn the essence of this novel mode of rule. The Empire was not a narrowly Roman but a genuinely universal government: a system the ramifications and reverberations of which are still with us today. The bimillennium of the death of its founder, Augustus, was marked in 2014. Arguably, his adoptive father Julius Caesar was Rome's first emperor *manqué*. But there is still room for argument over just how monarchic he intended to become, had he not been assassinated by Senators in the Senate House on the Ides (the 15th) of March, 44 BCE. The rule of Augustus, however, was unquestionably monarchic, for all that he went to enormous lengths to disguise it with the forms of a Republican commonwealth. In his own very long lifetime (63 BCE—CE 14) he was mostly known as Caesar, and it is one of history's little ironies that 'Caesar' modulated into 'Kaiser' and 'Czar', since Augustus wished be thought of as anything but that. Ironic too that his adoptive father had once punned—because a relative bore the surname Rex—that he was not 'Rex' ('king') but 'Caesar': it was precisely because he was thought to be aiming at becoming a king that he was assassinated where and by whom he was.

That fatal error Augustus strove more or less subtly to avoid, employing several different ruses. Whenever he attended the Senate, for example, he wore a breastplate. He made a huge song and dance about being the saviour of the old Republic and restorer of the old, Republican order, and emphatically not the instigator of any newfangled, un- or anti-Republican regime—as an acknowledged monarchy, however constitutional or mild, would inevitably have been seen to be. Although he willingly adopted the title 'Imperator', from which our 'emperor' is directly derived, by it Augustus intended to signal that he was the holder of Republican *imperium* (power), especially military, a power legitimately conferred by the Senate and Roman People only on two ranks of magistrates: in ascending order—praetors and consuls. Augustus chose to rule the Roman world not as an emperor but as a kind of Republican super-consul, both within and outside *Urbs Roma*, the capital city of Rome.

The other most important constituency for his overall rule besides the army were the plebeian citizen masses of Rome, the *plebs Romana*. So important indeed were they that in 23 BCE Augustus assumed, for life, a kind of power from which his status as a patrician ought legally to have debarred him: the power of a tribune of the plebs. This provided him with certain symbolic benefits, partly mythological, partly mundanely pragmatic, including personal inviolability. To the plebs of Rome he doled out lavishly what the later satirist Juvenal contemptuously labelled 'bread and circuses': a subsidised grain dole and fancy chariot races. But Augustus' largesse was far from limited to them. Besides the occasional cash donatives, he also permanently improved the basic housing of the poor, and backed that up with a rudimentary fire brigade and police force. However, as a later imperial functionary tellingly observed, grain and entertainments did not only feed and amuse the Roman people, they also controlled (literally 'held') them; or, to put it in another way, they 'were far from a welfare program'.

More directly relevant to our basically constitutional concerns, Augustus positively flaunted his tribunician power by including the year of its conferral among his titles when documenting his official, legal acts. This was picked up far afield among his subjects: for example, in 9/8 BCE a romanized Gaulish prince made a dedication, on an arch erected near the summit of the Mt Cénis pass, to Augustus 'in his fifteenth year of tribunician power'. Moreover, by its judicious conferral on others, Augustus marked out his closest colleagues and intended imperial successors, from Agrippa (d. 11 BCE) to Tiberius (r. CE 14–37). The disabused Senatorial historian Tacitus, looking back a century later from the reigns of Trajan (98–117) and Hadrian (117–138), referred shrewdly to Augustus' tribunician power as the 'the title given to the topmost summit' of his power: that is, it was a largely—but crucially—symbolic name, as opposed to the truly effective legal basis of his supremacy, which was his *imperium* in its various military and non-military manifestations.

The major contemporary witness to and propagandist for Augustus' 'deeds done' or 'accomplishments' (*res gestae*), apart from the documents themselves, is his autobiographical text named exactly that. The *Res Gestae* was originally inscribed towards the end of his long life on bronze tablets stationed prominently outside the Mausoleum that he had had built for himself and members of his household at Rome as early as 28 BCE. The original bronze tablets have, not surprisingly, disappeared long since. But Augustus also caused copies of the text to be distributed outside Rome, and these were intended presumably for public inscription throughout the empire. Yet as it happens, just four copies of the original have survived, all from the Greek-speaking Eastern half of the Empire: one small fragment from the province of Asia, the other three from the province of Galatia, the most complete of which—a bilingual Greek-Latin version—is preserved in a temple dedicated to 'Rome and Augustus' at Ancyra (today's Ankara).

Throughout the document Augustus, although he was sole commander-in-chief of the army and also its paymaster, keeps very quiet indeed about the actual basis of his sovereign power, his unique *imperium*—ultimately the power of life and death, usable both in Rome (consular) and outside (proconsular *imperium*, and superior to anyone else's in case of a clash). Instead, he puts on a show of which the 'mad men' of Madison Avenue would not have been ashamed, emphasizing that it was he who had brought an end to civil war, he who had ushered in the blessings of peace, and he who had in some sense restored the Republic. But in what sense, precisely? Like the apt pupil schooled in Roman rhetoric that he was, he leaves the climax for the very end of the document, in the two key chapters 34 and 35.

To interpret these properly, we would be well advised to compare and contrast the much later biography of Augustus, written in the reign of Hadrian, by Suetonius, who as an imperial bureaucratic functionary had access to original documents no longer extant. Suetonius as it were took Augustus' life and career for his doctoral research subject and, distanced in both time and political space, could afford to draw back the veil of Augustan propaganda to reveal the less cosy truth beneath. In the *Res Gestae* Augustus paints himself as the ultimate patriot and constitutional conservative, who as merely the 'first citizen' (Princeps) had in 28 BCE transferred the Republic from his power (*potestas*) to the *arbitrium* (see below) of the SPQR, had never held any greater power than any colleague in any one office, and had been granted in 2 BCE the honorific title of 'father of the fatherland' by decree of the Senate.

The meaning of *potestas* is unambiguous enough, since Augustus did in 28 BCE hold supreme de facto power both in Rome and throughout the empire, although the legal basis of that power was deeply questionable in strictly Republican terms. But what was meant by the weasel word *arbitrium*? Its literal sense is something like 'free disposition' and thus the power of decision, and presumably the wily Augustus aimed to suggest thereby that the SPQR formula once again meant what it had done before Julius Caesar's assumption of the title of Dictator Perpetuus in 44, and the ensuing civil wars of 43 to 31 BCE, had rendered it null and void. But actually, as Suetonius acutely observed, Augustus had merely 'thought about' genuinely restoring the Republic in some authentically traditional sense, on two occasions—but had decided against doing so both times. Moreover, towards the end of the biography Suetonius blows the lid off the whole Augustan fabrication, exposing the real source of power in this supposedly 'restored' Republic. For this in fact lay not with the Roman People nor even the reconstituted Senate but with Augustus and his chancery, which was managed not by Senators but by his own personally appointed and directly responsible staff, chiefly his own ex-slave freedmen. These powerbrokers, merely first-generation Roman citizens, were as far removed from being Senators as was remotely thinkable then, and yet it was they who knew, managed, and controlled all the relevant administrative details of imperial commands and finances.

To that brutal exposure Suetonius adds a crucial detail that brings out the full implication of the grant to Augustus of the title of 'father of the fatherland' in 2 BCE, with which Augustus climaxes his *Res Gestae*. As the colourless Senatorial stooge who formally proposed the award obsequiously stated, it was to be conferred for the benefit not only or merely of Augustus personally but also and more importantly for the benefit of his entire 'house'. In other words, by 2 BCE Augustus had contrived, after a process of trial and error going back at least to the construction of his Mausoleum in 28 BCE, to induce or rather compel the Senate officially to recognise his own family as a kind of royal family: a dynasty at the very heart of the Roman state, ruling over a *res publica* that was in fact no longer 'free'. It was no mere coincidence therefore that the family-dynastic Temple of Mars Ultor (Mars, god of war, honoured as the 'avenger' of Julius Caesar's murder) was publicly dedicated in that very same year; it had been commissioned by Augustus to celebrate his ancestral lineage stretching all the way back to Venus. What unhappily for Augustus exposed the blatant contradiction between his proclamation of a 'restored Republic' and his de facto sovereign rule over it was the 'succession problem'.

Strictly, legally, there could be no successor in a non-monarchical political regime: for there to be a succession problem, there has to be a position of supreme power to succeed to. But actually without an imperial successor to Augustus Rome was all too likely to dissolve once more into civil war. Augustus sought to resolve this problem first in 23 BCE (by a dynastic marriage of his daughter Julia to his nephew Marcellus), but Marcellus soon after died—and thus became the first occupant of the family Mausoleum. He tackled it again, much more firmly, in 17 BCE. Not only did Augustus then adopt as his sons Gaius and Lucius, his two grandsons from Julia's second dynastic marriage, to Agrippa, but this year was trumpeted as the inauguration of a new era, and hymned as such in Horace's specially commissioned poem. But it proved to be a false dawn. Gaius and Lucius also died prematurely, and so finally, grudgingly, and unsatisfactorily, Augustus solved his and Rome's problem in CE 4 by the odd expedient of adopting not only his stepson Tiberius (son of Livia) but also jointly with him the only surviving son of Julia and Agrippa, the less than fully sane Agrippa Postumus. Perhaps the joint adoption was a pale gesture towards

Republican collegiality, but, if so, it was never going to be workable, and one of the first acts of Tiberius' (in fact) reign was the murder of his adopted brother.

Taking Augustus' career since 28 BCE all in all, I believe that Edward Gibbon was quite correct to label Augustus a 'subtle tyrant'. In reaching that judgment Gibbon was hugely influenced by his reading of the imperial historian Tacitus, whose *Histories* and *Annals* between them originally covered the years CE 14 to 96. His sly take on Augustus' tribunician power has already been noticed, but no less acute was his imagined scenario of Augustus' state funeral right at the start of the *Annals* (1.9–10). As they looked upon the pyre of the late emperor, who was about to be formally deified, allegedly 'prudent' men argued the toss for and against the merits and demerits of his reign. Tacitus places the negative arguments second, for emphasis, and they are expressed both at greater length and more memorably than the positive arguments. Above all, his prudent critics rip holes in Augustus' façade, exposing his ruthless opportunism and ambition and dwelling on the many deaths that he had directly or indirectly caused and about which Augustus himself was so carefully silent in the *Res Gestae*. One of these negative criticisms is particularly telling: he had brought peace to the Roman world, certainly, after the horrendous bloodletting of the civil wars; the peace he brought, however, was itself also 'bloody'. The civil wars might have ended in 31 BCE, but foreign wars had not, nor had political assassinations.

Tacitus of course wrote with 20:20 hindsight. Five decades and eight reigns after that of Augustus, the true legal nature of the so-called Principate was finally enshrined in permanent public record in the Law on the *Imperium* of Vespasian. For after performing sterling military service for the Empire in among other places Britannia (made into a province by Claudius in CE 43), Titus Flavius Vespasianus, to give him his full name, was chosen by his loyal troops as Emperor of Rome. But he had to fight for the position. More precisely, he triumphed, as the fourth and last in the Year of the Four Emperors (CE 69), in the civil wars following upon the suicide of Emperor Nero in CE 68. Vespasian reigned until 79, and he managed to found a dynasty of sorts known as Flavian, after his middle name. But of Vespasian's two sons and successors, Titus (79–81) and Domitian (81–96), the latter proved a tyrant, and his reign gave to the Principate as a whole the bad name that Tacitus has made immortal.

The civil wars of 68–69 had given the Principate a nasty jolt. A public gesture reconfirming the imperial power was required. The law passed on the *Imperium* of Vespasian spells out—as Augustus could not or would not have done—what had in fact been the case since 27 BCE: 'He shall have the power ... to transact and do whatever things divine, human, public and private he deems to serve the advantage and the overriding interest of the state—just as Augustus, Tiberius and Claudius had'. Tacitus was not fooled. Vespasian was no less of an absolutist ruler than his son Domitian, regardless of any cloak of supposed legality. Even Tacitus, however, was not immune from mythmaking. He himself became consul in the year after Domitian's assassination, probably already so nominated by none other than Domitian. To cover his tracks, he blithely heralded the short and not particularly sweet reign of the elderly Senator Nerva (96–98) as the dawn of yet another golden era: the first ever uniting of the Principate with 'freedom', as a Roman Senator understood that. Suetonius, who wrote his biographical series of *Twelve Caesars* after Tacitus, began it with Julius Caesar and ended, like Tacitus, with Domitian. But unlike Tacitus, Suetonius avoided the overoptimistic, post-Domitianic gloss. 'Freedom' was by now nothing but a name and shadow.

A contemporary of the brilliant Latin writers Tacitus and Suetonius was the equally brilliant and even more polymathic Greek intellectual Plutarch (Ploutarkhos, or ruler in wealth, in Greek), who lived from about 46 to 120. His Latin name, since he was also a Roman citizen, was Lucius Mestrius Plutarchus, and he bestrode the Greek and the Roman intellectual worlds alike. He is best known today, thanks partly to Shakespeare, as the writer of biographies, including most famously a series of 'parallel lives' of 'great' Greeks and Romans. In the preface to his pairing of Alexander the Great with Julius Caesar he took time out to emphasise that he was not a historian, as that term was by then understood in the Hellenistic-Roman world: 'I write lives, not histories'. His principal intellectual preoccupation was a philosophically informed moral didacticism, and that programmatic declaration exempted him from having to try to do anything like justice to the political and military achievements of his subjects. Although he was ferociously learned and read absolutely everything available, including 'big' narrative histories, what really interested him were anecdotes that revealed something special or unique about the chosen subject's moral character.

It is possible, of course, to read the *Lives* against the grain, as it were, in order to elicit information not otherwise preserved about the political deeds of, say,

Pericles (Chapter 7). But more rewarding for our immediate purposes is an essay of c. CE 100, the title of which may be translated alternatively as *Precepts for Statecraft* or *Advice on Public Life*. This belongs to the other main branch of Plutarch's voluminous corpus, his so-called *Moralia* (Moral Essays). It is written as a warning to ambitious young Greek would-be politicians, instructing them as to how they should best comport themselves in the political conditions of the high Roman imperial era. The message that comes across loud and clear is that politics, as it had once been understood in a free Greek *polis* before the conquests of Alexander the Great and of Rome, was now a dead letter. The word *polis* was indeed still in current use, but any *polis* that found itself within a province of the mainly Greek-speaking eastern Roman empire was—not to put a fine point on it—actually under the heel (Plutarch says military 'boot') of a proconsul: that is, of a Senatorial governor such as Tacitus, who rose to occupy the top provincial post of governor of Asia with the rank of proconsul ('instead of/functionally equivalent in power to a consul'). An expert on the period and region has sagely commented: 'The concreteness of his advice ... shows Plutarch to be concerned with real issues. An abundance of material, literary and documentary, shows the aptness of his advice to his own time'.

Plutarch is generally reckoned an ornament of the literary movement known as the Second Sophistic. (The First had been the era of the fifth- to fourth-century BCE Sophists, including the democrat Protagoras, against whom Plato had railed; see Chapter 6.) Adepts of this movement liked to peddle their wares in the form of public display lectures and declamations, or essays that they circulated among like-minded would-be intellectuals. Conspicuous among these was the Greek orator and propagandist Aelius Aristeides (117–c.180), who graced the Antonine age. The age's outstanding literary output has been well summarised as follows: 'The philosopher Epictetus. The historians Arrian and Appian. The Greek novels of Longus and Achilles Tatius. The travel narrative of Pausanias. The satirist Lucian. *A number of performing sophists, including Aelius Aristides, Favorinus and Polemo.* The Christian authors Justin and Clement. The philosophical meditations of the emperor Marcus Aurelius. The medical writings of Galen.'

Aelius came from Mysia (in northwest Turkey today) and developed an extremely intimate connection with the Roman imperial court, initially through sharing a tutor with future emperor Marcus Aurelius. There was no danger therefore that he might take an objective, or even an accurately comparativist, view of the system of governance of the Roman empire. But in c. 143, during the reign of Emperor Antoninus Pius, he surpassed even himself. Declaiming a rhetoric-infested paean, *To Rome* (Rome was not only a place but also a goddess), he roundly declared: 'There has been established throughout the world alike a democracy—under one man, namely the best ruler and controller *(kosmetes)*' (sec. 60). The choice of the word *kosmetes* was a nice conceit, since it captured both the notion of Rome as a universal, global empire and the original Greek sense of *kosmos* as meaning 'order'. (*Kosmetes* was also the title of the officials supervising the Athenian *ephebeia*: Chapter 12.) Yet even Aelius should surely have been ashamed at the flagrant logical contradiction he committed by his identification of a by then blatant *monarchia* as a *demokratia*.

Worse was yet to come. The essence of Greek *demokratia* in its original construction had been to define a polity of equal and free citizens. Citizenship, especially democratic citizenship, was jealously prized and guarded by Greeks. In contrast to the *poleis* of the Archaic and Classical Greek worlds, the Romans were, as noted (Chapter 15), relatively generous in the extension of their version of citizenship to people beyond the bounds of the City of Rome and of Italy; Emperor Claudius had made the point rather acerbically in 47/8, when advocating the admission of Gauls to the Senate. But in CE 212 the Romans went for broke. Under the terms of a decree promulgated by Emperor Caracalla, known legally as the *Constitutio Antoniniana*, all free-born people throughout Roman empire were declared by fiat to be of citizen status. At first sight this would appear to be a massively liberal, if not egalitarian move, a sure mark of generosity and political inclusiveness. Actually, this token gesture was the clearest possible indication of how politically insignificant the mere possession of Roman citizenship had by then become. What mattered was how rich or not a citizen was, and in any case the imperial measure was motivated not by lofty ideals of status enhancement or validation but by mundane considerations of improved tax collection. Once upon a time, in the early first century BCE, Italians, including Italians possessing relatively privileged Latin rights, had thought it worth fighting and dying to wrest from their Roman overlords the gift of full Roman citizenship, with its then very real political and economic advantages. Three centuries later, that thought would not have occurred to the huge numbers of new—but all equally powerless—Roman citizens, who had acquired their citizen status merely by the wave of an imperial hand.

In 324 Emperor and Christian convert Constantine founded a New Rome, at Constantinople, formerly known as Byzantium. The dominant language of Constantinople and the Byzantine empire, formerly the east Roman Empire, was Greek, but the Byzantines (as we call them) were proud to refer to themselves as Romans. It remains to trace the ultimate downwards trajectory of democracy in imperial Roman and early Byzantine discourse and ideology, that is, the degeneration of both the institution and the word 'democracy' beyond even the seeming nadir reached by Aelius Aristides. In 325/6 Eusebius, Bishop of Caesarea and competent documentary historian of early post-Constantinian Christianity, composed a panegyric on Constantine. In this work of piety he contrasted monarchy (*mon-archia*), which for him was a good thing, with the dreaded *poly-archia*, or 'rule of the Many': the latter, since it fails to make or duly recognise proper discriminations of rank, descends inevitably and inexorably into 'anarchy and civil strife'. Finally, ultimately, in the reign of Byzantine Emperor Justinian (527–565), the author of a *Chronographia* (c. 550) used and abused the term *demokratia* to mean riot, mob violence, insurrection: that is, exactly what it could not have meant in the fifth- to fourth-century BCE Greek world of its origins.

Justinian is justly remembered and celebrated for the codification of Roman jurisprudence that he set in train under the overall supervision of Tribonian. Within that codification is to be found a maxim of the late second- to early third-century Roman jurist Ulpian, which rather nicely encapsulates the message of this rather doleful chapter in democracy's life: 'What the Princeps (Emperor) decides has the full force of (a) Law'. The contrast with the way in which these things were managed in, say, the Athenian democracy, could hardly have been starker, at least from a pro-democratic point of view. There the *demos* had exercised its barely fettered *kratos* in the legal as in all other spheres: that is, they ruled themselves and they directly exercised *kratos* by taking democratic, simple-majority decisions in Assembly and Lawcourts, and by implementing them no less democratically. *Sic transit gloria mundi antiqui.*

17.

DEMOCRACY ECLIPSED

Late Antiquity, the European Middle Ages, and the Renaissance

---

TWO GENERAL OBSERVATIONS MUST preface any account of the life of democracy in the long, post-Antique, mediaeval twilight. First, after Aelius Aristeides' paradoxical praise of Imperial Rome as a *demokratia* in the mid-second century (Chapter 16), there stretches until as late as the seventeenth century a black hole of silence in the post-Roman imperial West on the subject of democracy as a potentially viable political system. Democracy in the sense of popular power was, we might say, on a life-support machine. Not even that much can be said for the post-Antique Byzantine Empire, the successor to the Roman Empire in the East. For the Byzantines, *demokratia* continued to carry the negative charge of political unrest, even riot, that it had been debited with in the sixth century (Chapter 16), although in the later centuries of Byzantium signs have been detected of an evolution from autocracy and outright aristocracy towards a lifestyle that included some populist elements.

Second, a combination of rigidly fixed, hierarchical status relations, including feudal tenures and Catholic-Orthodox Christianity, hardly favoured popular or indeed any politics, properly so called, let alone popular influence or power. In all three Synoptic Gospels of the Christian New Testament, Jesus had allegedly instructed his flock to 'render unto Caesar that which is Caesar's and unto God that which is God's', thereby both drawing a sharp distinction between the spiritual and the secular-political and encouraging an unquestioning passivity in face of both earthly and heavenly powers. (Saint) Paul, for some the true founder of Christianity, went even further by confounding the spiritual and the political domains in his implied injunction that 'the powers that be are ordained of God'.

Nevertheless, during these centuries prior to Renaissance humanism the nascent concept of the state and a notion of sovereignty resting on a general will or popular consent begin to provide a way back in for some idea of proto-democracy, although it would be democracy of a very non-ancient Greek kind.

Post-Antique Mediaeval West

Between c. 1000 and 1500 there flourished in northern Italy (Lombardy, Tuscany, Veneto) political entities broadly categorized as city-states that included an active *popolo* and enjoyed an intense urban history, although in size they were not much bigger than early twentieth-century Oxford. From the eleventh century on there are even hints, or anticipations, of popular politics; indeed, some speak of a 'period of the *popolo*'. This rebound has been ascribed to three factors: some persistent residue of the old Roman citizenship, in the sense of civility or civic consciousness rather than any active or passive notion of citizenship; ambitious thuggery on the part of landed feudal chieftains; and expansive trade connections. By 1200 these communities had gelled into instances of the *stato-città*, in which the members of a merchant class were the prime political movers, and the non-elite classes participated more directly and substantially in the political process, such as it was. But by 'politics' should be understood no more than the existence of peaceful assemblies and workable compromises with the people reached by the city-states' ruling councils (*commune*, led by a *podestà*); and these alternated with bitter intransigence and lawlessness, which led to the gradual triumph of despotism (*signoria*). To repeat, citizenship properly so labelled no longer existed, not even in an etiolated, post-*Constitutio Antoniniana* sense (Chapter 16).

However, the very state-form of the city-state did in itself constitute an explicit challenge to dominant Christian notions of god-given hereditary monarchy, and city-republics did on occasion seriously attempt to implement some notion of popular sovereignty. Thus from time to time an election for the top executive job threw up a successful popular candidate, for example, Simone Boccanegra ('Black Mouth'), a plebeian pirate who was elected doge of Genoa in 1339 (d. 1363); later on, such rare events could be an inspiration to the enemies of tyranny and absolutism. Yet to talk of democracy would be grossly anachronistic. The word existed in Latin transliteration from c. 1250 as a borrowing from the work of translated Aristotle, 'the master of those who know', as Dante famously called him; and it turned up in discussions of the 'mixed constitution'. But it was used more significantly in approval of Aristotle's generally negative take on the versions of fourth-century BCE *demokratia* that he knew and did not love.

As has been remarked aphoristically of the emergence of city-states of widely differing type in widely differing periods and places, 'there is no parallel in the age of the *poleis* to the role of bishops and clergy in medieval Italy'. For Thomas Aquinas (*On Princely Government*, c. 1270), characteristically, democracy was a case of a poor majority tyrannising over a rich minority (Shades of the Old Oligarch; Chapter 6). But the divinely ordained power of king and church was meeting with ever more potent, ever more secular challenges. Around 1300 the Dominican Ptolemy of Lucca composed his *de Regimine Principum* ('On the Government of Rulers'), which paid especial respect to Aristotle, whom he read in part through the lens of (his understanding of) the Roman Republic. Though by no means a republican, he saw virtue in the Republic's abhorrence of absolutist, dictatorial kingship. No more of a republican, but far more innovative, was his younger contemporary Marsilius of Padua. His advocacy of a concept of popular consent within a broadly secular framework of political analysis presaged a great future.

Outside Italy these long, democracy-free centuries should not be allowed to pass without honourable mention of two remarkable documents produced within these British islands: first, the Magna Carta (Great Charter) of 1215 and its later reimpressions, and, second, the Declaration of Arbroath issued in 1320. Both involved centrally a king (of England and Scotland respectively), his barons, and a pope (of Rome), and both are more important in the longer purview than in terms of their more immediate effects. Both are indeed quite regularly invoked even today as essential parts of the story, or staging posts along the journey, of democracy. But it has to be said that not even the most moderate or modest supporter of ancient Greek *demokratia* in any Aristotelian sense would have been at all keen to rely in court on either document, and that the connection of either with democracy as that is currently (post-1850, say) understood is also distinctly tenuous, if not actually factitious.

The Magna Carta that was very reluctantly sworn by King John with his barons in 1215 and reissued, substantially revised, in 1225 under Henry III, owes its fame in part to the fact of its unique survival; not dissimilar charters were issued in Germany, Sicily, and France in the thirteenth and early fourteenth centuries, but these have not survived. In even larger part, it owes its *éclat* to its echoings in the United States Bill of Rights. Yet it is in fact both textually and contextually problematic, and in order properly to appreciate it, subsequent mythical overlays and readaptations for quite other purposes than those originally intended have to be stripped away. It was, for example, cited anachronistically by Sir Edward Coke (died 1634) as enshrining England's ancient constitution and the English people's immemorial right to freedom, claims which were not unconnected to the great political upheaval that followed in the 1640s (Chapter 18). Three of its sixty-three original clauses are still legally valid, of which the most famous articulates the principle of *habeas corpus*: 'No free man [in the somewhat free translation offered by the British Library] shall be seized or imprisoned, or stripped of his rights or possessions, or outlawed or exiled ... nor will we [the royal 'we'] proceed with force against him ... except by the lawful judgement of his equals or by the law of the land'. But this statement of principle was 'buried deep in Magna Carta' and 'was given no particular prominence in 1215'. The real legacy of the document as a whole is that it established the crucial principle that the law was a power in its own right to which the king, like his people, was subject and thus limited the king's authority. True enough—as a statement of principle; but laws are general and have to be interpreted, as Aristotle insisted; and the ancient Greeks, especially the democrats among them, were well aware that is only when the people exercises its political power in and through the lawcourts that it may be said truly to rule.

A similar limitation of regal absolute power was claimed by the eight earls and thirty-one barons of Scotland who collectively put their name to a document addressed, in Latin, to Pope John XXII. Sometimes called a Declaration of Independence, it was in practical terms a response to the excommunication first of Robert the Bruce, then of the people of Scotland as a whole. What the signatories declared on the sixth day of April 1320 at the monastery of Arbroath rested chiefly on their refusal 'for so long as there shall but one hundred of us remain alive' to 'consent to subject ourselves to the dominion of the English'. They were thus imploring one sovereign to throw his weight into the scales against another. Again, a principle was at stake, but it was not even a strictly popular, let alone a democratic one.

The Renaissance

The fourteenth- to sixteenth-century European Renaissance (as Jules Michelet and Jacob Burckhardt, both nineteenth-century historians, respectively baptized and framed it) was in significant part a rediscovery, recuperation, or reinvention of Graeco-Roman Antiquity, including its pagan gods and goddesses. The discovery of metal movable-type printing was quickly dedicated to the cause, famously for instance by Aldus Manutius in Venice from the end of the fifteenth century. But the Renaissance movement was more especially a rediscovery of ancient Rome than of ancient Greece, and that applies particularly in the political sphere. An early, literally graphic example is Ambrogio Lorenzetti's fresco cycle of 1338–1339 commissioned by the Council of Nine that governed the Tuscan city-state of Siena. Originally regarded as an allegory on the virtues of peace set against the vices of war, it is now usually referred to as the Allegory of Good and Bad Government.

By 1500 Latin was no longer anyone's mother tongue, but it was the scholarly lingua franca, and that could not but reinforce the attention devoted to Roman rather than ancient Greek history and politics. Renaissance and later scholars who saw Rome as a democracy were concerned with the issue of sovereignty; that is, they recognized that 'the People' formally possessed it, or alternatively, if they saw it as a mixed constitution, that was because they were concerned rather with governance in practice, or how much power 'the People' did actually wield. Anything much like the democratic *polis* of the fifth or fourth centuries BCE had to wait to be recuperated until the eighteenth century, and only rather late in that century at that.

At the end of the fifteenth century, and also in Tuscany, a remarkable linguistic revolution may be detected in Florence: 'Republic' (used as a paraphrase for 'democracy') came to be understood in the sense of popular government. This linguistic turn is exemplified most strongly by the writings of Machiavelli. Besides his far better known *Il Principe* of 1513, which was a tract for enlightened autocracy at best, in 1519 Machiavelli also published *Discourses* on Livy's First Decade; that is, the opening ten books of his *Ab urbe condita* ('From the Foundation of the City of Rome'), which describe the period of the kings

(753–509 BCE) and the early Republican era. Machiavelli's choice of author and polity speaks worlds: nothing Greek or democratic (in a Greek sense) to worry about there. Moreover, although he was not uninterested in the ancient Greek world, especially through his reading of Polybius, and praises Sparta *en passant* for the longevity and alleged stability of its constitution, Machiavelli was pre-occupied less with constitutional niceties than with the thoroughly aristocratic notion of *virtù* and with civic greatness, which he associated with liberty. One scholar has spoken optimistically of 'Machiavellian democracy', but he also comments more soberly and accurately that 'Machiavelli suggests that the best one can hope for from a republic … or democracy is an alternation between rule and being ruled among citizens'. However, for an ancient Greek political commentator, that would be a defining condition of a *polis*, not specifically of any version of a democratic one.

'Civic humanism' of the type illuminated by Machiavelli flourished intellectually in a broadly Roman Republican—not Greek—tradition. For instance, the great sixteenth-century Dutch scholar Joost Lips (Justus Lipsius) wrote his *Politica*, a tract on 'civil doctrine', in six books (1589), in the tradition of Roman Stoicism. He was a great admirer of the sceptical, disabused, non-religious and ostensibly 'republican' (anti-Principate) Tacitus, as also was Machiavelli. Indeed, when Machiavelli was placed on the Papal Index of censored works, coded references to Tacitus could be substituted for mentions of Machiavelli, an intellectual tendency so prevalent that it has come to be dignified with the sobriquet of 'tacitism'. Such reappraisal of religious and secular thinking through the examination of the literary bases of theology and philosophy counts as 'humanism'. Its 'civic' dimension took the form of a revival of the old idea of Roman citizens' rights and privileges, but it would be a long time before that notion would issue eventually in the French Revolutionary Declaration of the Rights of Man—and Citizen (Chapter 18).

∽ V ∽

18.

DEMOCRACY REVIVED

England in the Seventeenth Century and France in the Late Eighteenth and Early Nineteenth Centuries

---

England in the Seventeenth Century

After a long sleep, democracy—as an idea, and in name, but not yet substance—began to reawaken in the seventeenth century in England. This was a century full of surprises, indeed of revolution in the eyes of some, the English Revolution. At any rate, it was certainly an epoch of massive political upheaval. Not inappropriately, the English Civil War period from 1642 was dubbed the Days of Shaking, and no institutions were more shaken up than those of the Stuart monarchy and the talking-shop of Parliament. Indeed, the concussive phrase could be applied quite aptly to the whole period from the regicide of 1649 to the so-called Glorious Revolution of 1688 and on to the accession of William III of Orange to the restored throne in 1689.

The Civil Wars of the 1640s had a naval as well as a land-based military dimension, but it is the members of Oliver Cromwell's New Model Army who, as we shall see, set the pace politically. They were at the heart of an ideological debate over what form of constitution or political regime should replace and supersede hereditary monarchy, and more particularly about what role in that new political order should be allocated to or assumed by the People (broadly so labelled). In polarised times ideologues lined up in numbers on either side of the republican-monarchist divide. There was a tradition of classical humanism going back to the late Renaissance in mainland Europe (Chapter 17) on which contenders could draw. But the debates that took place within the New Model Army, with Cromwell himself in the chair, in St Mary's Church Putney (by the banks of the river Thames) in October and November 1647 were something quite new, and indeed unrepeated. It is one of the unanticipated blessings of the anti-elite political tradition of this country that a tachygraphic record of the debates survived in an Oxford college archive to be transcribed and published only in the nineteenth century.

The Putney Debates are also known as the Levellers' Debates, since that was the derogatory tag attached (by their opponents) to those in favour both of a republic and of some widening of the franchise. Their leader John Lilburne understandably preferred Agitators. Whatever exactly they stood for, they stood well to the left of the mainstream of the New Model Army, though also to the right of Gerrard Winstanley's Diggers, who far more radically favoured the

FIGURE 18.1
Oliver Cromwell
Oliver Cromwell (1599–1658), the man who would be king, was a republican of a sort, but vehemently opposed the radical proto-democratic republicanism of the English Levellers, over whose Putney Debates (1647) he presided. © RMN-Grand Palais/ Art Resource, NY

abolition of all property qualifications for political entitlement and participation. Colonel Thomas Rainborough's declaration during the Debates that 'the poorest he hath a life to live, as the greatest he' has rung out down the ages as the most succinct and powerful clarion call to egalitarianism; for his pains, he was murdered in 1648. But the spirit of his declaration was echoed in a speech delivered, on the scaffold, by Colonel Richard Rumbold in 1685: 'I am sure ... none comes into the World with a Saddle on his back, neither any Booted and Spurred to ride him'. The Levellers were not yet nor in any precise sense democrats, but the Putney Debates did prompt talk by James Harrington of democracy (a word brought into English from French in the sixteenth century).

Harrington's *Oceana* of 1656 was dedicated to Cromwell, by then firmly established as Lord Protector since 1653, and constituted a call to him to become the new (Spartan) Lycurgus—not, be it noted, the Athenian proto-democratic Solon, let alone the democratic Cleisthenes. For Harrington was a 'firm believer in the leadership of the nobility and gentry', although he also approved the 'Antient Prudence' that had created mixed states such as that of Lycurgus' Sparta and more recently the republic of Venice. Cromwell himself ostensibly preferred liberty to 'tyranny', which he identified with the temporarily extinguished rule of the House of Stuart, a popish Church, and a legal system biased towards the rich. But the pull of regal ideology—as exemplified in *Eikon Basilike* of 1649, a plea for the 'divine right' of kings attributed posthumously to Charles I—was still so strong that in 1657 Cromwell agonised over whether or not to take the title 'king'. Another who harked back to antiquity for precedent and inspiration was the journalist Marchamont Nedham, but his *The Excellency of a Free State* (also 1656) more traditionally looked rather to Rome than to Greece for republican precedent.

Far more unconventionally republican was the poet and thinker who served as Cromwell's Latin Secretary under the post-regal Commonwealth: one John Milton. T. B. Macaulay powerfully observed in his 1826 *Essay on Milton* that 'he lived at one of the most memorable eras in the history of mankind, at the very crisis of the conflict between liberty and despotism, reason and prejudice'. A fervent defender both of Parliament versus the Crown and of the 1649 regicide, Milton responded fiercely to *Eikon Basilike*. But although he did quote from Euripides' *Suppliant Women* in the original Greek on the title page of his 1644 tract in favour of press freedom, he titled the tract *Areopagitica*, which drew attention to the least democratic of all the Athenian democracy's institutions (Chapter 12). And his post-Restoration manifesto *The Ready and Easy Way to Establish a Free Commonwealth* (1666) was prompted more by his familiarity with Roman classical authors, especially the historian Sallust, a client of Julius Caesar, than by any sympathy for Euripides' democratic Athenian republic.

No less fierce and in their way impressive were the opponents of the abortive republican experiment, and none more so than Thomas Hobbes (1588–1679). His first published work (1628) was a translation of Thucydides' *History*, the first done into English directly from the Greek rather than via a Latin translation. One of his last was an autobiography composed in Latin hexameter verse (1672), in which he made bold to claim that it was Thucydides who had 'taught him how superior was the rule of one wise man' to that of the ignorant, undisciplined mass. Yet despite—or because of—his knowledge of the ancient languages, he averred in his major work of political philosophy, *Leviathan* (1651), that 'there never was any thing so deerly bought' as the 'learning of the Greek and Latine tongues': for by reading these texts 'men from their childhood have gotten a habit (under a false shew of Liberty) of favouring tumults, and of licentious controlling the actions of their soveraigns; and again of controlling these controllers, with the effusion of so much blood'.

By such men Hobbes meant of course Milton and his despised, prorepublican kind. It is therefore somewhat ironic that some modern scholars have detected proto-democratic leanings even in Hobbes, or at any rate argued that in another of his works, the *De Cive* ('On the Citizen', 1642; English translation, 1651), Hobbes envisaged the state as having a democratic foundation in popular consent, which had—if only for practical reasons—to be overridden in favour of monarchic autocracy. But most of us prefer still to regard Hobbes as firmly authoritarian, indeed the first to put forward the needs of a State sovereign quite so vigorously, and as allotting to such a sovereign a central, commanding role for which 'the People' were deemed by him to be totally unqualified. The Athenian democratic practice of ostracism predictably drew his ire.

The Restoration of 1660 had terminated England's brief flirtation with a kind of republicanism, but the civil war continued on the ideological plane, if with diminishing vigour. The Glorious Revolution of 1688—actually not a revolution at all, let alone an obviously glorious one—did arguably establish a new kind of modern, that is, participatory state and thereby paved the way indirectly for parliamentary democracy. The principal ideologue of this formative era was John Locke, whose *Two Treatises of Civil Government* (1690) emphasised individual rights to life, liberty, and property, and the necessity of a voluntary social contract. He is often now seen as the intellectual godfather of liberal, parliamentary democracy—on both sides of the Atlantic. It is, however, still open to claim that the *Treatises* do not in fact look forward in that way, since the consent postulated by their author was envisaged as passive, not active, and therefore that any such idea of a public political contract, social or otherwise, must inevitably have been one-sided, loaded in favour of the State rather than the People.

At all events, it would probably be uncontroversial to claim that only a very few reputable thinkers or practical politicians have, since Locke, wished to advocate anything remotely resembling ancient Greek *demokratia* of the full-blooded, dictatorship-of-the-proletariat type in preference to some sort of liberal democracy, so far as the regular governmental practice of more or less normal modern states is concerned (see epilogue). Nevertheless, it remains to be seen how between 1690 and 1850 ancient Greece and especially ancient Athens did somehow figure in the fashioning of the modern Western, Euro-American political world: not least in bequeathing to us, rather paradoxically, the very word 'democracy' (see further the following section, and Chapters 19 and 20).

France in the Late Eighteenth and Early Nineteenth Centuries

The history of the revival or renascence of democracy as a desirably practical idea is also the history of the American and French Revolutions (properly so called): a major moment in democracy's life. The historical figure who links the two most directly was, however, neither American nor French. Thomas Paine, hailing from Thetford in East Anglia, directly supported first the US revolution (becoming a friend of founding father Thomas Jefferson), and then the French Revolution. But Paine, as we shall see (Chapter 20), was no democrat in any ancient Greek sense.

Chronologically, the American Revolution anticipated the French by over a decade, but the ideological inspiration that was common to both was in origin

FIGURE 18.2
Maximilien Robespierre
Maximilien Robespierre (1758–1794) encapsulated the indeterminate fervour at the heart of the French
Revolution; not afraid to lop the heads of the ancien regime both metaphorically and literally,
he was afraid of the newfangled democracy that revolutionaries further on the left than he were starting
to advocate. © Scala/ Art Resource, NY

mainly French or francophone, and I begin my discussion of both revolutions
with the French Enlightenment ('les Lumières') and its Euro-American impact.
In the remainder of this chapter and in the next, the major underlying focus
of our interest will be on the extent to which engagement with ancient Greek
ideas of democracy played any substantial role in enabling or furthering those
great political Revolutions.

The Enlightenment as a whole, in whatever country of Europe or part of
America, was far more preoccupied or engaged with Rome (both of the
Republic and of the Principate) than it was with ancient Greece. I begin with
the great Montesquieu, Charles-Louis de Secondat, Baron Montesquieu, who in
a relatively youthful work of 1734 had written on the 'grandeur and decadence'
of Rome—that is, the Roman Republic. In his major work of political theory,
De l'esprit des lois ('Of the Spirit of the Laws', 1748), Montesquieu used the word
'democracy', acknowledging its ancient Greek derivation. However—and not

surprisingly, since the gulfs in practice and scholarship were simply too great—he did not have a good historical understanding of Athenian democracy. At any rate, when he spoke approvingly of the 'good democracies' of Athens and Rome, it was the timocratic-aristocratic Athens of Solon rather than the truly democratic Athens of Pericles that he had in mind. Nor, arguably, did he properly understand the peculiar (in both senses) British 'constitution'. But from the perspective of his legacy and impact, what matters is that he identified as its key point of distinction and driving motor the checks and balances implied by the supposed separation of powers (legislative, executive, and judicial) of the post-1688 governmental settlement, not whether or not he correctly so identified them. That discovery is to be distinguished both from the two main versions of the ancient mixed constitution theory (i.e., 'pudding', 'seesaw'; Chapter 15) and from modern mixed constitution theorising. It was to bear spectacular if indirect fruit in the post-Revolutionary constitution of the United States of America.

Far more sympathetic to something resembling an ancient Greek notion of popular governance was the Swiss-born Jean-Jacques Rousseau. His posing of the question of human equality, and his trumpeting of the sovereign importance to public decision-making of something he called the General Will, were both somehow proto-democratic. Yet in the great eighteenth-century quarrel between the respective merits of Athens and Sparta as models to be imitated, he firmly preferred the supposedly self-denying, communally oriented Sparta to the luxuriously self-indulgent democratic Athens. This preference may have something to do with his otherwise puzzling notion that citizens of his ideal state must be forced to be free.

In some ways Rousseau's comrade in arms, in others his sworn enemy, François-Marie Arouet, alias Voltaire, launched a parallel intellectual crusade both against the entrenched ideological power of the Catholic Church—under the slogan 'écrasez l'infâme!' ('crush the infamous!')—and against the temporal power of the absolutist French monarchy. Strongly in favour of individual liberty of thought and, contra Rousseau, firmly on the side of 'luxury', Voltaire not unnaturally opted for Athens against Sparta, though for cultural, not political, reasons. It has to be added, however, that, unlike Montesquieu and other French Enlightenment luminaries, Voltaire was not much interested in looking to antiquity for political inspiration at all. In the 'quarrel of the Ancients and the Moderns' (sometimes referred to as 'the battle of the books'), he lined up squarely on the side of the Moderns. So too did the thinker to whose writings the origins of Greek republicanism can be traced, Iosipos Moisiodax: no invoking of an ancient Greek republican paradigm for him.

Two radical thinkers who were very interested in antiquity and in the ancient Greeks, however, were the Marquis de Condorcet and Dutch philosopher, geographer, and diplomat Cornelius de Pauw, author of *Recherches philosophiques sur les Grecs*. Condorcet approved Voltaire's attitude to religion and the Roman Catholic Church but did not share his distaste for the ancients. His radical political views drew the ire of John Adams, the second president of the United States. De Pauw was almost alone in preferring Athens politically, as well as culturally, to other ancient Greek states, especially to Sparta, and in demeaning both Montesquieu, because he didn't know ancient Greek, and Rousseau, whom he dismissed as an 'inconsequent' thinker.

However, exciting though Montesquieu, Voltaire, Rousseau, and De Pauw are, they pale in comparison to Denis Diderot and the openly atheistic Baron d'Holbach (organiser of a Parisian literary salon c. 1750–1780), who are known not least for their association with the multi-authored *Encyclopédie, ou Dictionnaire raisonné des Sciences, des Arts et des Métiers* (1751–1772). At least, those four pale into relative insignificance if Diderot and d'Holbach really do represent what has been provocatively dubbed the 'democratic Enlightenment'. The entry for 'démocratie' in the *Encyclopédie* (vol. V, 1754, 816–18), unfortunately, does nothing to bolster that claim: its author, the Chevalier de Jaucourt, did not consider democracy to be either a commodious or a stable form of government, or one that advantaged great states, and he defined it rather minimally as 'one of the simple forms of government in which the people as a body has the sovereignty'.

But is there more to be said for the claim that it was a certain elevated set of ideas traceable ultimately to Baruch Spinoza—democracy, religious toleration, human rights, and social, racial, and sexual equality—that drove the vast and complicated upheaval known compendiously as the French Revolution? The thesis seems to be vulnerable on both empirical and theoretical grounds. Yet it does have the merit of drawing attention to the important roles played by Camille Desmoulins together with Georges Jacques Danton, and by Maximilien Robespierre together with Louis-Antoine de Saint-Just—practical revolutionaries who, though initially forming just the minority left wing and divided amongst themselves, did nevertheless briefly dominate France at the height of the Revolution in the winter of 1791–1792. All were inspired by Rousseau, and they looked back, some more than others, to Greece as well as to Rome for revolutionary inspiration. For example, a February 1794 Report of the Committee of Public Safety on 'Principles of Political Morality' linked the promotion of active, participatory citizenship with democracy itself, claiming 'democratic or republican: these two words are synonymous'. But, as is too well known, the Revolution devoured its own children.

First, Danton and Desmoulins were executed at the behest of Robespierre; then Robespierre himself, accused of tyranny in 1794, was executed. The left-wing struggle was carried on by the splendidly named Gracchus Babeuf and his 1796 Conspiracy of the Equals: though his forename is Roman, he attempted to introduce what could be made to look like, and conceivably was intended to be, genuine, Greek-style political-civic equality. This notion, however, was found too threatening even by his left-wing comrades, since Greek democracy's major sin (according to its ancient as to its modern critics) was precisely that of treating unequals equally. In any case, all movement towards civic-political equality, whether on an ancient or a modern model, was soon terminated by the rise to autocratic power of Napoleon Bonaparte. His bewildered contempt for the magnificent history painting of the Battle of Thermopylae accomplished in c. 1814 by the neoclassicist Jacques-Louis David, his chief court painter, is a powerful commentary on Napoleon's conception both of the classical tradition and of his place in world history. The emperor simply could not understand why David had lavished so much time and effort on depicting so heroically a bunch of losers such as the Spartan king Leonidas and his doomed 300.

In one of the most elegant short studies of the changing meanings and modes of democracy, John Dunn has pertinently asked: 'Why ... has the word democracy changed so sharply in meaning from the days of Babeuf to those of Tony Blair?' One key part of the answer is to be found in a lecture titled 'Of the Liberty of the Ancients compared to that of the Moderns' delivered in Paris in 1819 by the Swiss liberal and pro-Revolution thinker and writer Benjamin Constant. Like Montesquieu, Constant was far from getting all his facts about the ancient Athenian democracy right, and, like many then and since, he took Athens, virtually his only comparandum, to stand in for 'ancient'. But his strong preference for what he took to be the modern understanding of liberty, privatised and bourgeois, over the ancient Athenian, that is public-political, notion was widely shared in its day. Indeed, in retrospect it may be seen to have anticipated somewhat Isaiah Berlin's distinction of 'two concepts' of liberty: the negative (freedom from) and the positive (freedom to). The hollowing out of democracy today, to which I shall return in the epilogue, is directly connected to the privatisation and individualising of the notion of liberty.

I end with two thinkers who, although of a very different stamp, both nicely represent this ever-growing distance between antiquity and modernity in the leading political thought of continental Europe. C. F. Volney in 1791 prophetically published his *The Ruins. A Survey of the Revolutions of Empires*; as an early globalist, he was dead set against what he saw as the particularism of the Greek city-states. He was also one of the first to give 'revolution' its new meaning of political, including socio-economic, transformation—a much more extensive and richer sense therefore than can be attributed to Aristotle's *metabole* (Chapter 2).

Finally, Karl Marx. He was classically educated; indeed, he obtained the degree of doctor of philosophy for a short thesis comparing the philosophical ideas of the atomist Democritus and Epicurus. His voluminous writings, both journalistic and scientific, are littered with references to Classical authors (he called Aristotle a 'giant thinker', but his favourite was Aeschylus) or allusions to Classical antiquity. In his *18th Brumaire of Louis Napoleon* (1857), for example, he memorably wrote that the French revolution had dressed itself up alternately as the Roman Republic (trumpeting the slogan of 'freedom', bringing death to a monarch and monarchy) and the Roman Empire (Napoleon seen as a rerun of first emperor Augustus). But that Marx's imagery and reference are automatically Roman is telling by itself. Even more so is the fact that unlike his British counterparts and indeed his German fellow countrymen, he nowhere couches an appeal for democracy in terms of appeal to its ancient Greek origins.

For Marx, the defining fact of chattel slavery by itself ruled the ancient Greek citizen-states out of consideration as potential political models. In the by then post-revolutionary United States, however, democracy and slavery were not yet seen as mutually incompatible, let alone as mutually contradictory, as we shall see in the next chapter.

19.

DEMOCRACY REINVENTED

The United States in the Late Eighteenth and Early Nineteenth Centuries and Tocqueville's America

---

The United States

It has been contended by an American scholar that to the US Founders, and to the French aristocrats Montesquieu and Alexis de Tocqueville, the intellectual heritage of ancient Greece was as important as, or even more important than, that of ancient Rome. Actually, few of the US Founders knew well, let alone were decisively influenced by, ancient Greek history or historians and political thinkers. At least, not in any positive way. What little they did know—mainly from Thucydides (as read by Hobbes, Chapter 18) and Plutarch (Chapter 16)—confirmed their instinctive or learned preference for Roman Republican 'order'. And this was a preference, moreover, thanks to their reading of the ubiquitous 'Tully' (Cicero), for an order of a Middle Republican rather than a Late Republican sort (Chapter 15). This also explains, for example, why Washington, DC, is blessed with a Capitol Hill and the US constitution with a Senate, and not with an Acropolis or Boule.

Among the leading ideologues of the American Revolution were the three authors of the *Federalist Papers*: James Madison, Alexander Hamilton, and John Jay. Madison's *Federalist* 10 (1787), following on Hamilton's no. 9, delivered a broadside against what he was pleased to deride as 'faction'. Adopting an almost early Byzantine notion of ancient Greek direct democracy as 'riot' and

FIGURE 19.1
Thomas Jefferson
The third president of the United States, and a learned classicist, Thomas Jefferson (1743–1826) was the chief author of the Declaration of Independence, but he was able to reconcile his advocacy of liberty with his own continuing slave ownership and, like almost all the Founding Fathers, had little time for ancient Greek-style direct democracy. © Gianni Dagli Orti / The Art Archive at Art Resource, NY

mob rule by the ignorant and fickle over their betters, and employing a classically Roman rhetorical trope, Madison opined that even 'had every Athenian citizen been a Socrates, every Athenian assembly would still have been a mob'. The practical inference for him, so far as the future of American governance was concerned, was that 'the people in their collective capacity' must be rigorously excluded from any active or direct share in it. Popular sovereignty might have lip service paid to it, as a theoretical abstraction, but it should go no further than that towards practical realisation. It would be very interesting to know what 'ordinary' Founders—those who fought for the Revolution especially between 1774 and 1776—thought about such elitist views, but as usual the thoughts of the common people are not reported reliably, if at all.

The US Founders were especially keen on John Locke's treatment of property ownership as a right (cf. Chapter 18). Hence Thomas Jefferson's famous reference in the Declaration of Independence that he largely composed to the 'unalienable rights' to 'life, liberty and the pursuit of happiness'. The last of those rights was understood as inseparable from the ownership of real property, which—contradictorily, one might have thought—did not exclude property in humans, in which the Virginian Jefferson himself generously indulged. Moreover, these rights were severally and collectively interpreted as trumping any version of the ideal of human equality. Jefferson's favourite ancient historian, not altogether surprisingly for a dedicated opponent of the allegedly tyrannical George III, was Tacitus—a critic, as he read him, of the absolutist monarchy of the Roman Principate, but of course no democrat (Chapter 16).

Yet at least the ancient Greek-derived word 'democratic' was put back on the political agenda, if in a profoundly non- or even anti-ancient Greek sense. This was demonstrated most vividly in 1791, when Jefferson in combination with Madison made bold to found a new political party and to call it the Democratic-Republican Party. (I well remember my sense of surprise when I first learned this fact, as the distinction and indeed opposition of a Democratic party and a Republican party had been drummed into my conscious and subconscious mind from the moment I became at all aware of American politics.) Of course, the nature, functions, and manifestoes of those parties have shifted, sometimes violently, over the more than two centuries since then, and there is now a quite widespread sense abroad that because of their limits and failures they have outlived their usefulness. But the main point to emphasise here is that, not just organisationally but ideologically too, parties as such are antithetical to any ancient Greek notion of citizenship: that is, citizenship in the active, participatory sense, enjoying both the legal and the pragmatic capacity to exercise an automatically prescribed share in ruling and in passing judgment. The modern party has several actual or potential functions in a modern political system: it may hold a group of people together as a distinct part of a larger and irreducibly divided configuration that it helps to define; it may have a quasi-military capacity for deliberate action or intervention, and an ability to win over dominant (though never complete) portions of a larger body of opinion. But the modern political party also flies in the face of the ancient, individualistic if not voluntarist, conception of democratic entitlement, empowerment, and participatory rule.

The foundation and formation of the Democratic Party in something like its modern incarnation are credited either to the seventh president, Andrew

Jackson, or to his successor, Martin van Buren, or to both. But it is salutary to recall that when the United States suffered its shocking bout of civil war in the 1860s, the Democrats were on the side of conservatism, fighting to retain slavery as a legal mode of human exploitation, against Abraham Lincoln's emancipatory Republicans. But in that, at any rate, they were more ancient than modern: ancient Greek democrats too had defended the institution of slavery, insofar as they thought it needed defending or even thinking about at all. Indeed, ancient (chattel) slavery and ancient Greek democracy could be said to be joined at the hip, inasmuch as a democrat's ideological commitment to freedom was premised on his freedom from legal servitude, and to equality on his being considered equal only to his (male) citizen peers, not to his society's more numerous unfree members, who were, legally and politically speaking, un-persons.

Tocqueville's America

One of the earliest positive uses of the word 'democracy' (in its French form) headlines a two-volume work by a declassed French aristocrat, Alexis de Tocqueville (born Paris 1805, died Cannes 1859); his crowded curriculum vitae included experience of and reflection upon the revolution of 1848, and service in 1849 as foreign minister to Louis Bonaparte, the future Napoleon III (and subject of Marx's *Eighteenth Brumaire*; Chapter 18). Tocqueville's *Democracy in America* (1835–1840) was based on the nine-month journey he undertook in 1831 and 1832 in the company of Gustave de Beaumont. Their task was to study and report home on the US penal system; among many other challenging adventures, they witnessed chattel slavery in Baltimore and were shipwrecked on the Ohio River. But the journey's principal outcome was this landmark publication, a unique book both in the field of political commentary and in the history of modern America. It has been extensively studied in anglophone scholarship, and translated into English more than once. It fully deserves reinvestigation and reappraisal in a life of democracy.

Tocqueville was notoriously slippery on what exactly he meant by democracy, understanding it loosely as comporting above all 'the largest possible amount of liberty accorded to each citizen, rich or poor, powerful or humble', and in that sense an 'equal liberty'. For by (political) equality he meant the absence of aristocratic hereditary political rights, an absence that he himself approved because, unlike many of his fellow aristocrat contemporaries, he did not equate it with anarchy and mob rule. His reflective text was intended as a kind of 'American lessons for French Republicans' manual. Significant chapter titles include 'On what tempers the tyranny of the majority in the United States', 'How, in the United States, religion knows how to make use of democratic instincts', and 'Equality naturally gives men the taste for free institutions'. But as a manual it was, as we shall shortly see, rather deeply flawed.

Tocqueville paid due attention to the character and spirit of the American people, that is, to what Aristotle might have referred to as the *bios* or *psyche* dimension of the American *politeia*. For example, he argued that the US revolutionaries, unlike his compatriots, had made the spirit of religion cohere with their spirit of liberty. Ever an acute critic of privilege, Tocqueville welcomed the fact that US society was more open than France's, and he praised its associational life ('civil society') for acting as a buffer to protect the liberty of individuals from the coercive instinct of the State. Conversely, and correlatively, he argued that self-government was a condition of (moral, individual) self-development, while at the same time he rightly emphasised the degree to which *embourgeoisement* had already occurred. For instance, he wrote that 'violent political passions have little hold on men who have so attached their whole soul to the pursuit of [individual, personal] well-being'; shades of Benjamin Constant. Yet he was also enough of a child of the Rousseauian strain of French revolutionary thought (Chapter 18) to believe that individualism had its limits and must not be pursued at the cost of neglecting the value of community. Aristotle would have approved Tocqueville's disapprobation of 'extreme' economic equalisation, but even he might well have found too extreme the Frenchman's profound lack of sympathy for the unemployed. Finally, because Tocqueville was very hostile to the centralisation of power, he was also inimical to the nascent socialism or social democracy that, as we shall see (Chapter 20), may be traced back to the writings of the radical Englishman Thomas Paine.

Tocqueville has been criticised sharply for omitting to discuss the US legislative Congress and even more sharply for not properly 'getting' America. Yet undeniably it was largely thanks to his work that 'democracy', the word, had come to stay in current American political parlance. In 1863, on the Civil War battlefield of Gettysburg in Pennsylvania, President Abraham Lincoln would refer back unforcedly if anachronistically to the Declaration of Independence and classify democracy unforgettably as 'government of the people by the people for the people', a form of popular self-rule. But actually America's post-revolutionary experience of democracy had been contradictory. On the one hand, the persistence of slavery made it only partial and reactionary, nullifying any claims to be pursuing let alone assuring genuine equality of persons (let alone any other kinds of equality). On the other hand, the absence of a monarchy absolved Americans from the laboriously self-defeating task of having to dream up such an oxymoron as 'constitutional monarchy', as was required in the home of the so-called Mother of Parliaments.

Which is a reminder that although political development in the United States in the nineteenth century roughly shadows that in Britain—consider only the reform acts of 1832 and 1867, in parallel with the foundation of Andrew Jackson's Democratic Party in the 1830s and the victory of the Northern states in the Civil War of the 1860s—massive differences between the two countries were also glaringly apparent. For my next and concluding chapter, therefore, I shall return to English or rather British versions of democracy, from Thomas Paine to John Stuart Mill. As we shall see, the English or British path to democracy was very different from either the French or the American.

20.

DEMOCRACY TAMED

Nineteenth-Century Great Britain

IN THE UNITED KINGDOM of Great Britain the leading intellectual and political opponent of the French Revolution—though not, a little surprisingly, of the American Revolution—was the Dublin-born Anglo-Irishman Edmund Burke (1729–1797). In the privately expressed view of his fellow parliamentarian and fellow member of Samuel Johnson's Literary Club, Edward Gibbon, Burke was 'the most eloquent and rational madman that I ever knew'. Burke placed his eloquence long term in the defence of the principles of representative government, as opposed to government by delegated elected officials; his 1774 *Speech to the Electors of Bristol at the Conclusion of the Poll* had made that plain quite early on in his career. But as to representative democracy, Burke shared pretty much the same three basic objections that had been voiced against democracy in its original, direct Greek form. First, 'the people'— meaning non-elite, non-aristocratic persons—lacked the requisite intelligence and knowledge to be capable of exercising proper governance. Second, common people—unlike, *ex hypothesi*, members of the social-political elite—were congenitally incapable of resisting the passions that were all too easily and dangerously aroused by demagogues, and such passions were likely to be directed against established traditions and institutions, in particular those of conventional religion. Third (shades of both Xenophon and Plato), democracy was for him intrinsically a form of collective, majoritarian tyranny—wielded heavy-handedly against minorities whose views were deemed unpopular.

FIGURE. 20.1
Thomas Paine
Thomas Paine (1737–1809) a man of humble English origins, uniquely played leading roles, theoretical
as well as practical, in both the American and the French Revolutions. A convinced republican, he was
as firmly opposed to direct democracy as he was to monarchical tyranny, and no less fervently in favour
of representative government. © The Art Archives at Art Resource, NY

It was against Burke's *Reflections on the Revolution in France* (1790) that
Thomas Paine penned in 1791 his *Rights of Man*, an appropriately eloquent
defence of not only liberal but also representative democracy. He completed
his three-pronged programme for radical political reform—*Common Sense*
had been published in 1776—with *The Age of Reason*, a religion-focused tract
published in three parts (1794, 1795, 1807). Or rather it was an *anti*-religion
tract, subtitled *An Investigation of True and Fabulous Theology*. This was a
source for nineteenth-century free thought that kept on giving. As Edward
Thompson brilliantly commented, Paine 'had taken the polite periods of the
comfortable Unitarian ministers and the scepticism of Gibbon, translated them
into literal-minded English, and thrown them to the groundlings. He ridiculed
the authority of the Bible with arguments which the collier or country girl
could understand'. It was not of course necessary to be an atheist or freethinker
to be a good democrat, but, if the goal was to open politics to the hitherto

disenfranchised working man and woman in an inclusively egalitarian way, then Paine's nostrums offered a viable if not painless programme.

By contending that all citizens could and should be protected by the State against the predictable hazards of poverty and insecurity, Paine arguably became, together with the French Marquis de Condorcet, a plausible if distant founding father of social democracy—the socialised (sometimes also socialist) version of liberal democracy. But he was no democrat in any ancient Greek sense. Unarguably, the kind of democracy he believed in and advocated was of the representative, not direct, variety. Against Paine, in a friendly written exchange of 1791, the French revolutionary Emmanuel-Joseph Sieyès (1748–1836) pertinently observed that it wasn't and couldn't possibly be democracy that he was promoting, since the people would be unable to speak or act except through their representatives. He himself, like Paine, was all for representative government, but, unlike Paine, wished to distinguish in theory and on principle between a representative regime and a republic—of which latter form he too was equally fervently an advocate.

Paine himself, however, never stood for office and so missed the chance or the necessity of attempting to translate his political ideas into mundane parliamentary practice. A younger contemporary and compatriot of his, George Grote (1794–1871), did just that, and a great deal more besides. He is the principal subject, if not hero, of this final chapter in our life of democracy. Grote was educated in Classics at Sevenoaks and Charterhouse schools, but did not go on to university. Instead, he helped to found one: the University of London, initially just University College, in 1826. He came from a banking family, and worked for a while in the family bank, but between 1832 and 1841 he served as an elected Member of Parliament (MP) at Westminster, where he joined a tendency sometimes known as the Philosophical Radicals.

These were momentous times: the first Reform Act was passed on his watch in 1832, and extended the franchise to an appreciable degree. From the 1830s to the 1850s the movement for a People's Charter—calling for manhood suffrage, pay for MPs, and secret ballots—gathered and then lost a head of steam under the leadership of William Jones. In 1839 Welsh Chartists, including Jones, actually led an armed uprising against Newport that resulted in more than twenty deaths. But the Chartists were ahead of their time, even if they made some impression upon Karl Marx and his *Communist Manifesto* of 1848. By that time, however, and clearly with a sense of relief, Grote had withdrawn from what Edward Gibbon, a historian-parliamentarian predecessor, had called a 'school of civil prudence', and taken up once again his bookish historical studies. For his *History of Greece*, eventually published in twelve volumes (1846–1856), had been begun as early 1822, when he was not yet thirty.

To place the *History* in the wider context of British historiography of ancient Greece, Grote's not altogether distinguished predecessors included John Gillies, Oliver Goldsmith, William Mitford (below), E. Bulwer Lytton, and, most seriously, Connop Thirlwall. Grote was a pioneer of ancient historiography in purely technical terms; he set new standards not least by his respect for the law of evidence. In his own day this prompted a furious riposte from one Richard Shilleto: in a thirty-page pamphlet titled *Thucydides or Grote* (published in London in 1851) he accused Grote of the grossest hubris in setting himself up as an authority above even Thucydides. This in turn provoked a more measured response, not from Grote himself but from his brother John.

However, Grote was also, and from our standpoint most importantly, a pioneer in the re-evaluation of ancient Athens as a democracy. Not least in this respect, Grote's *History* was a more than satisfactory rejoinder to William Mitford's four-volume Tory version of ancient Greek history (1796–1820). Grote, for example, did not shrink from defending the institution of ostracism that had attracted such ire from Aristotle onwards. He also spoke up in defence of the Athenians' treatment of their leaders. As a specialist in ancient philosophy, he devoted a whole long chapter (67) to a defence of the Sophists against their principal critic (or calumniator), Plato; this was also an integral part of his very nineteenth-century linkage of democracy with intellectual progress, to which he allied also a defence of the necessity of rhetoric as a means to enable ordinary people to make up their minds and thereby give their genuine consent to political decisions.

Chapter 67 of the *History*, moreover, follows immediately after Grote's description of the death in 404 BCE of Alcibiades, one of the two most prominent Athenians—the other being Plato's relative Critias—whom as youths Socrates could allegedly have corrupted (Chapter 10). And it is placed immediately before the chapter (68) that is devoted precisely to 'Sokrates'. Ever keen to defend the Athenian People against charges of corruption, Grote ends that chapter with a series of extenuations of the Athenians' guilty verdict and death sentence on Socrates in 399. Socrates himself, in the acidulous judgment of Grote the radical-liberal, pro-democratic historian, 'contributed quite as much to the outcome as all three accusers united'! In this regard, unusually, Grote's view clashed strongly with that of Thirlwall, who had sided with Socrates against the Sophists.

Some of those defences are, in the light of subsequent scholarship and reflection, more persuasive than others. But although Grote did more than anyone to rehabilitate the ancient Athenian democracy, he did so as a historian, and not as an advocate of a return to Athenian-style governance. Like Paine, but even more like his friend and disciple John Stuart Mill (1806–1873), Grote believed in representative, not direct democracy. Grote's *History* appeared in instalments over a ten-year period and at once attracted fierce criticism. Equally fiercely, Mill leaped to Grote's defence, both intellectually and politically, in a telling series of reviews published in the *Edinburgh Review*. For example, he wrote: 'The Athenian Many, of whose irritability and suspicion we hear so much, are rather to be accused of too easy and good-natured a confidence, when we reflect that they had living in the midst of them the very men who, on the first show of an opportunity, were ready to compass the subversion of the democracy'. This was in reference to the so-called Thirty Tyrants, who reigned with terror from 404 to 403 (Chapter 9), but the comment could be applied equally to the briefer but not much less terroristic regime of the Four Hundred in 411.

Mill himself not only approved Grote's take on the ancient Athenian democracy but, unlike his mentor, went back to ancient Athenian democracy to help him formulate certain aspects of his own theory of democratic government. Thus was unwittingly created what has been dubbed the 'myth' of ancient Athens—as a model for democracy today (see further in the epilogue). Yet actually Mill (like Tocqueville and Burke) greatly feared what he envisaged as the tyranny of the unenlightened, ignorant, fickle majority, and he was therefore, like Grote, much keener on representative than direct democracy. Indeed, so much keener was he that in *Representative Government* (1861) he elaborated a theory of what, and how, parliamentary representatives—as opposed to delegates—should represent. That work further developed the notions of 'liberal' democracy that he had expressed in his 1859 essay *On Liberty*: liberty of thought and discussion, limits set to the authority of society over the individual, and promotion of individuality. That essay was the proximate ancestor of Isaiah Berlin's theories of negative and positive liberty (Chapter 18).

For well over a century Mill's version of democracy—Greek-inflected but not Greek-infected, if I may so put it—prevailed, as the only viable model on offer within the context and increasingly globalised presence of liberal, representative, parliamentary democracy. Or, as Winston Churchill famously put it in the House of Commons on 11 November 1947 (Armistice Day):

> Many forms of Government have been tried, and will be tried in this world of sin and woe. No one pretends that democracy is perfect or all-wise. Indeed it has been said that democracy is the worst form of Government except for all those other forms that have been tried from time to time.

Events of our own day, however, have served to undermine—that is place a time bomb under—even that rather carefully guarded formulation, as we shall see in the epilogue.

EPILOGUE

Democracy Now: Retrospect and Prospects

I CONCLUDE THIS EXPLORATORY FORAY into the life of democracy with a brief consideration of the prospects for real-world democracy, in whatever sense. I do so from the viewpoint of the relevance of ancient democracy and democratic politics to modern, and on the disabused, get-real understanding that 'politics is the business of how we decide as a society what our priorities are and then set about achieving them'. There are many unanswered, possibly unanswerable questions here, but it is also such a vital topic for our age. We live under this system, democracy, even though paradoxically those who founded it in the late eighteenth and early nineteenth centuries were adamant that it was not democracy in any ancient sense and were just as adamant that—happily—it kept the masses from exercising direct influence on it, and indeed that this was precisely why it should be preferred. This paradox is or should be a serious problem for us moderns.

I begin with some of the grounds for being pessimistic about democracy's future, then consider a variety of grounds for optimism, before concluding, sadly, that pessimism is on balance the more rational of the two prospective outlooks.

Pessimism

In the year 2000, 120 out of the 192 members of United Nations were labelled as democracies. But so what, if under that classification Yemen was counted as a democracy? And how much did it mean when just one of those 192, China, accounted for one-quarter of the human race? Despite the state's official title being the Chinese People's Democratic Republic, there seems not to be much democracy of any description to be found there. As Mr Cheng Jin, the official in charge of elections to local 'people's congresses', rather nicely put it in 2011: 'There are 1.3 billion people in China. If they all expressed their opinions, who would we listen to?'

Arguably, democracy Beijing-style amounts to or is based essentially upon bribes and threats—though there is nothing unique to China about this. And that is not to mention the multiple uses of torture (walling, close confinement, water dousing, waterboarding, and rectal hydration, among other disgusting and degrading practices) used supposedly in defence of freedom and democracy by Western democracies, whether in Abu Ghraib, Guantanamo Bay, or The Maze in Northern Ireland. In short, at best democracy may well today merely occupy the space filled in classical Latin by *res publica*; that is, it identifies every legitimate form of government from Parliament to peshmergas but hardly washes its face as a meaningful, let alone pinpointedly accurate classificatory label.

At all events, democracy in stable governmental regimes on both sides of the Atlantic and elsewhere firmly means representative democracy and liberal (anti-Big State) democracy: that is, anything but 'pure', ancient Greek-style democracy. 'We, the People' in any mass-popular sense are normally kept well away from any direct access to—let alone the regular daily exercise of—governmental power. When the former Greek Prime Minister George M. Papandreou suddenly mooted the possibility of holding a referendum on a package of eurozone conditions for a financial bailout in 2011, he was widely greeted with astonishment at what seemed, and surely proved, a mere political manoeuvre and empty threat.

This is far from being entirely surprising. There is no direct institutional legacy of Athenian or any other ancient direct democracy to any modern form of democracy, and those moderns who wish to take it as a model of inspiration are usually, inevitably, very selective in what borrowings they recommend (e.g., lottery only, or use of new-communications technology to simulate face-to-face decision-making, and further examples, below). Some more full-blooded notion of direct, active, participatory democracy is often desiderated, but those who call for it often also dwell either on the democracy we have lost or on the managed, hollowed-out, or empty democracy we actually and fore-seeably have. Some even speak of the myth of ancient Athenian democracy.

Two further considerations have tended to operate in the same pessimistic direction. The modern world, especially when understood in a developed, glo-balised sense, is infinitely more complex than any ancient Greek polity. Sheer scale is indeed not a minor differentiating variable: such contemporary excep-tions as the direct democratic system of the German-speaking *Landsgemeinde* are surely feasible only on—and because they are on—the smallest scale, and because they speak to the traditions and perceptions of small, culturally homogeneous communities. Second, according to the conservative sociolo-gist Robert Michels and his followers, there exists an Iron Law of Oligarchy, whereby every political organization at every level or scale ultimately and nec-essarily for largely operational reasons begets functional oligarchy. Hence, to end this opening section with what is often taken to be the most realistic posi-tion, conceiving democracy in terms of results rather than principles can be made to seem the best or at any rate the only practicable option.

Optimism

However, if that sort of standpoint had been the only one viably on offer, this book would have been neither conceived nor undertaken. On the optimistic side of the fence there are reputable modern historians of ancient Greece who variously argue either that there are, if not continuities, at least relevant compa-rabilities between ancient (Greek) and modern (parliamentary, representative) democracies; or that regardless of the objectively determinable and unarguable differences between them, indeed *because of* those differences, ancient Greek democracies can still teach us something practically useful today. I discuss just three such historians: the late Moses Finley (American-British), Mogens Herman Hansen (Danish), and Josiah Ober (American), whose views may in all cases be traced ultimately back to those of George Grote (Chapter 20).

Moses Finley was a victim of 1950s McCarthyite witchhunting and anti-intellectual repression; for him a conception of democracy mattered a very great deal. It was therefore by no means a surprise that he should have cho-sen as the theme of the lectures he gave in 1972—at Rutgers, the university from which he had been dismissed two decades earlier—democracy ancient and modern. (The first published version of the three lectures appeared under that title in 1973; a second, much enlarged edition appeared in 1985.) The lectures can be read in many different ways—and that applies even more to the second edition, which included complementary essays. But whatever else they may have been, or intended as, they constituted a powerful tirade against the 'apathy' theory of democracy that Finley rightly perceived as the dominant trend current in the 1950s and beyond. A special target was Joseph Schumpeter, who, although he had advocated a minimalist, accountability model, had also rejected the 'classical theory' of democracy that postulated the superiority of decisions made collectively by the non-elite many rather than by an elite few (Chapter 3). Interpreting democracy instead in terms of results, not principles, he predicted that by means of a democratic process capitalism would come to be replaced by socialism.

Against Schumpeter and likeminded others Finley called in aid Grote and J. S. Mill (Chapter 20), counterposing with them the achievements of the Athenian 'Many'. Admittedly, they had made mistakes, not the least of them being to tolerate in their midst an unrelenting, unreconciled anti-democratic minority. The latter not only twice overthrew Athens' democratic system of self-governance, with a lot of help from foreign Greek and non-Greek friends and supporters, but were also ultimately responsible for the 'anti-democratic tradition in Western thought'. But then again, as another modern defender of the Athenian masses against their detractors has correctly remarked, 'No constitution has ever given more weight to the decisions of the ordinary man than did the Athenian'. Today, presumably, Finley would be turning his guns on technocrats, international bankers, and other unelected experts, along the lines of his devastating rejoinder to Plato's intellectualist, anti-democratic plea for government by specialists:

> When I charter a vessel or buy passage on one, I leave it to the
> captain, the expert, to navigate it—but *I* decide where I want to
> go, not the captain [emphasis original].

In 1989, at the bicentenary of the French Revolution, the Danish scholar M. H. Hansen—the most prolific expert on ancient Greek and Athenian democracy—asked, in his book of the same title, was Athens a democracy? That question seems odd at first sight, but what he meant to ask was not whether the ancient Athenian polity had ever been governed according to the norms of *demokratia*, but whether or not, from our modern perspectives on democracy, ancient Athens would significantly qualify as such. His answer was firmly positive, since it was—and is—his view that in the fundamental respect of its ideas of liberty Athens drew the line between public and private not so very differently from the way that line is drawn by liberal democracies today: that is, allowing considerable scope to individual and familial privacy and freedom from central social or political demands. In this he has been powerfully supported by those who believe it is helpful to apply concepts such as justice-as-fairness and political liberalism to interpret ancient Athenian democracy, and who argue that the Athenians took their public political obligations ever more seriously precisely in order to safeguard individual as well as collective liberty. I myself happen not to believe that ancient and modern can be so readily compared, or indeed identified, in this key regard, since I am far less confident than Hansen that there was an entity called 'the state' against which the liberty or freedom of an individual Athenian citizen needed to be safeguarded. But I respect the seriousness with which the comparison is drawn—and welcome the enlightenment that can ensue from such a comparativist exercise.

Still more enlightening, in my view, is the work of the scholar to whom I have chosen to dedicate this book. Also in 1989, not coincidentally, Josiah Ober published his prizewinning monograph *Mass and Elite in Classical Athens: Rhetoric, Ideology and the Power of the People*. Democratic Athens, he there argued, not only was by ancient standards an exceptionally large and complex society and polity but might also be best seen as a shining exception to Michels' Iron Law. In that same year he published a still eminently readable review article on the nature of Athenian democracy, a topic to which he has reverted many times since. But the shifts in his emphasis over the years are telling: from history to political science, and from primarily seeking to understand the ancient Athenian democracy on its own terms to extracting from that understanding positive guidance towards improving our own.

His broad overall message is that although ancient democracy was very unlike modern democracy both structurally and in its history, we can nevertheless learn from the ancients how to revise and reform modern democracy (defined as 'collective self-government that is at once stably effective and limited') by incorporating the sorts of insights highlighted in Herodotus 3.80

(the accountability of leaders, from the Persian Debate). Or, more generally, we may come to appreciate better that democratic knowledge—that is, the kind gained and disseminated through democratic structures of initiative and accountability—is more 'efficient' than other kinds, not least because it conduces to some beneficially utilitarian view of what politics should be ultimately about. I retain my doubts as to the viability or feasibility of treating the ancient Athenian democratic *polis* as if it were some sort of soulful corporation, but harbour none as to the wisdom of the notion that ancient—and modern—oligarchs should not be allowed the last word on the merits and demerits of Athenian-style democracy.

But arguably even the modernising approach of Ober does not go nearly far enough. A key challenge both theoretical and practical is to globalize democracy—or democratize globalization. Some might of course say this is putting the cart before the horse: can we even begin to think in global terms before we have radicalized local (national) democracy? If we can't make even the economically defined eurozone work politically, what hope is there for making democracy work globally? This is a fair enough objection, but modern technology does offer the possibility of some radical version of 'teledemocracy': the forced marriage of new digital and informational technology with ancient democratic practice. This probably also ought to be founded upon an international Bill of Digital Rights. And of course it must be not merely accompanied by but also premised upon a fundamental rethink about the quality of twenty-first-century politics and its appropriately amended mindset.

Such a rethink has indeed been undertaken fruitfully in principle by a Danish academic, Marcus Schmidt (1993), and his scheme has been given a seal of approval by fellow-Dane Mogens Hansen, precisely because it combines 'all the five most prominent aspects of Athenian democracy': direct popular vote on all major issues, sortition, rotation, political pay, and co-operation between professional policymakers in parliament and amateur decision-makers on an electronic panel. What was pure theory in that case has since been partly translated into actuality in Iceland. Citizens were invited to help redraft the national constitution, with some apparent success: 523 candidates stood for election to a 'constitutional assembly' consisting of up to 31 members. A more modest proposal involves reintroducing the ancient Greek democratic notion of the lottery, either for the filling of offices, or at least for the allocation of local government funds. Other prominent advocates of a renewed, revived democracy based upon citizen participation and deliberation by public consultation include Benjamin Barber and James Fishkin.

Conclusion

Yet for all those signs and wonders, and multiple glimmerings of neo-democratic hopes, even I have to confess defeat in the present and immediately foreseeable future, on three main counts.

First, political or civic rights or privileges are now often seen as secondary to, and indeed as opposed to, human rights. In my own university there exists a Centre of Governance and Human Rights, which aims to bring together relevant specialists to 'think critically and innovatively about pressing governance and human rights issues throughout the world', with a special focus on Africa. But the ancient Greeks certainly did not invent, and would not feel at all comfortable with, any notion of universal human rights—even if we were to grant them some understanding of 'rights' in the first place. This is a very recent, post-Enlightenment invention. One very interesting test case of the relevance of modern human rights conceptions as applied to practical democratic politics is the contentious issue of Prisoners' Right to Vote within the European Union. As reported in the London *Times* Law Report of 12 June 2012, the Grand Chamber of the European Court of Human Rights has argued that 'the rights guaranteed by article 3 of Protocol I were crucial to establishing and maintaining the foundations of an effective and meaningful democracy governed by the rule of law'. Yet the right to vote was not deemed to be an absolute and indefeasible right, so that 'the removal of a prisoner's right to vote was not a violation of his human rights provided that such a penalty had not been imposed automatically and indiscriminately'. That is a judgment on which the present British Government is keen to rely, whereas out-and-out human rights democrats see deprivation of the right to vote as a species of unfreedom.

Second, dearly as I would like to end this brief life of democracy on a harmonious note, far more closely in tune with our malodious times (if I may be permitted that pun), as it seems to me, is a chilling volume titled *They Can't Represent Us! Reinventing Democracy from Greece to Occupy*. The book is chilling not because of the laudable intention signalled in its subtitle, but because its title reflects the political actuality of a profoundly non- or anti-democratic world and age—as seen from a modern as well as an ancient Greek viewpoint. It deploys five contemporary case studies—from Greece, Spain, the United States, Argentina, and Venezuela, respectively—and uses, indeed transcribes, *vox pop* observations in order to illustrate its theme and message. In the second, prefatory chapter, there is a section titled 'Historical References', where a reassuringly accurate account is given of 'some of the basic concepts of [ancient] Athenian democracy'. This is done to show both that 'the similarities between many *principles* of ancient Athenian democracy and the democratic practices of *the new global movements* are evident' (my emphases), and yet that current democratic practice has betrayed the ancient ideals. To that end the authors quote from a work of 1996 titled *Radical Democracy*:

> 'Democracy' was once a word of the people, a critical word, a
> revolutionary word. It has been stolen by those who would rule
> over the people, to add legitimacy to their rule. It is time to take
> it back, to restore to it its radical power.

Hear, hear. Back to the future. But there is a third, possibly clinching reason for pessimism. Probably the single biggest difference that has been made in the twenty-first century to any discussion of the relevance or otherwise of ancient Greek democracy and politics to modern democracy is the post-9/11 re-injection of religion into a debate that is now global: political arguments based on transcendental, non-empirical sources are widely proclaimed in both East and West. In this regard, we are alas going backwards. Under the terms and conditions of the outcome of the American Revolution, religion had been on principle—though admittedly not in practice (see de Tocqueville)—excluded or at least separated off from and opposed to politics. There had been a comparable secularisation as a consequence of the French Revolution, and freedom of religious thought and practice has come to be seen as a cardinal principle of all Western liberal democracies. That is no longer by any means the case in lived actuality.

Against those like myself who wish for 'a fuller expression of the concept of democracy itself', we must constantly remind ourselves that there exist others who, though themselves brought up within a western liberal-democratic tradition, feel absolutely no sympathy whatsoever for its ideals, however etiolated those may now seem to some of us. Thus, for example, Mehdi Hassan, a late British jihadi, tweeted in November 2012 as follows:

> We should be supporting the mujahideen who are fighting for Shariah, no to DEMOCRACY.

Since then Daesh (also known as ISIS, ISIL, and Islamic State) has perpetrated numerous atrocities in the name of that same body of moral and religious law, against both human beings and their treasured, irreplaceable cultural artefacts.

In ancient Greece they had managed these things very differently. Socrates had been tried and convicted for impiety, true, but religion as such did not obstruct but rather was seen as complementary to the elaboration of norms of active, participatory, egalitarian, democratic citizenship. What price, now, the eternal vigilance upon which our too-fragile democratic liberties all depend?

AFTERWORD

*D*EMOCRACY: *A LIFE* WAS published on both sides of the Atlantic (New York City and Oxford, UK) in March/April 2016 and was shortlisted in 2017 for the two main book prizes on offer annually in the UK for ancient Greek studies (the Runciman Award and the London Hellenic Prize). In the interval between those relatively parochial occurrences, however, contemporary, Western-style democracy experienced no fewer than **four** decision-making events with potentially world-shattering implications: the so-called Brexit Referendum of June 2016 in the UK, the US presidential election of November 2016, the French presidential election of May 2017, all three drawn-out and quite unpredictable affairs, and lastly the no less unpredictable (in both timing and outcome) 'snap' UK general election of June 2017. That period of twelve to fifteen months is therefore the most extraordinary—politically speaking and on a global scale—in my adult lifetime as an actively participant democratic citizen. I was born in London in 1947, and so came of voting age in 1968.

1968 was itself a year of major global political turmoil, but it lacked what I take to be the major immediate consequence of the 2016–2017 upheavals, namely a deep questioning of the very validity and future viability of democracy in any recognizably traditional shape or form. Indeed, the universal political slogan of 1968 was 'we are all democrats now'—the Western more or less liberal democracies confronting what were advertised as the 'People's Democracies' of the Soviet and Chinese blocs. But if it's too soon (according to a dictum attributed to the late Chinese communist leader Zhou Enlai) to assess the impact of the French Revolution, whether of 1968 or 1789, it's far too soon to predict the eventual fallout from those four events of 2016–2017. Nevertheless, I have to say that the omens and runes as I write do not seem at all promising, either in the United States or in Europe (excepting possibly to some extent France), let alone globally, at least not to my possibly jaundiced eye.

On the strength of the book, I have during the past fifteen months reflected both orally and in written form, and in a wide variety of contexts and modes, on democracy ancient and modern—or rather, ancient *as distinct from and indeed opposed to* modern. For overall, and above all, I have incessantly sought to broadcast and inculcate the historically grounded message that direct democracy, invented by the ancient Greeks of Athens, and representative/parliamentary/indirect democracy, invented cumulatively in England, the United States, and France between in round figures 1650 and 1830, are two quite different, indeed often opposed, modes of political self-governance. They merely happen to share a name, itself a historical coincidence of considerable historical interest and impact but potentially grossly misleading. Thus, to take the most salient instance for a UK citizen of 2017, referendums (direct democracy) are potentially a disaster waiting to happen in most of our current Western systems of democracy—unless they're properly prepared for by deep education and are thoroughly debated in principle as well as in detail in parliament (indirect, representative democracy) and their results correctly interpreted and acted upon by politicians and voters alike. The fact of a mere 52 per cent of the actual voting electorate, or palpably less than 40 per cent of the total potential UK electorate, voting a crude 'Yes' to leaving the EU in the 2016 referendum, and that borderline, knife-edge outcome's being taken to equate to the unalloyed, unambiguous, undivided 'will' of (all) the miraculously unified 'people', is probably the most egregious and potentially disastrous counter-instance.

Which leads me to the second most important message that I would want my book to convey as forcefully as I may, namely that democracy—by which I mean, principally, evolved Western modes of democracy—is a tender plant, which requires constant tendance. For 'democracy is under assault'—in the words of Walter Newell, author of *Tyrants*, writing in *The Conversation*, July 18, 2017. And not only from the 'creeping crypto-oligarchy' rightly identified by Dr Roslyn Fuller (Trinity College Dublin), author of *Beasts and Gods: How Democracy Changed Its Meaning and Lost Its Purpose*, but also and more insidiously from 'populism'—a privileging of nonrational emotion over fact-based analysis and a crude appeal to the basest nationalistic instincts of the tribe—which has with alarming rapidity, aggravated by electronic-digital social media, become the order of the day in practical demagogic politics, whether those of the Left (e.g., those of the UK Labour Party leader, crypto-Brexiteer Jeremy Corbyn) or those of the Right (*imprimis* those of Mr Populism himself, President Trump). The impact of these assaults is surely reflected in the 2017 Freedom House report on democracy; Thorvaldur Gulfason's commentary on that report, headlined 'democracy under stress' and emphasizing that declining democracy in the US has a ripple effect on the wider world, makes for sobering reading: https://www.socialeurope.eu/2017/05/democracy-under-stress/. As I concluded the Epilogue to *Democracy: A Life*, 'What price, now, the eternal vigilance upon which our too-fragile democratic liberties all depend?'

However, to conclude this afterword on a more optimistic note, there are grounds for Pandora's residual Hope, even if we 'experts' do still have to contend with respected (on other grounds) colleagues who for one reason or another fall prey to the folly of impotent Euro- or America-first nationalism. The at least temporary termination of Daesh's abominable and execrable quest for a new caliphate may open the door to a resumption of more normal politics in the Middle East. The recent flurry of election- and referendum-holding in the West has done quite a lot to make up the previous 'democratic deficit' in practice—though not yet by any means enough: myself I'm inclined to favour the Australian (and also an ancient Greek) approach to compulsory voter registration and compulsory voting, on pain of having to pay a monetary fine for failure to do either. And in the sphere of more or less high political theory, Christopher Achen and Larry Bartels have published a major book exposing the downside of that supposed democratic shibboleth, elections, *Democracy for Realists: Why Elections Do Not Produce Responsible Government*. Contrariwise, a timely and suggestively plausible plea for making much more use of the lottery (the classic ancient Athenian democratic mode) in contemporary democratic politics has been issued by the Belgian theorist David Van Reybrouck, significantly entitled *Against Elections: The Case for Democracy*. Back to the future?

Paul Cartledge
Cambridge, August 2017

NOTES AND REFERENCES

PROLOGUE

Books on the ancient Athenian democracy are not in short supply; among those I have found most helpful are Jones 1957; Hansen 1999; Ober 1989a, 1996, 1998, 2008a; Sinclair 1988; Osborne 2010.

One useful attempt to place the Athenian democracy in a comparative ancient–modern perspective is Held 1996; for further conversations on ancient democracy and modern ideology, see Ober & Hedrick eds. 1996; Rhodes 2003a; Hansen 2005. Marcaccini 2012 is an inventive discussion of how democratic Athens became transformed within nineteenth- and twentieth-century socialist discourse into a bold and suggestive revolutionary paradigm.

CHAPTER 1

ANCIENT SOURCES AND SOURCEBOOKS

The Cambridge University Press Translated Documents series includes Fornara 1983, Harding 1985, and Burstein 1985, but the texts expertly translated and annotated therein are not all strictly documentary. For 403 to 323 BCE, see Rhodes & Osborne 2003. On the ideas and realities of democracy, Rodewald 1975; Asmonti 2014. On early Greek political thought from Homer to Aristotle, see Gagarin & Woodruff 1995. On social values in Classical Athens: Fisher 1976. The urban archaeology of Athens is well covered by Camp 1986, 1990. Kagan ed. 1966 (e.g., Section IX on 'Periclean Athens— Was It Democratic?', Section XI 'The Unpopularity of the Athenian Empire', and XII 'Demosthenes vs Philip of Macedon'), Robinson ed. 2004, and Samons ed. 1998 all contain both ancient sources in translation and modern work.

ARISTOTLE

Politics: useful translations include T. A. Sinclair, rev. T. J. Saunders (Penguin Classics, 1981); and E. Barker, rev. R. F. Stalley (Oxford World's Classics, 1995); cf. Cartledge 2009b. On the legacy of ancient politics more generally, Vlassopoulos 2009a; Vlassopoulos 2007b, by repositioning the *polis* within an interlinked history of the wider Mediterranean and Near Eastern world, has also argued for a major paradigm shift in the way ancient historians should conceive and treat ancient Greek political thought and practice.

Constitution of the Athenians or *Ath. Pol.*: trans. P. Rhodes, Penguin Classics 1984; on its date, purpose, authorship, relationship to *Politics*, and value, see Rhodes 1981/1993. Further on Aristotle as witness to and critic of democracy: Ober 1998; Ste. Croix 2004; as political sociologist of the *polis* in general, not just the democratic *polis*: Ste. Croix 1981: 69–80.

Aristotle as 'antiquary' and researcher: Huxley 1979.

Aristotle on poverty and wealth (*penia kai ploutos*): esp. *Politics* 1279b16ff, esp. 1279b34–80a3, with Ste. Croix 1981: 69–80 at 72–3. Aristotle and Marx: Ste. Croix 1981: 55–6, 74, 77–80.

Civil strife or war (*stasis*): Lintott 1982; Gehrke 1985; Hansen 2004; Gray 2015; cf. Funke 1980.

Literacy levels: Harris 1989 argues a low percentage of functional literates; contra: Missiou 2011; cf. Harvey 1965, 1966.

Eucrates decree, 336 BCE: Rhodes & Osborne 2003: no. 79; the relief at the top shows a symbolic representation of Demokratia (by then worshipped as a goddess) crowning a representation of the People of Athens; further Blanshard 2004a; Teegarden 2012, 2013, 2014.

Erythrae regulations, ?453/2: Fornara 1983: no. 71 (offers two different translations, based on rival restorations and interpretations of the damaged stone); Samons 1998: 122–3. On Athenian imperial officials, etc., see Osborne 2000; for interpretations, esp. Ste. Croix 1954 (repr. in Low ed. 2008); Ste. Croix 1972.

Thoricus stele: Daux 1983; Athenian religion: Mikalson 1987; Parker 1996, 2006.

Oath of Plataea stele from Acharnae: Cartledge 2013.

Standards decree, ?420s: Fornara 1983: no. 97, Samons 1998: 125–7. This is often referred to as the Coinage Decree, but it also concerns weights and measures, so Standards is more correct. Discussions include Starr 1970; Figueira 1998.

Owl coinage: an example is depicted on the cover of Samons 1998.

Cleinias [tribute-collection] Decree, ?440s, ?420s: Fornara 1983: no. 98; Samons 1998: 127–9; Ramou-Chapsiadi 2009.

Tyrannicides group: on our evidence for it, and for the twin statues' characteristic poses as represented in later, marble copies, see Webb 1997, www.brynmawr.edu/archaeology/guesswho/webb. html; cf. Anderson 2003: 198–206; 2007; Azoulay 2014. 'Tyrannicide' narrative: Thucydides 6.53–59: Thomas 1989.

On 'official' Athenian (democratic and public) art generally, see Castriota 1992; on democracy, imperialism, and the arts, Raaflaub & Boedeker eds. 1998; on especially the Parthenon and its political implications, Meiggs 1963; Connelly 2014. Also Neer 2002.

Roberts 1994: good rev. by E. Robinson, *Bryn Mawr Classical Review* 95.02.08.

Rarity of ideological democrats: Maloy 2013.

CHAPTER 2

Goody on alphabetic literacy as democratic: Goody & Watt 1962/1963.

Copenhagen Polis Project: Hansen & Nielsen eds. 2004; cf. Hansen 2006.

Polis as 'state'? in favour: Hansen 2002; against: Berent 2004 (stateless political community).

Rise of *polis*: Snodgrass 1980; Starr 1986.

City-state cultures: see an excellent review of Hansen ed. 2002 and 2004 by K-J. Hölkeskamp, *Bryn Mawr Classical Review* 2004.04.03.

Polis in Homer? Cartledge 2009: ch. 3.

Hector's 'patriotism': Greenhalgh 1972.

Hesiod *Works and Days*: translations include G. Most (Loeb Classical Library, Cambridge, MA, 2006).

Hesiod as 'semi-aristocrat': Starr 1986.

On Theognis: Figueira & Nagy eds. 1985; on oligarchy: Ostwald 2000a; Winters 2011: 72ff.

Hoplites and their rise: Kagan & Viggiano eds. 2013 encapsulates the main controversies.

Notes and References

Spartan Great Rhetra in its political context: Cartledge 1980/2001a.

Eunomia: Andrewes 1938. Sparta as 'alternative to tyranny': Andrewes 1956.

Dreros *polis* law: Fornara 1983: no 11. Laws in Archaic Crete: Gagarin & Perlman 2015. On early Greek *agorai*: Kenzler 1999, with the exhaustive review by K-J. Hölkeskamp, *Zeitschrift der Savigny-Stiftung für Rechtsgeschichte. Romanistische Abteilung* 2002: 389–96.

CHAPTER 3

Ath. Pol.: Wallace in Raaflaub, Ober, Wallace et al. 2007; Hansen 2010a gives too much credence to, e.g., Robinson 2001.

'Age of experiment': subtitle of Snodgrass 1980. Age of tyranny: de Oliveira Gomes 2007.

'Strong principle' of equality: Morris 1996. But see also Cartledge 2009a.

Solon in *Ath. Pol.*: chs 5–12 are devoted to Solon; see esp. the poem later titled 'Eunomia', *Ath. Pol.* 12; S. is mentioned also at 2.2, 3.5, 13.1, 14.1, 22.1, 28.2, 29.3, 35.2, 41.2, and 47.1. Freeman 1926 is still worth reading; more recently on his 'politics of exhortation', see Irwin 2005; R. Wallace in Raaflaub, Ober, & Wallace 2007 (S. as a genuine founder of democracy); Lewis 2008 (on S. as a moral-political philosopher along similar lines to Aristotle); Poddighe 2014 (S. in Aristotle, *Ath. Pol.*).

Solon as fourth-century talisman: Mossé 1979, repr. in translation in Rhodes ed. 2004. On the problem of what were, or were not, his reforms: Hansen 1999: 288–9.

Post-Solonian conception of Athenian citizenship: Manville 1990.

Significance and possible origins of the counting of votes: Larsen 1949. On the majority-decision principle, comparatively: Flaig ed. 2013.

Chios stele: Fornara 1983: no. 19.

The late Nikos Birgalias 2009 on *isonomia*: ch. 1 *isonomia* = the transformation of social into political majority, a compromise between elite and the masses; ch. 2 '*Isonomia* and Herodotus' discusses how *isonomia* evolved into democracy at Athens between 479 and 462; ch. 3 'From Aristocracy to *Isonomia*' offers six cases falling between 600 and 470: Chios, Heraclea Pontice, Eretria, Elis before 470, and Argos 494–470; there is a significant enlargement of the Assembly of citizens, who may now be elected to ruling positions; ch. 4 'From Tyranny to *Isonomia*' cites four cases: Cyrene, Megara, Erythrae, and Ambracia; ch. 5 '*Isonomia*: Ambiguous Cases'—four in number: Lipara 580–70, Mytilene after 580 to 525, Chalcis 506–446, and Naxos 506–500.

Robinson's—unsustainable—view of the appearance of several *demokratiai* by 550 (2011: 219–22; cf. Robinson 1997) is explicitly opposed by him to the misguidedly Athenocentric view that 'Athens was the one and only "true" democracy'.

Sources on Peisistratus include Herodotus 1.59–64; 5.62–5, 90–1, 93–5; 6.35ff, 39, 103, 108–9, 121, 123; 7.6.3; Thucydides 1.20; 2.15.5; 3.104.1 (Delos); *Ath. Pol.* 13–19; Aristotle *Politics* 1310b3–1128; 1313b18–29; 1315b21–2; 29–34; 1314a25–15b10; and Plutarch *Solon* 8; 13; 29–32. Modern work includes Andrewes 1956; Boersma 1970 (buildings); Shapiro 1989; Thomas 1989: ch. 5; and McGlew 1993.

Cleisthenes as eponymous Archon 525/4: Fornara 1983: no. 23 (a list of eponymous Archons spanning 527/6 to 522/1, inscribed about a century later, but there is no reason to doubt its accuracy).

'Tyrannicides' and their myth: Azoulay 2014. For 'popular tyranny', see Morgan ed. 2003; for the democratic 'struggle against tyranny', see Teegarden 2014.

CHAPTER 4

Vernant's 'intellectual revolution': Vernant 1982; 1985; cf. Snell 1953; Lloyd 1979; Seaford 2004; Cartledge 2009b.

Xenophanes: Gagarin & Woodruff 1995.

Sources for Cleisthenes include: Herodotus 5.66, 67.1, 69–70, 72–3; 6.131.1; *Ath. Pol.* 13.5, 20–22, 29.3; Arist. *Politics* 1275b34–7, 1319b19–27.

Cleisthenes' demotic turn, or manoeuvre: Camassa 2000.

Significance of the given name 'Demokrates': Hansen 1986.

The deme as the 'basis' of the Athenian democracy: Hopper 1957; cf. in great detail Whitehead 1986; Paga 2010 (deme theatres).

Ostracism: Fornara 1983: no 41; other translated ancient texts: see www.csun.edu/~hcflloo4/ostracis.html; procedure: *Ath. Pol.* 43.5; Plutarch *Aristeides* 7. Among modern discussions, see esp. Lang 1990; Ste. Croix 2004; Forsdyke 2005.

Literacy in the Athenian democracy: Goody & Watt 1962/1963; Harvey 1966; Harris 1989; Pébarthe 2006; Lagogianni-Georgakarakou & Buraselis eds. 2009; Missiou 2011.

Modern interpretations of Cleisthenes include: Lewis 1963 (family fiddles); Andrewes 1977; Cartledge 1996 (equality), 2007; Ober 1996; Lévêque & Vidal-Naquet 1964/1996 (in the later edition they resiled from attributing as many reforms as possible to Cleisthenes personally); Anderson 2003; Ste. Croix 2004; Hammer 2005 (an example of 'plebiscitary politics'); K. Raaflaub in Raaflaub, Ober, & Wallace 2007. See generally Osborne 2009b: ch. 9; and Azoulay & Ismard eds. 2011.

CHAPTER 5

On all cultural-political aspects of Aeschylus' *Persians*, Hall 1989; on Greek cultural responses more generally, Bridges et al. eds. 2007.

Reforms of Ephialtes and Pericles: *Ath. Pol.* 25–28, with Rhodes 1981/1993; Raaflaub et al. 2007.

Political pay for jury service: Markle 1985/2004 (but there was no pay for Assembly attendance until the 390s). The timing of the introduction of other forms of public political pay is uncertain, but not later than 411: Thucydides 8.69.4, with Rhodes 1981/1993: 304, 691–2.

Pericles' Citizenship Law: Patterson 1981; Blok 2009.

Autochthony myth: Loraux 1993; Sebillotte Cuchet 2006: ch. 9; Blok 2009: 150–4.

CHAPTER 6

Soviet communism: Eden & Cedar Paul (1920) optimistically labelled the post-Bolshevik revolutionary regime an 'ergatocracy', explaining that 'as usual in modern English, the coiner of a neologism must have recourse to the rich and expressive language of the Greeks'; their book was published, ironically, by the 'Plebs [Latin!] League' established in 1908.

Ideology of ancient imperialism: I disagree rather strongly here with Finley 1973/1985; cf. Robinson 2001; Ma et al. eds. 2009.

Absence of democratic theory: an extreme exponent of this view is Davies 2003.

On ancient Greek political thought: Raaflaub ed. 1993; Schuller ed. 1998; Rowe & Schofield eds. 2000; Balot 2006; Balot ed. 2009; Cartledge 2009b (in practice); Salkever ed. 2009.

Aristotle on *theoria* as the highest form of virtue: *Nicomachean Ethics* book 10.

A.H.M. Jones' 'The Athenian Democracy and Its Critics' (1953) is repr. in Jones 1957: ch. III.

Scholars postulating the existence of ancient democratic theory include: Ober 1996, 1998; Raaflaub 1989b; Roberts 1994.

Herodotus' 'Persian Debate': Cartledge 2009a. Accountability: Roberts 1982; Landauer 2012.

Herodotus as a political writer: Thompson 1996.

Thucydides on (his) speeches: 1.22; cf. Connor 1984. On the post-Renaissance reception of Thucydides: Harloe & Morley eds. 2012.

Isonomia: Vlastos 1953, 1964; Cartledge 1996; Rausch 1999; Lombardini 2013. On intellectualist equality arguments, see Plato's version of Protagoras' democratic theorising below.

Sortition, lottery: Taylor 2007a; Birgalias 2009b.

Plato's version of Protagoras' democratic theorising: *Protag.* 319b–324c; and for an explication of Protagoras' democratic theory, insofar as that can be recovered, see Farrar 1988; cf. Hall 2010: 178–81; Denyer 2013. Plato against the Sophists: Grote 1846–1856: ch. 67. On Plato as a political 'dissenter': Ober 1998.

All ancient Greek political philosophy as a response to democracy: Farrar 1992: ch. 2; see also Brock 1991, Ober 1998; Cartledge 2009a: ch. 6. On the Western political tradition as predominantly *anti*-democratic: Roberts 1994.

Oratorical defences of democracy: Demosthenes 20.106, 21.67, 24.59, 76, 39.10–11; Aeschines 1.4, 3.6; Lycurgus 1.4.

Thucydides' Athenagoras of Syracuse, 414 BCE: 6.39.

Epitaphios or Funeral Oration: Loraux 1986.

Lysias speech 2 is his Funeral Oration; he participated at great personal risk in the democratic liberation and restoration of 403, and his pro-democratic sentiment (2.18–19) was doubtless entirely genuine.

'Old Oligarch' (a sobriquet conferred by Gilbert Murray) is a familiar label for Pseudo-Xenophon *Ath. Pol.*: Osborne 2004, with review by J. J. Sullivan, *BMCR* 2005.07.79; J. Marr & Rhodes 2008; another trans. by G. Bowersock (Loeb Classical Library *Xenophon* Vol. VII: *Scripta Minora*, 1968). The author was certainly an oligarch, but far from certainly aged; his thread of argument is unpicked by Cartledge 2009a: Appendix 1. The reference to blameworthy class traitors is at 2.20.

Two kinds of equality: Harvey 1965, 1966.

Xenophon's anti-democratic dialogue: *Memorabilia* 1.2.40–6; cf. Ste. Croix 1981: 414–15, Cartledge 2009a: 96–7. On tyranny as anti-democracy: Morgan ed. 2003.

Utopianism: Cartledge 1996b. Eu-topia = place of well-faring. Ou-topia = no-place. Thomas More coined 'utopia' in 1516 to represent chiefly the latter.

Aristotle's political thought: most Greek polities of his day either a version of democracy or a version of oligarchy: *Pol.* 1296a22–4. Four species each of the respective genera *demokratia* and *oligarchia*: *Pol.* 1291b31–92a38, 1292a39–b10, 1292b2–93a34, 1318b6–19b32; cf. also Rhodes 1981/1993: 11–12; Ste. Croix 1981: 69–81; Lintott 1992, 2000; Ober 1998; Hansen 2010a. 'Last' democracy: *Pol.* 1292a28ff. Democracy = rule of poor, oligarchy = rule of rich: *Pol.* 1279b8–9, 1281b–82a, 1291–93a. Aristotle's 'middling polity': *Pol.* 1296a37–8; his 'well-blended oligarchy': *Pol.* 1320b20.

Stasis in the Greek world since the 420s: Thucydides 3.82. Violent anti-democratic oath: Aristotle *Pol.* 1310a8, with Ste. Croix 1981: 81.

Thucydides' 'moderate blending': 8.97.2.

CHAPTER 7

General summations of 'the Athenian democracy': Jones 1957: ch. I; Gomme 1962; Forrest 1966: ch. 1.

'Age of Pericles': Azoulay 2014 is a salutary corrective; see also Ferrario 2014.

Difference between pre- and post-403 democracy and democracies: Rhodes 1980; Hansen 1990b.

'Age of Demosthenes': e.g., Hansen 1987.

Aristotle's definition of 'the citizen': *Pol.* 1275, at 1275a32–4. Recent (controversial) discussion: Woods 2014.

Deme-residence: such evidence as there is suggests that though there inevitably was some internal movement out of one's hereditarily ascribed deme, yet there was also a high degree of continuity of residence: Osborne 1985; cf. Taylor 2007b.

Inspection of genitals: Davidson 2006.

Age of majority: Golden 1979.

Oath of the Ephebes: Blok 2009: 159–60; Cartledge 2013; Kellogg 2013.

Speech on appeal against disfranchisement: Demosthenes 57. Another case of skulduggery is the 'foolhardy surety' Meixidemus of Myrrhinous: Osborne 1985; Osborne 2010: 185.

Deme decrees for benefactors: e.g., *IG* ii.2 1175 = Fisher 1976: 156–7; *IG* ii.2 1187 = Fisher 1976: 157–8.

The deme as 'the basis of the Athenian democracy': (the title of) Hopper 1957; cf. Whitehead 1985 (but note 313–26: few major politicians seem to have cut their teeth in their demes); Jones 1999: chs 2–4; and for citizenship matters, Manville 1990.

Size of Greek city populations: Hansen & Nielsen eds. 2004; Hansen 1985. Athenian heavy loss of life in late fifth and early fourth century: Strauss 1987: 70–86.

On all matters to do with the Council of 500: Rhodes 1972, repr. 1985; cf. Taylor 2007a (sociology of the lot).

Accountability: Roberts 1982; cf. Ostwald 2000b. 'Divided power': Pasquino 2010.

Honorary citizenship votes: Vlassopoulos 2013: 116.

Assembly: Hansen 1987; cf. Hansen 1983 and 1989; Ruzé 1997: 525–38 (list of known proposers of decrees, amendments); Saxenhouse 2006: ch. 7 (Thucydides). Assembly pay (and jury pay): Markle 1985.

Political pay outside Athens: Ste. Croix 1975.

Peitho (persuasion) as goddess: Buxton 1982.

Cleon as a 'new politician': Connor 1971.

Athenian 'demagogues': Finley 1962, 1985; with Lane 2012.

Jurisdictional power of the *demos*: Cartledge, Millett & Todd eds. 1990; Todd 1993; Blanshard 2004. Legal change: Schwartzenberg 2004, 2007.

Heliastic or dicastic Oath: Christ 1998; Lanni 2006. Agora lawcourts: Boegehold 1995. Dicasts' bronze tokens (*pinakia*): Kroll 1967 (Athenian system exported to Sinope, Thasos, Epeirus, and Halieis).

Thucydides on Antiphon's treason defence speech: 8.68. On his own exile: 5.25.

Athenian legal procedure: Todd 1993.

'Sycophants': Harvey 1990; Darbo-Peschanski 2007.

Arginusae trial: Xenophon *Hellenica* 1.7 (a monstrously one-sided account).

Areopagus: on all aspects, see Wallace 1989.

CHAPTER 8

Tyrtaeus reference to *polieteon* ('citizens' in genitive plural): *P.Oxy.* XLVII.3316, ed. M. Haslam (Oxford, 1980).

Politeia as *taxis* in Aristotle: *Pol.* 1278b8–11, 1289a15, cf. 1274b26, 1289b27.

'Great Rhetra': the literature is huge; e.g., Cartledge 1980/2001.

'The secrecy of its *politeia*': Thucydides 5.68.2. This is the subtitle of Michell 1952. An important if opaque Spartan social institution was the Krypteia or 'secret service ritual': Cartledge *Der Neue Pauly* s.v.

Spartan *oliganthropia*: Cartledge 1979/2002: 263–72.

Spartans and Helots, according to Thucydides: 4.80 (interpretations of the ambiguous Greek text differ: does he mean to say that, so far as relations with the Helots were concerned, the Spartans' overriding priority was security? Or, more broadly, that the Spartans' overriding priority was security against the Helots?). On all aspects of Helot life: Cartledge 2011.

'Othering': Cartledge 2002.

Unusual piety and religiosity of the Spartans: Herodotus 5.63, 9.7; cf. Richer 2010.

Athenian religious festivals: Parker 1996, 2006.

Panathenaea: Neils ed. 1992, Neils 1994; Wohl 1996. Meaning of the Parthenon frieze: Connelly 2014. As good a short account as any of the Parthenon's political implications: Meiggs 1963; cf. Fehr 2011. On the 'Periclean' building programme as a whole: Azoulay 2014.

Dionysia: Cartledge 1985. Democratic function of plays: Goldhill 1986; cf. Winkler & Zeitlin eds. 1990; Cartledge 1997a; Cartledge 1990 (Aristophanes); Pritchard 2004 (dithyrambs); Villacèque 2008; Boedeker & Raaflaub eds. 2009; Burian 2011 (tragedy). *Contra*: Rhodes 2003b, 2011a. A fascinating modern riff on the ancients' tragic understanding of democratic politics: Johnston 2015.

Regulations for Eleusis, ?422/1: Fornara 1983: no. 140; cf. Gagné 2009.

'Sacred *Orgas*' decree of the Assembly: Rhodes & Osborne 2003: no. 58.

Aristotle's woman, and on Spartan women and wives: Cartledge 1981/2001.

For Athens as not only a (masculine) democracy but also a phallocracy, see Keuls 1985/1993. Women and religion: Jones 2008; cf. Jameson 1997/2004.

Property rights of Athenian women: Ste. Croix 1970. Index entry: Harrison 1968.

Wealthy Athenian families: Davies 1971, 1981. Domestic space at Athens: Nevett 1999, 2010. Family life: Katz 1998. Women and democracy: Jameson 1997/2004.

Trireme service as a 'school of democracy': Strauss 1996.

Slavery as a or the 'basis' of Greek civilization: Finley 1959/1981; cf. Wood 1988 (one of the 'foundations' of Athenian democracy); Garlan 1988; Bradley & Cartledge eds. 2011. Slaves good to think with: Cartledge 1993. Laureum mines: Nicias allegedly hired out 1,000 of his slaves to contractors for this literally servile work.

Public slaves: Ismard 2015. Xenophon in his pamphlet on revenues (*Poroi*, 355 BCE) advocated the purchase of large numbers of slaves directly by the Athenian community to work the silver mines. Slavery, freedom, and citizenship: Vlassopoulos 2009a. Advocate of extreme blurring of the status distinction between citizen and slave in the economic sphere: Cohen 2000. On status at Athens generally, Kamen 2013. On the Athenian 'extra-institutional public sphere': Gottesman 2014.

Nicomachus: see Lysias Speech 30. 'Old Oligarch': Ps.-Xenophon *Ath. Pol.* 1.10–12.

Athenian litigiousness: Cohen 1995 (feud by other means); Christ 1998; contra Herman 2006: 199–201. Rule of law: Lanni 2007. Generally Todd 1993; cf. Cartledge et al. eds. 1990. Lawcourts: Boegehold et al. 1995.

Sycophancy: Harvey 1990; Darbo-Peschanski 2007.

Athenian Agora: Camp 1986, 1990; Millett 1998; Vlassopoulos 2007a. An excellent series of Agora picture books is published by members of the American School of Classical Studies' Agora excavations team (excavating in the Agora since 1931). See also Ehrenberg 1962 for a sociology of Athenian Old Comedy (Aristophanes and his peers).

Peiraeus: Garland 1987/2001; as a deme: Whitehead 1985: 394–6. Trireme service: Strauss 1996. On the architectural development of Peiraeus: Wycherley 1978. 'A world apart': von Reden 1995. Isocrates on the Peiraeus: 4 (*Panegyricus*) 42; cf. Old Oligarch 2.7; Thucydides 2.38.2 (Periclean Funeral Speech); Hermippus fr. 63 Kassel-Austin (from *Phormophoroi*, 'Basket-bearers'). Maritime traders: Reed 2003.

Death: Humphreys 1993; Patterson ed. 2006. Eighth-century burial egalitarianism: Snodgrass 1977. Public civic funeral ritual: Loraux 1986; cf. Pritchard ed. 2010.

Dexileos monument: Low 2002, cf. 2010; Ferrario 2014: 179–81.

Atotas' epitaph: Bradley & Cartledge eds. 2011: 132. Funerary commemorations in general: Ferrario 2014 (honours for a slave: p. 211). Epitaphs and citizenship: Meyer 1993.

CHAPTER 9

Ober 2011 compares the 508/7 'Cleisthenic' democracy with the 320s Athenian democracy of the Aristotelian *Ath. Pol.*; cf. Azoulay & Ismard eds. 2011. Raaflaub et al. (including Cartledge) 2007 argue the toss over when the Athenian *politeia* first became a *demokratia* properly so called.

Democracies beyond Athens: Robinson 2011; cf. O'Neil 1995.

Delian League: Osborne 2000; Low ed. 2008; Ma et al. eds. 2009.

Athenian fifth-century support for democracy elsewhere: Old Oligarch 1.14, 16, 3.11, Thucydides 1.115, 3.27, 47 (Diodotus speech), 8.24, 38), both fifth-century; Lysias 2.56; Isocrates 4. 104–6, 12.68; and Aristotle *Pol.* 1307b23–5).

Athenian 'epigraphic habit': Hedrick 1999.

Samos 440/39: on balance I believe that Athens did impose a democracy in 439: Cartledge 1982. Athens-Samos isopolity agreement, 405: Osborne 2000: no. 183 (passed 405, inscribed 403/2).

Claudius' speech in Senate on comparative citizenship practices, in CE 46: Tacitus *Annals* 11.24. Ideologically motivated interventions: Thuc. 3.82.1.

Sparta and oligarchy: Thuc. 1.19.

Athenian speaker (Diodotus) alleges that the allied masses support Athens: Thuc. 3.47.

Brock's line: 2009: 161; also that of Ostwald 1993; contra Ste. Croix 1954/1972; Hunt 2010: 90. For the inscriptional evidence, including the Erythrae decree, see Lewis 1984/1997.

Argos-Sparta treaty, 417: Thuc. 5.77, 79.

Syracuse, fifth-century politics: Herodotus 7.155; Thuc. 6.34–41, 72–3; Diodorus 11.68.5–6, 11.86.3–87.6, 13.91.3–96.4; Aristotle *Pol.* 1302b, 1304a; democratic interlude: Finley 1979; see also Berger 1992; O'Neil 1995; Robinson ed. 2004: ch. 3 ('Popular politics in fifth-century Syracuse'); Camassa 2007b ('the tormented political life of fifth-century Syracuse'). Likeness of Syracuse to Athens: Finley 1979: 61. Post-413 transition: *Pol.* 1304a28–9.

Ancient democracies fighting each other: Robinson 2001.

Herodotus on Naxos: 5.30, 6.96. Thucydides on Naxos: 1.98.

Mantineia as a democracy: Thucydides 5.29, 47, backed up by inscriptional evidence; the evidence for Elis' early democracy is likewise epigraphic.

'Peloponnesian League': Ste. Croix 1972: 101–24; Cartledge 1987/2000: 242–73; Funke & Luraghi eds. 2009.

Aristophilidas as 'king' of Taras: Herodotus 3.136. Demonax of Mantinea legislates for Cyrene: Herodotus 4.161.

Transformation of Taras into a democracy: Aristotle *Politics* 1303a3–6; cf. Diodorus 11.52.

Foundation of Thouria/Thurii: Diodorus 12.11; cf. Diogenes Laertius *Lives of the Philosophers* 9.8.50 (Protagoras). Regime change at Thouria: Aristotle *Politics* 1307.

Camarina lead tablets: Cordano 1992; but see Shipley 2005: 400 n. 143. Camarina debate, 415: Thucydides 6.75–88; cf. Calabrese 2008: 192–212.

Thucydides on Pericles: 2.65; on the 5,000: 8.97. On all matters Thucydidean, see Connor 1984; Hornblower's *Commentary* 1997-2004-2008. Probably the best translation is that of J. Mynott (Cambridge, 2013).

Civil strife within the tribe (*stasis emphulios*): Herodotus 8.3.1; on the phenomenon of *stasis*, see Lintott 1982; Finley 1983; Gehrke 1985; Loraux 1997/2002; Gray 2015.

'Acknowledged lunacy': Thucydides 6.89 (but Alcibiades was supposedly addressing the Spartans in 414, and as an acknowledged traitor). Assembly decision-making as threatening *stasis*: Loraux 1997/2002.

Thucydides on *idiai diaphorai*: 2.65.

On all aspects of the origins and strategy of the Peloponnesian War: Ste. Croix 1972; on all aspects of Pericles' career and reputation: Azoulay 2014.

On Cleon as a 'new politician': Connor 1971; as a 'demagogue': Finley 1962/1985.

Thucydides on the 'Corcyra affair': 1.24–55; on the Corcyra *stasis*, 427: 3.71–84.

Reaction of the Athenian masses to the Sicilian disaster: Thuc. 8.1.1; their greed and ignorance: 6.24.

Allied cities 'receiving *sophrosune*': Thucydides 8.64.5. Attempted sell-out by the 400: 8.90. Athens 'best governed' under the 5,000: 8.97.2.

The 411 counter-revolution: Andrewes in Gomme 1981 (on Thuc. 8.45–97); Rhodes 1981/1993; Raaflaub 1992 (ideological fallout); Grigoriadou 2009; Shear 2011: 19–69.

Revision of democratic memory post-410: Shear 2011: 71. Revision of the laws under Nicomachus' commission: Todd 1996.

Xenophon on the Arginusae affair: *Hellenica* 1.7.

Lysias (a metic of Syracusan origin) Speech 20: Piovan 2011.

The Thirty Tyrants: Krentz 1982; Piovan 2010 (Xenophon); cf. Bultrighini 1999 (Critias); Shear 2011: 166–87. Execution of Theramenes: Xenophon *Hell.* 2.3.15–36; cf. *Ath. Pol.* 28, 34.3 (taking a 'Theramenist' line).

The Amnesty, 403: Wolpert 2002; Carawan 2013.

CHAPTER 10

Aristotle's citizen: *Politics* 1275a22–3. *Demos* controls courts: *Ath. Pol.* 9.

Democratic jurisdiction at Athens: Cartledge, Millett & Todd eds. 1990. Further bibliography at endnotes to Chapter 7.

Mass and elite engagement: Ober 1989a.

On Antiphon the politician as identical with the Sophist of that name: Gagarin 2002; on the pea-fowl trial: Cartledge 1990b.

Peisander: Thucydides Book 8, *passim*, with A. Andrewes in Gomme 1981.

Terms of indictment of Socrates: Diogenes Laertius *Lives of the Philosophers* 2.40.

Discussion of Socrates' trial with full bibliography: Cartledge 2009a: ch. 6; add Ismard 2013.

Aeschines' retrospect on the conviction of Socrates: *Against Timarchus*, sec. 173.

J. S. Mill: Urbinati 2002.

I. S. 'Izzy' Stone: 1988.

Graphe paranomon: Hansen 1999.

On the 'Crown' Speech of Demosthenes (no. 18), see the commentary of Yunis 2001, together with his translation 2005. Still the best modern account of Demosthenes' career, to my mind, is G. T. Griffith's contribution to Hammond & Griffith 1979. On Aeschines' politics, see Harris 1995.

CHAPTER 11

On Aristotle as a researcher: Huxley 1979; on how Aristotle's thought relates to the practicalities of *polis*-life, Cartledge 2009b.

Sparta's development as a *polis*: Cartledge 1980/2001; cf. Cartledge 1978/2001.

'Mixed constitution' theory, ancient and modern: Nippel 1980. See further Chapter 15.

Spartan upbringing: Ducat 2006 (somewhat exaggerating the amount of private as opposed to public education).

432 division in the Assembly: Thucydides 1.87; cf. Plut. *Lycurgus* 26.

Probouleusis of the Gerousia: Plut. *Agis* 11.

'Great Rhetra': a corrupt text is preserved in Plutarch *Lycurgus* 6, which almost certainly was derived from the lost Aristotelian *Politeia* of the Spartans.

Sparta's *eunomia*: Herodotus 1.65. Sparta champions oligarchy abroad: Thuc. 1.19.

Spartan religion and religiosity: Richer 2010.

Boeotians' attitude to Sparta in 420: Thuc. 5.31.

For all aspects of Sparta, Spartan society, and foreign policy between 404 and 360, see Cartledge 1987.

King's Peace/Peace of Antalcidas: Xenophon *Hellenica* 4.4.1ff, 5.1.34.

Xenophon on the Mantinea *dioikismos*, 385: *Hellenica* 5.2.1-7, 6.5.3-10.

Xenophon on Agesilaus' attitude to democratic Phleious: *Hell.* 5.2.8-10, 5.3.10-25; *Agesilaus* 2.23. Xenophon's own praise of the loyalty to Sparta of oligarchic Phleious: *Hell.* 7.2.

The oligarchic constitution of Thebes and the Boeotian federal state, 447-382: *Hellenica Oxyrhynchia* ch. 22.

Xenophon on Sparta's violation of its King's Peace oaths at Thebes, 382: *Hell.* 5.4.1.

Theban 'hegemony' of 371-362: Buckler 1980.

Thebes joins Second Athenian League 378/7: Harding 1985: no. 35.

Chios' alliance with Athens, 384: Harding 1985, no. 31; joins Second Athenian League: no. 35. On the League in general: Cargill 1985.

Locri Epizephyrii, a fourth-century democracy: Del Monaco 2011.

On Philip of Macedon: Cawkwell 1978.

Argos destroys Mycenae, 460s: Herodotus 6.83, 7.148; Thucydides 5.27, 38, 47.

New Argive hoard: *SEG* 54 2004, entry no. 427; Kritzas 2003/2004, 2006; on literacy and democracy: Harvey 1966; Missiou 2011.

'Socrates' on the oligarchic city as bifurcated: Plato *Rep.* 422. On the necessity for 'philosopher-kings': *Rep.* 473.

Utopiography: Cartledge 1996b.

Aristotle's 'mixed' Politeia: Yack 1993: ch. 7; Lockwood 2006.

Puffed-up donkeys under democracy: Plato *Republic* 563.

CHAPTER 12

Overall assessment of Lycurgus' career: Humphreys 1985; Wirth 1997; on his family and property, Davies 1971, s.v. On 'Lycurgan' Athens: Rhodes 2010a; Azoulay & Ismard eds. 2011.

Timeline 480-307 BCE: Scott 2010: 269-88.

Liturgies at Athens: Davies 1967; cf. 1971.

Result of Battle of Mantinea, 362: Xenophon *Hellenica* 7.5.27.

The personified Demos of the 350s: Lawton 1995: ch. 2 (interprets the appearance of Demos shortly before 350 and its frequent use thereafter, and of a figure of the Boule likewise, as a sign of the increased professionalism and self-consciousness of the democracy; Athena was no longer considered an adequate figurehead).

Revision of citizen-rolls (*diapsephisis*) at Athens, 346/5: Harding 1985: no. 85; Demosthenes speech 57.

On the international context (age of Alexander): Mitchel 1965; Mossé 1973: 80–101; Bosworth 1988: 204–15; Habicht 1997: 6–35; Faraguna 2003; Hunt 2010.

League of Corinth: G.T. Griffith in Hammond & Griffith 1979.

Law on Tyranny, 336: Harding 1985: no. 101; Rhodes & Osborne 2004: no. 79; Blanshard 2004; Teegarden 2014.

On Lycurgus as a conscientious student of Plato's political philosophy: Allen 2010.

On Lycurgus and Athenian public finance: Burke 1985. Athens' grain supply (*Ath. Pol.* ch. 51): Garnsey 1988. Problems of the early 320s: Harding 1985: no. 116; Rhodes & Osborne 2003: no. 96 (Cyrene provides free grain 331–324).

'Hidden' economy: Engen 2011; cf. Engen 2010.

Phoenicians and Egyptians permitted to worship respectively Astarte and Isis: Rhodes & Osborne 2003: no. 91.

Voluntary contributions: Rhodes & Osborne 2003: no. 94.

On the *Against Leocrates*: Allen 2000; Whitehead 2006. The citation of Tyrtaeus is at section 21.

Ephebeia, lists: *Ath. Pol.* 42; Harding 1985: no. 109.

Ephebic Oath: Lycurgus, *Against Leocrates* 76. Later sources: Plutarch *Alcibiades* 15.7; Pollux *Onomasticon* 8.105; cf. Kellogg 2013.

Acharnae stele: Cartledge 2013 (see also Chapter 1).

Little Panathenaea reorganization: Rhodes & Osborne 2003: no. 81.

Gift of Eudemus of Plataea: Rhodes & Osborne 2003: no. 94.

On Lycurgus and Attic tragic drama: Plutarch *Mor.* 841d; with Hanink 2014, e.g., ch. 3 ('Site of change, site of memory: the "Lycurgan" Theatre of Dionysus'); on Lycurgus and religion more generally: Parker 1996: 242–55; Mikalson 1998: 11–45.

Public awards for private donations: *IG* ii.2 1147 (a tribal award for the financing of plays); *IG* ii.2 1187 (the deme Eleusis awards Dercylus of Hagnous, a general, a crown worth 500 drachmas for funding the education of boys from a deme not his own but where perhaps he resided).

Linking payment of liturgies to office-holding: Arist. *Politics* 1321a31–42; with Ste. Croix 1981: 305–6.

Harpalus affair: Badian 1961; www.pothos.org/content/index.php?page=harpalus.

'Hellenic War' against Antipater: Ferguson 1911.

Revolt of Agis III: Badian 1967; Ste. Croix 1972: 376–8; countered by Badian 1994; see also Cartledge in Cartledge & Spawforth 2002.

Number of Athenian citizens struck off in 321: Diodorus 18.18.5 (22,000); Plutarch *Phocion* 28.7 (12,000); with Hansen 1985 (who favours Diodorus' prior total of 31,000).

CHAPTER 13

In favour of a qualitative, post-403 break: Hansen 1989c; see also Hansen 1983: ch. 13; cf. chs 11–12; 1999: ch. 13. Judicious review: Rhodes 1980.

Choice between 'completion' and 'decline': Eder ed. 1995.

The debate on when Athens first became a *demokratia*: Raaflaub et al. (including Cartledge) 2007.

Pericles as 'first man': Thuc. 2.65; *demokratia* used by 'Pericles' in the Funeral Oration: Thuc. 2.37. Thucydides on the 'Five Thousand': 8.97.2.

Graphe paranomon: Todd 1993. Aristophon: Aeschines 3.194, with Whitehead 1986.

Eleventh *metabole*: *Ath. Pol.* 41.

Notes and References

Codification: Lysias 30 (*Against Nicomachus*) with Todd 1993: ch. 14; 1996.

'Ancestral constitution': Finley 1971/1986; attributed to Solon: Mossé 1979/2004.

'Rule of Law': Sealey 1987. 'Sovereignty of the law': Ostwald 1986: esp. ch. 2. 'Sovereignty' of the People's Court: Hansen 1974. Against 'sovereignty': Pasquino 2010. Rule of the *demos*: *Ath. Pol.* 41.2 (via decrees and lawcourt judgements).

Athenian citizen demographics: Hansen 1985. Participation: Sinclair 1988.

Enlargement of Pnyx assembly space: Rotroff 1996.

Stasis: Gehrke 1985.

'Crisis of the Greek city'?: Welskopf ed. 1974; reviewed by R. Browning, *Philologus* 120 (1976).

'Evolutionary dead-end': Runciman 1990. Contrast Jones 1940.

Fourth century's 'failure'? Saunders 1969: 25. *Contra*: Rhodes 2011b; according to Rhodes 2012: 111, 'there was nothing fundamentally wrong with Athens in the fourth century'.

CHAPTER 14

A.H.M. Jones on the later Roman Empire: 1964b; on Athenian democracy: 1957. Quotation in text: Jones 1963/1974.

Jones on the Hellenistic age: 1964a; cf. Cartledge 1997b.

'Successor' kingdoms: Romm 2011; Waterfield 2011.

Droysen: Momigliano 1970; Nippel 2008b.

'Rehabilitation of the post-classical Greek cities': P. Rhodes *ZSS* 129 (2012) 676–82, at 682, reviewing Carlsson 2010; cf. Gauthier 1984; Dmitriev 2005: Part I; Fröhlich & Müller eds. 2005; Mann & Scholz eds. 2011; Giannokopoulos 2012.

Alexander establishes a democracy at Ephesus: Arrian *Anabasis* 1.17.

Proclamation of democracies: Arrian *Anab.* 1.18.

Chios rescript, ?332: Austin 2006: no 6; Rhodes & Osborne 2003: no. 84.

Restoration of Tegean exiles, ?324: Harding 1985: no. 124.

Lysimacheia democracy: Burstein 1985: no. 22, line 8. Seleucids 'eager to deprive cities of democracy', 278 BCE: Memnon *ap.* Burstein 1985: no. 16 (sec.11, line 4) and n.5. 'Restoration' of democracy at Miletus, 313: Burstein 1985: no. 25.4. Hellenistic Delphi a (moderate) democracy: Gauthier 2011: ch. 16; cf. chs 14–15.

'Freedom of the Greeks' slogan: Austin 2006: nos. 32, 169, 170; cf. Dmitriev 2011.

'Freedom, Independence and Political Procedures in Some East Greek States': Carlsson 2010.

Chersonesus, 155 BCE: Burstein 1985: no. 77 (treaty between Chersonesus and King Pharnaces I of Pontus), line 24. Earlier democracy: Hind 1998: 150–2.

Erythrae pro-tyrannicide decrees: *SIG* ed. 3, 284; with Ma 2009 (quotation from p. 250); and Teegarden 2014: ch. 5.

Strabo on Rhodes: *Geography* 14.2.5 = Austin 2006: no. 110. Naval aristocracy: Gabrielsen 1997; see further O'Neil 1981; Berthold 1984; Wiemer 2002 (but note the negative review of A. Moreno *BMCR* 2003.10.17); and cf. Fraser 1977 (funerary monuments illustrating a dense interethnic cultural mix).

Achaean League: Polybius *History* 2.37–8 = Austin 2006: no. 67; 4.26 = Austin 2006: no. 2; 22.7–10, 20 = Austin 2006: no. 240b; 23.5, 28.3, 29.23–5; Livy 31.25, 32.19–23, 38.30; Plutarch *Aratus* 24; Austin 2006: no. 157.

Aetolian League: Polybius 2.3, 20.9–10, 21.1–3, Livy 35.34–5, 45.28.

Larsen on federalism: 1955, 1968; on federal democracy: Larsen 1945. But see Beck & Funke eds. 2015.

Polybius on the Achaean League: 2.37.7–38.9. F.W. Walbank's three-volume *Historical Commentary on Polybius* (1957, 1967, 1979) remains indispensable; his is also the best short study of the historian: 1973. See further Chapter 15, first section.

Cercidas: Tarn 1923; Tarn & Griffith 1952: esp. 119–25.

Hellenistic Sparta: Cartledge in Cartledge & Spawforth 2002.

Conspiracy of Cinadon: Cartledge 1987.

'Revolution' of Cleomenes III: Cartledge in Cartledge & Spawforth 2002: ch. 4; Cartledge 2009b.

Nabis: Cartledge in Cartledge & Spawforth 2002: ch. 6.

Democracy restored at Athens, 287: Rhodes *apud* Lewis 1997: esp. 35–61, at 47; see further Index p. 638 s.v. democracy.

Rhodes on defining 'democratic': 2006: 38. Conclusion: 2006: 42. *Contra*: Dreyer 1999.

Phocion and Demetrius of Phaleron: Maddox 1982; Fortenbaugh & Schütrumpf eds. 2000.

Demetrius of Macedon: Plutarch, *Life of Demetrius* (Philippides' mockery: ch. 26); Demetrius also caused scandal by residing within the Parthenon.

Debt-servitude in Menander's *Hero*: Ste. Croix 1981: 163. On Menander's comedy as evidence for democratic culture in Hellenistic Athens: Lape 2004.

Official decree for Callias of Sphettus, 270/69: Burstein 1985: no. 55; Austin 2006: no. 55.

Honours for Euphron of Sicyon, 318/7: Austin 2006: no. 32, p. 75 n. 4. 'Liberation' from Demetrius of Phaleron, 307: Austin 2006: no. 42. See further Austin 2006: 611, index s.v. democracy.

Democratic atrophy: Habicht 1997: ch. 3.

Rome promotes oligarchy: Ste. Croix 1981: 526 & 660 nn.5–6; cf. Ferguson 1911: 440–59; Habicht 1997.

'Free' Hellenistic poleis: Grieb 2008. Durability and decline: Van der Vliet 2012. Devaluation and degradation: Ste. Croix 1981: 321–3.

CHAPTER 15

On the Roman Republican 'constitution': Lintott 1999; North 2006. On Roman 'constitutional thought' from the Late Republic onward: Straumann 2015

Polybius' patriotic concession: 16.14.6ff. For bibliography on Polybius, see also Chapter 14. There is a very good Oxford World's Classics translation by R. Waterfield, with an introduction by B. McGing, author of *Polybius*, 2010.

Not the first 'universal' historian: 5.33.2; but, thanks to *symploke* (1.4.11), his was the first truly Universal History: 3.32.

'Freedom of the Greeks' declaration: Dmitriev 2011.

Eulogy of Philopoemen: Polyb. 10.21.1–24.7; eulogy of Scipio: 10.2–3; with Champion 2004; Sommer 2013.

'Disorder and disturbance': Polyb. 3.4.13; cf. Xenophon *Hellenica* 7.5.27.

Polybius on how to write history: esp. 12.25. 'Pragmatic' history: 12.9.1–2.

Rise of Rome not due to mere chance: 1.63.

The 'pudding' and 'seesaw' metaphors: Walbank 1969 (review of Aalders 1968); cf. Nippel 1980; Hansen 2010a.

Polybius and Greek categories of political analysis: Sommer 2013; cf. Welwei 2002.

Provocatio: Livy 1.26, 2.8, Cicero *de re publica* 2.31.

Tribunes of the *plebs*: cf. Livy 2.32–3.

Group voting in the *Comitia Centuriata* and *Concilium Plebis*: Staveley 1972.

Rome favours oligarchies in the Greek cities: Briscoe 1967/1974; Ste. Croix 1981: App. IV; on the 'coming of Rome' generally, Gruen 1986.

Polybius on *deisidaimonia*: 6.56; on *okhlokratia*: 6.4.6, 57.9.

Thucydides on *nautikos okhlos*: 8.72. Plato on *theatrokratia*: Laws 701a.

Tacitus on 'mixed constitution' theory in general: *Annals* 4.32–3.

Millar quotation: Millar 2002a: 180. See also Millar 1984a, 1986, 1989, 1995.

Support for Millar: Walbank 1995: 222; Yakobson 1999.

On the democracy debate: North 1990, 2002, cf. 2009; Jehne ed. 1995; Mouritsen 2001: esp. 144–8; Tatum 2009; Hölkeskamp 2010, 2011; Hurlet 2012. Hammer ed. 2014 appeared too late for my consideration.

Aristotle on the proper size of a *polis*: *Pol.* 7.4, 1326a37–8.

Greek 'demagogues': Finley 1985; Mann 2007; Lane 2012. See also Chapter 7.

Cicero's *liber populus* or *populus*: *de re p.* 1.42–9, 53, 55, 69; cf. 66–8—the latter is a partial paraphrase of Plato *Rep.* 562aff; *civitas popularis*: 1.42; with Ste. Croix 1981: 322. See also Marshall 1997; Nicolet ed. 1983; Kharkhordin 2010.

Roman 'mob': Brunt 1966/1974: esp. 76–80. Roman assemblies and violence: David 2013; cf. Vanderbroeck 1987; Osborne 2009a: 114–18.

Roman living conditions: Yavetz 1958/1969.

<h2 style="text-align:center">CHAPTER 16</h2>

Josephus on the Roman Republic as a *demokratia*: *Ant. Jud.* 19.162, 187.

Devaluation of *demokratia*: Ste. Croix 1981: 323.

Julius Caesar: Stevenson 2014; cf. Weinstock 1971.

Rudimentary fire brigade and police force: Yavetz 1958/1969.

'Held': Fronto, *Princ. Hist.* 210 H.; 'far from a welfare program': Brennan 1990/2000: 48.

Gaulish prince's dedication: Ehrenberg-Jones 1976: no. 166 (9/8 BC).

Tacitus: Syme 1958; Woodman ed. 2010 (includes Cartledge 'Gibbon's Tacitus'); for a comparison of Tacitus to Montesquieu, cf. Hammer 2009: esp. ch. 4.

Tacitus on Augustus' tribunician power: *Annals* 3.24.

Res Gestae: Cooley 2009.

Augustus twice 'thought about' restoring the Republic: Suetonius *Aug.* 28. Augustus actually controlled the entire Empire: *Aug.* 101.

Suetonius on the grant of the 'Father of the Fatherland' (*pater patriae*) title: *Aug.* 58.2.

Gibbon on Augustus: *Decline and Fall of the Roman Empire* vol. I (1776).

Lex de imperio Vespasiani: Lewis & Reinhold 1990: 11–13.

Tacitus on the uniting of the Principate with *libertas* under Nerva: *Agricola* ch. 3.

Plutarch and history: Pelling 2002. Plutarch's *Precepts for Statecraft*: Jones 1971: 114; cf. Cartledge 2009b: ch. 10.

Literary output of the Antonine age: Whitmarsh 2004: 250 (my italics).

Aelius Aristides, *To Rome*: Ste. Croix 1981: 323 with 615 n.54, 386; Harris ed. 2009.

Claudius on admission of Gauls to the Senate, 47/8: Tacitus *Annals* 11.23–25.

Constitutio Antoniniana: Sherwin-White 1973.

Downwards trajectory of democracy in the early Byzantine Empire: Ste. Croix 1981: 300–326, esp. 321–3, 326, with Appendix IV (518–537);

Demokratia as 'riot': John Malalas *Chronographia* Book 18; cf. Watts 2010 (focused on the Alexandria riot of 485).

Notes and References

CHAPTER 17

General: Skinner 1992; Wood 2008 ch. 4.

'render unto Caesar': *Matthew* 22.15–22, *Mark* 12.13–17, *Luke* 20.20–26.

'powers that be': Paul *Romans* 13.1–6.

Eleventh-century rebound: Jones 1997.

democracy talk anachronistic: Skinner 1992: 59.

Dante on Aristotle: *Inferno*, 4.31.

Emergence of city-states: Athens & Rome, Florence & Venice compared: Molho, Raaflaub & Emlen eds. 1991; Davidson 1981 (Venice). Wood 2008: 195 (contrasts with Greek *polis*); cf. Burns ed. 1988: index s.v. 'Democracy, in mixed constitution; see also People/*populus*'.

'No parallel in the age of the *poleis*': Runciman 2009: 199.

Ptolemy of Lucca: Blythe 1997 ('period of the *populo*', Intro., p. 10). Marsilius of Padua: Skinner 1978: I. 49–65; Nederman 1995; Garnett 2006.

Magna Carta: Holt 1992. 'buried deep': Breay 2007: 8. Magna Carta Project blog: http://magnacartaresearch.blogspot.co.uk.

Declaration of Arbroath: McDonald-Lewis 2009 (but 'democracy' in her subtitle is grossly anachronistic).

'Renaissance': Aston 1996; Goody 2009.

Ambrogio Lorenzetti's *Buon Governo* frescoes: Skinner 1999.

Latin no longer a mother tongue: Sanson 2011: 32.

Sovereignty: Nippel 2008a; reviewed by B. Straumann *Bryn Mawr Classical Review* 2008.10.31; cf. Straumann 2015.

'Machiavellian democracy': McCormick 2011: 204 n.11 On Machiavelli's realism, see Maloy 2013: 168–70, and on comparison with Aristotle: Pasquino 2009; Maloy 2013: 103.

Renaissance civic humanism: Peltonen 1995; Hankins ed. 2004. On 'republicanism' ancient and (or as opposed to) modern: Koenigsberger ed. 1988; Nippel 1988; Rahe 1992; Nippel 1994. Not a Greek tradition, *pace* Nelson 2004.

Lipsius' *Politica*: Östreich 1989; Brooke 2012.

'Tacitism': Cartledge 2010.

Citizens' rights: Brett 2003.

CHAPTER 18

'English Revolution': Hill 1991. Surprises: Morgan 1988: 306.

English civil wars and Oliver Cromwell: Worden 2009, 2012; Rollison 2010. Naval dimension: Scott 2011.

Civic humanism tradition of 'republican' discourse, 1570–1640: Peltonen 1995.

'Putney Debates' (also known as Levellers' Debates): Sharp ed. 1998; Robertson ed. 2007; Mortimer 2015. Caryl Churchill's 1976 play, *Light Shining on Buckinghamshire* (re-staged in 2015, to coincide with Magna Carta's eight-hundredth anniversary), re-uses original dialogue from the Debates. Wootton 1992: 75 calls the Levellers 'nearly democrats'.

Diggers; and works of Winstanley: Corns et al. eds. 2010.

Rainborough: quoted Ste. Croix 1981: 441.

Harrington: Rawson 1969/1991: 192.

Milton and Nedham: Worden 2007. See also Scott 2011: ch. 4.

Macaulay on Milton: quoted in the *Encyclopaedia Britannica* vol. 7, 1959, s.v. democracy p. 181; cf. Hammond 2014. Milton and republicanism: Armitage et al. eds. 1995.

Quotation from Hobbes' *Autobiography* (my translation): see Ste. Croix 1972: 25–28. See also Skinner 1978, 2008; Berent 1996; Nelson ed. 2008; Hoekstra 2012.

Hobbes' *Leviathan*: quotation is from p. 150 of R. Tuck's 1996 Cambridge edition; pp. 267–8 of the Penguin edition by C. B. Macpherson; but the first properly critical edition is that of Noel Malcolm (Oxford, 2012); Hobbes published an abbreviated Latin version, c.1668.

Hobbes as proto-democrat: Tuck 2006.

Hobbes' sovereign: Skinner 2008.

On the 1688 'revolution' as introducing a new kind of state: Pincus 2009.

Montesquieu on Athens: Azoulay 2014: 178; cf. Nelson 2004.

Locke's *Two Treatises*: ed. P. Laslett (Cambridge, 1988); cf. http://plato.stanford.edu/entries/locke-political/.

On Locke's passive consent: Dunn 1969.

Montesquieu on the 'separation of powers': Rahe 2009.

Modern mixed constitution theory: Hansen 2010.

Rousseau on Athens versus Sparta: Cartledge 1999b; MacGregor Morris 2004; Shklar 2006.

Voltaire in general: Davidson 2012; on luxury: *Dictionnaire Philosophique* (1764) s.v. 'luxe'.

Iosipos Moisiodax: Kitromilides 2006: 51.

On the French Revolution and historiography: Vidal-Naquet 1995: ch. 5; Hartog 2003: 185–95. On the French Revolution and Antiquity in general: Parker 1937; Mossé 1989; Hartog 1993; cf. Nippel 2005: 264–9. On democracy and the French Revolution: B. Fontana in Dunn ed. 1992: ch. 7; Vidal-Naquet 1995: ch. 4 (with N. Loraux). On the changing significance, connotations and associations of democracy in France, America, Britain, and Ireland between 1750 and 1850: Innes & Philp eds. 2013.

Condorcet: Garlan 2000.

Cornelius de Pauw's 'Philosophical Researches on the Greeks' (Paris, 1788): Roberts 1994: 171–3; cf. Mossé 1979/2004.

'Democratic Enlightenment' and Spinoza: Israel 2011 (1152 pages); 2014 (870 pages). *Contra*: Furet 1981.

Chevalier Jaucourt's entry s.v. 'Démocratie' in the *Encyclopédie*: Lough ed. 1971: 280.

Committee of Public Safety Report, February 1794: quoted in Dunn 2005: 116.

Robespierre: Scurr 2006; McPhee 2012. 'Terror': Wahnich 2012.

Saint-Just: Williams 1991/1995.

Babeuf's manifesto: Courtois et al. eds. 2012.

Leonidas at Thermopylae by J-L. David: Rawson 1969/1991: facing 286.

Dunn's pertinent question: 2005: 150.

Constant's lecture (intended as a preface to a larger work), 1819: Fontamara ed. 1988; cf. Rosenblatt ed. 2009.

Isaiah Berlin's 'two concepts': 1958.

Volney: 1811.

Marx and Aristotle: Chapter 2, above. Marx and world literature: Prawer 1976. Marx's influence on subsequent conceptualisations of Athenian democracy: Marcaccini 2012.

CHAPTER 19

American scholar: Nelson 2004. The Founders and the Classics: Reinhold ed. 1984; Richard 1994; Nippel 2005: 260–4.

Roman Republic in the American Revolution: Sellers 2014.

Federalist papers: ed. J. R. Pole (Indianapolis, 2005); see also Wootton ed. 2003.

online: http://thomas.loc.gov/home/histdox/fedpapers.html.

Declaration of Independence: Allen 2014; for the Constitution eventually arrived at and—crucially—written down, see Bodenhamer 2012.

For a chronicle of waning Enlightenment and waxing democracy, see Wood 2009. The word 'democracy' 1789–1799: Palmer 1953; cf. Palmer 1959–1964/2014; Cotlar 2013; Dupuis-Déri 2013.

Parties have outlived their usefulness?: Guldi & Armitage 2014: 4.

Ancient Greek democracy and slavery: Finley 1959/1981; Cartledge 1993.

Tocqueville in general: Brogan 2007; Wolin 2001; Mansfield 2010; Ryan 2012: ch. 20; Jaume 2013; Runciman 2013: ch. 1; cf. Holmes 2009.

Tocqueville's US journey: Pierson 1938; Zunz ed. 2011; and Peter Carey's 2010 novel, *Parrot and Olivier in America*.

Democracy in America: 1-volume translation, ed. H. Mansfield and D. Winthrop (Chicago, 2000; repr. Folio Society, London, 2002); see also Bevan 2003. On democracy: Manent 2007.

Tocqueville's failure to discuss Congress: criticized by, e.g., Brogan 2007. Failure to 'get' America: G. Wills, *New York Review of Books*, 29 April 2004.

Lincoln at Gettysburg: Wills 1992.

CHAPTER 20

E. P. Thompson on Paine's *Age of Reason*: 1968: 106–7.

Paine and social democracy: Stedman Jones 2004.

Paine as advocate of representative democracy: Philp 2011; cf. 1989. On representative government: Manin 1997.

Grote's *History of Greece*: see Grote 2000 (a selection only on Athens from Solon down to 403 BCE), with new introduction by Cartledge; on Grote's *oeuvre* more generally, see Demetriou ed. 2014.

Paine in debate with Sieyès: Sieyès 2003.

Background to Grote: Ceserani 2011.

Great Reform Act of 1832: Brock 1973. 'Philosophical Radicals': Thomas 1979. 'Popular contention': Tilly 1995. Debate over democracy: Demetriou 1996/2011.

On Grote and reactions to him: Demetriou 1996/2011; ed. 2003: vols 1–2 (includes John Grote's response to Richard Shilleto); Turner 1981: 187–234.

On Grote's historiography: Momigliano 1952/1994. On his re-evaluation of the ancient Athenian democracy: Roberts 1994: 233–51; Demetriou 1999.

On Bulwer Lytton's incomplete *Athens. Its Rise and Fall* (1837), see O. Murray's introduction to Lytton 2004.

On Thirlwall (2 vols, 1835–44, 2nd edn 1845–52), see P. Liddel's 2007 selection (with a useful Appendix, 235–53, comparing and contrasting him with Grote).

Grote's Chapter 67 is hailed by Momigliano 1952/1994: 20 as his 'major discovery in the field of Greek thought'.

Mill's reviews of Grote are reprinted in Mill 1978. On Mill and antiquity, see Irwin 1998; and Urbinati 2002, with her reply to critics in *BMCR* 2003.06.51. On Mill and representation: Harlow 1985; cf. Rosen 1983 (Bentham).

Mill's remark on 'the Athenian Many' is aptly quoted by Finley 1962/1985; cf. Cartledge 2013.

Ancient Athenian democracy as a model: Euben et al. eds. 1994. Historical perspective on reception of the Athenian democracy from 1750 to 1990: Hansen 1992; cf. Dunn 2003.

EPILOGUE

'Get Real': Glaser 2012: 203.

Cheng Jin: the London *Times*, 12 November 2011; cf. Bell 2015.

'We, the people': Wood 1995.

Our relation to ancient Greek democracy: Hansen 2005; Wagner 2013: 63.

Swiss *Landsgemeinde*: Hansen 1983: 207–29; Fossedal 2001.

'Iron Law of Oligarchy': Michels 1915 (translated into French, 2015).

'Nature of Athenian democracy': Ober 1989b.

The democracy we've lost: Dunn 1993; Skocpol 2003; Ringen 2007; Wolin 2008; Mair 2009; Badiou 2012; Zarka ed. 2012. The 'myth' of ancient Athenian democracy: Haarmann 2013.

On Finley's *Democracy Ancient and Modern*: Cartledge 2013.

The 'anti-democratic tradition in Western thought': Roberts 1994.

'Decisions of the ordinary man': Forrest 1966: 16; cf. Woodruff 2005.

Finley's rejoinder to Plato: 1977: 87.

Hansen 1989a. Supported by esp. Liddel 2007 (focused on Athens between 355 and 317 BCE).

Can we learn from ancient Athenian democracy? Ober 1989; with Kallet-Marx 1994; Ober 2009; cf. Manville & Ober 2003. Democratic knowledge: Ober 2008a.

Globalization of democracy: Archibugi 2004, 2008, Archibugi et al. 2011.

International Petition of Digital Rights: this has been called for in a petition addressed to the UN by 562 writers who believe 'The basic pillar of democracy is the inviolable integrity of the individual', signed 10 December 2013 (International Human Rights Day) www.change.org/petitions/a-stand-for-democracy-in-the-digital-age-3. Cf. D-CENT, 'a Europe-wide project creating privacy-aware tools and applications for direct democracy and economic empowerment. Together with the citizens and developers, we are creating a decentralised social networking platform for large-scale collaboration and decision-making ... builds on Europe's latest experiments in direct democracy in Finland, Iceland and Spain'.

Danish academic: Marcus Schmidt's *Direkte Demokrati I Danmark—Om indførelse af et elektronisk andetkammer*(1993); cf. Hansen 2005: 54–5.

Iceland constitutional experiment: Landemore 2015; cf. Aitamurto 2012 (crowdsourcing in Finland).

Lottery: Barnett & Carty 1998; cf. www.imprint.co.uk/books/sortition.html.

Advocates of revived democracy: Barber 1984/2004; Euben et al. 1994; Fishkin 2009.

No 'rights' talk in ancient Greece: Ostwald 1996/2004.

They can't represent us: Sitrin & Azellini 2014; cf. Ogien & Laugier 2015. Quotation from Lummins 1996.

Impact of 9/11: Vlassopoulos 2009: esp. 144; cf. Buruma 2009.

'Fuller expression': Gulder & Armitage 2014: 75–6: 'A longer history of international government can even demonstrate that alternatives exist to our own political system, alternatives that might in turn offer a fuller expression of the concept of democracy itself'. On that note, see further: Dunn 2014 (we must be prepared to break democracy's spell); Meckstroth 2015 (struggles for democratic change have a history).

BIBLIOGRAPHY AND FURTHER READING

Aalders, G.J.D. 1968. *Die Theorie der gemischten Verfassung in Altertum*. Amsterdam.

Abdel-Nour, F. & B. L. Cook. 2014. 'As If They Could Be Brought to Account: How Athenians Managed the Political Unaccountability of Citizens'. *History of Political Thought* 35.3: 436–57.

Achen, C. H., & L. M. Bartels. 2016. *Democracy for Realists: Why Elections Do Not Produce Responsive Government*. Princeton.

Aitamurto, T. 2012. *Crowdsourcing for Democracy: New Era in Policy-Making*. Helsinki.

Allen, D. S. 2000. 'Changing the Authoritative Voice: Lycurgus' *Against Leocrates*'. *Classical Antiquity* 19: 5–33.

Allen, D. S. 2010. *Why Plato Wrote* (Blackwell Bristol Lectures on Greece, Rome and the Classical Tradition). Chichester & Malden, MA.

Allen, D. S. 2014. *Our Declaration: A Reading of the Declaration of Independence in Defense of Equality*. New York.

Anderson, G. 2003. *The Athenian Experiment: Building an Imagined Political Community in Ancient Attica, 508–490 B.C.* Ann Arbor.

Anderson, G. 2007. 'Why the Athenians Forgot Cleisthenes: Literacy and the Politics of Remembrance in Ancient Athens', in C. Cooper ed. *Politics of Orality* (Orality and Literacy in Ancient Greece vol. 6). Leiden: 103–27.

Anderson, G. 2009. 'The Personality of the State'. *Journal of Hellenic Studies* 129: 1–23.

Andrewes, A. 1938. 'Eunomia'. *Classical Quarterly* 32: 89–102.

Andrewes, A. 1956. *The Greek Tyrants*. London.

Andrewes, A. 1966. 'The Government of Classical Sparta', in Badian ed. 1966: 1–20.

Andrewes, A. 1977. 'Kleisthenes' Reform Bill'. *Classical Quarterly* n.s. 27: 241–8.

Apfel, L. 2011. *The Advent of Pluralism: Diversity and Conflict in the Age of Sophocles*. Oxford & New York.

Archibugi, D. 2004. 'Cosmopolitan Democracy and Its Critics: A Review'. *European Journal of International Relations* 10.3: 437–73.

Archibugi, D. 2008. *The Global Commonwealth of Citizens: Toward Cosmopolitan Democracy*. Princeton.

Archibugi, D. et al. 2011. *Global Democracy: Normative and Empirical Perspectives*. Cambridge.

Armitage, D., A. Himy, & Q. Skinner eds. 1995. *Milton and Republicanism*. Cambridge.

Arnason, J., K. Raaflaub, & P. Wagner 2013 eds. *The Greek Polis and the Invention of Democracy: A Politico-Cultural Transformation and Its Interpretation*. Malden, MA, Oxford, and Chichester.

Asmonti, L. 2014. *Athenian Democracy: A Sourcebook*. London.

Aston, M. 1996. *The Renaissance Complete*. London & New York.

Austin, M. M. 2006. *The Hellenistic World from Alexander to the Roman Conquest*, 2nd edn. Cambridge.

Azoulay, V. 2010/2014. *Périclès: la démocratie athénienne à l'épreuve du grand homme*. Paris (English translation by J. Lloyd, with foreword by P. Cartledge, Princeton).

Azoulay, V. 2014. *Les Tyrannicides d'Athènes: vie et mort de deux statues*. Paris.

Azoulay, V., & P. Ismard 2011. eds. *Clisthène et Lycurgue d'Athènes: autour du politique dans la cité classique*. Paris.

Badian, E. 1961. 'Harpalus'. *Journal of Hellenic Studies* 81: 15–43.

Badian, E. 1967. 'Agis III'. *Hermes* 95: 170–92.

Badian, E. 1994. 'Agis III: Revisions and Reflections', in I. Worthington ed. *Ventures Into Greek History*. Oxford: 272–7.

Badian, E. ed. 1966. *Ancient Society and Institutions: Studies Presented to Victor Ehrenberg on his 75th Birthday*. Oxford.

Badiou, A. 2012. *Polemics*. London.

Balot, R. 2006. *Greek Political Thought*. Oxford.

Balot, R. 2009. ed. *A Companion to Greek and Roman Political Thought*. Malden, MA.

Banning, L. 1996. *The Sacred Fire of Liberty: James Madison and the Founding of the Federal Republic*. Ithaca, NY.

Barber, B. 1984/2004. *Strong Democracy: Participatory politics for a new age*. Berkeley.

Barnett, A., & P. Carty. 1998. *The Athenian Option*. Exeter.

Beck, H. 2013. ed. *A Companion to Ancient Greek Government*. Malden, MA.

Beck, H., & P. Funke eds. 2015. *Federalism in Antiquity*. Cambridge.

Bell, D. 2015. *The China Model: Political Meritocracy and the Limits of Democracy*. Princeton.

Berent, M. 1994. 'The Stateless Polis. Towards a Re-Evaluation of the Classical Greek Political Community'. Unpublished Cambridge PhD diss.

Berent, M. 1996. 'Hobbes and the "Greek Tongues"'. *History of Political Thought* 17: 36–59.

Berent, M. 1998. '*Stasis*, or the Greek Invention of Politics'. *History of Political Thought* 19.3: 331–62.

Berent, M. 2000. 'Anthropology and the Classics: War, Violence and the Stateless Polis'. *Classical Quarterly* n.s. 50: 257–89.

Berent, M. 2004. 'In Search of the Greek State: A Rejoinder to M. H. Hansen [sc. Hansen 2002]'. *POLIS* 21: 107–46.

Berger, S. 1992. *Revolution and Society in Greek Sicily and Southern Italy*. Stuttgart.

Berlin, I. 1958. *Two Concepts of Liberty*. Oxford.

Berthold, R. M. 1984. *Rhodes in the Hellenistic Age*. Ithaca, NY.

Bettini, M. 2011/2000 '*Mos, Mores* and *Mos Maiorum*: The Invention of Morality in Roman Culture', in *The Ears of Hermes: Communication, Images, and Identity in the Classical World*, trans. W. M. Short. Columbus, OH: 87–130.

Bevan, G. trans. 2003. *Democracy in America and Two Essays on America, by Alexis de Tocqueville*. London.

Birgalias, N. 2009a. *Apo ten koinonike sten politike pleionopsephia. To stadhio tes Isonomias—Politeiakes metaboles ston arkhaio elleniko kosmo 550–479 pro Khristou*. Athens.

Birgalias, N. 2009b. 'Organisation and Competencies of Magistrates of the Athenian State Down to the End of the Classical Period', in M. Lagogianni-Georgakarakos & K. Buraselis eds. *Athenian Democracy Speaking Through Its Inscriptions*. Epigraphic Museum, Athens: 25–33.

Blanshard, A. 2004a. 'Depicting Democracy: An Exploration of Art and Text in the Law of Eukrates'. *Journal of Hellenic Studies* 124: 1–15.

Blanshard, A. 2004b. 'What Counts as the Demos? Some Notes on the Relationship Between the Jury and "the People" in Classical Athens'. *Phoenix* 58: 28–48.

Blok, J. 2009. 'Perikles' Citizenship Law: A New Perspective'. *Historia* 58.2: 141–70.

Blythe, J. M. trans. 1997. *Ptolemy of Lucca On the Government of Rulers (de Regimine Principum)*. Philadelphia.

Bodenhamer, D. 2012. *We the People. The Revolutionary Constitution*. New York.

Boedeker, D., & K. Raaflaub eds. 1998. *Democracy, Empire and the Arts in Fifth-Century Athens*. Washington, DC.

Boedeker, D., & K. Raaflaub. 2009. 'Tragedy and City', in R. Bushnell ed. *A Companion to Tragedy*. Malden, MA: 109–27.

Boegehold, A. L. et al. 1995. *The Lawcourts at Athens: Sites, Buildings, Equipment, Procedure, and Testimonia* (Athenian Agora vol. XXVIII). Princeton.

Boegehold, A. L., & A. Scafuro eds. 1994. *Athenian Identity and Civic Ideology*. Baltimore.

Boersma, J. S. 1970. *Athenian Building Policy from 561/0 to 405/4 B.C.* Groningen.

Bordes, J. 1982. *Politeia dans la pensée grecque jusqu'à Aristote*. Paris.

Bosworth, A. B. 1988. *Conquest and Empire: The Reign of Alexander the Great*. Cambridge.

Breay, C. 2007. *Magna Carta: Treasures in Focus*. London.

Breaugh, M. 2007. *L'expérience plébéienne. Une histoire discontinue de la liberté politique*. Paris.

Breen, T. H. 2004. 'Ordinary Founders: Forgotten Men and Women of the American Revolution', *Times Literary Supplement*, 8 May.

Brennan, T. C. 1990/2000. '*Principes* and *Plebs*: Nerva's Reign as Turning-Point?' *American Journal of Ancient History* 15: 40–66.

Brett, A. 2003. 'The Development of the Idea of Citizens' Rights', in Q. Skinner & B. Stråth eds. *States & Citizens*. Cambridge: 97–112.

Brickhouse, T., & N. Smith. 2002. *The Trial and Execution of Socrates: Sources and Controversies*. Ithaca, NY.

Bridges, E., E. Hall, & P. Rhodes eds. 2007. *Cultural Responses to the Graeco-Persian Wars*. Oxford.

Briscoe, J. 1967/1974. 'Rome and the Class Struggle in the Greek States 200–146 BC' (*Past & Present* 1967), repr. in Finley ed. 1974: ch. 3.

Brock, M. 1973. *The Great Reform Act*. London.

Brock, R. 1991. 'The Emergence of Democratic Ideology'. *Historia* 40: 160–9.

Brock. R. 2009. 'Did the Athenian Empire Promote Democracy?', in J. Ma, N. Papazardakas, & R. Parker eds. *Interpreting the Athenian Empire*. Oxford: 149–66.

Brock, R. 2013. *Greek Political Imagery from Homer to Aristotle*. London.

Brock, R., & S. Hodkinson eds. 2000/2002. *Alternatives to Athens. Varieties of Political Organization and Community in Ancient Greece*. Oxford.

Brogan, H. 2007. *Alexis de Tocqueville: A Life*. New Haven.

Brooke, C. 2012. *Philosophic Pride: Stoicism and Political Thought from Lipsius to Rousseau*. Princeton.

Brüggenbrock, C. 2006. *Die Ehre in den Zeiten der Demokratie. Das Verhältnis von athenischer Polis und Ehre in klassischer Zeit*. Göttingen.

Brunt, P. A. 1966/1974. 'The Roman Mob'. *Past & Present* 35: 3–27, repr. in Finley ed. 1974: 74–102.

Buckler, J. 1980. *The Theban Hegemony, 371–362 BC*. Cambridge, MA.

Bultrighini, U. 1999. '*Maledetta democrazia*'. *Studi su Crizia*. Alessandria.

Bultrighini, U. ed. 2005. *Democrazia e Antidemocrazia nel mondo greco*. Alessandria.

Burian, P. 2011. 'Athenian Tragedy as Democratic Discourse', in D. M. Carter ed. *Why Athens? A Reappraisal of Tragic Politics*. Oxford: 95–117.

Burke, E. 1756. *A Vindication of Natural Society, or A View of the Miseries and Evils Arising to Mankind*. London.

Burke, E. 1790. *Reflections on the Revolution in France*. London.

Burke, E. M. 1985. 'Lycurgan Finances'. *Greek Roman and Byzantine Studies* 26: 251–64.

Burns, J. H. ed. 1988. *The Cambridge History of Medieval Political Thought, c. 350–c.1450*. Cambridge.

Burstein, S. ed. & trans. 1985. *The Hellenistic Age from the Battle of Ipsos to the Death of Kleopatra VII (301–30)*. Cambridge.

Buruma, I. 2010. *Taming the Gods: Religion and Democracy on Three Continents*. Princeton.

Buxton, R.G.A. 1982. *Persuasion in Greek Tragedy: A Study in Peitho*. Cambridge.

Calabrese, B. E. 2008. *Fear in Democracy: A Study of Thucydides' Political Thought*. Ann Arbor.

Camassa, G. 2000. 'Cronaca degli anni fecondi: Clistene, il Demos e le Eterie'. *Quaderni di Storia* 51: 41–56.

Camassa, G. 2007a. *Atene. La Costruzione della democrazia*. Rome.

Camassa, G. 2007b. *Forme della vita politica dei Greci in età arcaica e classica*. Bologna.

Camassa, G. 2011. *Scrittura e Mutamento delle leggi nel mondo antico*. Rome.

Cammack, D. 2013. 'Rethinking Athenian Democracy'. PhD diss., Harvard University.

Cammack, D. 2014. 'Deliberation in Classical Athens: Not Talking, but Thinking (and Voting)'. Unpublished paper.

Camp, J. M. 1986. *The Athenian Agora: Excavations in the heart of Classical Athens*. London & New York.

Camp, J. M. 1990 *The Athenian Agora. Guide*, 4th edn. Athens.

Canfora, L. 2006. *Democracy in Europe. A History of an Ideology*. Oxford.

Carawan, E. 2013. *The Athenian Amnesty and Reconstructing the Law*. Oxford.

Cargill, J. L. 1985. *The Second Athenian League: Empire or Free Alliance?* Chicago.

Carlier, P. 1998. 'Observations sur la décision politique en Grèce, de l'époque mycénienne à l'époque archaïque', in Schuller ed.: 1–18.

Carlsson, S. 2010. *Hellenistic Democracies: Freedom, Independence and Political Procedure in some East Greek City-States* (*Historia* Einzelschr. 206). Stuttgart.

Carter, D. M. 2010 'The *Demos* in Greek Tragedy'. *Cambridge Classical Journal* 56: 47–94.

Cartledge, P. A. 1978/2001. 'Literacy in the Spartan Oligarchy'. *Journal of Hellenic Studies* 98: 11–27 (repr. with add. in Cartledge 2001).

Cartledge, P. A. 1979/2002. *Sparta and Lakonia. A Regional History 1300–362 BC*, 2nd edn. London & New York.

Cartledge, P. A. 1980/2001. 'The Peculiar Position of Sparta in the Development of the Greek City-State'. *Proceedings of the Royal Irish Academy* 80C: 91–108 (repr. with add. in Cartledge 2001).

Cartledge, P. A. 1981/2001. 'Spartan Wives: Liberation or License?' *Classical Quarterly* n.s. 31: 84–105 (repr. with add. in Cartledge 2001).

Cartledge, P. A. 1982/2001. 'Sparta and Samos: A Special Relationship?' *Classical Quarterly* n.s. 32: 243–65 (repr. with add. in Cartledge 2001).

Cartledge, P. A. 1985. 'The Greek Religious Festivals', in P. Easterling & J. Muir eds. *Greek Religion and Society*. Cambridge: 98–127, 223–6.

Cartledge, P. A. 1987. *Agesilaus and the Crisis of Sparta*. London & Baltimore (repr. 2000).

Cartledge, P. A. 1990a. *Aristophanes and his Theatre of the Absurd*. London (revised, with index, 1999).

Cartledge, P. A. 1990b. 'Fowl Play: A Curious Lawsuit in Classical Athens (Antiphon frr. 57–59 Thalheim)', in Cartledge et al. eds: 41–61.

Cartledge, P. A. 1993. "'Like a Worm i' the Bud"? A Heterology of Classical Greek Slavery'. *Greece & Rome* 40: 163–80.

Cartledge, P. A. 1996a. 'Comparatively Equal: A Spartan Approach', in Ober & Hedrick eds. Princeton: 175–85 (updated repr. in Cartledge 2001: ch. 6).

Cartledge, P. A. 1996b. 'Utopie et Critique de la politique', in *Le Savoir grec. Dictionnaire critique*, ed. J. Brunschwig & G.E.R. Lloyd. Paris (E. T. Cambridge, MA, 2001).

Cartledge, P. A. 1997a. "'Deep Plays": Theatre as Process in Greek Civic Life', in Easterling ed.: 3–35.

Cartledge, P.A. 1997b. 'Introduction' to Cartledge, Garnsey, & Gruen eds: 1–19.

Cartledge, P. A. 1998. 'Writing the History of Archaic Greek Political Thought', in N. Fisher & H. van Wees eds. *Archaic Greece: New Approaches and New Evidence*. London: 379–99.

Cartledge, P. A. 1999a [publ. 2000]. 'Democratic Politics Ancient and Modern: From Cleisthenes to Mary Robinson', *Hermathena* 166 (Summer): 5–29.

Cartledge, P. A. 1999b. 'The Socratics' Sparta and Rousseau's', in S. Hodkinson & A. Powell eds. *Sparta: New Perspectives*. London: 311–37.

Cartledge, P. A. 2000. 'The Historical Context'. Inaugural chapter of *The Cambridge History of Ancient Political Thought*, ed. C. Rowe & M. Schofield. Cambridge: 11–22.

Cartledge, P. A. 2001. *Spartan Reflections*. London & California.

Cartledge, P. A. 2002. *The Greeks. A Portrait of Self and Others*, 2nd edn. Oxford.

Cartledge, P. A. 2007. 'Democracy, Origins of', in Raaflaub, Ober, & Wallace eds: 155–69 .

Cartledge, P. A. 2008. *Demokratie—Eine Trilogie*. Stuttgart.

Cartledge P. A. 2009a. *Ancient Greece. A History in Eleven Cities*. Oxford (pb. repr. as *Ancient Greece: A Very Short Introduction*, 2011).

Cartledge, P. A. 2009b. *Ancient Greek Political Thought in Practice*. Cambridge.

Cartledge, P. A. 2010. 'Gibbon's Tacitus', in A. J. Woodman ed. *The Cambridge Companion to Tacitus*. Cambridge: 269–79.

Cartledge, P. A. 2011. 'The Helots: A Contemporary Review', in *The Cambridge World History of Slavery*, vol. 1: *The Ancient Mediterranean World*, ed. P. Cartledge & K. R. Bradley. Cambridge: 74–90.

Cartledge, P. A. 2013. 'Finley's Democracy/Democracy's Finley', in W. V. Harris ed. *Moses Finley and Politics*. Leiden & Boston: 93–105.

Cartledge, P. A., & M. Edge. 2009. "'Rights", Individuals, and Communities in Ancient Greece', in R. Balot ed. *A Companion to Greek and Roman Political Thought*. Malden, MA & Oxford: 149–63.

Cartledge, P. A., & A. Spawforth 2002. *Hellenistic and Roman Sparta: A Tale of Two Cities*, rev. edn. London & New York.

Cartledge, P. A. ed. 1998. *The Cambridge Illustrated History of Ancient Greece*. Cambridge (rev. edn, 2002).

Cartledge, P. A., P. Garnsey, & E. Gruen eds. 1997. *Hellenistic Constructs: Essays in Culture, History, and Historiography*. Berkeley.

Cartledge, P. A., P. Millett, & S. Todd eds. 1990, repr. 2002. *NOMOS. Essays in Law, Politics and Society in Classical Athens*. Cambridge.

Cartledge, P. A., P. Millett, & S. von Reden eds. 1998, repr. 2002. *KOSMOS. Essays in Athenian Order, Conflict and Community*. Cambridge.

Castriota, D. 1992. *Myth, Ethos, Actuality: Official Art in 5th-Century Athens*. Madison.

Cawkwell, G. L. 1978. *Philip of Macedon*. London.

Ceserani, G. 2011. 'Modern Histories of Ancient Greece: Genealogies, Contexts and Eighteenth-Century Narrative Historiography', in A. Lianeri ed. *The Western Time of Ancient History*. Oxford: 138–55.

Champion, C. B. 2004. *Cultural Politics in Polybius's Histories*. Berkeley.

Christ, M. R. 1998. *The Litigious Athenian*. Baltimore & London.

Christ, M. R. 2006. *The Bad Citizen in Classical Athens*. Cambridge.

Christ, M. R. 2012. *The Limits of Altruism in Democratic Athens*. New York.

Coggan, P. 2013. *The Last Vote: The Threats to Western Democracy*. London.

Cohen, D. 1995. *Law, Violence and Community in Classical Athens*. Cambridge.

Cohen, D. ed. 2003. *Demokratie, Recht und Soziale Kontrolle im klassischen Athen*. Munich.

Cohen, E. E. 2000. *The Athenian Nation*. Princeton.

Colvin, S. C. 2004. 'Social Dialect in Attica', in J.H.W Penney ed. *Indo-European Perspectives: Studies in Honour of Anna Morpurgo Davies*. Oxford: 95–108.

Connelly, J. 2014. *The Parthenon Enigma: A Journey into Legend*. New York.

Connolly, J. 2014. *The Life of Roman Republicanism*. Princeton.

Connor, W. R. 1971/1992. *The New Politicians of Fifth-century Athens*. Princeton (repr. Indianapolis).

Connor, W. R. 1984 *Thucydides*. Princeton.

Connor, W. R. 1989. 'City Dionysia and Athenian Democracy'. *Classica et Mediaevalia* 40: 7–32.

Constant B. 1819/1988. 'On the Liberty of the Ancients Compared with that of the Moderns', in *Political Writings*, ed. B. Fontana. Cambridge: 307–28.

Cooley, A. ed. & comm. 2009. *Res Gestae Divi Augusti*. Cambridge.

Cordano, F. 1992. *Le tessere plumbee del tempio di Atena a Camarina*. Rome.

Corns, T. N. et al. eds. 2010. *The Complete Works of Gerrard Winstanley*, 2 vols. Oxford.

Cotlar, S. 2013. 'Languages of Democracy in America from the Revolution to the Election of 1800', in Innes & Philp eds: ch. 1.

Coulson, W. et al. eds. 1994. *The Archaeology of Athens and Attica under the Democracy*. Oxford.

Courtois, S., J-P. Deschodt, & Y. Dilas-Rocherius eds. 2012. *Démocratie et révolution. Cent manifestes de 1789 à nos jours*. Paris.

Cranston, M. 1985. 'Rousseau on Equality', in E. Frankel Paul, F. D. Miller Jr & J. Paul eds. *Liberty & Equality*. Oxford: 115–24.

Crick, B. 2002. *Democracy. A Very Short Introduction*. Oxford.

Csapo, E. et al. eds. 2014. *Greek Theatre in the Fourth Century B.C.* Berlin & Boston.

Dabdab Trabulsi, J. A. 2006. *Participation directe et Démocratie grecque. Une histoire exemplaire?* Besançon.

Dahl, R. 2002. *How Democratic is the American Constitution?* New Haven.

Darbo-Peschanski, C. 2007. 'Pour une poignée de figues. Judiciarisation moderne et sycophantie ancienne', in P. Schmitt Pantel & F. de Polignac eds. *Athènes et le politique. Dans le sillage de Claude Mossé*. Paris: 147–78.

Daux, G. 1983. 'Le calendrier de Thorikos au Musée J. Paul Getty'. *L'Antiquité Classique* 52: 150–74.

David, J-M. 2013. 'Les règles de la violence dans les assemblées populaires de la République romaine'. *Politica Antica* 3: 11–29.

Davidson, J. 2006. 'Revolutions in Human Time. Age-Class in Athens and the Greekness of Greek Revolutions', in S. Goldhill & R. Osborne, eds, *Rethinking Revolutions Through Ancient Greece*. Cambridge: 29–67.

Davidson, I. 2012. *Voltaire: A Life*. London.

Davidson, N. 1981. *Politics in Renaissance Venice*. London.

Davies, J. K. 1967. 'Demosthenes on Liturgies: A Note'. *Journal of Hellenic Studies* 87: 33–40.

Davies, J. K. 1971. *Athenian Propertied Families 600–300 B.C.* Oxford.

Davies, J. K. 1977/1978. 'Athenian Citizenship: The Descent Group and the Alternatives'. *Classical Journal* 73: 105–21.

Davies, J. K. 1981. *Wealth & the Power of Wealth in Classical Athens*. Salem, NH.

Davies, J. K. 2003. 'Democracy without Theory', in P. Derow & R. Parker eds. *Herodotus and his World*. Oxford: 319–35.

Del Monaco, L. 2011. 'Riflessioni in margine all'organizzazione civica di Locri Epizefirii', in C. Antonetti ed. *Lo spazio ionico e la comunità della Grecia nord-occidentale: Territorio, società, istituzioni*. Pisa: 461–75, Eng abstract 624–5.

Demetriou, K. 1996/2011. 'In Defence of the British Constitution: Theoretical Implications of the Debate over Athenian Democracy in Britain, 1779–1850'. *History of Political Thought* 27.2: 280–97, repr. as *Studies on the Reception of Plato and Greek Political Thought in Victorian Britain*. Farnham, Surrey & Burlington, VT, 2011: ch. 1.

Demetriou, K. N. 1999. *George Grote on Plato and Athenian Democracy: A Study in Classical Reception*. Oxford.

Demetriou, K. N. 2008. *O Platonikos Mythos. Kritiki Anadhromi sti neoteri Platoniki Ermineia* (*The Myth of Plato or The Platonic Myth. A Critical Retrospect on the More Recent Scholarship*). Athens.

Demetriou. K. N. ed. 2003. *Classics in the Nineteenth Century: Responses to Grote*, 4 vols. London (vols 1–2: *A History of Greece*).

Demetriou. K. N. ed. 2014. *The Brill Companion to George Grote*. Leiden.

Denyer, N. 2013. 'The Political Skill of Protagoras', in V. Harte & M. Lane eds. *Politeia in Greek and Roman Philosophy*. Cambridge: 155–67.

Detienne, M. 2001. 'Public Space and Political Autonomy in Early Greek Cities', in Henaff & Strong eds: 41–52.

Detienne, M. 2007. *The Greeks and Us: A Comparative Anthropology of Ancient Greece*. Cambridge, MA.

Detienne, M. 2009. *Comparer l'incomparable*, new edn. Paris.

Diamond, L. 2008. 'The Democratic Rollback: The Resurgence of the Predatory State'. *Foreign Affairs* (March/April).

Diamond, L. 2011. 'A Fourth Wave or False Start? Democracy after the Arab Spring'. *Foreign Affairs* (May).

Di Palma, G. 1991. *To Craft Democracies: An Essay in Democratic Transitions*. Berkeley.

Dmitriev, S. 2005. *City Government in Hellenistic and Roman Asia Minor*. Oxford.

Dmitriev, S. 2011. *The Greek Slogan of Freedom and Early Roman Politics in Greece*. Oxford.

Dreyer, B. 1999. *Untersuchungen zur Geschichte des spätklassischen Athen: 322–ca.230 v. Chr.* (*Historia* Einzelschr. 137). Stuttgart.

Ducat, J. 2006. *Spartan Education: Youth & Society in the Classical Period*. Swansea.

Dunn, J. 1969. *The Political Thought of John Locke*. Cambridge.

Dunn, J. 1993. *Western Political Theory in the Face of the Future*, 2nd edn. Cambridge.

Dunn, J. 2003. 'Democracy as a European Inheritance', in *The Idea of European Community in History* (Education Research Centre of Greece: Conference Proceedings) Vol. I. Athens: 33–41.

Dunn, J. 2005. *Setting the People Free: The Story of Democracy*. London.

Dunn, J. 2007. 'Capitalist Democracy: Elective Affinity or Beguiling Illusion?' *Daedalus* (Summer): 5–13

Dunn, J. 2014. *Breaking Democracy's Spell*. New Haven.

Dunn, J. ed. 1992. *Democracy: The Unfinished Journey 508 BC to AD 1993*. Oxford.

Dupuis-Déri, F. 2013. *Démocratie: Histoire politique d'un mot aux Etats-Unis et en France*. Montréal.

Easterling, P. E. ed. 1997. *The Cambridge Companion to Greek Tragedy*. Cambridge.

Eder, W. 1991. 'Who Rules? Power and Participation in Athens and Rome', in Molho, Raaflaub, & Emlen eds: 169–98.

Eder, W. 1998. 'Aristocrats and the Coming of Athenian Democracy', in Morris & Raaflaub eds. 1998: 105–40.

Eder, W. ed. 1995. *Die athenische Demokratie im 4. Jahrhundert v. Chr. Vollendung oder Verfall einer Verfassungsform?* (Akten eines Symposiums 3.–7, August 1992). Stuttgart.

Eder, W., & K-J. Hölkeskamp eds. 1997. *Volk und Verfassung im vorhellenistischen Griechenland.* (Beiträge auf dem Symposium zu Ehren von Karl-Wilhelm Welwei in Bochum, 1.–2. März 1996). Stuttgart.

Edge, M. 2009 .'Athens and the Spectrum of Liberty'. *History of Political Thought* 30: 1–45.

Edge, M. 2010. *Liberty.* Exeter.

Ehrenberg, V. 1962. *The People of Aristophanes: A Sociology of Old Attic Comedy,* 3rd edn. New York.

Ehrenberg, V. 1969. *The Greek State,* 2nd edn. London.

Ehrenberg. V., & A.H.M. Jones. 1976. *Documents Illustrating the Reigns of Augustus and Tiberius,* 2nd edn. Oxford.

Elster, J. 2013. *Securities Against Misrule.* Cambridge.

Engen, D. T. 2010. *Honor and Profit: Athenian Trade Policy and the Economy and Society of Greece, 415–307 B.C.E.* Ann Arbor.

Engen, D. T. 2011. 'Democracy, Knowledge, and the Hidden Economy of Athens'. *Journal of Economic Asymmetries* 8.1: 93–106.

Estlund, D. M. 2009. *Democratic Authority: A Philosophical Framework.* Princeton.

Euben, P., J. Wallach, & J. Ober eds. 1994. *Athenian Political Thought and the Reconstruction of American Democracy.* Ithaca, NY.

Evans, G. 1958/1966. 'Ancient Mesopotamian Assemblies'. *Journal of the American Oriental Society* 78: 1–11 (repr. in Kagan ed. 1966: 20–29).

Evans, N. 2010. *Civic Rites: Democracy and Religion in Ancient Athens.* Berkeley.

Faraguna, M. 2003. 'Alexander and the Greeks', in Roisman ed.: 118–24.

Farrar, C. 1988. *The Origins of Democratic Thinking: The Invention of Politics in Classical Athens.* Cambridge.

Farrar, C. 1992. 'Ancient Greek Political Theory as a Response to Democracy', in Dunn ed.: 17–39.

Farrar, C. 2013. 'Putting History in Its Place: Plato, Thucydides, and the Athenian *Politeia*', in Harte & Lane eds: 32–56.

Fehr, B. 2011. *Becoming Good Democrats and Wives: Civil Education and Female Socialisation on the Parthenon Frieze.* Berlin.

Ferente, S. 2013. 'The Liberty of Italian City-States', in Skinner & Van Gelderen 2013, vol. I: 157–75.

Ferguson, W. S. 1911. *Hellenistic Athens: An Historical Essay.* London.

Ferrario, S. B. 2014. *Historical Agency and the 'Great Man' in Classical Greece.* Cambridge.

Ferrary, J-L. 1987–1989. 'Les Romains de la République et les démocraties grecques'. *OPVS* 6–8: 203–16.

Figueira, T., & G. Nagy eds. 1985. *Theognis of Megara: Poetry and the Polis.* Baltimore.

Figueira, T. 1998. *The Power of Money: Coinage and Politics in the Athenian Empire.* Philadelphia.

Finley, M. I. 1959/1981. 'Was Greek Civilization Based on Slavery?' (*Historia* 8, 1959) repr. in his *Economy and Society in Ancient Greece,* ed. B. Shaw & R. Saller. London: 97–115.

Finley, M. I. 1962/1985. 'Athenian Demagogues'. *Past & Present* 21: 3–24, repr. in Finley 1973/1985 and in Rhodes ed. 2004.

Finley, M. I. 1971/1986. *The Ancestral Constitution* (Cambridge), repr. as *The Use and Abuse of History,* 2nd edn. London: ch. 2.

Finley, M. I. 1973/1985. *Democracy Ancient & Modern,* 2nd ed. London.

Finley, M. I. 1977. *Aspects of Antiquity: Discoveries and Controversies,* 2nd edn. Harmondsworth.

Finley, M. I. 1979. *Ancient Sicily (A History of Sicily,* vol. 1), 2nd ed. London.

Finley, M. I. 1981. 'Politics' in Finley ed., *The Greek Legacy. A New Appraisal.* Oxford: 22–36.

Finley, M. I. 1983. *Politics in the Ancient World*. Cambridge.

Finley, M. I. ed. 1974. *Studies in Ancient Society*. London & Boston.

Fisher, N. ed. 1976. *Social Values in Classical Athens*. London & Toronto.

Fisher, N. 1992. *Hybris. A Study in the Values of Honour and Shame*. Warminster.

Fishkin, J. 2009. *When the People Speak: Deliberative Democracy and Public Consultation*. Oxford.

Flaig, E. ed. 2013. *Genesis und Dynamiken der Mehrheitsentscheidung*. Munich.

Flannery, K., & J. Marcus. 2012. *The Creation of Inequality: How Our Prehistoric Ancestors Set the Stage for Monarchy, Slavery, and Empire*. Cambridge, MA.

Fleming, D. 2004. *Democracy's Ancient Ancestors: Mari and Early Collective Governance*. Cambridge.

Flower, H. A. ed. 2004. *The Cambridge Companion to the Roman Republic*. Cambridge.

Fontana, B. 1988. 'Introduction', in Fontana ed. *Constant: Political Writings*. Cambridge: 307–28.

Fontana, B. 1992. 'Democracy and the French Revolution', in Dunn ed.: 107–24.

Fornara, C. W. 1983 *Archaic Greece to the End of the Peloponnesian War*, 2nd edn. Cambridge.

Fornara, C., & L. Samons II. 1991. *Athens from Cleisthenes to Pericles*. California & Oxford.

Forrest, W. G. 1966. *The Emergence of Greek Democracy 800–400 B.C.* London.

Forrest, W. G. 1983. 'Democracy and Oligarchy in Sparta and Athens'. *Classical Views* 3: 285–96.

Forsdyke, S. 2002. 'Greek History, *c.* 525–480 BC', in E. J. Bakker, I. de Jong, & H. van Wees eds. *Brill's Companion to Herodotus*. Leiden: 521–49.

Forsdyke, S. 2005. *Exile, Ostracism and Democracy: The Politics of Expulsion in Ancient Greece*. Princeton.

Fortenbaugh, W. W., & E. Schütrumpf eds. 2000. *Demetrius of Phalerum: Text, Translation and Discussion*. New Brunswick, NJ.

Fossedal, G. A. 2001. *Direct Democracy in Switzerland*. Piscataway, NJ & London.

Foxhall, L., & A. Lewis eds. 1996. *Greek Law in its Political Setting: Justifications Not Justice*. Oxford.

Foxley, R. 2013. 'Democracy in 1659: Harrington and the Good Old Cause', in S. Taylor & G. Tapsell eds. *The Nature of the English Revolution Revisited: Essays in honour of John Morrill*. Woodbridge: 175–96.

Foxley, R. 2015. 'The City and the Soul in James Harrington's Republicanism'. Unpublished paper, Cambridge.

Fraser, P. M. 1977. *Rhodian Funerary Monuments*. Oxford.

Freeman, C. 1999/2001. *The Greek Achievement: The Foundation of the Western World*. London.

Freeman, K. 1926 *The Work and Life of Solon*. Cardiff.

Fröhlich, P., & C. Müller eds. 2005. *Citoyenneté et participation à la basse époque hellénistique*. Geneva.

Fröhlich P. 2013. 'Governmental Checks and Balances', in Beck ed.: 252–66.

Fukuda, A. 1997. *Sovereignty and the Sword: Harrington, Hobbes, and Mixed Government in the English Civil Wars*. Oxford.

Fuller, R. 2015. *Beasts and Gods: How Democracy Changed Its Meaning and Lost Its Purpose*. London.

Funke, P. 1980. 'Stasis und politischer Umsturz im Rhodos zu Beginn des 4.Jhdts v. Chr.', in W. Eck et al. eds. *Studien zur antiken Sozialgeschichte*. Cologne & Vienna: 59–70.

Funke, P., & N. Luraghi eds. 2009. *The Politics of Ethnicity and the Crisis of the Peloponnesian League*. Washington, DC.

Funke, P. 2015. 'The Aitolian League', in Beck & Funke eds. ch. 5.

Furet, F. 1981. *Interpreting the French Revolution* (*Penser la révolution française*, 1978). Cambridge.

Gabrielsen, V. 1997. *The Naval Aristocracy of Hellenistic Rhodes*. Aarhus.

Gagarin, M. 2002. *Antiphon the Athenian: Oratory, Law, and Justice in the Age of the Sophists.* Austin, TX.

Gagarin, M., & P. Woodruff. 1995. *Early Greek Political Thought from Homer to the Sophists.* Cambridge.

Gagarin, M., & P. Perlman. 2015. *The Laws of Ancient Crete c. 650–400 BCE.* New York & Oxford.

Gagné, R. 2009. 'Mystery Inquisitors: Performance, Authority and Sacrilege at Eleusis'. *Classical Antiquity* 28.2: 211–47.

Gamble, A. 2009. *The Limits of Politics* (Cambridge Inaugural lecture, 2008).

Garlan, Y. 1988. *Slavery in Ancient Greece*, 2nd edn. Ithaca, NY.

Garlan, Y. 2000. 'La démocratie grecque vue par Condorcet', in A. Avlami ed. *L'Antiquité grecque au XIXe siècle: un "exemplum" contesté.* Paris: 55–69.

Garland, R. 1987. *The Piraeus.* London (repr. with bibl. add. 2001).

Garland, R. 1992. *Introducing New Gods: The Politics of Athenian Religion.* London.

Garnett, G. 2006. *Marsilius of Padua and "the Truth of History".* New York.

Garnsey, P. 1988. *Famine and Food Supply in the Graeco-Roman World. Responses to Risk and Crisis.* Cambridge.

Garnsey, P. 1996. *Ideas of Slavery from Aristotle to Augustine.* Cambridge.

Garnsey, P. 2007. *Thinking About Property: From Antiquity to the Age of Revolution.* Cambridge.

Gauthier, Ph. 1984. 'Les Cités Hellénistiques: Épigraphie et Histoire des Institutions et des régimes politiques'. *Acts of the 8th International Congress of Greek and Latin Epigraphy* (Athens, 3–9 October 1982). Athens: 82–107.

Gauthier, P. 2011. *Etudes d'histoire et d'institutions grecques: choix d'écrits*, ed. D. Rousset. Geneva.

Gehrke, H.-J. 1985. *Stasis. Untersuchungen zu den inneren Kriegen in den griechischen Staaten des 5. und 4. Jh. v. Chr.* (Vestigia 35). Munich.

Gehrke, H.-J., & A. Möller eds. 1996. *Vergangenheit und Lebenswelt. Soziale Kommunikation, Traditionsbildung und historische Bewusstsein.* Tübingen.

Giannokopoulos, N. 2012. *Thesmoi kai leitourgia ton poleon tes Euboias kata tous ellenistikous kai tous autokratorikous khronous.* (Sources and Studies of Greek and Roman Law, 7.) Thessaloniki.

Gibson, B., & T. Harrison eds. 2013. *Polybius and His World: Essays in Memory of F. W. Walbank.* Oxford & New York.

Glaser, E. 2012. *Get Real: How to See Through the Hype, Spin and Lies of Modern Life.* London.

Goette, H. R. 2007. 'Choregic Monuments and the Athenian Democracy', in P. J. Wilson ed. *The Greek Theatre and Festivals: Documentary Studies.* Oxford: 122–49.

Golden, M. 1979. 'Demosthenes' Birthdate and the Age of Majority at Athens', *Phoenix* 33: 25–38.

Goldhill, S. 1986/1988. *Reading Greek Tragedy.* Cambridge.

Goldhill, S. 1990. 'The Great Dionysia and Civic Ideology' (originally *Journal of Hellenic Studies* 107, 1987: 58–76), repr. in J. Winkler & F. Zeitlin eds. *Nothing to do with Dionysos? Athenian Drama in its Social Context.* Princeton: 97–129.

Goldhill, S., & R. Osborne eds. 2006. *Rethinking Revolutions Through Ancient Greece.* Cambridge.

Gomme, A. W. 1945, 1956 (2), 1970, 1981. *Historical Commentary on Thucydides*, 5 vols (vol. 4 ed. by K. J. Dover & A. Andrewes, vol. 5 by A. Andrewes). Oxford.

Goody, J. 2007. *The Theft of History.* Cambridge.

Goody, J. 2009. *Renaissances: The One or the Many.* Cambridge.

Goody, J., & I. Watt. 1962/1963. 'The Consequences of Literacy'. *Comparative Studies in Society and History* 5: 304–35, repr. in Goody ed. 1968.

Goody, J. ed. 1968. *Literacy in Traditional Societies.* Cambridge

Gottesman, A. 2014. *Politics and the Street in Democratic Athens.* Cambridge.

Graeber, D. 2013. *The Democracy Project: A History, a Crisis, a Movement*. New York.

Gray, B. 2015. *Stasis and Stability: Exile, the Polis, and Political Thought, c. 404–146 B.C.* Oxford.

Greaney, G. L. trans. 2005. *Aeschines On the False Embassy*. Lewiston.

Green, J. E. 2010. *The Eye of the People: Democracy in an Age of Spectatorship*. Oxford.

Greenhalgh, P. 1972 'Patriotism in the Homeric World'. *Historia* 21: 528–37.

Grieb, V. 2008. *Hellenistische Demokratie: Politische Organisation und Struktur in freien griechischen Poleis nach Alexander dem Grossen*. Stuttgart.

Grigoriadou, P. 2009. 'Athens on the Morrow of the Oligarchy of the 400 …', in M. Lagogianni-Georgakarakos & K. Buraselis eds. *Athenian Democracy Speaking Through Its Inscriptions* (Epigraphic Museum). Athens: 102–4.

Grote, G. 1846–1856. *A History of Greece*, 12 vols. London (repr. in 10 vols, 1888).

Grote, G. 2000. *A History of Greece: From the Time of Solon to 403 BC* (1-vol. abridgment by J. M. Mitchell & M.O.B. Caspari, originally 1907, with a new introduction by P. Cartledge).

Gruen, E. S. 1991. 'The Exercise of Power in the Roman Republic', in Molho et al. eds: 251–67.

Gruen, E. S. 1986. *The Hellenistic World and the Coming of Rome*. California & London.

Guldi, J., & D. Armitage. 2014. *The History Manifesto*. Cambridge.

Haarmann, H. 2013. *Mythos Demokratie: Antike Herrschaftsmodelle im Spannungsfeld von Egalitätsprinzip und Eliteprinzip*. Frankfurt/Main.

Habicht, C. 1997. *Athens from Alexander to Antony*. Cambridge, MA.

Hahm, D. E. 2009. 'The Mixed Constitution in Greek Thought', in Balot ed.: ch. 12.

Hall, E. 1989. *Inventing The Barbarian: Greek Self-Definition Through Tragedy*. Oxford.

Hall, E. 2010. *Greek Tragedy: Suffering Under the Sun*. Oxford.

Hammer, D. 2005. 'Plebiscitary Politics in Archaic Greece'. *Historia* 54: 107–31.

Hammer, D. ed. 2014. *A Companion to Greek Democracy and the Roman Republic*. Malden, MA.

Hammond, N.G.L., & G. T. Griffith. 1979. *A History of Macedonia* vol II: 750–336 B.C. Oxford.

Hammond, P. 2014. *Milton and the People*. Oxford.

Hamon, P. 2005. 'Le conseil et la participation des citoyens: les mutations de la basse époque hellénistique', in Fröhlich & Müller eds: 21–44.

Hanink, J. 2014. *Lycurgan Athens and the Making of Classical Tragedy*. Cambridge.

Hankins, J. ed. 2004. *Renaissance Civic Humanism: Reappraisals and Reflections*. Cambridge.

Hansen, M. H. 1974. *The Sovereignty of the People's Court in Athens*. Odense.

Hansen, M. H. 1983–1989. *The Athenian Ecclesia*, 2 vols. Copenhagen.

Hansen, M. H. 1985. *Democracy & Demography: The Number of Citizens in Athens in the Fourth Century*. Herning.

Hansen, M. 1986. 'The Origin of the Term Demokratia'. *Liverpool Classical Monthly* 11.3: 35–6.

Hansen, M. 1987. *The Athenian Assembly in the Age of Demosthenes*. Copenhagen.

Hansen, M. H. 1989a. *Was Athens a Democracy? Popular Rule, Liberty and Equality in Ancient and Modern Political Thought*. Copenhagen.

Hansen, M. H. 1989b. 'On the Importance of Institutions in an Analysis of Athenian Democracy', in *The Athenian Ecclesia II. A Collection of Articles 1983–1989*. Copenhagen: 263–9.

Hansen, M. H. 1989c .Review article of J. Bleicken, *Die athenische Demokratie* (1985), *Classical Philology* 84: 137–48.

Hansen, M. H. 1990a. 'Solonian Democracy in Fourth-Century Athens', in J. Rufus Fears ed. *Aspects of Athenian Democracy*. Copenhagen: 71–99.

Hansen, M. H. 1990b. Review of Ober, *Mass and Elite* 1989. *Classical Review* 40: 348–56.

Hansen, M. H. 1992. 'The Tradition of the Athenian Democracy A.D. 1750–1990'. *Greece & Rome* 39.1: 14–30.

Hansen, M. H. ed. 1997. *The Polis as an Urban Centre and as a Political Community*. Copenhagen.

Hansen, M. H. 1991/1999. *The Athenian Democracy in the Age of Demosthenes*, new, augmented edn. Bristol.

Hansen, M. H. 2002. 'Was the Polis a State or a Stateless Society?', in T. H. Nielsen ed. *Even More Studies in the Ancient Greek Polis* (Copenhagen Polis Centre Papers 6 = *Historia* Einzelschr. 162). Copenhagen & Stuttgart: 17–48.

Hansen, M. H. 2004. '*Stasis* as an Essential Aspect of the *Polis*', in Hansen & Nielsen eds: 124–9.

Hansen, M. H. 2005. *The Tradition of Ancient Greek Democracy and its Importance for Modern Democracy*. Copenhagen.

Hansen, M. H. 2006. *POLIS: An Introduction to the Ancient Greek City-State*. Oxford & New York.

Hansen, M. H. 2010a. 'The Mixed Constitution versus the Separation of Powers: Monarchical and Aristocratic Aspects of Modern Democracy'. *History of Political Thought* 31.3: 509–31.

Hansen, M. H. et al. 2010b. *Démocratie athénienne—démocratie moderne: tradition et influences* (Entretiens Hardt 56). Vandoeuvres.

Hansen, M. H. 2012. *Demokratiets Historie fra Oldtid til Nutid*. Copenhagen.

Hansen, M. H. 2013. *Reflections on Aristotle's Politics*. Copenhagen.

Hansen, M. H. ed. 1993. *The Ancient Greek City-State*. Copenhagen.

Hansen, M. H. ed. 2002. *A Comparative Study of Six City-State Cultures*. Copenhagen.

Hansen, M. H. ed. 2004. *A Comparative Study of Thirty City-State Cultures*. Copenhagen.

Hansen, M. H. ed. 2005. *The Imaginary Polis* (Copenhagen Polis Centre Acts 7). Copenhagen.

Hansen, M. H., & T. H. Nielsen eds. 2004. *An Inventory of Greek Poleis*. Oxford.

Harding, P. ed. & trans. 1985. *From the End of the Peloponnesian War to the Battle of Ipsus (404–301)*. Cambridge.

Harding, P. 2008. *The Story of Athens: The Fragments of the Local Chronicles of Attika*. London & New York.

Harloe, K., & N. Morley eds. 2012. *Thucydides and the Modern World: Reception, Reinterpretation and Influence from the Renaissance to the Present*. Cambridge.

Harlow, C. 1985. 'Power from the People? Representation and Constitutional Theory', in *Law, Legitimacy and the Constitution*, ed. P. McAuslan & J. F. McEldowney. London: 62–81.

Harrington, T. 1656/1992. *The Commonwealth of Oceana*, ed. J. Pocock. Cambridge.

Harris, E. M. 1995. *Aeschines and Athenian Politics*. Oxford.

Harris, E. M. 2006. *Democracy and the Rule of Law in Classical Athens: Essays on Law, Society and Politics*. Cambridge.

Harris, W. V. 1989. *Ancient Literacy*. Cambridge, MA.

Harris, W. V. ed. 2009. *Aelius Aristides: Between Greece, Rome, and the Gods*. New York.

Harrison, A.R.W. 1968. *The Law of Athens* [I]: *Family and Property*. Oxford.

Harte, V., & M. Lane eds. 2013. *Politeia in Greek and Roman Philosophy*. Cambridge.

Hartog, F. 1993. 'La Révolution française et l'Antiquité: l'Avenir d'une illusion ou cheminement d'un quiproquo?' in M. Gauchet, P. Manent, & P. Rosenvallon eds. *Situations de la démocratie: Démocratie: l'ancien et le neuf, l'historicisme et ses ennemis, passé present*. Paris: 30–61.

Hartog, F. 2003. *Régimes d'historicité: Présentisme et expériences du temps*. Paris.

Harvey, D. 1965. 'Two Kinds of Equality'. *Classica et Medievalia* 26: 101–47 (with add. in *Classica et Mediaevalia* 27, 1966: 99–100).

Harvey, F. D. 1966. 'Literacy in the Athenian Democracy'. *Revue des Études Grecques* 79: 585–635.

Harvey, F. D. 1990. 'The Sykophant and Sykophancy: Vexatious Redefinition?' in Cartledge, Millett, and Todd eds: 103–21.

Hawkesley, H. 2009. *Democracy Kills: What's So Good About the Vote?* London.

Headley, J. 2007. *The Europeanization of the World: On the Origins of Human Rights and Democracy*. Princeton.

Hedrick, C. W. 1999. 'Democracy and the Athenian Epigraphic Habit'. *Hesperia* 68: 387–439.

Held, D. 1996 *Models of Democracy*, 2nd edn. Cambridge.

Herman, G. 2006. *Morality and Behaviour in Democratic Athens*. Cambridge.

Herman, G. ed. 2011. *Stability and Crisis in the Athenian Democracy* (*Historia* Einzelschr. 220). Stuttgart.

Herrman, J. ed. 2009. *Hyperides: Funeral Oration* (APA/American Classical Studies 52). Oxford & New York.

Hesk, J. P. 2000. *Deception and Democracy in Classical Athens*. Cambridge.

Hill, C. 1991. *The World Turned Upside Down: Radical Ideas during the English Revolution*, new edn. Harmondsworth.

Hind, J.G.F. 1998. 'Megarian Colonisation in the Western Half of the Black Sea (Sister—and Daughter-Cities of Herakleia)', in G. R.Tsetskhladze ed. *The Greek Colonisation of the Black Sea Area. Historical interpretation of Archaeology* (*Historia* Einzelschr. 121). Stuttgart: 131-152.

Hoekstra, K. 2012. 'Thucydides and the Bellicose Beginnings of Modern Political Theory', in Harloe & Morley eds: 25–54.

Hölkeskamp, K-J. 1996. 'Exempla und *mos maiorum*. Überlegungen zum kollektiven Gedächtnis der Nobilität', in Gehrke & Möller eds: 301–38.

Hölkeskamp, K-J. 2004a. *SENATVS POPVLVSQVE ROMANVS. Die politische Kultur der Republik—Dimensionen und Deutungen*. Stuttgart.

Hölkeskamp, K-J. 2004b. *Rekonstruktionen einer Republik. Die politische Kultur des antiken Rom und die Forschung der letzten Jahrzehnte* (*Historische Zeitschrift*, Beiheft 38). Munich.

Hölkeskamp, K-J. 2006. 'Konsens und Konkurrenz: Die politische Kultur der roemischen Republik in neuer Sicht'. *Klio* 88: 360–96.

Hölkeskamp, K-J. 2010. *Reconstructing the Roman Republic: An ancient political culture and modern research*. Princeton (rev., updated, and augmented edn of 2004b).

Hölkeskamp, K-J. 2011. 'What's in a Text? *Reconstructing the Roman Republic*—Approaches and Aims Once Again'. *Bulletin of the Institute of Classical Studies* 54.2: 115–24.

Holland, T., trans., with P. Cartledge. 2014. *Herodotus: The Histories*. London.

Holmes, S. 2009. 'Saved By Danger/Destroyed By Success: The Argument of Tocqueville's Souvenirs'. *Archives Européennes de Sociologie* 50: 171–99.

Holt, J. C. 1992. *Magna Carta*, rev. edn. Cambridge.

Hopper, R. J. 1957. *The Basis of the Athenian Democracy* (Inaugural Lecture). Sheffield.

Hornblower, S. 1997–2004-2008. *Commentary on Thucydides*, 3 vols, rev. Oxford.

Humphreys, S. C. 1985. 'Lycurgus of Butadae. An Athenian Aristocrat', in J. W. Eadie & J. Ober eds. *The Craft of the Ancient Historian. Essays in Honour of Chester G. Starr*. Lanham, MD: 199–252.

Humphreys, S. C. 1993. *The Family, Women and Death: Comparative Studies*. London & New York.

Hunt, P. 2010. *War, Peace and Alliance in Demosthenes' Athens*. Cambridge.

Hunter, V. J. 1994. *Policing Athens. Social Control in the Attic Lawsuits 420-320 BC*. Princeton.

Hurlet, F. 2012 'Démocratie à Rome? Quelle démocratie?' in S. Benoit ed. *Rome, A City and its Empire in Perspective: The Impact of the Roman World through Fergus Millar's Research/Rome, une cité impérialiste en jeu. L'impact du monde romain selon Fergus Millar*. Leiden: 19–43.

Huxley, G. 1979. *On Aristotle and Greek Society*. Belfast.

Innes, J., & M. Philp eds. 2013. *Re-imagining Democracy in the Age of Revolutions: America, France, Britain, Ireland 1750-1850*. Oxford.

Irwin, E. 2005. *Solon and Early Greek Poetry: The Politics of Exhortation*. Cambridge.

Irwin, T. 1998. 'Mill and the Classical World', in J. Skorupski ed. *The Cambridge Companion to Mill*. Cambridge: 423–63.

Isakhan, B. 2011 'What Is So "Primitive" about Primitive Democracy? Comparing The Ancient Middle East and Classical Athens', in Isakhan & Stockwell eds: 19–34.

Isakhan, B., & S. Stockwell eds. 2011. *The Secret History of Democracy*. Houndmills & New York.

Isakhan, B., & S. Stockwell eds. 2012. *The Edinburgh Companion to the History of Democracy*. Edinburgh.

Ismard, P. 2013. *L'Evénement Socrate*. Paris.

Ismard, P. 2015. *La démocratie contre les experts. Les esclaves publics en Grèce ancienne*. Paris.

Israel, J. I. 2011. *Democratic Enlightenment: philosophy, revolution, and human rights 1750–1790*. Oxford.

Israel, J. I. 2014. *Revolutionary Ideas: An Intellectual History of the French Revolution from The Rights of Man to Robespierre*. Princeton.

Jameson, M. 1997/2004. 'Women and Democracy in Fourth-Century Athens', repr. in Robinson ed. 2004: 281–92.

Jaume, L. 2013. *Tocqueville: The Aristocratic Sources of Liberty*. Princeton.

Jehne, M. ed. 1995. *Demokratie in Rom? Die Rolle des Volkes in der Politik der römischen Republik*. Stuttgart.

Johnston, S. 2015. *American Dionysia: Violence, Tragedy, and Democratic Politics*. Cambridge.

Johnstone, S. 1999. *Disputes and Democracy: The Consequences of Litigation in ancient Athens*. Austin, TX.

Jones, A.H.M. 1940. *The Greek City from Alexander to Justinian*. Oxford.

Jones, A.H.M. 1957/1978 *Athenian Democracy*. Oxford.

Jones, A.H.M. 1963/1974. 'The Greeks under the Roman Empire'. *Dumbarton Oaks Papers* XVII: 3–19 (repr. in *The Roman Economy*, ed. P. A. Brunt. Oxford: 90–113).

Jones, A.H.M. 1964a. 'The Hellenistic Age'. *Past & Present* 27: 3–22.

Jones, A.H.M. 1964b. *The Later Roman Empire AD 284–602*, 3 vols. Oxford.

Jones, C. P. 1971. *Plutarch and Rome*. Oxford.

Jones, N. F. 1999. *The Associations of Classical Athens: The Response to Democracy*. New York & Oxford.

Jones, N. F. 2008. *Politics and Society in Ancient Greece*. New York.

Jones, P. 1997. *The Italian City-State: From Commune to Signoria*. Oxford.

Jones, W.R.D. 2005. *Thomas Rainborowe (c. 1610–1648): Civil War Seaman, Siegemaster and Radical*. Woodbridge.

Jordan, B. 1979. *Servants of the Gods: A Study in the Religion, History, and Literature of Fifth-century Athens*. (*Hypomnemata* 55). Göttingen.

Judge, E. A. 1997. 'The Second Thoughts of Syme on Augustus'. *Ancient History: Resources for Teachers* 27: 43–75.

Kagan, D. 1991. *Pericles of Athens and the Birth of Democracy*. New York.

Kagan, D. ed. 1966. *Problems in Ancient History*. New York & London.

Kagan, D., & G. Viggiano eds. 2013. *Men of Bronze: Hoplite Warfare in Ancient Greece*. Princeton.

Kallet-Marx, L. 1994. 'Institutions, Ideology, and Political Consciousness in Ancient Greece: Some Recent Books on Athenian Democracy'. *Journal of the History of Ideas* 55.2: 307–35.

Kamen, D. 2013. *Status in Classical Athens*. Princeton.

Katz, M. 1998. 'Women, Children and Men', in Cartledge ed. 1998: 100–38.

Keane. J. 2009. *The Life and Death of Democracy*. New York.

Kellogg, D. 2013. 'The Place of Publication of the Ephebic Oath and the "Oath of Plataia"'. *Hesperia* 82: 263–76.

Kenzler, U. 1999. *Studien zur Entwicklung und Struktur der griechischen Agora in archaischer und klassischer Zeit*. Frankfurt/Main.

Keuls, E. 1985/1993 *The Reign of the Phallos. Sexual Politics in Ancient Athens*. California & London.

Kharkhordin, O. 2010. 'Why *Res Publica* is Not a State: the Stoic Grammar and Discursive Practices in Cicero's Conception'. *History of Political Thought* 31.2: 221–45.

Kitromilides, P. 2006. 'From Republican Patriotism to National Sentiment: A Reading of Hellenic Nomarchy'. *European Journal of Political Theory* 5.1: 50–60.

Koenigsberger, H. ed. 1988. *Republiken und Republikanismus im Europe der frühen* Neuzeit. Munich.

Krentz, P. 1982. *The Thirty at Athens*. New Haven.

Kritzas, Ch. 2003/2004. 'Literacy and Society: The Case of Argos'. *Kodai* 13/14: 53–60.

Kritzas, Ch. 2006. 'Nouvelles inscriptions d'Argos: Les archives des comptes du trésor sacré (IVe s. av. J-C.)'. *Comptes Rendus de l'Académie des Inscriptions et Belles-Lettres*: 397–434.

Kroll, J. H. 1967. 'Dikasts' pinakia from the Fauvel Collection'. *Bulletin de Correspondence Hellénique* 91: 379–96.

Lagogianni-Georgakarakos, M. 2009. 'The Visissitudes of the Athenian Democracy in the 5th c. BC', in Lagogianni-Georgakarakos & Buraselis eds: 97–101.

Lagogi anni-Georgakarakos, M., & K. Buraselis eds. 2009. *Athenian Democracy Speaking Through Its Inscriptions* (Epigraphic Museum). Athens.

Lamb, R. 2014. 'Virtue, Rights and Publicity: Thomas Paine's Democratic Thought'. Unpublished paper, Cambridge.

Lambropoulos, V. 1997. 'Justice and Good Governance'. *Thesis* 11: 1–30.

Landauer, M. 2012. '*Parrhesia* and the Demos Tyrannos: Frank Speech, Flattery and Accountability in Democratic Athens'. *History of Political Thought* 33.2: 185–208.

Landemore, H. 2015. 'Inclusive Constitution-Making: The Icelandic Experiment'. *Journal of Political Philosophy* 23.2: 166–91.

Lane, M. S. 2012. 'The Origin of the Statesman-Demagogue Distinction In and After Ancient Athens'. *Journal of the History of Ideas* 73.2 179–200.

Lang, M. L. 1990. *Ostraka* (Athenian Agora XXV). Princeton.

Lanni, A. 2006. *Law and Justice in the Courts of Classical Athens*. Cambridge.

Lape, S. 2004. *Reproducing Athens: Menander's Comedy, Democratic Culture, and the Hellenistic City*. Princeton.

Lape, S. 2010. *Race and Citizen Identity in the Classical Athenian Democracy*. Cambridge.

Larsen, J.A.O. 1945. 'Representation and Democracy in Hellenistic Federalism'. *Classical Philology* 40: 65–96.

Larsen, J.A.O. 1948. 'Cleisthenes and the Development of the Theory of Democracy at Athens', in M. R. Konvitz & A. E. Murphy eds. *Essays in Political Theory presented to George H. Sabine*. Ithaca, NY: 1–16.

Larsen, J.A.O. 1949. 'The Origin and Significance of the Counting of Votes'. *Classical Philology* 44: 164–81.

Larsen, J.A.O. 1955. *Representative Government in Greece and Rome*. California & London.

Larsen, J.A.O. 1968. *Greek Federal States*. Oxford.

Lauriola, R. 2009. 'The Greeks and the Utopia: An Overview through Ancient Greek Literature'. *Revista Espaço Acadêmico* 97 (June): 109–24.

Lawton, C. 1995. *Attic Document Reliefs: Art and Politics in Ancient Athens*. Oxford.

Lévêque, P., & P. Vidal-Naquet 1964/1996 .*Cleisthenes the Athenian*, ed. D. A. Curtis. Atlantic Highlands.

Lévy, E. 2005. 'Isonomia', in Bultrighini ed.: 119–37.

Lewis, D. 1963. 'Cleisthenes and Attica'. *Historia* 12: 22–40.

Lewis, D. 1984/1997. 'Democratic Institutions and Their Diffusion', in *Selected Papers in Greek and Near Eastern History*, ed. P. Rhodes. Cambridge: 51–59.

Lewis, D., with P. J. Rhodes 1997. *The Decrees of the Greek States*. Oxford.

Lewis, J. D. 2008. *Solon the Thinker: Political Thought in Archaic Athens*. London.

Lewis, N., & M. Reinhold eds. 1990/1955. *Roman Civilization*, 3rd edn. vol 2. *The Roman Empire*. New York.

Lewis, S. 2002. *The Athenian Woman: An Iconographic Handbook*. London & NewYork.

Lewis, S. 2009. *Greek Tyranny*. Exeter.

Liddel, P. 2007. *Civic Obligation and Individual Liberty in Ancient Athens*. Oxford.

Liddel, P. 2009. 'Democracy Ancient and Modern', in Balot ed. 2009: 133–48.

Linke, B., & M. Stemmler eds. 2000. *Mos maiorum. Untersuchungen zu den Formen der Identitätsstiftung und Stabilisierung in der römischen Republik*. Stuttgart.

Lintott, A. 1982. *Violence, Civil Strife and Revolution in the Classical City 750–330 BC*. London & Sydney.

Lintott, A. 1992. 'Aristotle and Democracy'. *Classical Quarterly* 42: 114–28.

Lintott, A. 1999. *The Constitution of the Roman Republic*. Oxford.

Lintott, A. 2000. 'Aristotle's Mixed Constitution', in Brock & Hodkinson eds: ch. 8.

Lipset, S. M. ed. 1996. *The Encyclopedia of Democracy*, 4 vols. London & New York.

Lipset, S. M., & J. M. Lakin. 2004. *The Democratic Century*. Norman, OK.

Lloyd, G.E.R. 1979. *Magic, Reason and Experience: Studies in the Origins and Development of Greek Science*. Cambridge.

Lockwood, T. C. Jr. 2006. 'Polity, Political Justice and Political Mixing'. *History of Political Thought* 27.2: 207–22.

Lombardini, J. 2013. '*Isonomia* and the Public Sphere in Democratic Athens'. *History of Political Thought* 34.3: 393–420.

Loomis, W. T. 1998. *Wages, Welfare Costs and Inflation in Classical Athens*. Ann Arbor.

Loraux, N. 1986. *The Invention of Athens: The Funeral Speech in the Classical City*. Cambridge, MA (French original 1981).

Loraux, N. 1987/1997. 'Le lien de la division'. *Le Cahier du Collège International de Philosophie* 4:101–24 (repr. as Loraux 1997: ch. 4).

Loraux, N. 1991. 'Reflections of the Greek City on Unity and Division', in Molho, Raaflaub, & Emlen eds: 33–51.

Loraux, N. 1993. *Children of Athena: Athenian Ideas about Citizenship and the Division between the Sexes*. Princeton.

Loraux, N. 1997. *La cité divisée*. Paris. (Eng. trans. *The Divided City. Memory and Forgetting in Ancient Athens*, 2002).

Loraux, N. 2005. *La tragédie d'Athènes. La politique entre l'ombre et l'utopie*. Paris.

Lough, J. ed. 1971. *L'Encyclopédie*. Geneva..

Low, P. 2002. 'Cavalry Identity and Democratic Ideology in Early Fourth-Century Athens'. *Proceedings of the Cambridge Philological Society* 48: 102–19.

Low, P. 2010. 'Remembering Defeat and Victory in Democratic Athens', in Pritchard ed.: 341–58.

Low, P. ed. 2008. *The Athenian Empire*. Edinburgh.

Lummins, C. D. 1996. *Radical Democracy*. Ithaca, NY.

Lytton, E. B. 2004 [1837]. *Athens: Its Rise and Fall with Views of the Literature*, ed. O. Murray. London.

Ma, J. 2009. 'The City as Memory', in G. Boys-Stones, B. Graziosi, & Ph. Vasunia eds. *The Oxford Handbook of Hellenic Studies*. Oxford: 248–59.

Ma, J. 2013. *Statues and Cities: Honorific Portraits and Civic Identity in the Hellenistic World*. Oxford.

Ma, J., N. Papazarkadas, & R. Parker eds. 2009. *Interpreting the Athenian Empire*. London.

McClelland, J. S. 1988. *The Crowd and the Mob: From Plato to Canetti*. London.

McCormick, J. S. 2006. *Contain the Wealthy and Patrol the Magistrates. Restoring Elite Accountability to Popular Government*. Chicago.

McCormick, J. S 2011. *Machiavellian Democracy*. Cambridge.

McDonald-Lewis, L. 2009. *The Warriors and Wordsmiths of Freedom: The Birth and Growth of Democracy*. Edinburgh.

McGlew, J. F. 1993. *Tyranny and Political Culture in Ancient Greece*. Ithaca, NY.

McGlew, J. F. 2003. *Citizens on Stage: Comedy and Political Culture in the Athenian Democracy*. Ann Arbor.

MacGregor Morris, I. 2004. 'The Paradigm of Democracy: Sparta in Enlightenment Thought', in T. J. Figueira ed. *Spartan Society*. Swansea: 339–62.

McPhee, P. 2012. *Robespierre: A Revolutionary Life*. New Haven.

Maddox, J. 1982. 'Athens Without Democracy: The Oligarchy of Phocion and the Tyranny of Demetrius of Phalerum, 302–307 B.C.' Unpublished PhD diss., Yale.

Mair, P. 2009. *Ruling the Void: The Hollowing of Western Democracy*. London.

Maloy, J. S. 2013. *Democratic Statecraft: Political Realism and Popular Power*. Cambridge.

Manent, P. 2007. *Tocqueville et la nature de la démocratie*. Paris.

Manin, B. 1997. *The Principles of Representative Government*. Cambridge.

Mann, Chr. 2007. *Die Demagogen und das Volk: Zur politischen Kommunikation im Athen des 5. Jahrhunderts v. Chr*. Berlin.

Mann, Chr., & P. Scholz eds. 2011. *'Demokratie' im Hellenismus: Von der Herrschaft des Volkes zur Herrschaft der Honoratioren?* (Die hellenistische Polis als Lebensform, 2). Berlin.

Mansfield, H. 2010. *Tocqueville: A Very Short Introduction*. New York & Oxford.

Manville, B. 1990. *The Origins of Citizenship in Ancient Athens*. Princeton.

Manville, B., & J. Ober 2003. *A Company of Citizens: What the World's First Democracy teaches Leaders about Creating Great Organizations*. Cambridge, MA.

Marcaccini, C. 2012. *Atene sovietica: Democrazia antica e rivoluzione communista*. Pisa & Cagliari.

Markle, M. M. III 1985/2004. 'Jury Pay and Assembly Pay at Athens', repr. In Rhodes ed. 2004: ch. 4.

Marr, J. L., & P. J. Rhodes eds. 2008. *The 'Old Oligarch': The Constitution of the Athenians Attributed to Xenophon*. Oxford.

Marshall, B. A. 1997. '*Libertas Populi*: The Introduction of Secret Ballot at Rome and its Depiction on Coinage'. *Antichthon* 31: 54–73.

Martin, M. III, & D. C. Snell 2004. 'Democracy and Freedom', in Snell ed. *A Companion to the Ancient Near East*. Oxford: 397–407.

Mattusch, C. 2014. *Enduring Bronze: Ancient Art, Modern Views*. Los Angeles.

Mazower, M. 2012. *Governing the World: The History of an Idea*. London.

Meckstroth, C. 2015. *The Struggle for Democracy: Paradoxes of Progress and the Politics of Change*. Oxford.

Meier, C. 1980/1990. *The Greek Discovery of Politics*. Cambridge, MA (abridgement of German original 1980).

Meier, C. 1982/2004. 'The Greeks: The Political Revolution in World History', in Rhodes ed.: ch. 14.

Meier, C. 2011. *A Culture of Freedom: Ancient Greece and the Origins of Europe*. Oxford.

Meiggs, R. 1963. 'The Political Implications of the Parthenon', in G. Hooker ed. *Parthenos and Parthenon* (*Greece & Rome* Supp. X). Oxford: 36–45.

Meiggs, R. 1972. *The Athenian Empire*. Oxford.

Meyer, E. A. 1993. 'Epitaphs and Citizenship in Classical Athens'. *Journal of Hellenic Studies* 113: 99–121.

Michels, R. 1915. *Political Parties: A Sociological Study of the Oligarchical Tendencies of Modern Democracy*. New York (German original, 1911).

Mikalson, J. D. 1987. *Athenian Popular Religion*. Chapel Hill, NC.

Mikalson, J. D.1998. *Religion in Hellenistic Athens*. Berkeley.

Mill, J. S. 1978. *Collected Writings* vol. XI: *Essays on Philosophy and the Classics*. Toronto.

Millar, F. 1984a. 'The Political Character of the Classical Roman Republic, 200–151 B.C.' *Journal of Roman Studies* 74: 1–19 (repr. as 2002b: 109–42).

Millar, F. 1984b. 'State and Subject: The Impact of Monarchy', in Millar & E. Segal eds. *Caesar Augustus: Seven Aspects*. Oxford: 37–60.

Millar, F. 1986. 'Politics, Persuasion, and the People before the Social War (150–90 B.C.)'. *Journal of Roman Studies* 76: 1–11 (repr. as 2002b: 143–61).

Millar, F. 1989. 'Political Power in mid-Republican Rome: Curia or Comitium?' *Journal of Roman Studies* 79: 138–50 (repr. as 2002b: 85–108).

Millar, F. 1995. 'Popular Politics at Rome in the Late Republic', in I. Malkin & Z. Rubinsohn eds. *Leaders and Masses in the Roman World. Studies in Honor of Zvi Yavetz*. Leiden: 91–113 (repr. as 2002b: 162–82).

Millar, F. 1998. *The Crowd in Rome in the Late Republic*. Ann Arbor.

Millar, F. 2002a. *The Roman Republic in Political Thought*. Hanover, NH & London.

Millar, F. 2002b. *Rome, the Greek World, and the East*. Vol. I. *The Roman Republic and the Augustan Revolution*, ed. H. Cotton & G. M. Rogers. Chapel Hill, NC.

Miller, F. D. Jr. 1996. *Nature, Justice, and Rights in Aristotle's 'Politics'*. Oxford.

Millett, P. 1998. 'Encounters in the Agora', in Cartledge et al. eds: 203–28.

Missiou, A. 2011. *Literacy and Democracy in Fifth-Century Athens*. Cambridge.

Mitchel, F. W. 1965. 'Athens in the Age of Alexander'. *Greece & Rome* 12: 189–204.

Mitchell, L., & P. Rhodes eds. 1997. *The Development of the Polis in Archaic Greece*. London & New York.

Molho, A., K. A. Raaflaub, & J. Emlen. eds. 1991. *Athens and Rome, Florence and Venice: City-States in Antiquity & Medieval Italy*. Stuttgart.

Momigliano, A. D. 1952/1994. 'George Grote and the Study of Greek History' (an Inaugural Lecture delivered at University College London, 19 February 1952), repr. in Momigliano 1994: 15–31.

Momigliano, A. D. 1970/1994. 'J. G. Droysen between Greeks and Jews'. *History & Theory* 9.2: 347–65, repr. in Momigliano 1994: 147–61.

Momigliano, A. D. 1994. *Studies on Modern Scholarship*, ed. G. W. Bowersock and T. J. Cornell. Berkeley.

Morgan, E. S. 1988. *Inventing the People: The Rise of Popular Sovereignty in England and America*. New York & London.

Morgan, K. ed. 2003. *Popular Tyranny: Sovereignty and Its Discontents in Ancient Greece*. Austin, TX.

Morris, I. 1996. 'The Strong Principle of Equality and the Archaic Origins of Greek Democracy', in Ober & Hedrick eds: 19–48.

Morris, I., & K. A. Raaflaub eds. 1998. *Democracy 2500? Questions and Challenges*. (Archaeological Inst. of America, Colloquium and Conference Papers 2.) Dubuque, IA.

Mortimer, S. 2015. 'What Was at Stake in the Putney Debates?' *History Today* (January): 50–55.

Mossé, C. 1973. *Athens in Decline, 404–86 B.C.* London.

Mossé, C. 1979/2004. 'How a Political Myth Takes Shape: Solon, "Founding Father" of the Athenian Democracy', in Rhodes ed. 2004: ch. 10.

Mossé, Cl. 1989. *L'Antiquité dans la Révolution française*. Paris.

Mossé, Cl. 2013. *Regards sur la démocratie Athénienne*. Paris.

Mouritsen, H. 2001. *Plebs and Politics in the Late Roman Republic*. Cambridge.

Murray, O., & S. Price eds. 1990. *The Greek City: From Homer to Alexander*. Oxford.

Nederman, C. J. 1995. *Community and Consent: The Secular Political Theory of Marsilio of Padua*. Lanham, MD.

Neer, R. 2002. *Style and Politics in Athenian Vasepainting: The Craft of Democracy, ca. 530–460 BC*. Cambridge.

Neils, J. ed. 1992. *Goddess and Polis: The Panathenaea Festival in Ancient Athens*. Princeton.

Neils, J. 1994. 'The Panathenaia and Kleisthenic Ideology', in Coulson et al. 1994:152–9.

Nelson, E. 2004. *The Greek Tradition in Republican Thought*. Cambridge.

Nelson, E. ed. 2008. *Thomas Hobbes, Translations of Homer*, 2 vols. Oxford & New York.

Nevett, L. 1999. *House and Society in the Ancient Greek World*. Cambridge.

Nevett, L. 2010. *Domestic Space in Classical Antiquity*. Cambridge & New York.

Newell, W. R. 2016. *Tyrants: A History of Power, Injustice, and Terror*. Cambridge.

Nicolet, C. ed. 1983. *Demokratia et aristokratia. A propos de Caius Gracchus: mots grecs et réalités romaines*. Paris.

Nippel, W. 1980. *Mischverfassungstheorie und Verfassungsrealität in Antike und der Früher Neuzeit*. Stuttgart.

Nippel, W. 1988. 'Bürgerideal und Oligarchie. "Klassischer Republikanismus" aus althistorischer Sicht', in Koenigsberger ed. 1988: 1–18.

Nippel, W. 1993. 'Macht, Machtkontrolle und Machtentgrenzung. Zu einigen Konzeptionen und ihrer Rezeption in der frühen Neuzeit', in J. Gebhardt & H. Münkler eds. *Bürgerschaft und Herrschaft. Zum Verhältnis von Macht und Demokratie im antiken und neuzeitlichen politischen Denken*. Baden-Baden: 58–78.

Nippel, W. 1994. 'Ancient & Modern Republicanism: "Mixed Constitution" and "Ephors"', in B. Fontana ed. *The Invention of the Modern Republic*. Cambridge: 6–26.

Nippel, W. 2005. 'Die Antike in der amerikanischen und französischen Revolution', in G. Urso ed. *Popolo e Potere nel mondo antico* (Friuli conference, September 2004). Pisa: 259–69.

Nippel, W. 2008a. *Antike oder moderne Freiheit? Die Begründung der Demokratie in Athen und in der Neuzeit*. Frankfurt/Main.

Nippel, W. 2008b. *Johann Gustav Droysen: Ein Leben zwischen Wissenschaft und Politik*. Munich.

North, J. 1990. 'Democratic Politics in Republican Rome', *Past & Present* 126: 3–21 (repr. with postscript in Osborne ed. 2004b: 140–58).

North, J. 2002. 'Pursuing Democracy', in A. K. Bowman et al. eds. *Representations of Empire: Rome and the Mediterranean World. Fest. F. Millar*. Oxford: 1–12.

North, J. 2006. 'The Constitution of the Roman Republic', in N. Rosenstein & R. Morstein-Marx eds. *A Companion to the Roman Republic*. Malden, MA: 256–77.

Ober, J. 1989a. *Mass and Elite in Classical Athens: Rhetoric, Ideology and the Power of the People*. Princeton.

Ober, J. 1989b. 'Review Article: The Nature of Athenian Democracy', *Classical Philology* 84: 322–34 (of Hansen 1987).

Ober, J. 1993/1996. 'The Athenian Revolution of 508/7 B.C.: Violence, Authority, and the Origins of Democracy', in C. Dougherty & L. Kurke, eds. *Cultural Poetics in Archaic Greece: Cult, Performance, Politics*. Cambridge: 215–32 (repr. in Ober 1996: ch. 4 and in Rhodes ed. 2004).

Ober, J. 1996. *The Athenian Revolution: Essays on Ancient Greek Democracy and Political Theory*. Princeton.

Ober, J. 1998. *Political Dissent in Democratic Athens: Intellectual Critics of Popular Rule*. Princeton.

Ober, J. 2005. *Athenian Legacies*. Princeton.

Ober, J. 2008a. *Democracy and Knowledge: Innovation and Learning in Classical Athens*. Princeton.

Ober, J. 2008b. 'What the Ancient Greeks Can Tell Us about Democracy'. *Annual Review of Political Science* 11: 67–91.

Ober, J. 2009. 'Can We Learn from Ancient Athenian Democracy? Historical and Modern Perspectives', in A. Chaniotis, A. Kuhn, & C. Kuhn eds. *Applied Classics: Comparisons, Constructs, Controversies* (HABES 46). Stuttgart: 207–30.

Ober, J. 2011. 'Comparing Democracies', in Azoulay & Ismard 2011: 307–24.

Ober, J., & C. Hedrick eds. 1996. *Dēmokratia: A Conversation on Democracies, Ancient and Modern*. Princeton.

Östreich, G. 1989. *Antiker Geist und moderner Staat bei Justus Lipsius (1547–1606): Der Neustoizismus als politische Bewegung*, ed. N. Mout. Göttingen.

Ogien, A., & S. Laugier. 2015. *Le principe démocratie: Enquête sur les nouvelles formes du politique*. Paris.

De Oliveira, G. 2007. *La Cité tyrannique: Histoire politique de la Grèce archaïque*. Rennes.

O'Neil, J. L.1981. 'How democratic was Hellenistic Rhodes?' *Athenaeum* 59: 468–73.

O'Neil, J. L. 1995. *The Origins and Development of Ancient Greek Democracy*. Lanham, MD & London.

Oppeneer, T. 2012. 'Democratic Elements in the Greek Cities of the Roman Empire'. MA thesis, Universiteit Gent.

Osborne, R. 1985. *Demos. The Discovery of Classical Attika*. Cambridge.

Osborne, R. 1987. *Classical Landscape with Figures*. London.

Osborne, R. 1993/2004. 'Competitive Festivals and the Polis: A Context for Dramatic Festivals at Athens', in Rhodes ed. 2004: ch. 8.

Osborne, R. 2006. 'When was the Athenian Democratic Revolution?' in S. Goldhill & R. Osborne eds. *Rethinking Revolutions through Ancient Greece*. Cambridge: 10–28.

Osborne, R. 2009a. 'Economic Growth and the Politics of Entitlement'. *The Cambridge Classical Journal* 55: 97–125.

Osborne, R. 2009b. *Greece in the Making, 1200–479 BC*, 2nd edn. London & New York.

Osborne, R. 2010. *Athens and Athenian Democracy*. Cambridge.

Osborne, R. 2011. *The History Written on the Classical Body*. Cambridge.

Osborne, R. G. ed. 2000. *The Athenian Empire*, 4th edn (LACTOR vol 1). London.

Osborne, R. ed. 2004a. *The Old Oligarch*, rev. edn (LACTOR vol. 2). London.

Osborne, R. ed. 2004b. *Studies in Ancient Greek and Roman Society*. Cambridge.

Osborne, R. ed. ed. *The World of Athens*, 2nd edn. Cambridge.

Osborne, R., & S. Hornblower eds. 1994. *Ritual, Finance, Politics: Athenian Democratic Accounts Presented to David Lewis*. Oxford.

Ostwald, M. 1969. *Nomos and the Beginnings of the Athenian Democracy*. Oxford.

Ostwald, M. 1986. *From Popular Sovereignty to the Sovereignty of the Law: Law, Society and Politics in Fifth-Century Athens*. California & London.

Ostwald, M. 1993. '*Stasis* and *Autonomia* in Samos: A Comment on an Ideological Fallacy'. *Scripta Classica Israelica* 12: 51–66.

Ostwald, M. 1996/2004. 'Shares and Rights: "Citizenship" Greek Style and American Style', in Ober & Hedrick eds: 49–61 (repr. in Robinson ed. 2004).

Ostwald, M. 2000a. *Oligarchia: The Development of a Constitutional Form in Ancient Greece*. Stuttgart.
Ostwald, M. 2000b. 'Popular Sovereignty and the Problem of Equality'. *Scripta Classica Israelica* 19: 1–13.
Ostwald, M. 2005. 'The Sophists and Athenian Politics', in Bultrighini ed.: 35–51.
Paga, J. 2010. 'Deme Theaters in Attica and the Trittys System', *Hesperia* 79: 351–84.
Palmer, R. R. 1953. 'Notes on the Use of the Word "Democracy" 1789–1799'. *Political Science Quarterly* 68.2: 203–26.
Palmer, R. R. 1959-1964/2014. *The Age of the Democratic Revolution: A Political History of Europe and America, 1760-1800*, 2 vols. Princeton (repr. 2014, with new foreword by D. Armitage).
Parker, H. T. 1937. *The Cult of Antiquity and the French Revolutionaries: A Study in the Development of the Revolutionary Spirit*. Chicago.
Parker, R. 1996. *Athenian Religion: A History*. Oxford.
Parker, R. 2006. *Polytheism and Society at Athens*. Oxford.
Pasquino, P. 2009. 'Machiavelli and Aristotle: The Anatomies of the City'. *History of European Ideas* 35.4: 397–407.
Pasquino, P. 2010. 'Democracy Ancient and Modern: Divided Power', in Hansen ed. 2010b: 1–40 (discussion, 41–9).
Patrikin, L. 2015. *Economic Equality and Direct Democracy in Ancient Athens*. New York.
Patterson, C. 1981. *Pericles' Citizenship Law of 451-0 B.C.* New York.
Patterson, C. ed. 2006. *Antigone's Answer: Essays on Death and Burial, Family and State in Classical Athens* (= *Helios* 33). Lubbock, TX.
Paul, E., & C. Paul. 1920. *Creative Revolution: A Study of Communist Ergatocracy*. New York.
Paul, E. F., F. D. Miller, Jr., & J. Paul eds. 1985. *Liberty & Equality*. Oxford.
Pébarthe, C. 2006. *Cité, démocratie et écriture: Histoire de l'alphabétisation d'Athènes à l'époque classique*. Paris.
Pelling, C. 2002. *Plutarch and History: Eighteen Studies*. London.
Peltonen, M. 1995. *Classical Humanism and Republicanism in English Political Thought 1570-1640*. Cambridge.
Philp, M. 1989. *Paine*. Oxford.
Philp, M. 1998. 'English Republicanism in the 1790s'. *Journal of Political Philosophy* 6: 235–62.
Philp, M. 2011. 'Revolutionaries in Paris: Paine, Jefferson & Democracy'. Unpublished paper.
Pierson, G. 1938/1966. *Tocqueville and Beaumont in America*. New York.
Pincus, S. 2009. *1688: The First Modern Revolution*. New Haven & London.
Piovan, D. 2010. *Senofonte: L'antidemocrazia al potere. La tirannia dei trenta in Senofonte*. Pisa.
Piovan, D. 2011. *Memoria e oblio della Guerra civile: strategie giudiziarie e racconto del passato in Lisia*. (Studi e testi di storia antica, 19). Pisa.
Pocock, J.G.A. 2009. *Political Thought and History: Essays on Theory and Method*. Cambridge.
Poddighe, E. 2014. *Aristotele, Atene e le metamorfosi dell'idea democratica. Da Solone a Pericle (594-451 a.C.)*. Rome.
Podlecki, A. 1998. *Pericles and His Circle*. London & New York.
Prawer, S. S. 1976. *Karl Marx and World Literature*. Oxford.
Pritchard, D. 2004. 'Kleisthenes, Participation, and the Dithyrambic Contests of Late Archaic and Classical Athens'. *Phoenix* 58: 208–28.
Pritchard, D. 2005. 'Kleisthenes and Athenian Democracy—Vision from Above or Below?' *POLIS* 22: 136–57 (review article of Anderson 2003).
Pritchard, D. 2013. *Sport, Democracy and War in Classical Athens*. Cambridge.
Pritchard, D. ed. 2010. *War, Democracy and Culture in Classical Athens*. Cambridge.

Przeworski, A. 2010. *Democracy and the Limits of Self-Government*. Cambridge.

Raaflaub, K. A. 1983. 'Democracy, Oligarchy and the Concept of the "Free Citizen" in Late Fifth-Century Athens'. *Political Theory* 11: 517–44.

Raaflaub, K. A. 1989a. 'Die Anfänge des politischen Denkens bei den Griechen'. *Historische Zeitschrift* 248: 1–32.

Raaflaub, K. A. 1989b. 'Contemporary Perceptions of Democracy in Fifth-Century Athens'. *Classica et Mediaevalia* 40: 33–70.

Raaflaub, K. A. 1992. *Politisches Denken und Krise der Polis. Athen im Verfassungskonflikt des späten 5. Jahrhunderts v. Chr.* Munich.

Raaflaub, K. A. 1993. 'Homer to Solon: The Rise of the *Polis* (the Written Sources)', in Hansen ed.: 41–105.

Raaflaub, K. A. 1994. 'Democracy, Power, and Imperialism in Fifth-Century Athens', in Euben, Wallach, & Ober eds. 1994: 103–46.

Raaflaub, K. A. 1998 'Power in the hands of the People: foundations of Athenian democracy' in Morris & Raaflaub eds: 31–66

Raaflaub, K. 2003. 'Between a Rock and a Hard Place: Reflections on the Role of Ancient History in a Modern University'. *Classical Journal* 98.4: 415–31.

Raaflaub, K. 2004. *The Discovery of Freedom in Ancient Greece*. 2nd edn. Chicago.

Raaflaub, K. A. 2014. 'Why Greek Democracy? Its Emergence and Nature in Context', in Hammer ed.: ch. 2.

Raaflaub, K. A., J. Ober, & R. Wallace, with C. Farrar and P. Cartledge. 2007. *Origins of Democracy in Ancient Greece*. Berkeley.

Raaflaub, K. A. ed. 1993. *Anfänge politischen Denkens in der Antike*. Munich.

Rahe, P. 1992. *Republics Ancient and Modern: Classical Republicanism and the American Revolution*, 2 vols. Chapel Hill, NC.

Rahe, P. 2009. *Montesquieu and the Logic of Liberty*. New Haven.

Ramou-Chapsiadi, A. 2009. 'The Cleinias Decree', in Lagogianni-Georgakarakos & Buraselis eds: 63–6.

Rausch, M. 1999. *Isonomia in Athen. Veränderungen des öffentlichen Lebens vom Sturz der Tyrannis bis zweiten Perserabwehr*. Frankfurt/Main.

Rawson, E. 1969/1991. *The Spartan Tradition in European Thought*. Oxford (repr. With introduction by K. Thomas).

Reden, S. von. 1995. 'Peiraeus—A World Apart'. *Greece & Rome* 42: 24–37.

Reed, C. M. 2003 *Maritime Traders in the Ancient Greek World*. New York.

Reinhold, M. ed. 1984. *Classica Americana: The Greek and Roman Heritage in the United States*. Detroit.

Reinmuth, O. W. 1971. *The Ephebic Inscriptions of the Fourth Century B.C.* (*Mnemosyne* Supp. 14). Leiden.

Rhodes, P. J. 1972/1985. *The Athenian Boule*. Oxford.

Rhodes, P. J. 1980. 'Athenian Democracy after 403 B.C.' *Classical Journal* 75: 305–23.

Rhodes, P. J. 1981/1993. *A Commentary on the Aristotelian Athenaion Politeia*, rev. ed. Oxford.

Rhodes P. J. 2003a. *Ancient Democracy and Modern Ideology*. London.

Rhodes, P. J. 2003b. 'Nothing to Do with Democracy: Athenian Drama and the *Polis*'. *Journal of Hellenic Studies* 123: 104–19.

Rhodes, P. J. 2006. '"Classical" and "Hellenistic" in Athenian History'. *Electrum* 11: 27–43.

Rhodes, P. J. 2007. *The Greek City States. A Sourcebook*, 2nd edn. Cambridge.

Rhodes, P. J. 2009a. 'How Seriously Should We Take the Old Oligarch?' *Pegasus* 52: 8–13.

Rhodes, P. J. 2009b. 'State and Religion in Athenian Inscriptions'. *Greece & Rome* 56: 1–13.

Rhodes, P. J. 2010a. '"Lycurgan" Athens', in *Philathenaios: Studies in Honour of M. J. Osborne.* Athens: 81–90.

Rhodes, P. J. 2010b. 'Stability in the Athenian Democracy after 403 B.C.', in B. Linke, M. Meier, & M. Strothmann eds. *Zwischen Monarchie und Republik: gesellschaftlichen Stabilisierungsleistungen und politische Transformationspotentiale in den antiken Stadtstaaten (Historia* Einzelschr. 217). Stuttgart: 67–75.

Rhodes, P. J. 2011a. 'The Dionysia and Democracy Again'. *Classical Quarterly* 61: 71–4.

Rhodes, P. J. 2011b. 'Learning from the Past in Classical Athens', in Herman ed.: 13–30.

Rhodes, P. J. 2012. 'The Alleged Failure of Athens in the Fourth Century'. *Electrum* 19: 111–29.

Rhodes, P. J. ed. 2004. *Athenian Democracy.* Edinburgh.

Rhodes, P. J., & R. Osborne ed. & trans. 2003/2007. *Greek Historical Inscriptions 404–323 B.C.* Cambridge.

Richard, C. J. 1994. *The Founders and the Classics.* Cambridge, MA.

Richer, N. 2010. 'The Religious System at Sparta', in D. Ogden ed. *A Companion to Greek Religion.* Malden, MA: 236–52.

Ringen, S. 2007. *What Democracy Is For: On Freedom and Moral Government.* Princeton.

Rizakis, A. 2015. 'The Achaian League', in Beck & Funke eds: ch. 6.

Roberts, J. T. 1982. *Accountability in Athenian Government.* Madison.

Roberts, J. T. 1994. *Athens on Trial: The Antidemocratic Tradition in Western Thought.* Princeton.

Robertson, G. 2007. *The Putney Debates: The Levellers.* London.

Robespierre, M. 2007. *Virtue and Terror: Texts Selected and Annotated by Jean Ducange,* trans. John Howe. London.

Robinson, E. W. 1997. *The First Democracies: Early Popular Government Outside Athens.* Stuttgart.

Robinson, E. W. 2001. 'Reading and Misreading the Ancient Evidence for Democratic Peace'. *Journal of Peace Research* 38.5: 593–608.

Robinson, E. W. 2011. *Democracy Beyond Athens: Popular Government in the Greek Classical Age.* Cambridge & New York.

Robinson, E. W. ed. 2004. *Ancient Greek Democracy: Readings and Sources.* Cambridge, MA, & Oxford.

Rodewald, C. A. ed. 1975. *Democracy: Ideas and Realities.* London & Toronto.

Roisman, J. ed. 2003. *Brill's Companion to Alexander the Great.* Leiden.

Rollison, D. 2010. *A Commonwealth of the People: Popular Politics and England's Long Social Revolution, 1066–1649.* Cambridge.

Romm, J. S. 2013. *Ghost on the Throne: The Death of Alexander the Great and the War for Crown and Empire.* New York.

Rosen, F. 1983. *Jeremy Bentham and Representative Democracy: A Study of the 'Constitutional Code'.* Oxford.

Rosenblatt, H. ed. 2009. *Cambridge Companion to Constant.* Cambridge.

Rosenvallon, P. 2008. *Counter-Democracy: Politics in an Age of Distrust.* Cambridge.

Rosenvallon, P. 2014. *The Society of Equals.* Cambridge, MA.

Rotroff, S. I. 1996. 'Pnyx III: Pottery and Stratigraphy', in B. Forsen & G. Stanton eds. *The Pnyx in the History of Athens.* Helsinki: 35–40.

Rowe, C. J., and M. Schofield eds. 2000. *The Cambridge History of Greek and Roman Political Thought.* Cambridge.

Runciman D. 2013. *The Confidence Trap: A History of Democracy in Crisis from World War I to the Present.* Princeton.

Runciman, W. G. 1990. 'Doomed to Extinction: The Greek Polis as an Evolutionary Dead-End', in Murray & Price eds: 347–67.

Runciman, W. G. 2009. *The Theory of Cultural and Social Selection*. Cambridge.

Ruschenbusch, E. 1985. 'Die Zahl der griechischen Statten und Arealgrösse und Bürgerzahl der "Normalpolis"' *Zeitschrift für Papyrologie und Epigraphik* 59: 253–63.

Ruzé, F. 1997. *Délibération et pouvoir dans la cité grecque de Nestor à Socrate*. Paris.

Ryan, A. 2012. *On Politics: A History of Political Thought*, 2 Books in One: Book One. *Herodotus to Machiavelli*; Two: *Hobbes to the Present*. New York.

Saïd, S. 1979. 'Aristophane, les femmes et la cité'. *Cahiers du Fontenay* 17: 33–69.

Ste. Croix, G.E.M. de. 1954. 'The Character of the Athenian Empire'. *Historia* 3: 1–41 (repr. in Low ed. 2008).

Ste. Croix, G.E.M. de. 1970. 'Some Observations on the Property Rights of Athenian Women'. *Classical Quarterly* n.s. 20: 273–8.

Ste. Croix, G.E.M. de. 1972. *The Origins of the Peloponnesian War*. London.

Ste. Croix, G.E.M. de. 1975. 'Political Pay Outside Athens'. *Classical Quarterly* n.s. 25: 48–52.

Ste. Croix, G.E.M. de. 1981. *The Class Struggle in the Ancient Greek World: From the Archaic Age to the Arab Conquests*. London & Ithaca, NY.

Ste. Croix, G.E.M. de. 2004. *Athenian Democratic Origins and Other Essays*, ed. D. Harvey & R. Parker. Oxford.

Salkever, S. ed. 2009. *The Cambridge Companion to Ancient Greek Political Thought*. Cambridge.

Samons, L. J. II. 1998. 'Mass, Elite, and Hoplite-Farmer in Greek History'. *Arion*, 3rd ser. 5: 99–123.

Samons, L. J. II. 2004. *What's Wrong With Democracy? From Athenian Practice to American Worship*. California.

Samons, L. J. II. ed. 1998. *Athenian Democracy and Imperialism*. Boston.

Sanson, H. 2011. *Women, Language and Grammar in Italy, 1500–1900*. Oxford.

Saunders, A.N.W. ed. & trans. 1969. *Greek Political Oratory*. Harmondsworth.

Saxenhouse, A. 2006. *Free Speech and Democracy in Ancient Athens*. Cambridge.

Schaffer, F. 1998. *Democracy in Translation: Understanding Politics in an Unfamiliar Culture*. Ithaca, NY.

Schmidt, M. 1993. *Direkte Demokrati I Danmark*. Copenhagen.

Schmitt-Pantel, P. 1992 *La cité au banquet. Histoire des repas publics dans les cites grecques*. Rome.

Schofield, M. 1999. *Saving the City: Philosopher-Kings and Other Paradigms*. London & New York.

Schuller, W. ed. 1998. *Politische Theorie und Praxis im Altertum*, Darmstadt.

Schwartzenberg, M. A. 2004. 'Athenian Democracy and Legal Change'. *American Political Science Review* 2 (May): 311–25.

Schwartzenberg, M. A. 2007. *Democracy and Legal Change*. New York.

Scott, J. 2004. *Commonwealth Principles: Republican Writing of the English Revolution*. Cambridge.

Scott, J. 2011. *When the Waves Ruled Britannia: Geography and Political Identities, 1500–1800*. Cambridge.

Scott, M. 2010. *From Democrats to Kings: From the Downfall of Athens to the Epic Rise of Alexander the Great*. London.

Scott, T. 2012. *The City-State in Europe, 1000–1600: Hinterland, Territory, Region*. Oxford.

Scurr, R. 2006. *Fatal Purity: Robespierre and the French Revolution*. London.

Seaford, R. 2004. *Money and the Early Greek Mind: Homer, Philosophy, Tragedy*. Cambridge.

Sealey, R. 1987. *Athenian Democracy: Republic or the Rule of Law?* University Park, PA.

Sealey, R. 1993. *Demosthenes: A Study in Defeat*. New York.

Sebillotte Cuchet, V. 2006. *Libérez la patrie! Patriotisme et politique en Grèce ancienne*. Paris.

Sellers, M.N.S. 2014. 'The Roman Republic and the French and American Revolutions', in Flower ed.: 401–18.

Sen, A. 1999. 'Democracy as a Universal Value'. *Journal of Democracy* 10.3: 3–17.

Sen, A. 2006. *Identity & Violence: The Illusion of Destiny*. New York.

Sen, A., & J. Drèze 2013. *An Uncertain Glory: India and its Contradictions*. Princeton.

Shapiro, H. A. 1989. *Art and Cult under the Tyrants in Athens*. Mainz/Rhein.

Sharp, A. ed. 1998. *The English Levellers*. Cambridge.

Sherwin-White, A. N. 1973. *The Roman Citizenship*, 2nd edn. Oxford.

Shipley, G. 2005. 'Little Boxes on the Hillside: Greek Townplanning, Hippodamos and Polis Ideology', in Hansen ed.: 335–403.

Shklar, J. 2006. 'Rousseau's Two Models: Sparta and the Age of Gold', in J. T. Scott ed. *Jean-Jacques Rousseau: Paradoxes and Interpretations*. New York: 224–46.

Sickinger, J. 2009. 'Nothing to Do with Democracy: "Formulae of Disclosure" and the Athenian Epigraphic Habit', in L. Mitchell & L. Rubinstein eds. *Greek History and Epigraphy: Essays in honour of P. J. Rhodes*. Swansea: 87–102.

Sieyès, E. J. 2003. *Political Writings: Including the Debate between Sieyès and Tom Paine in 1791*, ed. and trans. M. Sonenscher. Indianapolis.

Sinclair, R. K. 1988 *Democracy and Participation in Athens*. Cambridge.

Sitrin, M., & D. Azellini 2014. *They Can't Represent Us! Reinventing Democracy from Greece to Occupy*. London.

Skinner, Q. 1978. *The Foundations of Modern Political Thought*, 2 vols. Cambridge.

Skinner, Q. 1992. 'The Italian City-Republics', in Dunn ed.: ch. 4.

Skinner, Q. 1999. 'Ambrogio Lorenzetti's *Buon Governo* Frescoes: Two Old Questions, Two New Answers'. *Journal of the Warburg and Courtauld Institutes* 62: 1–28.

Skinner, Q. 2008. *Hobbes and Republican Liberty*. Cambridge.

Skinner, Q., & M. Van Gelderen eds. 2013. *Freedom and the Construction of Europe*, 2 vols. Cambridge.

Skocpol, T. 2003. *Diminished Democracy: From Membership to Management in American Civic Life*. Norman, OK.

Smith, A. 2011. *Polis and Personification in Classical Athenian Art*. Leiden.

Snell, B. 1953. *The Discovery of the Mind: The Greek Origins of European Thought*, trans. T. G. Rosenmeyer. Oxford.

Snodgrass, A. M. 1980. *Archaic Greece: The Age of Experiment*. London.

Snodgrass, A. M. 1993. 'The Rise of the Polis: The archaeological Evidence', in Hansen ed.: 30–9.

Sommer, M. 2013 'The Mighty and the Sage: Scipio Aemilianus, Polybius and the Quest for Friendship in Second-Century Rome', in Gibson & Harrison eds: 307–18.

Spivey, N. J. 1994. 'Psephological Heroes', in Osborne & Hornblower eds: 39–51.

Starr, C. G. 1970 *Athenian Coinage 480–449 B.C.* Oxford

Starr, C. G. 1986 *Individual and Community. The Rise of the Polis, 800–500 B.C.* New York & Oxford

Staveley, E. S. 1972. *Greek and Roman Voting and Elections*. London & New York.

Stedman Jones, G. 2004. *An End to Poverty?* London.

Stein-Hölkeskamp, E. 2014. '"Immer der Beste sein"—Konkurrenz in der athenischen Demokratie', in R. Jessen ed. *Konkurrenz in der Geschichte. Praktiken-Werte—Institutionalisierungen*. Frankfurt & New York: 119–40.

Steinhauer, G. 2009. *Marathon and the Archaeological Museum*. Athens.

Stevenson, T. 2014. *Julius Caesar and the Transformation of the Roman Republic*. London.

Stone, I. F. 1988. *The Trial of Socrates*. London.

Straumann, B. 2015. *Roman Law in the State of Nature: The Classical Foundations of Hugo Grotius' Natural Law*. New York.

Strauss, B. S. 1987. *Athens after the Peloponnesian War: Class, Faction and Policy 403-386 B.C.* Ithaca, NY.

Strauss, B. S. 1996. 'The Athenian Trireme, School of Democracy', in Ober & Hedrick eds: 313-25.

Surowiecki, J. 2004. *The Wisdom of Crowds: Why the Many Are Smarter Than the Few*. New York.

Syme, R. 1958. *Tacitus*, 2 vols. Oxford.

Tarn, W. W. 1923. 'The Social Question in the Third Century', in E. Bevan et al. *The Hellenistic Age*. Cambridge: 108-41.

Tarn, W. W., & G. T. Griffith. 1952. *Hellenistic Civilisation*, 3rd edn. London.

Tatum, W. J. 2009. 'Roman Democracy?' in Balot ed.: 214-27.

Taylor, C. 2007a. 'From the Whole Citizen Body? The Sociology of Election and Lot in the Athenian Democracy'. *Hesperia* 76: 323-45.

Taylor, C. 2007b. 'The Sociology of Athenian Democracy: A Prosopographical Approach', in K. Keats-Rohan ed. *Prosopography Approaches and Applications: A Handbook*. Oxford: 313-24.

Teegarden, D. 2012. 'The Oath of Demophantos: Revolutionary Mobilization, and the Preservation of the Athenian Democracy'. *Hesperia* 81.3: 433-65.

Teegarden, D. 2013. 'Tyrant-Killing Legislation and the Political Foundation of Ancient Greek Democracy'. *Cardozo Law Review* 34.23: 965-82.

Teegarden, D. 2014. *Death to Tyrants: Ancient Greek Democracy and the Struggle Against Tyranny*. Princeton.

Teegarden, D. Forthcoming. 'Acting like Harmodios and Aristogeiton: Tyrannicide in Ancient Greek Political Culture', in C. Verhoeven & C. Dietze eds. *The Oxford Handbook of the History of Terrorism*.

Thirlwall, C. 1835-1844/1845-1852. *A History of Greece*. London (*A Selection*, ed. P. Liddel, Bristol 2007).

Thomas, R. 1989 *Oral Tradition and Written Record in Classical Athens*. Cambridge.

Thomas, W. 1979. *The Philosophical Radicals: Nine Studies in Theory and Practice*. Oxford.

Thompson, E. P. 1968. *The Making of the English Working Class*, rev. ed. Harmondsworth.

Thompson, N. 1996. *Herodotus and the Origins of the Political Community: Arion's Leap*. New Haven.

Thompson, N. 2001. *The Ship of State: Statecraft and Politics from Ancient Greece to Democratic America*. New Haven.

Tilly, C. 1995. *Popular Contention in Britain 1758-1834*. Cambridge, MA.

Tocqueville, de, A. 1835-1840. *De la démocratie en Amérique*, 2 vols. Paris.

Todd, S. C. 1993. *The Shape of Athenian Law*. Oxford.

Todd, S. C. 1996. 'Lysias *Against Nicomachus*: The Fate of the Expert in Athenian Law', in Foxhall & Lewis eds: ch. 7.

Tuck, R. 2006. 'Hobbes and Democracy', in A. Brett & J. Tully with H. Hamilton-Bleakley eds. *Rethinking the Foundations of Modern Political Thought*. Cambridge: ch. 10.

Tully, J. 2009. *Public Philosophy in a New Key*, 2 vols. Vol 1. *Democracy and Civic Freedom*. Cambridge.

Turner, F. M. 1981. *The Greek Heritage in Victorian Britain*. New Haven.

Urbinati, N. 2002. *Mill on Democracy: From the Athenian Polis to Representative Government*. Chicago.

Urbinati, N. 2011 'Representative Democracy and Its Critics', in S. Alonso, J. Keane, & W. Merkel eds. *The Future of Representative Democracy*. Cambridge: ch. 1.

Urbinati, N. 2012. 'Thucydides the Thermidorian: Democracy on Trial in the Making of Modern Liberalism', in Harloe & Morley eds: 55–76.

Vanderbroeck, P.J.L. 1987. *Popular Leadership and Collective Behavior in the Late Roman Republic (ca. 80–50 B.C.)*. Amsterdam.

Van der Vliet, E.Ch.L. 2012. 'The Durability and Decline of Democracy in Hellenistic Poleis', *Mnemosyne* 65: 771–86.

Van Reybrouck, D. 2016. *Against Elections: The Case for Democracy*. London.

Vernant, J.-P. 1985. 'Espace et organisation politique en Grèce ancienne', in *Mythe et pensée chez les Grecs*, 3rd edn. Paris: 238–60.

Vernant, J.-P. 2000. 'The Birth of the Political'. *Thesis Eleven* 60: 87–91.

Vernant, J.-P., & P. Vidal-Naquet. 1971/1986/1988. *Myth and Tragedy in Ancient Greece*, 2 vols in 1. New York.

Vidal-Naquet, P. 1995. *Politics Ancient and Modern*. Cambridge.

Vidal-Naquet, P. 2000. 'The Tradition of Greek Democracy', *Thesis Eleven* 60: 61–86.

Villacèque, N. 2008. 'Theatai logon. Histoire de la démocratie comme spectacle. Politique et théâtre à Athènes à l'époque classique'. PhD diss., Université deToulouse-Le Mirail.

Vlassopoulos, K. 2007a. 'Free Spaces: Identity, Experience, and Democracy in Classical Athens'. *Classical Quarterly* 57: 33–52.

Vlassopoulos, K. 2007b. *Unthinking the Greek Polis: Ancient Greek History beyond Eurocentrism*. Cambridge.

Vlassopoulos, K. 2009a. *Politics. Antiquity & Its Legacy*. London.

Vlassopoulos, K. 2009b. 'Slavery, Freedom and Citizenship in Classical Athens: Beyond a Legalistic Approach'. *European Review of History/Revue européenne d'histoire* 16.3: 347–63.

Vlassopoulos, K. 2013. *Greeks and Barbarians*. Cambridge.

Vlastos, G. 1953. 'Isonomia'. *American Journal of Philology* 74: 337–66.

Vlastos, G. 1964. 'Isonomia Politike', in J. Mau & E. G. Schmidt eds. *Isonomia. Studien zur Gleichheitsvorstellung im griechischen Denken*. Berlin: 1–35.

Vlastos, G. 1994. 'The Historical Socrates and Athenian Democracy', in *Socratic Studies*, ed. M. Burnyeat. Cambridge: 87–108.

Volney, C. F. 1811/2000 *The Ruins: Or A Survey of the Revolutions of Empires*. Otley & Washington, DC (French original 1791).

Wagner, P. 2013. 'Transformations of Democracy: Towards a History of Political Thought and Practice in Long-Term Perspective', in Arnason, Raaflaub, & Wagner eds: 47–68.

Wahnich, S. 2012. *In Defence of the Terror: Liberty or Death in the French Revolution*. London.

Walbank, F. W. 1957/1967/1979. *A Historical Commentary on Polybius*, 3 vols. Oxford.

Walbank, F. W. 1964. 'Polybius and the Roman State'. *Greek, Roman & Byzantine Studies* 5: 239–59.

Walbank, F. W. 1966. 'The Spartan Ancestral Constitution in Polybius', in Badian ed.: 303–12.

Walbank, F. W. 1969. Review of Aalders 1968, *Classical Review* n.s. 19: 314–17.

Walbank, F. W. 1973. *Polybius*. Berkeley.

Walbank, F. W. 1985. *Selected Papers* vol. I. Cambridge.

Walbank, F. W. 1995. 'Polybius' Perception of the One and the Many'. *Fest Z. Yavetz*. Leiden: 201–22 (repr. in Walbank 2004).

Walbank, F. W. 1998. 'A Greek Looks at Rome: Polybius VI Revisited'. *Scripta Classica Israelica* 17: 45–59.

Walbank, F. W. 2004. *Selected Papers* vol. II. Cambridge.

Wallace, R. W. 1989. *The Areopagos Council, to 307 BC*. Baltimore.

Wallace, R. W. 1994. 'Private Lives and Public Enemies: Freedom of Thought in Classical Athens', in Boegehold & Scafuro eds: 127–55.

Waterfield, R. 2011. *Dividing the Spoils: The War for Alexander the Great's Empire*. Oxford.

Watson, J. M. 2010. 'The Origin of Metic Status at Athens'. *Cambridge Classical Journal* 56: 259–78.

Watts, E. J. 2010. *Riot in Alexandria: Tradition and Group Dynamics in Late Antique Pagan and Christian Communities*. Berkeley.

Webb, E. Kent 1997. 'The Athenian Tyrannicides: Icons of a Democratic Society'. www.brynmawr.edu/archaeology/guesswho/webb.html.

Weeber, K-W. 2011. *Fièvre à Pompeii*. Paris.

Weed, R. L. 2007. *Aristotle on Stasis: A Moral Psychology of Political Conflict*. Berlin.

Weinstock, S. 1971. *Divus Julius*. Oxford.

Welskopf, E-C. ed. 1974. *Hellenische Poleis: Krise-Wandlung-Wirkung*, 4 vols. Berlin.

Welwei, K-W. 2002. 'Demokratische Verfassungselemente in Rom aus der Sicht des Polybius', in J. Spielvogel ed. *Res Publica Reperta. Zur Verfassung und Gesellschaft der römischen Republik und des frühen Prinzipats. Fest. J. Bleicken zum 75. Geburtstag*. Stuttgart: 25–35.

West, C. 2004. *Democracy Matters: Winning the Fight against Imperialism*. New York & London.

Whitehead, D. 1977. *The Ideology of the Athenian Metic (Proceedings of the Cambridge Philological Society*, Supp.). Cambridge.

Whitehead, D. 1985. *The Demes of Attica, 508/7–ca. 250 BC. A Political and Social Study*. Princeton.

Whitehead, D. 1986. 'The Political Career of Aristophon'. *Classical Philology* 81: 313–19.

Whitehead, D. 2006. 'Absentee Athenians: Lysias *Against Philon* and Lycurgus *Against Leocrates*'. *Museum Helveticum* 63.3: 132–151.

Whitmarsh, T. 2004. *Ancient Greek Literature*. Cambridge & Malden, MA.

Wiemer, H-U. 2002. *Krieg, Handel und Piraterie: Untersuchungen zur Geschichte des hellenistischen Rhodos*. Berlin.

Wilentz, S. 2005. *The Rise of American Democracy*. New York.

Williams, B.A.O. 1991/1995. 'St Just's Illusion', repr. in *Making Sense of Humanity*. Cambridge: 135–50.

Wills, G. 1992. *Lincoln at Gettysburg: The Words That Remade America*. New York.

Wilson, E. 2007. *The Death of Socrates: Hero, Villain, Chatterbox, Saint*. Cambridge, MA.

Wilson, P. J. 2000. *The Athenian Institution of the Khoregia*. Cambridge.

Wilson, P. J. 2008. 'Costing the Dionysia', in M. Revermann & P. J. Wilson eds. *Performance, Iconography, Reception: Studies in Honour of Oliver Taplin*. Oxford: 88–122.

Winstanley, G. 2010. *The Complete Works*, 2 vols, ed. T. N. Corns, A. Hughes, & D. Loewenstein. Oxford.

Winters, J. A. 2011. *Oligarchy*. Cambridge.

Wirth, G. 1997. 'Lykurg und Athen im Schatten Philipps II', in Eder & Hölkeskamp eds: 191–225.

Wiseman, T. P. 2002. 'The Ideological Vacuum', in Wiseman ed. *Classics in Progress: Essays on Ancient Greece and Rome* (British Academy). Oxford: 285–310.

Wohl, V. 1996. '*Eusebeias heneka kai philotimias*: Hegemony and Democracy at the Panathenaia'. *Classica et Mediaevalia* 47: 25–88.

Wohl, V. 2010. *Law's Cosmos: Juridical Discourse in Athenian Oratory*. Cambridge.

Wolin, S. S. 2001. *Tocqueville between Two Worlds: The Making of a Political and Theoretical Life*. Princeton.

Wolin, S. S. 2008. *Democracy Incorporated: Managed Democracy and the Specter of Inverted Totalitarianism*. Princeton.

Wolpert, A. 2002. *Remembering Defeat: Civil War and Civic Memory in Ancient Athens*. Baltimore & London.

Wood, E. M. 1988. *Peasant-Citizen and Slave: The Foundations of Athenian Democracy*. London.

Wood, E. M. 1995. 'The Demos versus "We, the People": From Ancient to Modern Conceptions of Citizenship', in *Democracy Against Capitalism: Renewing Historical Materialism*. Cambridge: 204–37.

Wood, E. M. 2008. *Citizens to Lords. A Social History of Western Political Thought from Antiquity to the Middle Ages*. London.

Wood, E. M. 2012. *Liberty and Property. A Social History of Western Political Thought from Renaissance to Enlightenment*. London.

Wood, G. S. 1992. 'Democracy and the American Revolution', in Dunn ed.: 91–105.

Wood, G. S. 2009. *Empire of Liberty: A History of the Early Republic, 1789–1815*. New York.

Woodman, A. J. ed. 2009. *The Cambridge Companion to Tacitus*. Cambridge.

Woodruff, P. 2005. *First Democracy: The Challenge of an Ancient Idea*. New York & Oxford.

Woods, C. 2014. 'The Limits of Citizenship in Aristotle's *Politics*'. *History of Political Thought* 35.3: 399–435.

Wootton, D. 1992. 'The Levellers', in Dunn ed.: ch. 5.

Wootton, D. ed. 2003. *The Essential Federalist and Anti-Federalist Papers*. Indianapolis.

Worden, B. 2007. *Literature and Politics in Cromwellian England: John Milton, Andrew Marvell, Marchamont Nedham*. London.

Worden, B. 2009. *The English Civil Wars 1640–1660*. London.

Worden, B. 2012. *God's Instruments: Political Conduct in the England of Oliver Cromwell*. Oxford.

Worthington, I. 2014. *By the Spear: Philip II, Alexander the Great, and the Rise and Fall of the Macedonian Empire*. Oxford.

Wycherley, R. E. 1978. *The Stones of Athens*. Princeton.

Yack, B. 1993. *The Problems of a Political Animal: Community, Justice, and Conflict in Aristotelian Political Thought*. Berkeley & London.

Yack, B. 2012. 'Democracy and the Love of Truth', in J. Elkins & A. Norris eds. *Truth and Democracy*. Philadelphia: 165–80.

Yakobson, Y. 1999 *Elections and Electioneering in Rome: A Study in the Political System of the Late Republic* (*Historia* Einzelschr. 128). Stuttgart.

Yavetz, Z. 1958/1969. 'The Living Conditions of the Urban Plebs in Republican Rome'. *Latomus* 17: 500–17 (repr. in R. Seager ed. *The Crisis of the Roman Republic. Studies in Social and Political History*. Cambridge).

Yunis, H. 1997. *Taming Democracy: Models of Political Rhetoric in Classical Athens*. Ithaca, NY.

Yunis, H. ed. 2001. *Demosthenes, On The Crown*. Cambridge.

Yunis, H. trans. 2005. *Demosthenes, Speeches 18 and 19*. Austin, TX.

Zarka, Y. C. ed. 2012. *La Démocratie, état critique*. Paris.

Zizek, S. ed. 2007. 'Introduction: Robespierre, or, the "Divine Violence" of Terror', in Robespierre 2007: vii–xxxix.

Zunz, O. ed. 2011. *Alexis de Tocqueville and Gustave de Beaumont in America: Their Friendship and their Travels*. Charlottesville.

INDEX

Byzantium (city)
  leader of Social War, 206
  Second Athenian League, 196, 198

Callias, 241, 243
Calymna, 235
Camarina, 157
Cannae, battle of (216), 249, 250
Caracalla (Roman Emperor), 273
Carthage
  annihilation, 252
  compared to Rome by Polybius, 257
  Roman wars with (*See* Punic Wars)
Catholic Church, 289
Cato the Elder, 252
Cercidas, 239
Chaeronea, battle of (338), 106, 196, 207–8
  armed service as result of, 29
  emergence of Lycurgus, 203
Chalcis, 55, 78
Chartists, 301
Cheng Jin, 306
Chersonesus, 236
Chinese People's Democratic Republic, 306
Chios
  Alexander and, 233
  in Athens anti-Persian naval empire, 159
  innovation in governance, 54–5
  leader of Social War, 206
  in Second Athenian League, 196–7, 328
   defection, 198
Chremonidean War, 244
Christians, first labelling of, 232
Churchill, Winston, 304
Cicero, 259, 262
Cimon
  admiral of the fleet, 82
  dissension with Pericles, 159
  son of Miltiades, 80, 81
citizens, Athenian, 37
  according to Aristotle, 69
   definition in *Politics*, 107
  imposition of minimum wealth qualification, 217, 242
  as jurors, 117
  number of, 224
  reforms

   of Cleisthenes, 87–8
   law of double-descent (Periclean law), 88–90, 137
   of Solon, 53
  rolls
   in deme, 66
   revision of, 207
   validation of credentials, 107
citizens, Roman, 260
  in Empire, 273–4
  levels of property-owning, 247
  in Republic, 259
citizens, Spartan, 43
Citizenship Law (451), 87, 88–90, 137
citizen-state as translation for *polis*, 15, 38
City Dionysia festival. *See* Great Dionysia festival
City Panathenaea. *See* Great Panathenaea
city-state as translation of *polis*, 37–9
city-states
  between c. 1000 and 1500, 276–7
  challenge to notion of god-given hereditary monarchy, 276–7
civic humanism, 280
civic religion, Lycurgus and, 214–15
civil war. *See* stasis
Clearidas, 157
Cleinias Decree, 31
Cleisthenes. *See also* reforms of Cleisthenes
  as Archon, 57
  modern interpretations, 322
  ostracism attributed to, 70, 72–3
Cleomenes I of Sparta, 78
  ending the tyranny in Athens, 59
Cleomenes III of Sparta, 240
Cleon, 115
  Aristophanes on, 119
  critical of Pericles, 160
  prosecution of Thucydides, 119
  Thucydides on, 158, 160
Clouds (Aristophanes)
  on Athenians as litigious, 139
  on Socrates, 175
coinage as evidence in history of the Athenian democracy, 30–1
Coinage Decree. *See* Standards Decree
Coke, Edward, 278
colonization, map of Greek, *48*

necessary wealth for equipment, 75, 103, 162
training of ephebes as, 213
transformation of nature of politics, 41
Hyperbolus, 72, 120
Hyperides, 216–17
Epitaphios, 97
on numbers of slaves, 138
speeches, 17

Iasus, 235
Iceland, 310
iconography and democracy in Athens, 31–2
ideology in Roman politics, 262
Iliad (Homer), 39
imperialism, ancient *versus* modern, 91–2
impiety
Alcibiades and, 131, 176
legal procedure, 177
Socrates and, 117, 118, 176
individualism, Tocqueville on limits of, 297
International Petition of Digital Rights, 336
Ion, 66
Ionian Revolt (499–494), 79
preliminaries to outbreak of, 153
Iron Generation, 40
Iron Law of Oligarchy, 307, 309
Isagoras, 65
Isakhan, Benjamin, 2, 3, 35
isegoria, 78, 114, 129
Isocrates, 202
Areopagiticus, 202, 206
documentary evidence on Athenian
democracy, 17
on the Peiraeus, 142
use of *politeia*, 123
isokratia, 75, 78
isonomia
Birgalias on, 55, 317
Cleisthenes' system as, 32, 75
Thucydides' use of, 161
Tyrannicides and introduction of, 32
use in Persian Debate, 94–5
isonomia politike, 161
isopolity
between Argos and Corinth, 150, 198
between Athens and Samos, 148–9
Isthmian Games, 56, 125

Jackson, Andrew, 295–6, 298
Jaucourt, Louis de, 290
Jay, John, 293
Jefferson, Thomas, *294*
and Declaration of Independence, 294–5
Jeffery, L. H., 54
Jewish Antiquities (Josephus), 265
John (King of England), 278
Jones, A. H. M.
on absence of Greek democratic
theory, 92
on Hellenistic democracy, 231
Jones, William, 301
Josephus, 265
Journey Around the World (Hecataeus), 63
Julius Caesar, 265, 268
jurors in Athenian courts, 117. *See also* People's
Courts (Athens)
annual selection of 6,000 citizens by lot,
170, 224
pay for, 87, 117–18, 169
religious oath, 131
justice, Homer on mortal, 39
justice system
in democratic Athens, 169–70
in spectrum of *demokratia* to
oligarchia, 102
Justinian (Byzantine Emperor), 274
Juvenal, 266

King's Peace (Peace of Antalcidas) (386),
190–1, 204
Thebes in, 194–5
Knights (Aristophanes), 140, 160, 174
on Cleon, 119
kratos, ambiguous meaning, 3

Lambropoulos, Vassilis, 54
Landsgemeinde, Swiss, direct democracy
in, 307
Larsen, Jakob, 238
Latin as Renaissance scholarly lingua
franca, 279
Law of Eucrates on Tyranny (336), *18*, 21, 22, 24,
105, 106, 320
both a law and a decree, 121
explicit mention of Areopagus in, 121, 209